Dearest Friend
A Life of Abigail Adams

Dearest Friend
A Life of Abigail Adams

Lynne Withey

THE FREE PRESS
A Division of Macmillan Publishing Co., Inc.
NEW YORK

Collier Macmillan Publishers
LONDON

Copyright © 1981 by The Free Press
A Division of Macmillan Publishing Co., Inc.

The Free Press
A Division of Macmillan Publishing Co., Inc.
866 Third Avenue, New York, N.Y. 10022

Collier Macmillan Canada, Ltd.

Library of Congress Catalog Card Number: 80-70694

Printed in the United States of America

printing number
1 2 3 4 5 6 7 8 9 10

Library of Congress Cataloging in Publication Data

Withey, Lynne
        Dearest friend.

        Bibliography: p.
        Includes index.
        1. Adams, Abigail, 1744–1818. 2. Adams, John, 1735–
1826. 3. Presidents—United States—Wives—Biography.
I. Title.
E322.1.A38W56   973.4′4′0924 [B]   80-70694
ISBN 0-02-934760-2   AACR2

For Michael

Contents

Preface

Abigail Adams was a tiny woman, little more than five feet tall, with dark hair, piercing dark eyes, and a forceful personality that belied her size. Quiet and reserved as a child, she nonetheless displayed a brilliant mind and fierce determination even then. As she matured, these qualities broke through her quiet exterior and she became voluble and outspoken, never afraid to assert her opinions whether in the company of friends, family, or heads of state.

To the modern observer, she is maddeningly contradictory. On the one hand, she was a fiery revolutionary, denouncing British tyranny in blistering rhetoric. She refused to be intimidated by the specter of British attack, even as she could hear the cannon and see the smoke of nearby battles; she raised four children, managed a farm, and conquered her intense feelings of loneliness and depression while her husband spent years away from her serving in the Continental Congress and negotiating with European powers. Her husband, John, called her a "heroine" for her courage, and indeed she was. Yet after the war she turned into a reactionary; she denounced all opposition to the new federal government as dangerous, blamed all political dissent on "foreign influence," and advocated the suppression of freedom of the press.

She was just as contradictory in other ways too. She argued for improved legal rights and education for women long before they became popular issues; but she always believed that a woman's place was in the home and, as she got older, became more and more obsessed with "delicacy" and moral purity in women. She professed to hate politics, and yet obviously thrived in her role as a politician's wife. Even in her relationships with her family, she displayed contradictory behavior. She tried to control the lives of everyone around her but instilled in her children a spirit of independence that made them resist—though not always successfully—her overwhelming influence. They often showed signs of resenting her interference in their lives, but they were also deeply attached to her. Despite her sometimes overbearing personality, she was a loving and generous woman. Her concern for her family and friends knew no bounds, and they, in turn, loved her unreservedly.

One may try to explain away the contradictions in Abigail's life by pointing out that she was essentially conservative, that as a feminist she was limited by the constraints of her times, that her professed distaste for politics was mostly talk. There is some truth in all these statements, but they are hardly sufficient to explain Abigail's complex personality. How does one explain a conservative who advocated independence for America and equality for women?

Abigail herself would not have appreciated having anyone try to force a pattern of consistency on her life. She was the first to admit that she was temperamental and changeable; she also believed that anyone with an independent mind would not ever try to be consistent. And she was nothing if not independent.

On some things, however, she never wavered. She was, throughout her life, temperamentally and philosophically conservative, despite her outspoken advocacy of the American Revolution. In general, she feared revolution; she valued stability, believed that family and religion were the essential props of social order, and considered inequality a social necessity. But at the same time she abhorred injustice—whether it was British control of the American colonies, women's subjection to their husbands, the enslavement of black people, or the antiquated laws that kept European peasants from owning their own land. These were all injustices, in her mind, that could be ended without threatening the underlying social order.

The American colonies rebelled against England, she believed, because their continued subjection to British rule was neither just nor necessary. The formation of a new American government seemed to her a perfect opportunity for ending women's inferior legal status and for abolishing slavery. But she saw no reason to change basic social relationships or to introduce "democracy." People who did advocate such changes, she believed, were guilty of undermining the government and betraying the ideals of the Revolution.

She approached the issue of women's rights from a similar perspective. She believed that women were the intellectual equals of men and had a right to an education; she hinted that they also had the right to vote. She talked about the "tyranny" of men and compared women's condition to "Egyptian bondage." Yet she also believed that women by nature were fundamentally different from men and were best suited to be housewives and mothers. To her way of thinking, there was nothing inconsistent about those views. Women had a clearly defined role caring for their homes and families, just as men had their role as breadwinners. Families needed both to survive, and families were the cornerstone of society. Better education and legal independence would do nothing to change this situation; indeed, education would only make women better wives and mothers.

But, as clear as these points seemed to Abigail, the issues she raised about women's rights did potentially undermine their traditional role, a dilemma that she herself could never quite escape. Although she never actually stepped outside her role as wife and mother, she carried it to its limits. She managed all the family property and investments—including buying land, planning additions to houses and farm buildings, hiring and firing laborers, contracting with tenants, and supervising farm work. Most of these things were accomplished without John's advice and in many cases without his knowledge. She often disagreed with him on the best way to invest their money, and she generally got her way. She also served as John's unofficial, unpaid, but most influential political adviser.

Abigail often felt uneasy about the extent to which she stepped out of women's traditional sphere. She constantly asked for John's advice about farm matters, usually without any response except his assurances that she managed brilliantly without his help. She admired women who achieved success in fields generally reserved for men, but she expected them to sacrifice some of their femininity as a result. Even more significant, she admired women who were more conventionally feminine than she was. She worried, for example, that she would not live up to Martha Washington's example as First Lady, although by all accounts Abigail was a far more interesting person. She admired in her own daughter those qualities that were most unlike herself: her quiet, demure manner, her selflessness, her delicate beauty. Late in life, when she compared two of her granddaughters who were entering their teens, she praised the one who was feminine and self-effacing while criticizing the other, who was stubborn and contentious, even though she admitted that the second girl was much more like herself as a child.

Abigail's ambivalence about her position as a woman affected her attitudes about politics too. On the one hand, she always said that she wished John would give up politics so they could return to their quiet rural life; but she clearly loved political debate and the sense of importance that went with being a public figure. John expressed the same conflicting feelings, as he struggled with his ambition for public recognition and his belief that such ambition must be checked.

For Abigail, however, the conflict was more complex. As a woman, she could not be accused of ambition; it was simply not a female quality. But in fact she was ambitious, almost without knowing it, and she acted out her ambition in the only way that an eighteenth-century woman could: through her husband. In that sense she enjoyed basking in John's reflected glory. But she also valued a traditional home and family life, which was largely denied to her because of John's political career.

This ambivalence about politics can be understood only in light of her commitment to her family. Abigail was most strongly opposed to John's involvement in politics during the Revolutionary years, when he was away from home for long periods of time. His absences not only disrupted their family life but also excluded her completely from his work. In later years, when they were together and she shared in his work, she complained much less about his attachment to politics. She continued to regret the disruption to her family—long absences from their children and from friends and relatives at home—but as long as she and John were together and she felt herself a part of his political career, rather than excluded from it, she did not regret his decisions to remain in politics. The gratification of being involved in public affairs, however indirectly, made up for the personal sacrifices she made.

Abigail Adams was, in many ways, a prisoner of the times in which she lived, and her views on women's role in society and on politics reflect that fact. She believed that women should have better education and more independence than the attitudes of the time permitted, and she managed to achieve both through her own determination. But she also accepted the social standards that confined women to the home. She enjoyed her role as wife and mother; she was passionately devoted to her husband and children. Sometimes, however, her devotion to her family and her sense of independence came into conflict. She tried to believe the prevailing notion that women were naturally suited to function in the restricted sphere of the home rather than in the world outside. She often prefaced her comments on politics with an apology for meddling in men's business. But the fact remained that she enjoyed being part of the "busy world," as she liked to call it, and did everything she could to keep herself squarely in the midst of it.

Abigail was largely self-taught, a fact that shows in her writings. Her handwriting is bold and distinctive but in no way resembles the regular, clear script of an educated man of the eighteenth century. Her spelling is unorthodox, her capitalization random, and her punctuation almost nonexistent. She herself was well aware of these facts and attributed them to her lack of formal education. When her son Thomas teasingly criticized her punctuation, she called him a "sausy Lad" but admitted that he had cause for his criticism. "As to points and comma's," she remarked, "I was not taught them in my youth, and I always intend my meaning shall be so obvious as that my readers shall know where they ought to stop." Unfortunately, her meaning is not always clear, and in direct quotes from her correspondance I have occasionally changed commas to periods in order to make more sense of her sentences. I have also capitalized the first words of sentences where she did not, but left all other capitalization and spelling unchanged.

I would like to thank the staffs of the Massachusetts Historical Society, the American Antiquarian Society, the Boston Public Library, the Library of Congress, and the Essex Institute for assistance in using the papers of Abigail Adams in their collections and for permission to quote from them. Several institutions provided photographs and granted permission to publish them: The Massachusetts Historical Society, the Museum of Fine Arts in Boston, the New York State Historical Association, the Library of Congress, the Adams National Historic Site, the British Museum, the Art Collections of Arizona State University, the Boston Atheneum, and the National Gallery. I am particularly grateful to Mrs. Lewis Greenleaf of Nantucket for permission to publish a photograph of a portrait in her private collection.

Many friends and relatives offered advice and encouragement during the writing and rewriting of this book. Robert Middlekauff gave generously of his time in reading and commenting on earlier versions of the manuscript. My husband, Michael Hindus, not only read every draft, but also followed me around the countryside in search of scenes from Abigail's life, always with good advice and good cheer.

And, finally, Catherine Scholten exercised her considerable historical judgment and editorial talent to help transform a rambling manuscript into a book. Tragically, she died before she could see the results of her efforts, or complete her own important work. Her premature death has deprived me of one of my best critics and one of my closest friends.

L. W.
Berkeley, California
February 1981

Chapter 1

A Minister's Daughter

~

Weymouth parsonage in Massachusetts in the 1750s was a lively, hospitable place, with four active young children and visitors coming and going all the time. The Reverend William Smith, the genial, popular minister to Weymouth's North Parish, and his wife Elizabeth presided over the rambling house, which itself was a rather odd mixture of old and new. The smaller wing dated back to the 1680s and had once stood as a house by itself. The Smiths had eventually outgrown its tiny, cramped rooms and had built on a much larger addition. The two wings formed an L, with the imposing new wing looking down on the older house with its slightly sagging roof line and irregular window panes. From its position at the crest of a low hill, it commanded a fine view of the surrounding farmlands. In the distance one could see Weymouth's marshy, deeply indented coastline.

Weymouth was already an old and well-established community. First settled in 1623 as an offshoot of the original New England settlement at Plymouth, it now had a population of about two thousand people. For the most part, the families stayed on in Weymouth for generations, farming land that took more and more effort every year to produce a decent crop. Few newcomers settled in town, because there was no land for them.

Despite its age and population, Weymouth was not a

crowded town. Houses sat on one-acre, two-acre, and larger lots; roads meandered around trees and pastures. Most of the houses were old and rather small, faced with clapboards weathered by age. The smell of salt water was always in the air, for Weymouth faced the sea, and a long estuary spread fingers of salt water through much of the town.

The people were mostly farmers, a taciturn lot who valued traditional ways. Deeply religious, most of them were descendants of the original Puritan settlers of New England, though they wore their faith more quietly than their forebears. Religion was an ingrained part of their existence but not a subject of much discussion or debate; the Great Awakening of the early 1740s had passed Weymouth by. Back in the 1720s—long before William Smith came to town—the congregation had divided into two parishes, but even that decision was accomplished with little conflict.

Few people here could be called either rich or poor, aside from the farmhands who came and went with the seasons, transient laborers about whom the townspeople knew and cared little. Most residents owned some land, a house, and a few animals; even the tradesmen and shopkeepers were part-time farmers. Once a year—more often if necessary—the men gathered in a town meeting to elect their officials, vote taxes, and direct the town's affairs. Any man legally resident in town could vote and hold office, but mostly the same men were elected year in and year out. The town's money went largely to maintain its minister, the school, and its few impoverished residents. Chores like mending fences, repairing roads, and rounding up stray livestock were done by the citizens themselves, with each man expected to put in a certain amount of labor for the town each year.

Everyone in town knew everyone else and a good many of the residents of the surrounding towns as well. Children generally settled close by when they married; few ever traveled more than 40 or 50 miles from home. To be sure, some young men were moving out to the frontiers of New England, to western Massachusetts, inland New Hampshire, and remote areas of Connecticut. But on the whole the people of Weymouth and other old, established New England towns lived much as their parents had and expected their children to do the same.

William Smith, an imposing man in his mid-forties, had been ministering to the town of Weymouth for more than twenty years. He was a warm-hearted, gregarious man, beloved by his parishioners. His wife was more reserved—some even called her snobbish—but was respected by the townspeople just the same. She was a superb cook and housekeeper, kept her large household running smoothly, and still found time to look after the sick and needy of the parish.

Smith doted on his three daughters. Mary was a pretty but sensible and intelligent girl, already old enough to handle most of the chores about the house. She was a serious child, with none of the giddy frivolity of many girls her age. Abigail, the middle daughter—Nabby to her family—was a small, frail child with fair skin, dark hair, and wide brown eyes. Her parents worried about her, because she seemed to catch more than her share of the usual childhood fevers and coughs. Shy and reserved like her mother, Nabby also displayed a certain stubbornness of spirit that dismayed her mother and delighted her father. Betsey, the baby, already showed signs of a sharp intelligence and lively spirit, or so her proud parents thought. Of their children, only William, the only son, was something of a disappointment. Born between Nabby and Betsey, he seemed to lack the drive, the spirit, and the quick mind of his sisters.

Girls growing up in the 1740s and 1750s could expect to live a rather narrowly circumscribed existence. They would be taught to read and write (New England Puritans believed that everyone should be able to read the Bible) and to do simple arithmetic, because women had to be able to keep track of their household accounts. But most of their learning would take place at home. They learned from their mothers how to cook, sew, keep a house clean, tend a vegetable garden, raise chickens, concoct medicines from herbs, and nurse the sick—all the tasks that a competent eighteenth-century woman was expected to handle. When she reached her early twenties, she would marry; almost certainly she would marry a young man from her own town or a neighboring one. They would settle down somewhere nearby, and she would bear children—one every other year or so until her fertile years were over. Family parties and an occasional trip to Boston would be her only diversions.

The Smith girls, however, were different. To be sure, they learned women's domestic chores at a tender age, and they expected to follow in their mother's footsteps, to become mistresses of households and mothers of children just as she had.

But they also spent hours in their father's library, learning from him how to read seriously—not just the meanings of the words and sentences, but the thoughts that lay behind them—and gaining from him an appreciation of literature, history, and theology.

Nabby, in particular, spent every moment she could snatch from her household chores sitting by the library fire and reading Shakespeare or Pope or even Locke. Her mother thought such reading was a waste of time for girls, but her father encouraged it. To the casual visitor Nabby appeared to be a shy, demure child, but her parents and others close to her knew better. She was stubborn and determined; obedient to her parents but clever at getting her own way. A close friend, exasperated by her love of argument, once said, "Nabby, you will either make a very bad, or a very good woman." With a child's logic, she saw no conflict in becoming both a good housewife and an educated woman.

William Smith was the son of a well-to-do Boston merchant. Instead of following his father into a commercial career, as his brother Isaac did, he attended Harvard to study for the ministry. In 1734, shortly after his graduation, he went to Weymouth to become minister to the North Parish. Four years later he bought the old parsonage, which had been home to a succession of Weymouth's ministers, and several acres of land around it.

Secure in his position, with a house and land of his own, Smith could think seriously about taking on the responsibilities of a family. In 1740 he married Elizabeth Quincy of Braintree, the neighboring town. A year later she bore their first child, Mary. Abigail followed in 1744; William in 1746; and Elizabeth in 1750.

Miss Quincy had been a fine catch for a young man, particularly one without long-standing family ties in town. The Quincy family traced its ancestry back to the founders of New England, to the landed gentry of England, and even to one of the signers of the Magna Carta. John Quincy, Elizabeth's father, was Braintree's leading citizen. He owned the estate known as Mount Wollaston, an enormous house perched on one of Braintree's highest hills, with sweeping views of the sea. The town invariably elected him moderator of the town meeting every year; he was also a justice of the peace and served several terms in the Massachusetts legislature.

Elizabeth herself was an attractive young woman, accomplished in the domestic arts and pious—as befitted a minister's wife. In manner she was inclined to the austere, but she was kind and compassionate despite her outward formality. Some said she married beneath her, but William's family background was impeccable too, if a bit unusual in rural towns like Weymouth and Braintree.

Both William and Elizabeth enjoyed a certain inherited status and enough independent income to ensure them a comfortable, if not extravagant, standard of living. Their independent incomes meant that they were not completely dependent on William's salary as a minister—an asset at a time when penny-pinching town fathers tried to keep taxes down by driving hard bargains over their ministers' compensation.

Financial security was one reason for Smith's long tenure in office—forty-nine years. At the time, such job stability was unusual for ministers, who could always be fired by vote of their congregations. But it was more than the absence of financial conflict that accounted for his success. His genial personality, moderate theology, and attentiveness to his parishioners also went a long way toward making him popular with his congregation.

Like all Congregational ministers at the time, he was part of an intellectual elite, one of a tiny minority of men with a college degree. Unlike many of his fellow ministers, however, he was not particularly ambitious intellectually, never published any of his sermons or engaged in theological debates. He was concerned more with the day-to-day needs of his parishioners than with establishing his professional position as a clergyman or making his mark as a scholar. Like the people he served, he spent much of his time farming. Most ministers had to be part-time farmers, both to put food on their tables and to supplement their often meager salaries. Smith took his agricultural pursuits more seriously than most. He not only supervised the planting of crops on the acres surrounding the parish house but also owned farms in Medford and Lincoln, several miles west of Boston.

On religious issues William Smith was a moderate. As a young man, he had not gone through the psychological torment over the state of his soul that many Puritans experienced. He opposed the evangelical revivalism of the Great Awakening and yet managed to avoid becoming embroiled in the quarrels it generated. That in itself was a remarkable feat; throughout New England, churches and towns were divided, sometimes irrevocably, over the revival, and many ministers were dismissed by their congregations as a result. Smith's ability to weather the storm was an indication not only of his generally moderate and conciliatory position but also of his strength within his parish. At a time when ministers often tried to place themselves above their parishioners, to establish themselves as socially and spiritually superior, he maintained easygoing and friendly relations with his congregation. He cared about their problems, and they in turn respected and supported him.

When John Adams first met William Smith, he did not particularly like him, but he noted Smith's friendly manner and the affection his parishioners felt for him. Adams's description suggests that Smith was an astute observer and judge of people and that his understanding of their feelings contributed greatly to his success as a minister. And Abigail, as an adult, observed of her father that he stressed to his children never to speak unkindly about anyone but "to say all the handsome things she could of Persons but not Evil—and to make things rather than Persons the Subjects of Conversation"—a wise policy for a minister trying to keep peace with his congregation.

William and Elizabeth raised their children with a firm but gentle hand. They believed that children should be indulged while they were very young, that they should not be pushed into grown-up responsibilities too quickly. Eighteenth-century children, however, were expected to grow up faster than modern children. Nabby and her sisters and brother were no exceptions.

By the time she was five or six, Nabby had her responsibilities around the house. Already she could stitch a hem, embroider a little, and help her mother with any number of household tasks. The Smith household had an ample supply of servants, including two black slaves—a young woman named Pheby and an older man named Tom—to help with domestic work, but that didn't exempt the children from their chores. Puritan parents, even well-to-do parents, believed that it was important for children to learn the value of work at an early age. Helping around the house not only kept little girls out of mischief and taught them the evils of idleness but helped prepare them for their future role in life as well.

From the time she was very young, Nabby went with her mother to church and learned to sit quietly through her father's long prayers and sermons. Going to church—or to meeting, as Congregationalists called it—was an all-day affair. Morning services, which could go on for two or three hours, were followed by a break for dinner and then an equally long service in the afternoon. Sermons were the principal feature of both services, and children, even very young children, were expected to pay attention without fidgeting. As the minister's daughter, Nabby had to learn this discipline well.

Both her father and her mother were deeply religious people, the sort who accepted God's will as the governing force in their lives without question. Nabby grew up with the same quiet and restrained but strongly felt faith, and it remained unshaken throughout her life. Like her father, she never experienced religious conversion in the sense that more evangelical Puritans did, nor did she ever question her ultimate salvation. Her God was sometimes unfathomable and sometimes angry with mortals' backsliding, but he was not the harsh God of the strict Calvinists and revivalists. She was not particularly emotional in her religious expression, and she had little patience with hair-splitting theological debates. Religion, as far as she was concerned, was most important in providing a set of moral standards for behavior and a source of hope in troubled times.

When she was a little older, Abigail went with her mother on her rounds to visit the sick and the poor of the parish. Elizabeth Smith was renowned for her compassion toward those less fortunate than herself. She called on the sick to offer words of comfort or to help with the nursing if the family was shorthanded, and she kept track of elderly widows who needed an extra cord of wood to get through the winter or laborers out of work who needed food for their families. Such kindnesses were no more than what was expected of ministers' wives, but it seems that Elizabeth did not stop with the routine duties. She also organized work at spinning yarn and weaving cloth to employ indigent women. She supplied the materials, parceled out the work, and marketed the finished products.

Accompanying her mother on visits to the sick and helping with her weaving projects made a deep impression on Abigail.

They became for her an outward expression of religious principles, and she grew up thinking that a women of means, even very modest means, had a responsibility to look out for the poor of her neighborhood as well as care for her own family.

Practically as soon as she was able to talk, Abigail began to learn to read. Her mother was her first teacher, but when she progressed beyond letters, numbers, and simple children's stories, her father took over. She never went to school, partly because her parents worried so much about her delicate health, but mostly because schools for girls ranged from poor to nonexistent. Every Massachusetts town was required by law to maintain a school, but those schools were for boys only. Sometimes girls were allowed to attend usually only early in the morning or late in the afternoon, before and after the boys' classes. Most towns had informal primary schools too, often called "dame schools" because they were run by women. Those schools were often conducted in the teacher's kitchen, and accomplished little more than teaching children the barest rudiments of reading and writing. Many parents, including Elizabeth Smith, preferred to teach their children these basics themselves.

A wealthy girl might be tutored at home in history, English literature, French, painting, dancing, and music—subjects calculated to give her a bit of polish and make her a more interesting wife. Girls rarely learned Latin or Greek, the staples of a boy's education, nor did they read extensively or seriously in literature or history. The vast majority of girls received no formal education past the age of seven or eight; they were doing well if they could read the Bible and write a simple letter.

Abigail and her sisters were more fortunate. In the hands of their father instead of a hired tutor, their education, if not very systematic, was serious and thorough. William Smith may have been less intellectually minded than some of his fellow ministers, but he loved books and had an excellent library. He managed to convey his enthusiasm for reading to his daughters and encouraged them to read whatever volumes struck their fancy. Abigail, who had an insatiable curiosity about everything, went through books of every description—the classical writers in translation; Shakespeare, Dryden, Pope, and Milton; historians, both ancient and modern; and works on political theory and theology. As a young child, she knew only that she loved to read; as she got older, she became determined to educate herself, despite prevailing views about women's intellectual capacities, and tried to read more systematically.

With her father's help and her own determination, Abigail became one of the best-read women of her time. She still felt the lack of a formal, systematic education, however, and was keenly aware of the deficiencies in her schooling as compared with that of a young man of her social class and ability. The differences showed up in such simple things as her handwriting, which was not particularly good at a time when good handwriting was considered the mark of an educated person, and in her spelling, whch was irregular even by the standards of the time. In retrospect it is clear that her intelligence and continued efforts to develop her mind far outweighed any disadvantages of her unorthodox education. Still, she remained sensitive all her life about what she imagined to be her intellectual limitations, and improved education for women was always one of her prime interests.

As a young child, Abigail spent almost as much time with her grandparents at Mount Wollaston as she did at home. She visited them for days or even weeks at a time, sometimes alone and at other times with her sisters. Abigail adored her grandparents. She was particularly close to her grandmother, who seemed to understand this shy but obstinate child better than anyone.

It was common enough to send children to stay with grandparents or other relatives, sometimes for extended periods. Seventeenth-century New Englanders had all but institutionalized the practice, routinely sending their children to live with other families as early as age seven or eight. By the time Abigail was born, the custom was less common but survived in a more informal way. Sending a child to stay with a relative broadened her experience a bit and gave her a chance to be the center of attention for a while. It relieved some of the burdens on her mother and provided some diversion for her grandparents. In a time when the pace of life moved slowly and outside amusements were limited, visits with relatives or friends helped fill the time, especially during the long winter months.

In Abigail's case, her mother hoped that Grandmother Quincy might get her to settle down. Elizabeth Smith worried about her daughter. Nabby obeyed her mother and performed her household tasks competently, but she had a stubborn streak that was disturbing. She did not have that gentle, docile disposition that turned girls into ladylike young women. And she spent altogether too much time poring over books of the sort that young ladies should not be interested in reading.

Grandmother Quincy viewed the situation differently. "Wild colts make the best horses," she was fond of saying. She found Abigail's spirit refreshing, even if she was sometimes hard to manage. She was proud of her granddaughter's quick mind and never said a word about being too bookish. Young Abigail, who loved her mother but always felt a certain distance from her, never felt any such reserve with her grandmother. Over the years, it was her grandmother who became her most important feminine model; to the end of her life she talked about the words and examples of Grandmother Quincy.

When she was a bit older, Abigail also spent a good deal of time with her aunt and uncle, Isaac and Elizabeth Smith, in Boston. The Quincys were the closest thing to landed gentry in colonial New England; the Smiths, by contrast, represented the newer wealth connected with the commercial expansion of the eighteenth century. Young Abigail, although born into the rather secluded and restricted atmosphere of a country parsonage, grew up with an appreciation of both these worlds.

Life in Boston was much different from life at Weymouth or Braintree. Boston was bigger, noisier, more crowded, dirtier; it also provided never-ending entertainment. Abigail could go down to the harbor to watch ships come in, wander among the warehouses and shops, or get lost in the city's maze of narrow, crooked streets. The Smiths lived every bit as elegantly as the Quincy's, but the pace was faster and the style more formal compared with the easygoing country hospitality of Braintree and Weymouth.

Weymouth could be very lonely for Abigail, so she looked forward to her visits to Mount Wollaston and Boston. In Weymouth she had no friends her own age. She knew everyone in town, of course; a minister had to know all his parishioners, and the Smith home was always open to visitors. But an unspoken social barrier separated the minister's famly from most of the families of the town, and the Smith children could not romp freely through the fields and meadows of Weymouth with other children. Elizabeth Smith's firm awareness of such social distinctions, along with her constant concern about Nabby's health, induced her to keep her daughter away from other children. Abigail and her sisters had to rely on each other for companionship. She and Mary, three years apart in age, became especially close.

A few people in Weymouth were intimates of the Smiths—mostly other members of the family. Cotton Tufts, in particular, was one of Abigail's favorites. In one of those complicated family ties that often occurred in small towns, he was related to her twice over. Cotton was William Smith's nephew, and his wife was Elizabeth's younger sister. Twelve years older than Abigail, he had come to Weymouth to practice medicine when she was just eight years old. "Uncle Tufts," as she always called him, a tall, lanky, rather homely looking man and an excellent physician by the standards of the day, was devoted to his young cousin/niece. His home—not far from the parsonage—was one of the few in Weymouth where she could feel completely at ease.

As a teenager Abigail spent much of her time with her aunt and uncle in Boston, where she finally found friends outside her immediate family circle. Her cousin, Isaac Jr., was five years younger but already preparing for Harvard; he shared with her his books and his ideas. Hannah Storer, Aunt Elizabeth's younger sister, was six years older but became Abigail's closest friend and confidante next to Mary, her older sister. Mary Palmer, or Polly, as she was called, became another close friend; she introduced Abigail to Mary Nicholson and Eunice Paine. Their friendship added a new dimension to Abigail's visits to Boston. Now it was not just the company of her aunt and uncle and the fast pace of Boston life that made these visits a welcome change. For the first time, she began to feel a bit of independence from her family.

When she went home to Weymouth, she maintained a "literary" correspondence—exchanges of letters designed to improve their minds and polish their writing styles—with Isaac and some of her women friends. She prized these letters. They gave her a chance to practice expressing her thoughts and removed some of her sense of isolation as she pursued her solitary studies in her father's library.

To Isaac she expressed her conviction of the importance of education. "In youth the mind is like a tender twig," she observed, "which you may bend as you please, but in age like a sturdy oak and hard to move." Knowledge, she believed, was essential to happiness; the ability to expand one's knowledge through life depended on laying a strong intellectual foundation in youth. Characteristically, however, she tempered her praise of learning with a reminder of the importance of the "Creator" and of the uncertainties of life.

Her correspondence with Hannah Storer was also intended to be "literary," but, woman to woman, they exhanged confidence about their men and their domestic concerns too. She and Hannah, Eunice Paine, Mary Nicholson, Polly Palmer, and Mary Smith adopted classical names for themselves that they used in all their correspondence with each other. Abigail was Diana, Roman goddess of the moon, patron of virgins and hunting; her sister was Aurelia, the mother of Julius Caesar; Hannah called herself Calliope, the muse of heroic poetry; Eunice Paine was Silvia, a shepherdess in Roman mythology; Polly Palmer was Myra, mother of Adonis, and Mary Nicholson took the name of Aspasia, mistress of the Athenian general Pericles and intellectual companion of Socrates. Eventually they involved their men in this circle of friendship too. They dubbed John Adams Lysander, a Spartan statesman; and Hannah Storer's future husband, Joshua Green, was Ardelio, whose identity remains a mystery.

Classical pen names were common among writers of pamphlets and newspaper columns who wished to preserve their anonymity. For Abigail and her friends, these names were a way of expressing intimacy with each other and their ideal conceptions of themselves. Using their pen names, they could shed the formality of eighteenth-century letter writers and adopt a more familiar tone. They identified with the classical characters whose names they had chosen; the choice of names was not random or capricious. Years later, as mature women, they still occasionally referred to each other by the pen names of their teens.

These girlhood friendships were lasting ones; they survived marriage, children, moves to other towns, and political upheaval. For Abigail they helped to broaden the restricted world of Weymouth parsonage. Her friendships not only provided opportunities for adolescent confidences but also introduced her to other women, outside her family, who shared her interest in ideas as well as in men, her imagination as well as her sense of feminine duty. All of these women expected to marry, to have children, and to spend most of their adult years looking after large households. They did not ever expect to see a world beyond New England. But as Diana and Silvia and Calliope they were able, for the time being, to indulge themselves in flights of imagination.

Chapter 2

John

Abigail first met John Adams when she was fifteen, although she certainly knew about him long before that. John had grown up in Braintree and was struggling to set up a law practice there. Almost everyone in Weymouth and Braintree knew each other, at least in passing. John was courting Abigail's cousin, Hannah Quincy—although perhaps "courting" was too strong a word for it. He and Hannah flirted with each other, but neither seemed ready to think seriously about marriage, certainly not John.

When he first met Abigail at a party, John was not impressed. She and her sister Mary suffered by comparison with his beloved Hannah. "Good nature is H's universal character," he observed. "She will be a fond, tender Wife, and a fond indulgent Mother. . . . Are S Girls either Frank or fond, or even candid. —Not fond, not frank, not candid."

What Abigail thought of this brash and arrogant youth went unrecorded. He was certainly not the sort of young man to set a girl's heart pounding; short, a bit overweight, with a round, chubby face, he had an unfortunate tendency to talk too much and to press his opinions on others. With her sharp mind, Abigail probably sensed his disapproval of her and gave him a wide berth. In fact, for the time being she had other interests. She had grown into a pretty, delicate-looking teenager with a slender figure and clear, pale skin—while losing none of her childhood stubbornness or curiosity. She was meeting plenty of young men in Boston, although none of them particularly interested her. Hannah Storer Green was the only one of her friends who was married by then. Although she and her other friends might talk about men and about marriage, they did not expect to settle down in the near future.

When Abigail was eighteen, she began to see more of John Adams. One of his best friends, Richard Cranch, began courting Mary; Richard often brought John along on his visits to the parsonage. The two of them made a strange pair—Cranch was tall, handsome, and charming, in contrast to John's short stature and brusque manner—but the two of them were practically inseparable, so John was a frequent caller at the Smiths almost in spite of himself.

Abigail adored Richard Cranch, who was practically the first man other than her father and her cousin Isaac to take her passion for learning seriously. Cranch taught her the rudiments of French, loaned her French books that she struggled to get through, discussed English literature with her, and introduced her to the popular contemporary novels of Samuel Richardson.

In time, Abigail came to enjoy John's visits as much as Richard's. He was now prepared to look with more tolerance upon the Smith girls—he had long since gotten over his infatuation with Hannah Quincy—and he had always admired a good mind wherever he found it. Never one to believe that women should be merely decorative, he grew to be impressed with Abigail's knowledge and her determined pursuit of an education. Following Cranch's example, he began bringing books for her too.

Abigail was shy with him at first, intimidated by his manner; but as she got to know him better, she found something strangely attractive about his bold and forthright behavior. He was opinionated, argumentative, and quick to anger; too often he spoke first and thought later. Abigail was like that too, although her mother's attempts to turn her into a lady had suppressed those inclinations to a considerable degree. She and John discovered that they were much alike, and before long they had fallen in love.

By the time Richard and Mary were married in November 1762, John no longer needed his friend as an excuse to visit. Now, analyzing his lady, his picture of her was changed radically from the one he had held three years earlier: "Tender feelings, sensible, friendly. A friend. Not an imprudent, not an indelicate, not a disagreeable Word or Action. Prudent, modest, delicate, soft, sensible, obliging, active." Within a few months, they were discussing marriage. Teasing Abigail, John wrote, "I never did [refuse marriage] and never will, but on the Contrary am ready to *have you* at any Time."

It was to be a long courtship, however. John, who was twenty-eight and reasonably well established as a lawyer, had recently inherited a house and some land from his father and was ready to marry; but Abigail, at eighteen, was still young to marry by contemporary standards. Legend has it that her parents did not approve of the match. Mrs. Smith in particular thought that John's family background was not prestigious enough to make him a suitable match for Abigail and hoped that her daughter would do better than marry a lawyer.

Objections to John turned out not to be serious in the long run. While he may not have enjoyed high social status, his college degree in itself stamped him as a member of the elite, and the house and land that he inherited at his father's death in 1761 provided him with the means to support a family in at least a modest style, despite his difficulties in establishing himself as a lawyer.

For the moment, however, Abigail and John had to be content with seeing each other as often as they could and with planning for a wedding sometime in the future. John's house was no more than 5 miles away from the parsonage, so he rode over often on his horse. When he couldn't get away, they sent love letters to each other.

Often addressing each other by their adopted classical names, Diana and Lysander, they gave free rein to their feelings. John told Abigail about his dreams of her: "I saw a Lady," he once wrote, "tripping over the Hills, on Weymouth shore, and Spreading Light and Beauty and Glory, all around her. At first I thought it was Aurora . . . But I soon found it was Diana, a Lady infinitely dearer to me and more Charming.—Should Diana make her Appearance every morning instead of Aurora, I should not sleep as I do, but should be all awake and admiring by four, at latest." Abigail could be just as whimsical. She teased John about a rumor that two "Apparitions" bearing a strong resemblance to John and his cousin had been seen haunting Weymouth. But she did not witness the specters and therefore "had not that demonstration which generally convinces me, that you are not a Ghost."

Courtship customs then were freer than they became in succeeding generations. When John came to visit, he and Abigail were left pretty much to themselves. If there were too many people underfoot in the house, they could always walk across the meadows or through the orchard to a secluded spot to exchange long kisses and confidences. In the fall of 1763 she went with him on one of his trips to the circuit court in Worcester. They stayed with friends and had little enough time to themselves, but still Hannah Green hoped they wouldn't be the victims of any lewd jokes. Abigail joked that the rocky, bumpy roads between Boston and Worcester were good practice for the hazards of matrimony.

The dictates of religion and propriety, however, prevented John and Abigail from indulging their passion too far. Other young people were not always so restrained, and an increasing number of young women were pregnant when they marched to the altar. But Abigail, the minister's daughter, would not be so indiscreet and John shared her strict moral values.

After a while, it became more difficult to restrain their feelings, and they both wearied of the long courtship. When a snowstorm kept John at home, he wrote to Abigail, "Cruel, Yet perhaps blessed storm!—Cruel for detaining me from so much friendly, social Company, and perhaps blessed to you, or me or both, for keeping me at *my Distance*. . . . the steel and the Magnet or the Glass and feather will not fly together with more celerity, than somebody and somebody, when brought within striking Distance—and, Itches, Aches, Agues, and Repentance might be the Consequences of a Contact in present Circumstances." Another time, when the circumstances had kept them apart longer than usual, he admonished her, "Patience my Dear! Learn to conquer your Appetites and Passions! . . . the Government of ones own soul requires greater Parts and Virtues than the Management of Kingdoms." Such advice was directed more at himself than at Abigail, for it was John who expressed constant concern about keeping his passions—of all sorts—in check.

John's and Abigail's attraction for each other—like the "steel and the Magnet or the Glass and feather"—never abated during their long life together. Understanding why they were so strongly attracted to each other is far more complicated than understanding why their initial reactions were negative. It seems that the qualities John scorned in fifteen-year-old Abigail were, in the long run, the qualities he admired.

Her wit and intelligence were foremost among them. John Adams was very much a man of his times and shared the prevalent notions about female inferiority, but he admired intelligence above all else. In Abigail he met his intellectual match. Her learning and her insatiable thirst for knowledge made her a fit companion for an aspiring lawyer who was interested more in the intellectual demands of studying law than in the day-to-day drudgery of drawing writs and wills. At the same time, however, Abigail had a clear sense of her place in society as a woman. She was "prudent, modest, delicate, soft, sensible, obliging." In more practical terms as well, Abigail Smith was certainly a good match. A minister's daughter and descendant of an old and prominent family, she could not help but be an asset to an upwardly mobile professional man.

For her part, Abigail thought that their hearts were "cast in the same mould." She could hardly fail to see that John Adams was unlike other young men of her acquaintance. Harvard-educated, ambitious, always demanding perfection from himself, he was clearly a man who would not be content, like most of his contemporaries, with following in the footsteps of his father. Abigail was ambitious too, in her own way. Her later life would show that she was not content with the lot of an ordinary woman, despite those womanly qualities John so admired. But for an eighteenth-century woman, ambition was seriously circumscribed, and the best she could expect was to act out her aspirations within her husband's orbit.

Perhaps young Abigail could sense that her life would not be quite so ordinary as the wife of John Adams. How out of the ordinary, she could not possibly have known in 1762 and 1763. But John had other attractive qualities too. He was sensitive and understanding—if at times a little too sensitive where his own feelings were concerned. He was passionate and emotional, and although, like all good Puritans, he tried to keep his passions in check, he was not afraid to express his feelings. He did not scorn Abigail's interest in books but rather encouraged it. And his sense of humor was remarkably like her own.

Abigail became increasingly impatient as the months dragged on and still they had not set a wedding date. By the end of 1763, when she and John had been seriously courting for about a year, she harbored hopes of a spring wedding. At that point John's concern about being able to provide adequately for a family, rather than any family objections, was apparently what delayed the marriage. John never thought he had enough money. Hannah Green sympathized with Abigail's frustrations. "I know of nothing more irksome than being just at the door of Bliss, and not being in a capacity to enter," she wrote. She also teased John about his reluctance, suggesting that April was an excellent month for weddings.

Just when it seemed that they might finally set a spring wedding date, however, a smallpox epidemic broke out in Boston. Residents of rural Braintree and Weymouth had little reason to fear this dreaded disease, for epidemics rarely spread outside the largest cities. But John's work often took him to Boston. Rather than curtail his work or risk his health, he decided to have himself inoculated. The wedding would have to be postponed.

This was no minor decision for John. Inoculation amounted to being deliberately infected with smallpox in a controlled environment in order to gain immunity. It was an uncomfortable, time-consuming, and potentially dangerous process. When inoculation was first introduced in Boston in the early eighteenth century, it generated enormous controversy because of its dangers; by the 1760s it was still by no means a universally accepted procedure. But the risk of inoculation by that time seemed slight enough compared to the very serious risks of death or disfigurement from the disease itself, so many Bostonians submitted to the procedure. Abigail wanted to go with John and be inoculated herself, but her mother, who was old-fashioned on the subject, as on so many others, refused to allow it.

John had to set aside his work for at least six weeks, seclude himself at home for several days under medication preparing for inoculation, and arrange lodgings in Boston for three weeks or more while the inoculaton actually took place. During that time he would be isolated from anyone not previously inoculated; popular belief held that even letters could transmit smallpox, unless smoked before touching the recipient's hands. John worried about leaving his farm and his practice for several weeks but decided that he "must permit the little Villains call'd the small Pox to have their Feast this Spring."

He began his preparation the first week in April. Conversations with Abigail's brother and her uncle, Cotton Tufts, reassured the couple considerably, as both men had recently undergone inoculation. "I am not affraid of your Virmin," Abigail wrote to Tufts during his own inoculation, "if you roast them well, otherways fear they will be too hard for my Digestion." She took great interest in the medical procedures and sent John medicines with admonitions to take them. He obliged with full details. Since preparation for inoculation involved measures that seemed calculated to make the patient as weak as possible, the details were not always very pleasant, but John managed to make sport of his own discomfort. "Did you ever see two Persons in one Room Iphichacuana'd together? . . . I assure you they make merry Diversion. [Iphichacuana was an emetic.] We took turns to be sick and to laugh. When my Companion was sick I laughed at him, and when I was sick he laughed at me." But the worst part of it all, he assured Abigail, was the separation "from my Diana."

Some weeks later, after enduring the mild version of smallpox that inoculation produced, he was less sanguine about the experience. "Don't conclude from any Thing I have written that I think Inoculation a light matter. —A long and total Abstinence from every Thing in Nature that has any Taste, Two heavy Vomits, one heavy Cathartick, four and twenty Mercurial and Antimonial Pills, and Three Weeks close Confinement to an House, are, according to my Estimation of Things, no small matters." Nevertheless, he added, it was far preferable to living in fear of the disease.

The several weeks apart were difficult for two lovers accustomed to frequent visits. John proposed, soon after arriving in Boston, "sending . . . a Nest of Letters like a Nest of Basketts; tho I suspect the latter would be a more genteel and acceptable Present to a Lady." For Abigail, "The Nest of Letters which you so undervalue, were to me a much more welcome present than a Nest of Baskets, tho every stran of those had been gold and silver." John had to smoke his letters before sending them from the smallpox-infested house, and insisted that Tom, the Smith's slave, smoke them again before Abigail read them, for "I would not you should take the Distemper, by Letter from me, for Millions." "Did you never rob a Birds nest?" Abigail responded. "Do you remember how the poor Bird would fly round—just so they say I hover round Tom whilst he is smokeing my Letters." Eventually she would show his letters to her family, but "Miser like I hoard them up, and am not very communicative."

In these letters Abigail and John expressed their deepest feelings for each other, sometimes under the cover of light-hearted banter, but at other times quite seriously and candidly. Abigail, who admitted that she found it easier to write than to speak her feelings, for the first time laid bare her apprehensions about living up to John's expectations of her. She chided him gently about being "too severe" in his judgments of people and worried that his severity would be directed against her. "You sometimes view the dark side of your Diana," she wrote, "and there no doubt you discover many Spots—which I rather wish were erased, than conceal'd from you." Criticism and self-criticism became persistent themes in their correspondence during these weeks. It was a subject they could not easily discuss face to face, and the extended forced separation brought these anxieties into the open. But all this probing into each other's personal qualities was tempered by their deep affection for each other and their sense of humor, so that the dialogue strengthened rather than threatened their relationship.

As the time drew near for John to return home she wrote him a description of a meeting she had witnessed (or invented) between a "Gentleman and his Lady" who had been separated some time. "Cloathe[s] all shifted—no danger—and no fear. A how do ye, and a how do ye, was exchanged between them, a Smile, and a good naturd look. Upon my word I believe they were glad to see each other. A tender meeting. I was affected with it. And thought whether Lysander, under like curcumstances could thus coldly meet his Diana, and whether Diana could with no more Emotion receive Lysander. What think you. I dare answer for a different meeting on her part were She under no restraint." She could hardly stand the separation any longer— "For should I see thee, 'Were I imprison'd e'en in paridice/I should leap the crystal walls.'"

John finally came home in May, and they then began preparing for a fall wedding. The last few weeks before their marriage were hectic, filled with complicated preparations for organizing a new household. Abigail went to Boston for a brief visit with the Smiths and promptly got sick, leaving John to hire household help and get furnishings in order by himself. They would move into the house John had inherited from his father, only yards away from where he had been living with his mother, so the logistical problems of moving furniture and other household effects were minimal. Finding servants, however, was another story. It was unthinkable to try to run a house without at least one or two servants, but help was scarce and their finances were limited. John related some of his problems to Abigail, still sick in Boston: "I have this Evening been to see the Girl. —What Girl? Pray, what Right have you to go after Girls? —Why, my Dear, the Girl I mentioned to you, Miss Alice Brackett. But Miss has hitherto acted in the Character of an House-Keeper, and her noble aspiring Spirit had rather rise to be a Wife than descend to be a Maid." In the end, they made do with one of John's mother's servants, a black woman named Judah, who could be spared for a few months. Abigail did not particularly like the arrangement, but there seemed to be no alternative.

The marriage preparations were complicated not only by Abigail's illness but also by the demands of John's work. In the midst of his efforts to find servants, he had to go to the circuit court session at Plymouth, where he expected to find "a Number of bauling Lawyers, drunken Squires, and impertinent and stingy Clients." On this trip John felt especially intolerant of his clients and fellow lawyers: "Oh my dear Girl," he wrote, "I thank Heaven that another Fortnight will restore you to me—after so long a separation. My soul and Body have both been thrown into Disorder, by your Absence, and a Month or two more would make me the most insufferable Cynick, in the World. . . . But you who have always softened and warmed my Heart, shall restore my Benevolence as well as my Health and Tranquility of mind. You shall polish and refine my sentiments of Life and Manners, banish all the unsocial and ill natured Particles in my Composition, and form me to that happy Temper, that can reconcile a quick Disernment with a perfect Candour."

On October 25, 1764, Abigail and John were married in the Weymouth meetinghouse. She was a month shy of twenty; he was twenty-nine. Abigail's father, William, presided at the marriage, as he did at the marriages of his other two daughters. According to family tradition he preached at Mary's wedding from the text, "Mary hath chosen that good part which shall not be taken from her." At Betsey's wedding, his text was, "There was a man sent from God, whose name was John." At Abigail's wedding, he chose the passage, "John came neither eating nor drinking, and they say he hath a devil."

Afterward, the newlyweds—tiny, dark-haired and brown-eyed Abigail, looking very young, and John, stocky, fair-haired, and ruddy-cheeked—took leave of their friends and rode along the familiar road to Braintree, and their new home.

Chapter 3

Wife and Mother

Abigail and John moved into a modest saltbox-style cottage next door to John's childhood home. The house was nearly a hundred years old, and decades of salt air had weathered its clapboards to a dull gray. John's mother still lived in the house opposite, nearly a twin to theirs. The two cottages, spaced well apart from their neighbors', faced the main road through Braintree, less than 2 miles from the ocean. Slightly farther inland was Penn's Hill, which on a clear day commanded a fine view of the countryside.

Their new home looked much smaller than Weymouth parsonage from the outside, but inside there was a surprising amount of room. One of the large rooms downstairs served as John's office. Abigail spent much of her time in the kitchen with its enormous fireplace, baking, sewing, or, when time permitted, reading. There was also a parlor downstairs, and a room off the kitchen for Judah, their servant. A narrow, steep stairway led from the front hall to the second floor, which had two spacious front bedrooms and two tiny rooms nestled under the eaves. The third-floor attic could be pressed into service for extra space when needed.

Their farm was small too—about 10 acres—but over the years the Adamses acquired small adjoining parcels as they came on the market. Like all New England farms, theirs was a mixture of different types of land of widely varying quality. John and Abigail never expected to make a living from their farm, only to provide for some of their own needs. They did not pro-

duce a surplus for market. Not all of the land could be cultivated, but every inch was used for something.

Livestock grazed on land too steep or rocky for growing
crops. The marshy coastal areas yielded grass for animal feed and
mud for fertilizer. Apple orchards produced an abundant harvest
every fall for the hard cider that was the New Englanders' favorite drink. Wooded acres were especially valuable; they produced
fuel for heating and cooking. Wood was a scarce commodity in
eastern New England, where the forests had long since been
cleared, and people who were not blessed with their own supply
paid a high price to stay warm in the winter.

The surroundings were familiar, and that helped to ease Abigail's adjustment to married life. Her new home was only about
5 miles from her old one, and her grandparents at Mount Wollaston were even closer. Mary and Richard Cranch, her sister and
brother-in-law, lived nearby too, in the section of Braintree
called Germantown. Almost every week she visited her parents
and grandparents, and she saw Mary even more often. Her sister,
especially, with two years experience as a wife, provided a sympathetic ear and friendly advice when Abigail needed it.

Even with a small house and a servant to help her, Abigail's
domestic responsibilities were heavy. But she had been well
taught by her mother and assumed her new duties with a minimum of difficulty. Cooking and sewing consumed the bulk of
her time. Tending the garden and caring for livestock were traditionally women's responsibilities too. Gradually the Adamses
accumulated a half dozen cows, twenty sheep, and a flock of
chickens, along with the two horses used for plowing and transportation.

The farm produced most of the young couple's daily needs—
fresh vegetables and fruit in season, poultry, and milk. They
grew most of their own animal feed and pressed their own cider.
Abigail had to buy her cornmeal, rye, and meat from other
farmers or order it from Boston; fish came from either the local
fishermen or the Boston markets; such staples as sugar, molasses, tea, and spices had to come from the Boston merchants,
who imported them from Europe or the West Indies. There were
no stores in Braintree or the surrounding towns, so when Abigail
wanted something that the local farmers couldn't provide, she
either went into Boston or sent a note to ask one of her relatives
there to procure what she needed.

Abigail cooked over a blazing fire in the huge kitchen fireplace, using heavy, cumbersome cast-iron pots and skillets. A hollowed-out area at the side of the fireplace, heated from below with coals, served as an oven.

"Puddings" made of cornmeal and molasses, cooked for hours over low heat, were a staple of their diet. Usually they ate the pudding first, before a main course of meat, potatoes, and vegetables. Unlike many of their contemporaries, the Adamses could afford to eat meat every day—Abigail cooked it on a spit over the fire or stewed it in a pot with vegetables. Pork, veal, and mutton were most common, whereas beef was seldom served. Fish and lobster were cheap substitutes for meat; the coastal waters abounded with them. Because fresh meat and fish could not be preserved for long, large quantities of them were salted and smoked.

Abigail bought white flour, imported from New York or Philadelphia, to bake bread and pies, although she also baked with cornmeal and rye, the staple grains of New England. Their garden provided vegetables in the summer, and some of the hardier varieties—potatoes, squash, pumpkins, onions—would keep for months in a cool cellar.

She also made most of their everyday clothes and linens. Abigail knew how to spin and weave, but they were arduous, time-consuming tasks and produced at best a plain, coarse cloth. For most of their needs she ordered dry goods from Boston— linen, cotton, and wool of various weights and qualities, depending on the purpose. Nor did she have to make such household necessities as soap and candles. Women in more remote areas or in less prosperous homes made all such household goods from scratch, but Abigail could afford to buy them and lived close enough to Boston to do so conveniently. She was also fortunate in having a servant to help with the cooking and heavy housework; over the years she and John hired more household help. Still, no self-respecting New England housewife, whatever her social status, would think of letting the servants do everything. There was no household chore that Abigail didn't to herself at least some of the time, from making puddings to scrubbing floors.

John's law practice grew rapidly, but he too still spent hours working on the farm and supervising the hired hands. With his office in the front room, he was rarely far away from Abigail, and the two always found time to be together. When the sun was bright and the snow packed hard on the roads, they went sleighing; in the spring they took long walks or climbed Penn's Hill to admire the view of the sea and the surrounding towns. On a clear day, they could see all the way to Boston, 10 miles away.

Their time together as carefree newlyweds, absorbed entirely with each other, was short. They conceived a child immediately, and Abigail gave birth to a daughter in mid-July, eight and a half months after their wedding. "Your Diana become a Mamma—can you credit it?" she wrote delightedly to Hannah Green. Her "pretty Smiles already delight my Heart, who is the Dear Image of her still Dearer Pappa." They named the child Abigail.

The new mother stayed in bed for three weeks or so, as was the custom, to recover her strength. Meanwhile, her mother, mother-in-law, and sisters took over the household chores and looked after the baby. Once she was up and about again, she adjusted quickly to her new role. Little Nabby wrought a great change in the household, but Abigail had felt no doubts about wanting a child as soon as possible. Nabby was a cheerful, docile baby, and so far married life had lost none of its magical quality for Abigail.

Shortly after Nabby's birth, news reached Braintree of events that in time would shatter the Adamses tranquil existence. The English Parliament had passed the Stamp Act, which imposed tax on all sorts of legal transactions and documents—even on newspapers. It was not a burdensome tax, but the principle behind it was pernicious to American colonists. For the first time, the British government asserted its right to tax the colonies on transactions that were strictly internal matters and had nothing to do with trade. As such, it was a dangerous precedent.

Americans, particularly New Englanders, had been disgruntled for some time with British policies toward the colonies. Since the early 1760s Parliament had been sporadically trying to extend its control over them, generally by taxing and regulating trade more heavily. With their dependence on commerce for economic survival, New Englanders were the first to object to these departures from tradition, and Boston became a center of debate over the new policies. John Adams was caught up in the discussions at an early stage. As one of the colony's up-and-coming young lawyers and an eloquent public speaker, he soon became one of the principal spokesmen for the American point of view.

Up to that time, public debate over British rule and American rights had been sporadic and tentative, but the Stamp Act was to unleash violent protest throughout the colonies. Bostonians led the way. A well-organized mob gathered at a stout tree—known forever afterward as the Liberty Tree—and hanged an effigy of Andrew Oliver, the newly appointed stamp distributor for Massachusetts. Next to it they strung up a boot with the devil sticking out of it, a pun on the Earl of Bute, one of King's most hated Ministers.

The mob then cut down Oliver's effigy, marched noisily past the Town House, where the Governor's Council was meeting, and on to the waterfront, where they burned Oliver's warehouse. They continued on to Oliver's house, beheaded the effigy, and threw stones at Oliver's windows. Finally they burned the image in a fire made with wood from the damaged warehouse. Several days later the mob spent its fury in a violent attack on the home of Thomas Hutchinson, the Crown-appointed lieutenant governor, and on the homes of two other royal officials.

The demonstration against Oliver succeeded in forcing him to resign, and no one else would take on the job of distributing the stamps. Without stamps no court business could legally be conducted, so no ships were able to enter or leave the harbor. John served on a committee to petition the governor to allow the courts to reopen. Its efforts did not succeed, however. John lamented that, just as he was building up a prosperous practice, all legal business had come to a grinding halt, leaving him worried about how to provide for his family.

Meanwhile politics helped fill the void left by the temporary halt in legal business. John became involved in the "Monday Night Club"—which discussed political issues weekly at Boston's coffee houses—wrote articles for the Boston *Gazette*, and joined the Sons of Liberty, a radical organization that grew out of the Stamp Act controversy.

In the spring of 1766 he was elected one of Braintree's selectmen, replacing a man who had been thought too sympathetic to the British side on the Stamp Act issue. Open campaigning was considered bad form in town elections, but John's brothers and a friend quietly drummed up votes for him. The contest clearly turned on questions of colonial rights and British policy. By the time the Stamp Act was repealed later in 1766 and he was able to resume his practice, John was well established as a political figure on both the local and the provincial levels.

With repeal, relative calm descended on Massachusetts, and John professed to lose interest in politics. For the moment, the three Adamses resumed some semblance of a normal family life. During the next year and a half John's practice grew rapidly as his name became better known. On that score, his public exposure during the Stamp Act crisis undoubtedly helped further his career. He spent more time "riding circuit"—attending court sessions in other districts of the colony. These sessions, which he attended almost monthly, kept him away from home for a week or two at a time. Financially, the Adamses' status improved substantially. For all his chronic complaints about low fees, John managed to buy more land and to lend some of his money at profitable interest rates.

In August 1766 Abigail and John took some time off, left Nabby with relatives, and took a trip to Salem to visit Mary and Richard Cranch. The Cranches had moved to Salem earlier in the year, after Richard's various business ventures in Braintree had failed. Richard hoped to make a new start in Salem.

Abigail and Mary, who had never been separated before, missed each other terribly. "Tis a hard thing to be weaned from any thing we Love," Abigail wrote her sister. "I think of you ten times where I used to once." Mary, living in a strange town and cut off from friends and family, felt the separation even more keenly. "I would give a great deal only to know I was within Ten Miles of you if I could not see you," she told Abigail. The conservative political atmosphere of Salem compounded her feeling of isolation, for Mary shared her sister's antipathy to the latest British policies. A copy of Boston's radical newspaper was "a Sight here rare enough to cure sore Eues as they say."

Abigail had never been to Salem, which was about 15 miles north of Boston and was Massachusetts's second largest seaport. They set off early in their small open chaise, had dinner with friends in Boston, and then drove on a few miles to Medford, where they spent the night. They made the 10 miles or so to Salem by noon the next day.

They stayed a week, spending long hours taking with Mary and Richard, and seeing the sights of Salem and its surroundings. They marveled at the homes of wealthy merchants, visited "witches' hill," where the victims of the Salem witchcraft trials had been hanged, and explored the winding, muddy streets of Marblehead, a fishing village adjacent to Salem.

The distance between Braintree and Salem did not seem so formidable after one trip, and the couple returned for another visit in the fall. This time both Abigail and John had their portraits painted by Benjamin Blyth, a local artist. It was the first time either of them had sat for a portrait. The twenty-two-year-old Abigail, her dark hair pulled neatly back from her pale face, looked reserved and thoughtful, with just a hint of a smile on her lips. Her brown eyes betray none of her childhood mischievousness. John's plump, round face and pink cheeks gave him an air of youthful innocence.,

On July 14, 1767, almost two years to the day after Nabby's birth, Abigail bore a son. They named him John Quincy after her grandfather, who had died just a few days earlier. With two children to care for now, Abigail felt the responsibilities of motherhood more keenly. John spent more and more time on his practice, often away from home riding circuit, and consequently the sole responsibility for home and children fell on her shoulders. John did share her concern about raising the children properly, but he worried most about working harder and making more money to support them.

The children's physical and moral well-being he left to Abigail. She had no difficulties with the practical matters of childrearing; the details of feeding, clothing, and caring for infants were passed down from mother to daughter just like recipes for making puddings and preserving fruit, and Abigail had any number of examples to follow. She was familiar with the childrearing theories of John Locke, whose ideas were popular in New England, but advice manuals for mothers were rare, and most women followed tradition and their own instincts rather than Locke's or anyone else's theories.

Abigail nursed her babies for about a year and then took care not to start them on too rich a diet too soon. A little cornmeal and water was their first solid food; meat came much later. Some mothers didn't feed their children meat until they were three or four years old. A baby's clothing was simple—diapers and sheets of linen or wool. When her children were old enough to crawl and then walk, Abigail would dress them in loose, smock-type gowns, which were easy to make, easy to wash, and comfortable for the children. Little boys wore them until they were six or seven.

Nabby's and Johnny's health was Abigail's most serious worry. An appalling number of children died in their first year or two or life. The cold baths that Locke advised for infants and children certainly didn't help their chances, nor did the crude medical methods of the day. Fortunately both of her children were strong babies, and a country town like Braintree was a healthy place for them to grow up. Abigail's herb medicines— she had one for every ailment—may not have always been very effective against childhood sicknesses, but at least they did no harm.

Her children's education and moral development were much more serious problems for Abigail than their physicial wellbeing. The tangible, practical ways of raising a child were easily mastered and produced obvious, visible results. It was far more difficult to shape a child's character, and any mistakes might not show themselves until it was too late. Abigail believed very seriously that mothers were primarily responsible for training their children to become moral, God-fearing, useful adults. As Mary put it, after relating an anecdote about her daughter, "What strang Ideas they have ours is the task to fix them right, that they may surpass thire mothers in every [thing]."

Traditional ideas about childrearing in the New England of the time started with the assumption that children were inherently sinful and emphasized the importance of breaking a child's will, preferably by age two, in order to instill habits of obedience. But such ideas, which stemmed from the strict Calvinism of seventeenth-century Puritans, were becoming obsolete by Abigail's time. Newer ideas urged instead that children's personalities be molded gradually and gently, with discipline to be employed sparingly and rationally and obedience for its own sake never demanded of children. At the heart of this shift in attitudes was a belief that children's personalities developed and changed as they grew older, in contrast to the earlier notion that every individual's personality was fixed from birth.

Such ideas were not entirely new in the mid-eighteenth century, nor did they completely supplant earlier, harsher views about childrearing. Both the strict Calvinist view of children as inherently evil and the more rationalistic view of children as developing personalities, along with the theories of childrearing associated with them, existed side by side throughout the colonial period. As in any time, many styles of raising children existed simultaneously, but some became more and some less fashionable. By the time Abigail became a mother, the rationalist, developmental theories about childrearing were most popular. But her parents had held similar views twenty and thirty years earlier. She adopted these ideas in large part because they described her own upbringing, but she was also quite conscious of new ideas that emphasized the importance of a mother's early care in her children's development.

She consulted with her friends and her sister Mary, who felt their maternal responsibilities just as seriously. They read and discussed the handful of books being published about childrearing and women's responsibilities in society and shared their ideas with each other. One of their favorites, a series of sermons addressed to young women by an English minister named James Fordyce, stressed mothers' lasting influence over their children and helped popularize rationalist methods of childrearing. He counseled mothers to instruct their children in a gentle fashion, relying on their own good example rather than "awful admonitions." Innocent childish behavior was to be overlooked, and children's minds were not to be pushed too fast too soon.

This new emphasis on personal growth and development in raising children fitted well with Abigail's instinctive views on the subject, but it also placed a special burden on mothers. Children were like "plants" who had to be "raised and cultivated" carefully. As their little "plants" spread, they would diffuse "virtue and happiness through the human race." Women, in short, had a unique opportunity to influence the world by raising good citizens. Unfortunately, while such views elevated women to a position of greater importance, they also saddled them with the ultimate responsibility for their children's development. Rationalist theories of childrearing left very little to heredity or chance. The "plants" would grow according to the quality of care they received: If their growth was stunted, it had to be their mother's fault. For Abigail the weight of responsibility sometimes seemed impossibly great, especially as the children got older.

John continued to spend long evenings in the Boston coffee houses after his days in court, haranguing his listeners about American rights and the best ways to protect them. It was clear to both John and Abigail that these political discussions took valuable time away from his work and his family. In January 1768, reflecting on his past, the New Year, and what it might bring, he asked himself the questions that troubled him throughout his career: What were the goals of his life—money or power? Was it more important for him to serve his country or to concentrate on supporting his family? He had two children now, and there would be more. He would earn money for his family if he spent his time on law rather than politics, and yet he felt compelled to play a role in public affairs.

Despite twinges of guilt over his duties to his family, politics and public service became, and remained, John's main commitment. His political activities in the 1760s were only the beginning of a career in public service that took up an increasing proportion of his time; his soul-searching in January 1768 was only the first of many occasions when he questioned his motives and lamented the time lost from Abigail and the children.

The demands of John's legal practice and his increasing involvement in provincial politics finally forced a decision to move to Boston in March 1768. John was reluctant to leave his quiet country home, but he also hated the constant traveling back and forth to Boston. And there was the inescapable fact that Boston was the legal and political center of the colony. If he were ever to amount to anything more than a country lawyer, he would have to move to the capital. For her part, Abigail felt none of John's apprehensions. She had visited Boston often as a child and enjoyed the city. She would be farther away from her parents, but they would still be close enough for frequent visits. Besides, she would be closer to Mary, who now lived in Boston, and she had plenty of other friends and relatives there too.

The Adamses rented a house on Brattle Square, right in the heart of Boston. Known around town as the "white house," it was a large, square structure, much roomier than the Braintree cottage. The Brattle Street Church, for years the center of the liberal, less Calvinistic brand of Congregationalism that Abigail and John espoused, was just across the way. The Town House, headquarters for the provincial government and courts, and Faneuil Hall, Boston's main market and meeting place, were only two blocks away.

Boston in 1768 was a lively, crowded city of about 16,000 people jammed onto a tiny, hilly peninsula. Since Abigail's time, most of its hills have been leveled, and much of the harbor and river surrounding it have been filled in to create more land. In her day, one entered Boston either along a narrow neck of land connecting the peninsula with the town of Roxbury, or by boat. The city itself covered an area slightly more than 3 miles long and 2 miles wide, most of it crisscrossed with narrow winding streets and alleys, heavily built up with houses.

Boston's irregular shape encouraged the formation of distinct neighborhoods. The North End was a peninsula unto itself, linked to the center of town by a neck of land hardly more than one street's width. It was the oldest part of town, heavily built up with houses dating back to the seventeenth century. In the 1760s it was a favorite neighborhood for merchants, who liked living a block or two away from their wharves and warehouses, which lined the waterfront.

The South End was the most recently settled section. Houses there were large and relatively new, and much of the land was still open. Both the North and the South End, as well as the central part of town where the Adamses lived, counted among their residents people of all occupations and social classes. Residents of the North and the South End, however, considered their neighborhoods distinctive, and a lively rivalry was carried on by the young men of the two sections. Each had its gang of young journeymen and laborers; they organized rival parades every November 5—Guy Fawkes Day, or Pope's Day, as it was called in New England, traditionally a day of rioting and merriment. These same gangs had formed the nucleus of the Stamp Act mob.

To the west and north were the Common, where any resident could graze sheep or cows, and the row of hills sometimes called the Trimountain. Beacon Hill, the tallest, rose 138 feet above sea level, separating the center of Boston from the Charles River to the west. Flanking it were Pemberton Hill and Mount Vernon, colloquially known in the 1770s as "Mount Whoredom." It was impractical to build on such steep terrain, so the Trimountain remained sparsely settled.

From her house on Brattle Square, Abigail was only steps away from the market where she bought fresh meat and produce and the merchants' shops where she bought her flour, tea, and dry goods. She had room for a small garden behind the house, but still she had to buy many of the things she had produced herself in Braintree. Sometimes she would send to Braintree for special things—a barrel of the cider stored in their cellar or cheese produced by one of the farmer's wives in their old neighborhood. It was an odd sort of reverse to her former situation, when she was forever sending to Boston for supplies.

The noise was the hardest thing to get used to in Boston. Carts clattered by the Adamses' front door constantly, at all hours of the day and night. The streets were filled with people, horses, and stray livestock. Even Bostonians kept chickens and pigs. For a long time Abigail couldn't sleep at night, but eventually she got acclimated. Sometimes she missed the solitude and clean, fresh air of Braintree—dirt streets, crowded conditions, and primitive sanitation gave Boston a distinctive pungent odor—but most of the time she enjoyed the change of pace.

Her friends were only a five- or ten-minute walk away, so they could see each other as often as they liked. She could read the newspapers before the news was stale. And she could watch the endless scene of activity at the waterfont. From her house it was just a short walk past the Town House and down King Street to the Long Wharf, which jutted nearly half a mile into the harbor. The main unloading point for ships from distant ports, it was lined with shops selling cloth and china from London, molasses from the West Indies, and fish from the coastal waters far to the north. Even though she saw little of John, with his constant attendance at the courts, coffee houses, and political clubs, she felt less isolated here than in Braintree.

Abigail and John had been in Boston only a few months when two regiments of British troops arrived in town, sent by the royal government in an attempt to nip Boston's radical activity in the bud. A show of force, the British believed, would stop this political poison before it spread to other colonies. But the troops served only to antagonize Bostonians. Conspicuous in their red uniforms, they were an ever present symbol of British oppression. Sooner or later, it was clear, the soldiers would create trouble. Unfortunately too for John and Abigail, they picked Brattle Square for their daily drills, and the thud of marching feet was soon added to the usual din of carts, horses, and people outside their windows.

Soon after they moved to Boston, Abigail conceived again, and in December she gave birth to a second daughter, named Susanna after John's mother. From the beginning she was a sickly child, and Abigail's time was totally absorbed in caring for her and their two toddlers.

John's reputation as both a lawyer and a politician increased as he took on significant, politically charged cases. He continued to write newspaper articles and to engage in casual coffee-house debates, but it was essentially through his legal work that he established his political reputation. That winter he defended John Hancock, one of Boston's wealthiest merchants and an ardent supporter of American rights, on a smuggling charge, and in the spring he defended four sailors accused of killing a Royal Navy officer while resisting impressment.

Abigail occasionally found time to attend court to hear him argue one of his political cases, and their home—they had moved again in the spring to a house on Cold Lane, four blocks west of Brattle Square—was always open to friends who wanted to discuss political ideas and strategies. Sam Adams, John's distant cousin, came often, always advocating more serious resistance against Britain. John, more cautious, was dubious about some of these ideas but enjoyed Sam's company and had to admit that he was a genius at politics. Abigail liked Sam's wife, Betsey. The two quickly became good friends.

The aristocratic-looking John Hancock, the renowned lawyer James Otis—who, it was said, was beginning to go mad—and Abigail's young cousin, Josiah Quincy, Jr., another aspiring lawyer, were all frequent visitors. Tall, handsome, blond Joseph Warren became a particular favorite with Abigail and the children. A young physician, he was rapidly achieving an excellent reputation. He not only talked politics with the Adamses but also nursed them through their colds and fevers. Politics might be men's business, but Abigail couldn't help but be drawn into the discussions in her parlor.

Through the fall and winter Susanna's already precarious health worsened. A tiny baby, she seemed unable to put on weight, and neither the doctor's remedies nor Abigail's home-brewed herb medicines did any good. By January it was clear that nothing more could be done. Abigail, pregnant again, spent anxious nights watching for the slightest improvement in the baby's condition, but to no avail. In February Susanna, barely more than a year old, died. Infant deaths were commonplace at that time; hardly any family escaped losing at least one of its children. But knowing that they were not alone was no consolation for the parents.

While Abigail and John struggled with their grief, Boston's tense calm began to break apart. Gangs of youths taunted the British soldiers, calling them "lobsterbacks" and other insulting names. So far, the troops had kept their composure, but the mood of the town became increasingly ugly. At the ropewalks along the waterfront, a few workers grew bolder in their insults, and drew nasty responses from the redcoats.

On March 5 several ropemakers left work together early in the evening. In an angry mood, they set out to attack the British sentry on duty, collecting other young men on the way. The sentry called for reinforcements; the young men, who had become a full-fledged mob, responded with insults and snowballs. Suddenly someone in the crowd yelled "Fire!" To this day, no one is certain who it was. The soldiers, thinking they had heard an order from their commander, fired their muskets into the crowd. When the smoke subsided, three Americans lay dead and two more were mortally wounded. The outraged citizens called the incident the Boston Massacre.

Abigail heard the shouts and screams of the crowd. Frightened, she watched as more troops poured down the street toward the center of town, but the violence subsided quickly. The crowd dispersed, and the bodies were carried away. But the troops remained, lined up in formation, as if to scare the townspeople off the streets and back into their homes.

John spent the evening with a group of men who met regularly to discuss politics. Hearing the bells that signaled a fire alarm, the group rushed toward the Town House. Along the way they heard wild reports of shooting, but it was all over by the time they reached the scene. Worried about Abigail, John hurried home, picking his way past the lines of soldiers. By the time he reached home, she had calmed down. But the two of them discussed well into the night their fears about where the violence would end.

Thomas Preston, captain of the British troops, and eight of his men were arrested for the shootings and were nearly lynched in the process. The next day a Tory merchant nicknamed the "Irish infant" by the radicals came to see John. It had been impossible to find anyone to defend Captain Preston and his men, he said. Even the Tory lawyers wouldn't touch the case, fearing reprisals by the mob. Tearfully, he begged John to take their case. John had a few momentary qualms about what the mob might do to him if he took the case. At the very least, his reputaton as one of the colony's leading patriots would be tarnished. But he believed in the accused man's right to legal counsel at least as strongly as he believed in the cause of American rights. A fair trial for the soldiers would show Britain and the other colonies that Bostonians still believed in the preservation of constitutional rights, that they had not completely degenerated into lawlessness and violence. Without even taking time to think about it, he agreed to take the case. Josiah Quincy, Jr., promised to assist him. Abigail, even though she knew that they might become targets of the mob, approved John's decision.

Preparations for what John termed the most important case of his career dragged on for months. By the time the men came to trial in October and November, passions surrounding the Massacre had died down. John argued that the soldiers had been deliberately attacked and had fired in self-defense. After two long trials—Preston was tried separately from his men—Preston and six of the soldiers were acquitted. Two others were convicted of manslaughter, branded on their thumbs, and released. Eighteenth-century legal usage allowed first offenders to get off with only this token punishment.

In June, while John had still been preparing the case, the Boston Town Meeting had elected him representative to the Massachusetts legislature, an indication that the Boston Massacre defense was not damaging his reputation. John was well aware of what his election would mean. Up to now, his participation in politics had been casual and sporadic—coffee-house discussions in the evenings, occasional newspaper articles, politically charged legal cases. His reputation as one of the leaders of the patriot cause was based primarily on his legal work, which was, after all, his profession. Now he was being called to play a much more active role. Attendance at legislative sessions would take time away from his work and reduce his income just when his family's needs were growing. Their third child, Charles, was just a week old.

More seriously, as a member of the legislature he would be marked by the British government as one of the treasonous radicals. "I considered the Step as a devotion of my family to ruin and myself to death, for I could scarce perceive a possibility that I should ever go through the Thorns and leap all the Precipices before me, and escape with my Life. . . . I was throwing away as bright prospects [as] any Man ever had before him: and had devoted myself to endless labour and Anxiety if not to infamy and to death, and that for nothing, except, what indeed was and ought to be all in all, a sense of duty." Yet he did not hesitate but accepted election immediately.

After the town meeting adjourned, John went home to break the news to Abigail. He poured out all his fears and misgivings about the step he had taken—fears and misgivings that she understood perfectly well and felt just as deeply. Abigail "burst into a flood of Tears." But she would not have had him decline the election. She feared more for him than for herself and the children; they could make do on a reduced income, but she knew only too well what would happen to John if the British government decided to unleash all its might against the colonial radicals. "She was very sensible of all the Danger to her and to our Children as well as to me," John noted in his diary, "but she thought I had done as I ought, she was very willing to share in all that was to come and place her trust in Providence."

She could hardly know, on that night in June 1770, how sorely she would be tried in the years to come.

Chapter 4

Politics

In the weeks after John's election, Abigail saw little of her husband. The legislature normally met in the Town House but sat through summer of 1770 in Cambridge, across the river. Governor Hutchinson ordered the move to get the legislators out of the politically charged atmosphere of Boston and away from the influence of the mob. John spent every waking moment riding the ferry back and forth to Cambridge, attending the sessions, and preparing for the Boston Massacre trial.

Abigail had her hands full with three children under the age of five, but her domestic responsibilities didn't stop her from following political events closely and demanding full details from John on his visits home. While convention barred women from any public role in politics, she was deeply engaged in the debate on the sidelines, among family and friends. Every bit as anti-British as John and the rest of the Boston radicals, and free of the restrictions felt by men in public life, she sometimes expressed herself a good deal more colorfully than they in denunciations of the mother country.

In the course of her thinking about American relations with Britain, she also began to question the position of women in American society. She became particularly interested in women who stepped outside the boundaries that society established for them. It is significant that the women she most admired in this regard—Mercy Otis Warren and Catharine Macaulay—both achieved recogniton for their anti-British writings. In the 1770s

Abigail's thinking about women and her thinking about American politics were inseparable.

When her cousin Isaac Smith, Jr., set off to visit England toward the end of 1770, Abigail felt envious of a young man's freedom to travel. Despite her hatred for "our (cruel) Mother Country," she heartily approved twenty-two-year-old Isaac's plan to visit England and wished she could go too. "From my Infancy I have always felt a great inclination to visit the Mother Country," she declared, ". . . and had nature formed me of the other Sex, I should certainly have been a rover." She asked Isaac to write her in detail his observations about England. Women might be considered "Domestick Beings," but their curiosity about the world beyond their homes and families was a match for any man's.

In her request to her cousin she could not resist adding a discourse on the obstacles that prevented most women from traveling. "The Natural tenderness and Delicacy of our Constitutions, added to the many Dangers we are subject to from your Sex, renders it almost imposible for a Single Lady to travel without injury to her character." Married women generally had family responsibilities sufficient to "prevent their Roving. . . . To your Sex are we most of us indebted for all the knowledg we acquire of Distant lands."

Abigail might defer to masculine superiority up to a point, but she was still Isaac's elder cousin and the mother of three, which apparently entitled her to hand out motherly advice. He would encounter many temptations on his travels, she told him, but he should resist them rather than hide behind the shield of youth and inexperience. Nor should he give in to pressure from his companions: "If your Gay acquaintance assault you with ridicule for persisting in a Laudable practice, dispise their contempt, and be only fearful of encurring your own." He should hold fast to the values instilled in him by his family and exhibit prudence beyond his years. Finally, the observations she wanted from him were not the usual sort made by the casual traveler but "instructive" comments on the state of English society.

John, perhaps aware of a touch of pomposity in Abigail's advice to Isaac, appended a note endorsing the "Exhortations of Dame Adams" but expressing his conviction that a man of Isaac's character had no need for such instructions. He too asked Isaac to send his observations about England, especially its politics. All signs showed that there would be more conflict with the mother country before their differences were ironed out.

Abigail's various postures in her correspondence with Isaac hint at some of the contradictions she felt about her place as a woman. As a married woman and mother she enjoyed some status and respectability, which allowed her to adopt a motherly or at least big-sisterly attitude toward a cousin who was not, after all, that much younger than she. On the other hand, as a woman there were always things to which she could not aspire, regardless of age, wisdom, or status. Hence the mixture of deference and admonition in her relationship with Isaac.

The detailed observations about England that she expected from Isaac were what concerned her most. Despite the mother country's "unnatural treatment" of the colonies, she wished to know the good as well as the bad about society and politics there. Perhaps it was rationalizing her inability to travel herself, but she told Isaac that she could not believe any other country was superior to America as a place to live, nor did she believe that one could learn anything substantial about human nature in Europe that could not be learned at home. "Dont you think this little spot of ours better calculated for happiness than any other you have yet seen or read of? Would you exchange it for England, France, Spain or Ittally?" she asked. Consistent with her general beliefs, she thought that education constituted the only significant difference among people—and there was nothing to stop Americans from being just as well educated as anyone else. But at the bottom of her comments about observing other nations was a political conviction: Americans were more nearly equal in status than the citizens of any other country, and they enjoyed greater liberty, though that liberty was now seriously endangered.

Little did Abigail realize, in 1771, that those threats to liberty would end in war or that, in the wake of that war, she would finally have her chance to observe Europe firsthand. She would, in fact, undertake an almost unthinkable task—traveling to England with only her daughter for a companion, to join John and John Quincy, who had been involved in American diplomacy in Europe.

Overwork and anxiety about politics took their toll on John. The Boston Massacre trials exhausted him; criticism from some of the more radical partisans disturbed him deeply, for he considered himself a staunch patriot. His health deteriorated, and he and Abigail finally decided to return to Braintree in the spring, three years after their move to Boston. John would keep his office in Boston, let his two clerks handle routine, day-to-day business, and ride his horse into town as often as necessary, returning in the evenings. The exercise would help to restore him, and he could always stay in town overnight if work kept him there late. With his family in Braintree, he would not be tempted to spend his evenings at coffee houses and political clubs. He would devote himself to business and to his family. "Farewell politics!" he wrote in his diary.

Something of a lull in the conflict between America and Britain in 1771 and 1772 was all that permitted John to keep his resolution to forsake politics. It was also a relatively slow period for legal business. He explained the slack period as an effect of New Englanders' animosity toward Britain, which made them frugal in their consumption of British goods. With a decline in trade, there were fewer occasions for lawsuits. Nevertheless, he observed in the fall of 1771 that "the hourly Arrival of Ships from England deeply loaden with dry Goods, and the extravagant Credit that is dayly given to Country Traders, opens a Prospect very mencholly to the public, tho profitable to Us, of a speedy revival of the suing Spirit." As usual, John was torn between two concerns, politics and personal finances. As a radical, he approved of nonconsumption of British goods; as a family man, he recognized that his financial interests were intimately linked to the revival of trade.

He continued to ride circuit. These frequent trips to other parts of the province were necessary to maintain his practice, but the time away from home grew increasingly tiresome. On a trip to Plymouth, even the company of good friends did not prevent homesickness. "I want to see my Wife and Children every Day," he wrote to Abigail. "I want to see my Grass and Blossoms and Corns, &c. every Day. I want to see my Workmen, nay I almost want to go and see the Bosse Calfs's as often as Charles does."

Years of marriage did not make periods of separation any easier for Abigail and John. The language of their letters to each other became more temperate in their mature years, but the emptiness of time spent apart remained. Abigail took solace in the company of her children when John was away, but occasionally visits to her family in Weymouth took her away from them too. "Alass! How many snow banks divide thee and me and my warmest wishes to see thee will not melt one of them," she wrote John when a storm delayed her return home. "I nev[er] left so large a flock of little ones before. You must write me how they all do. . . . I feel gratified with the immagination at the close of the Day in seeing the little flock round you inquiring when Mamma will come home—as they often do for thee in thy absence."

The flock of little ones grew to four by the end of 1771, with the birth of Thomas Boyston. Charles was still less than two years old, John Quincy four, and Nabby six. Some months later, in November 1772, the whole family packed up and moved back to Boston. A year and a half of country solitude had been enough to restore John's health, at least for the moment, and to convince both John and Abigail that the demands of business made living in the city more practical for them.

Soon after they returned to Boston, the uneasy calm of the last two years collapsed. Parliament had repealed the 1767 Townshend Acts, which had levied new taxes on imports, but had retained a tax on tea as a symbolic measure asserting England's right to tax the colonies. That was bad enough, but in 1773 they passed the Tea Act which renewed the tax on tea and granted a monopoly of the tea trade to the British East India Company. It was a measure designed to reduce the price of tea and therefore undercut American merchants who were smuggling tea to avoid paying the tax. Predictably, Americans were outraged. Plans were laid in Boston for a complete boycott of tea. The radicals engaged in protracted negotiations with merchants and provincial officials, but their usual tactics did not seem to work this time. Not even memories of the violence that had followed passage of the Stamp Act sufficed to persuade the merchants not to unload their tea.

By the time the first load of East India Company tea actually arrived in Boston Harbor in December, the contending parties had reached an impasse, and the radicals decided to take matters into their own hands. One cold night a small band of men dressed up as Indians quietly dumped the tea into the harbor. No one knows exactly who the "Indians" were; rumor had it that John Hancock and Sam Adams had been spotted in the crowd. John Adams, however, was not one of them. He was off riding circuit and missed all the excitement. Abigail heard all about the "Tea Party" soon after it happened. She heartily approved the action and the general movement to boycott "that bainfull weed," as she called it.

The British government retaliated quickly and harshly. They chose to ignore general American opposition to the Tea Act and concentrated instead on the illegal activities of the Boston Tea Party. Top British officials had always thought of Boston as a hotbed of radicalism and predicted that the American troubles would subside quickly if only the Boston radicals could be suppressed. To that end, Parliament passed the Boston Port Bill, prohibiting all shipping into and out of Boston until the town paid for the damaged tea. It was a measure designed to cripple the city's economy and bring it to its knees quickly. With its trade eliminated, Boston would be like a city under seige and could not hope to survive long.

British officials did not expect the other colonies to come to Boston's aid by sending money and supplies overland, but that was exactly what happened. Opposition to British policies did indeed extend beyond Boston; the colonies were not quite as fragmented as they appeared to be at first glance. Consequently, the retaliatory measures against Boston backfired; they only increased the other colonies' anger against Britian. The Coercive Acts, passed shortly after the Boston Port Bill, strengthened the general opposition. They required Americans to quarter British troops when necessary, made it easier to prosecute people who organized riots, and, in another measure directed specifically at Massachusetts (the so-called Regulation Act), placed more power in the hands of the royal governor.

The events of 1773 and early 1774 made it inevitable that John would again become deeply involved in politics, an involvement that Abigail supported. She too was giving more and more thought to the implications of current political developments. Both Adamses were pessimistic about the prospects for the future of American liberty. In the wake of the passage of the Boston Port Bill, John wrote to Abigail, "The Town of Boston, for ought I can see, must suffer Martyrdom: It must expire: And our principal Consolation is, that it dies in a noble Cause. The Cause of Truth, of Virtue, of Liberty and of Humanity." Probably they would be forced to leave their home in Boston; in any case, they would have to exercise the utmost frugality as business declined. Still, dark as the future looked, in his heart John thought that the American cause would triumph and Boston "will probably have a glorious Reformation, to greater Wealth, Splendor and Power than ever. . . . I look upon this, as the last Effort of Lord Norths Despair. And he will as surely be defeated in it, as he was in the Project of the Tea."

Abigail's political thinking was in close agreement with John's, and the two of them discussed politics extensively during these years. But her political discussions were not confined to her own home or letters to John. In the spring of 1773 she met Mercy Otis Warren, who became a close friend, a strong influence on her thinking, and a sounding board for her ideas. Mercy Warren had impeccable revolutionary credentials: She was the sister of James Otis, one of John's old heroes, and husband of James Warren, another leading Massachusetts radical and later an officer in the Continental Army. More important, she became a literary and political figure in her own right as a writer first of plays and later of history, all written with clear political intent. Abigail met Mercy through John, who knew the Warrens through political business. He often visited them while attending court sessions at Plymouth. On one of these trips, Abigail went along and met them for herself.

She was instantly attracted to Mercy, and soon came to regard her as a model for her own life. Like many of Abigail's friends, Mercy was considerably older: Abigail was twenty-nine and Mercy forty-five when they first met. The older woman seemed to have resolved many of the problems of managing a home and family that seemed so pressing to Abigail. She thought the Warren children—all of them, of course, somewhat older than her own—quite remarkable, a credit to Mercy's capability in raising them. At the same time she admired Mercy for her accomplishments outside the traditional sphere of home and family. Abigail did not herself aspire to anything more than being a good wife and mother, but she felt a special appreciation for women who did. Mercy Warren was the first such woman that she actually met and counted among her friends.

At the time they met, Mercy was just beginning to expand her literary interests and to publish some of her writings. She had written poetry—considered the only suitable literary form for female writers—for years but had never attempted to publish anything. Early in 1772, inspired by her desire to comment on political issues, she wrote a satirical play called *The Adulateur*, which was published serially in the *Massachusetts Spy*, a radical newspaper. It marked her first attempt at playwriting, satire, and political commentary. It was also her first important publication. *The Adulateur*, in which the characters were thinly disguised versions of contemporary political figures, was published in pamphlet form in 1773. Later that year she published *The Defeat* and, in 1775, her most famous play, *The Group*.

Reading *The Adulateur* had first inspired Abigail to accompany John to Plymouth to meet the Warrens. Although she looked up to Mercy as a model and admired her intellectual achievements, their relationship was never one-sided. Abigail and John were substantial sources of encouragement to Mercy in her new role as political satirist and playwright. Mercy, for all her talent and accomplishments, shared Abigail's belief that women's primary responsibility was caring for a home and family. It was one thing to write poetry privately, in her spare time, but wouldn't writing and publishing satire make her unfeminine? It was a question that nagged her off and on for years. She published her plays under a male pen name, and, until her fame spread and her style became familiar, it was widely assumed that the plays were in fact written by a man.

Mercy became Abigail's closest confidante during the Revolutionary years. Always conscious of women's supposed intellectual inferiority when she expressed her thoughts to men, Abigail was able to give freer rein to her ideas in correspondence with another woman. Her tone of deference to Mercy, as to an older woman of great intellectual accomplishment, faded quickly as the two became intimate. Their common concerns—raising children, supporting the American cause, and, later, coping with loneliness during their husbands' long absences—made their friendship an important source of strength for both women during a difficult time.

From the beginning of their friendship, children and politics were equally compelling concerns. Abigail opened her correspondence with Mercy by expressing her admiration for the Warren children and asking for advice. Their letters on this subject are indication of how seriously eighteenth-century women took their childrearing responsibilities, believing literally that they were primarily responsible for the kinds of adults that their children became. Abigail and Mercy were also of like mind on political issues—both squarely in the radical camp along with their husbands. Like them, Abigail imbibed her radical ideas from a variety of sources, including the classical writers Livy, Tacitus, and Cicero and Enlightenment philosophers, particularly Locke. The most significant influences on them, however, were several generations of theorists and propagandists critical of the British political system. From Milton, Sidney, and Harrington, radical writers of the English Civil War era, to critics of Crown policies in the early decades of the eighteenth century, to the radicals of the 1760s, the English tradition of political opposition helped shape American views on government and on their proper relationship to the mother country. The arguments of eighteenth-century writers—whether of the 1720s or the 1760s—had a particularly strong impact on American radicals, because they described and criticized changes in English politics that seemed to explain the evils of the current English administration and its attacks on American liberties.

Their arguments were rooted in the beliefs that all Englishmen had certain traditional, inalienable rights; that kings were accountable to their subjects; and that those subjects had a right to resist the king if he violated those rights. But there were also strong moral overtones to their arguments, and it was this aspect of their writings that so appealed to Americans. "Power corrupts" was their most persistent message. Unchecked power in the hands of a small group of individuals would inevitably bring disaster, and popular rights and liberties would be sacrificed. Unfortunately, highly placed officials showed a natural tendency to try to assume more and more power. Only the eternal vigilance of a virtuous people could prevent such an accumulation of power.

These ideas were tremendously influential among Americans, who saw themselves as the victims of corrupt royal ministers who usurped power and exerted a pernicious influence over

the King. The emphasis on moral issues in politics—the preoccupation with power, corruption, and virtue—especially appealed to Americans, among whom the Puritan tradition remained strong. For Abigail, as for her fellow New England
radicals, this juxtaposition of a corrupt government and a virtuous people seemed the only sensible way to explain the current state of affairs.

Throughout her life Abigail would explain political events
in terms of the moral character of individuals. Whether it was
King George and his Ministers or, much later, John Adams's political rivals, vice, corruption, and unchecked passions explained
their behavior. She believed that many of the qualities of human
nature were essentially neutral; whether they were put to good
or bad use depended on whether they were harnessed by virtue
and reason or by passion and personal interest. Take ambition,
for example—a quality about which eighteenth-century men
and women expressed great ambivalence. Most people possessed
it, Abigail explained to Mercy Warren, and in an "honest mind"
it could produce great service to the world. "Yet there is nothing
in Nature so amiable but the passions and interest of Men will
pervert to very base purposes." Ambition controlled by passion
would produce evil consequences; the ambition of "artfull and
designing men" was responsible for the disagreements between
America and England. Whatever the situation, individuals were
always to be judged by the yardsticks of virtue and vice. Abigail
even criticized Molière for ridiculing evil without at the same
time emphasizing virtue; but Mercy, the budding playwright,
chided her gently for demanding such a literal comparison of
right and wrong.

Among the various English radicals writing about current
politics, Abigail was particularly interested in Catharine Macaulay—partly because she was the most outspoken advocate of
the American cause, but mostly because she was a woman. She
admired Macaulay, just as she admired Mercy Warren, for having achieved a reputation as a writer and intellectual who expressed in a formal way the same convictions that Abigail felt so
strongly. Macaulay was among the most radical of the English
political writers of the 1760s and 1770s; unlike most, she went
so far as to advocate a republican form of government. She took a
particular interest in American events, because it was in America that she saw the promise of significant political reform. Her

writings were reprinted and enjoyed considerable popularity in the colonies, and when she toured America just before the Revolution, her celebrity there flourished still more.

Abigail had first expressed her interest in Catharine Macaulay in 1771, when Isaac Smith departed for Europe. "I have a great desire to be made acquainted with Mrs. Macaulay's own history," she wrote him. "One of my own Sex so eminent in a tract so uncommon naturally raises my curiosity . . . I have a curiosity to know her Education, and what first prompted her to engage in a Study never before Exhibited to the publick by one of her own sex and Country." Her curiosity was partly satisfied shortly afterward, when John began corresponding with Macaulay. He introduced her by letter to Mercy Warren in 1774, much to Macaulay's pleasure, because she was especially interested in American women and liked Warren's political ideas. Not to be outdone, Abigail took Macaulay's expressed interest in American women as an occasion to begin her own correspondence with the distinguished Englishwoman. Although she did not consider herself as accomplished as Mercy Warren, she told Macaulay that she was in "no ways deficient in her esteem for a Lady who so warmly interests herself in the cause of America."

She then proceeded to give Macaulay her version of American problems. The people of New England were suffering seriously because of Parliament's actions, so seriously that the possibility of war was ever-present in their minds. "We are invaded with fleets and Armies, our commerce not only obstructed, but totally ruined, the courts of Justice shut, many driven out from the Metropolis, thousands reduced to want, or dependant upon the charity of their neighbors for a daily supply of food, all the Horrours of a civil war threatening us on one hand, and the chains of Slavery ready forged for us on the other," she concluded.

It was easy for Abigail to get carried away on the subject of American grievances; the situation was not really quite so bad as she described. But in her rhetorical exaggeration she was in good company—"the chains of slavery" in particular was a very popular metaphor in the colonies.

Abigail knew, in writing to Catharine Macaulay, that she had a sympathetic audience, someone who would take her at her word when she said that American opposition to Britain had become so serious that the colonists' grievances must be speedily redressed. "The only alternative which every american thinks of is Liberty or Death." It was quite clear, however, that she did not really expect a peaceful redress of grievances.

One of the reasons that Abigail liked Macaulay's writings so much was that both of them viewed political events in terms of individual character. Macaulay's multivolume history of England was a tale of the ebb and flow of liberty from ancient times to the then present; her heroes were the leaders who promoted liberty, and her villains those who suppressed it. The heroes were motivated by reason and virtue and the villains by base passion and corruping power. It was a vision of history that stressed morality and individual motivation, and it fitted well with Abigail's ideas about human nature and historical causation.

In corresponding with Macaulay, she took particular care to stress the virtuousness of Americans even in the face of disorder produced by the current political debate. In part, she wanted to counter stories circulated by American opponents that the Americans were badly divided politically and that chaos reigned as British-appointed officials were for all practical purposes stripped of their power. More significantly, she believed that the Americans' virtue would ultimately help their cause triumph. Americans were filled "with that firmness, that fortitude, that undaunted resolution which ever attends those who are conscious that they are the injured not the *injurer*, and that they are engaged in a righteous cause." The courts may have been temporarily suspended, but "Honour and conscience" proved more powerful than judicial proceedings. Virtuous character, in other words, kept Americans from falling into disorder and conflict with each other in this unprecedented and troubled time. And virtuous character would be their strongest support in the fight against the British.

None of this was shocking to Catharine Macaulay. In her own view, virtue and liberty went hand in hand, and in the 1770s Americans seemed to have a monopoly of both. Nor would she disagree with Abigail's declaration that, if America were conquered, it would be the end of the English Constitution as well. For Macaulay, and for many other English radicals too, the future of liberty and constitutionalism in England as well as in the colonies seemed to lie in American hands.

Abigail's comments to Macaulay were filled with revolutionary bravado, but they also betrayed a very real fear of impending war. As early as 1773, in the wake of the crisis over tea, she was convinced—as were most New England radicals—that there would be no peaceful resolution of the conflict between America and Britain. "Altho the mind is shocked at the Thought of shedding Humane Blood," she wrote Mercy, "more Especially the Blood of our Countrymen, and a civil War is of all Wars, the most dreadfull Such is the present Spirit that our Heroes will spend their lives in the cause, With the Speach of Cato in their Mouths, 'What a pitty it is, that we can dye but once to save our Country.' "

Although America's plight was never far from Abigail's thoughts in 1773 and 1774, there were lighter moments too. Her younger sister Betsey was having troubles with men. She was at an age when most women were married, but was still living at home with no apparent intention of changing her status in the near future. Abigail confessed to Mary her disappointment when Betsey broke up with one man and then showed no interest in another, whom Abigail happened to like very much. "What a pitty tis we cannot reason ourselves into love," she commented. But she knew better than to urge Betsey into a match that she obviously did not want.

When Betsey finally did show some interest in a man—John Shaw, a young schoolmaster who boarded in the Smith household—Abigail scolded her for showing excessive familiarity with him. Apparently she had forgotten her own impetuosity as a teenager in love for the first time. Perhaps also she thought that living under the same roof with this youug man would expose Betsey to intolerable temptations. In any case, she tried to offer some big-sisterly advice and was told, in no uncertain terms, to mind her own business. As a woman living in isolation with few opportunities for intellectual conversation, Betsey asserted her right to cultivate any interesting company without regard to sex. She absolutely refused to "purse up the Mouth, look demure, commence Prude (which by the way I wonder I have not) keep at a Chimney's length, never suffer onself to get within the power of attraction. . . . And can a Sister blame me, who is every Day tasting the calm Pleasures, annexed to such a

Course of life." Just in case she hadn't made her point, she appended a statement "certifying" that she and John Shaw had no interest in each other beyond simple friendship, duly signed and witnessed by her parents—whose signatures were forged.

Betsey may have been telling the truth at the time, but friendship blossomed into love, and she and John Shaw were married in 1777. Abigail never did reconcile herself to the match; apparently she disliked Shaw intensely. In the meantime, however, she made no further efforts to interfere with her sister's love life.

In June 1774 John Adams was chosen as one of five delegates from Massachusetts to the Continental Congress, the first intercolonial political assembly to be convened since the short-lived Stamp Act Congress in 1765. The Congress was organized largely at the instigation of Massachusetts radicals, still reeling from the British attempts to squelch all opposition emanating from Boston. It was to be held, however, in Philadelphia.

Massachusetts by this time was practically in a state of rebellion. The port was closed, and the courts no longer sitting. Citizens held town meetings, and militia companies drilled in defiance of the Regulation Act, which prohibited such gatherings. The Committee of Correspondence, first organized in 1772 to maintain communication among radicals throughout the colony and in other colonies, took on many of the day-to-day functions of government. Still, anti-British sentiment in rural New England was considerably milder than in Boston, and it was milder yet in other colonies. There were plenty of people around who were quite prepared to believe, along with the officials of the British government, that Bostonians were just a pack of troublemakers.

In this atmosphere of political tension and uncertainty John accepted, with some misgivings, his nomination to the Continental Congress. In the weeks between his election and his departure for Philadelphia, he attended the circuit court in Maine (then part of Massachusetts), which was the only district court still in session. At the same time, Abigail and the children returned to Braintree, where they would remain for the duration of the Revolution.

Court business was sluggish, and political opinion in Maine was generally critical of Boston. The time dragged slowly for John, but he felt the need to earn money, however little it might be, to augment funds Abigail and the children would have to live on in his absence. Delegates to the Congress received only their expenses, and sometimes not even that. He was away longer than usual this time, about a month, and felt more than usually annoyed by the delays of trials. Abigail, for her part, had to contend with problems on the farm, manage the chidren by herself, and keep John informed of the latest local political developments. It was almost as if they were rehearsing for the much longer separation that lay ahead of them.

The farm demanded a considerable amount of attention. Frustrated at not being able to look after these things himself, John fired off letter after letter with instructions to Abigail. She should talk to one of several men in the neighborhood about getting marsh or creek mud for fertilizer; he explained how to use it. A week later he reminded her, "Pray remember my Marsh Mudd." She should extract as much work out of the tenants as possible; several men who owed them money might also be put to work. He reminded her that it was time for the hay to be mowed. More seaweed, marsh mud, and sand were needed. Always he urged her to be frugal.

Meanwhile, the lack of business in Maine did nothing to reassure John about the family finances, and the state of political opinion there gave him a good deal of distress. Especially upsetting was the widespread opinion that "the better sort" of Bostonians sided with the British, whereas the radicals were all part of a "vulgar mob." He was at this time arguing the case of a man whose house had been vandalized by a mob for no particular reason. "These private Mobs, I do and will detest," he noted. "If Popular Commotions can be justifyed, in Opposition to Attacks upon the Constitution, it can be only when Fundamentals are invaded, nor then unless for absolute Necessity and with great Caution. But these Tarrings and Featherings, these breaking open Houses by rude and insolent Rabbles, in Resentment for private Wrongs or in pursuiance of private Prejudices and Passions, . . . cannot be even excused upon any Principle." Most people did not understand the distinction between "private mobs" and justifiable "Popular Commotions," and the likes of John Adams found themselves classified with the vulgar rabble.

Not only were the people John encountered critical of the Boston mobs, but, worse yet, many of them did not see the point of fighting the tax on tea. Both Whigs and Tories engaged in inflammatory rhetoric; "We very seldom hear any solid Reasoning." No one, it seemed, understood that the essential question was whether the American colonies were a "distinct Community" with the power to determine when its rights were infringed, or were instead completely subject to the control of Parliament. All around him he saw evidence of extravagance and display, which suggested that people were concerned more about their pocketbooks than about their freedom.

On this point Abigail could not have agreed more, for it was the moral dimension of the conflict that excited her most impassioned statements. John was usually more concerned with the theoretical and political implications of the conflict, but he too believed that Americans had to rely on the simple virtues of industry, frugality, and faith in God to get them through the crisis.

Still, there were some bright spots on the horizon even in Tory-dominated Maine. One day, after a long ride on horseback, John asked a woman tavern keeper if he might have a cup of tea, providing, of course, that it had been "honestly smuggled" and had borne no tax. She informed him that she served no tea but would be happy to make coffee for him. In telling the story to Abigail, he announced, "Tea must be universally renounced. I must be weaned, and the sooner, the better."

John was especially sensitive about the wealth and extravagance that he observed, because he still worried that he was neglecting his family and his fortune in favor of his involvement in politics. He was also jealous of the success enjoyed by country bumpkins practicing law in the outlying areas. He knew of several Maine and New Hampshire men who had started with fewer advantages than he but were now wealthy. John berated himself for not doing as well; he had enjoyed an inheritance from his father and some financial assistance from Abigail's father, and he had worked very hard for sixteen years. He had an extensive practice and many rich clients, but still he was poor compared to the lawyers he was meeting on this trip. He blamed himself for spending too much money—his extensive library and the house in Boston were "indiscretions" that had turned to "disasters" because of the decline in business resulting from the political crisis. But it was not just the books and the house that prevented the Adamses from enjoying more financial security. The political crisis had virtually shut down Boston's commerce, and with it most legal business. The lawyers who succeeded were those who sided with the British government. John feared that his politics, rather than his extravagance, would bring financial disaster down upon his family. No wonder he resented people who pursued wealth with no concern for the good of their country. And no wonder that, on the eve of his departure for the Continental Congress, he felt guilty about neglecting his family for politics.

In his gloomy moments, John fell back on the importance of frugality and the virtues of a simple life on the farm. "I sometimes think I must come to this—to be the Foreman upon my own Farm, and the School Master to my own Children . . . I shall arouse myself ere long I believe, and exert an Industry, a Frugality, a hard Labour, that will serve my Country. . . . If I cannot serve my Children by the Law, I will serve them by Agriculture, by Trade, by some Way, or other."

The impending Congress inspired such thoughts in John because it seemed to be such an irrevocable step. It was the first substantial effort by the colonies to organize to assert their rights, and the men who participated in it would be forever labeled as the leaders of the rebellion—*if* rebellion ensued, as John thought it would. His attendance at the Congress would also be his first trip outside New England, no small undertaking in the days of horse-and-buggy transportation. He would be consorting with the most distinguished men of the provinces; he worried that their "Educations, Travel, Experience, Family, Fortune, and every Thing" would be superior to his. And he would be separated from his family for weeks, perhaps months, the longest time they had ever been apart.

But despite his doubts—about himself, his career, his ability to support his family, the future of America—there was never any question that John would go to Philadelphia, and Abigail never tried to dissuade him. Indeed, she urged him on. After ten years of marriage she was used to John's self-doubt and his periodic renunciations of politics in favor of the life of a simple farmer. And so, while he was in Maine arguing cases and taking the political pulse of the countryside, she helped prepare the things he would need for his journey to Philadelphia. Many details had to be attended to; John heard a rumor that washing was badly done in New York and Pennsylvania, so he decided he should carry a large supply of linen. Perhaps he should get a new suit. And he had to figure out the best means of transportation to Philadelphia.

This mixture of domestic details and burning political issues had occupied Abigail's thoughts for many months and would continue to occupy them for the next several years. John summed it up when he urged, "I must intreat you, my dear Partner in all the Joys and Sorrows, Prosperity and Adversity of my Life, to take a Part with me in the Struggle." Then, practically in the same breath, he said "rouse your whole Attention to the Family, the stock, the Farm, the Dairy. Let every Article of Expence which can possibly be spared be retrench'd." His words were hardly necessary, for she had been part of the struggle from the beginning.

Chapter 5

War

Abigail went into Boston with John on August 9, the day before he was to leave for Philadelphia with his fellow delegates. Early the next morning they said their private goodbyes, and then she joined the crowd gathering in the streets to wish the delegates well. The four of them—John, Sam Adams, and the prominent lawyers Thomas Cushing and Robert Treat Paine—made an impressive sight in their new clothes and freshly powdered wigs as they rode through the town in their coach-and-four. Two white servants on horseback preceded them, and four black servants in livery followed. Cheering crowds lined the streets as they rode through town.

When they were out of sight, Abigail turned back to her uncle's house and tried not to think about the separation that lay ahead. Proud of John's election to Congress and hopeful about this new sign of colonial unity, she nevertheless could not suppress a certain fear for the future.

Abigail dreaded war and yet saw no alternative. "The great anxiety I feel for my Country, for you and for our family renders the day tedious, and the night unpleasant," she wrote John only days after he left. "The Rocks and quick Sands appear upon every Side. . . . Uncertainty and expectation leave the mind great Scope. Did ever any Kingdom or State regain their Liberty, when once it was invaded without Blood shed? I cannot think of it without horror."

John's absence, of course, aggravated her anxieties. Although they had been separated often during their marriage, neither Abigail nor John had ever grown used to it. Their love for each other strengthened with the years. They shared everything—their views on politics, their fears for their country, their ideas about the farm, their hopes for their children—and depended on each other for comfort in any crisis. Now separated by a greater distance than ever before, for an indefinite length of time, and just when their world appeared to be most unsettled, each would have to survive alone.

Letters were their only consolation. They were a poor substitute for conversation, but Abigail had nothing else. She wrote often, with an ease and grace that made her letters as close to conversation as the written word could be. She poured out her worries about everything from planting corn to the possibility of war with Great Britain. Just putting her thoughts on paper helped relieve her mind, but it could take weeks for John's answers to come—when they came at all.

John wrote less often, citing the pressure of work as the reason. When he did write, his letters were generally brief and less emotional than Abigail's. But he always reassured her about her efforts with the farm and the children, and kept her informed about the deliberations of Congress. He entertained her with stories about his experiences in Philadelphia and descriptions of the people he met. Occasionally he gave vent to his frustrations over the petty quarrels among delegates and the slow pace of their discussions, feelings he could entrust to no one else.

Their letters traveled slowly. Braintree was about 300 miles from Philadelphia, a distance that could easily take two weeks to cover. Intercolonial postal service was poor at best and extremely expensive besides. Worried, with some justification, that his letters might be intercepted, John preferred to send them by personal messenger. Abigail could write several letters before getting a single reply; some were lost altogether. She could never count on getting a specific answer to any question— what to plant, when to plant it, which laborer to hire, where to send Johnny to school—in time to act on it. So she had to make many decisions on her own, and gradually she gained confidence in her ability to run the farm by herself. But even if John's letters were of little practical help, she depended on them tremendously to keep up her spirits and to maintain some sense of continity in their marriage.

John depended on Abigail's letters not only for the same

kind of emotional support but also for up-to-date, reliable information about events in New England. Philadelphia was far removed from the menace of British troops and was much more conservative politically. He contended daily with men who advocated a cautious and conciliatory policy toward Britain; it was good to be reminded that New England was ready to explode into war. With her passionate interest in political events and her skill at observation, Abigail was John's best informant. Newspapers were unreliable, and friends in Boston wrote erratically, but Abigail could be counted upon for detailed, accurate information.

She reported that government continued as usual in Massachusetts, although town meetings were technically illegal. Preparations for war were uppermost in most people's minds. Governor Gage fulfilled everyone's worst predictions when he began to fortify Boston—placing cannon on Beacon Hill, digging trenches on the neck connecting Boston with the mainland, and stationing a regiment there. Rumors about a British plot to seize all of Boston's gunpowder enraged the local population and posed the threat of violence. Only the great importance attached to the deliberations of Congress, according to Abigail, quieted the hostile feelings for the moment.

Feelings ran high between Patriots and Tories, sometimes even within the same families. Abigail went to dinner at her uncle Josiah Quincy's, along with her cousins Samuel and Josiah, Jr. Young Josiah, who had assisted John on the Boston Massacre case, was an ardent patriot; his brother favored the Crown side. To make matters even more heated, Samuel's wife supported the Patriots. "A little clashing of parties you may be sure," Abigail observed to John. "Mr. Sam's wife said she thought it high time for her husband to turn about."

In Braintree the patriots had the upper hand and the Tories were running scared, sometimes literally. Abigail recounted a story about an Anglican minister who hid in his attic when he thought the patriots were after him. "An other jumpt out of his window and hid among the corn whilst a third crept under his bord fence," she told John.

The Braintree patriots might have the Tories cowed with fear, but in Boston, headquarters for the British regiments, the situation was more serious. Fear and rumor had escalated to such a point that reports of a conspiracy of slaves circulated like wildfire. Abigail believed the rumor (although in fact there is no evidence that such a conspiracy existed) and was prompted to express her opposition to slavery. "I wish most sincerely there was not a Slave in the province. It allways appeard a most iniquitous Scheme to me—fight ourselfs for what we are daily robbing and plundering from those who have as good a right to freedom as we have." It was a conviction that came to be widespread among northern Americans during and after the Revolution. The implications of the rhetoric about being "slaves" of the British were not lost on these particular men and women.

But regardless of the threat of imminent war, Abigail had to look after the farm, see that the children continued their studies—even though schools were in disarray—and somehow hold together the threads of John's law practice.

Hired men did most of the day-to-day work on the farm, but Abigail saw to it that their tasks were accomplished and made the important decisions about the harvesting of crops.

Farming took on particular importance, both practical and symbolic, as the threat of war became more serious. Self-sufficiency was important to the opponents of Britain, and "industry" and "frugality" were the watchwords of the day. As John noted to Abigail, "I hope our Husbandry is prudently and industriously managed. Frugality must be our Support." Such prudence was partly a matter of necessity; with trade cut off and business in decline, families had to rely more heavily on their own production. This was especially true for the Adamses, for John could not provide financial support for his family while he served in Congress. But the emphasis on frugality had another purpose as well. Frugality—the denial of material possessions and pleasures—was equated with virtue. And virtue, to Americans, equaled strength. A virtuous America struggling against a corrupt England was one of the patriots' favorite images. Abigail and John, and most of their fellow countrymen, sincerely believed that ultimately God rewarded the virtuous, that high moral standards must be maintained if the cause of liberty was to triumph.

As the cause of virtue demanded careful management of the farm, no less did it demand the careful raising of children. With John gone and schools disrupted because of the crisis, Abigail carried the entire burden of educating the children just at the time when all her other domestic responsibilities had increased.

She worried most about John Quincy, the eldest son, because at seven he was old enough to begin his education in a serious way. Nine-year-old Nabby posed fewer problems, because a daughter's education was primarily the responsibility of her mother, and Abigail had very clear ideas about the education of young women. Charley and Tommy, aged five and three, were still young enough to be taught entirely at home.

In normal circumstances it would be time for Johnny to begin grammar school, where boys learned Latin and Greek. None of the schools in the area were functioning on a regular basis, however, and Abigail hesitated to send him to the makeshift local school. With too many children of all ages and abilities crammed into one room, she feared he would not learn much and would pick up bad influences there. She decided instead to have John Thaxter tutor him. Protecting him from potential corrupting influences more than made up for any educational deficiencies in the arrangement, she believed. "Children should in the early part of life be unaccustomed to such examples as would tend to corrupt the purity of their words and actions that they may chill with horrour at the sound of an oath, and blush with indignation at an obscene expression," she observed to John. "These first principal[s] which grow with their growth and strengthen with their strength neither time nor custom can totally eradicate." John agreed with her views and told her to tell Johnny "to keep himself out of the Company of rude children."

The weeks of separation were hard for both Abigail and John, but John at least had plenty of activity and new experiences to occupy his mind. Abigail, on the other hand, felt the pain of separation much more severely. John's absence, the burden of running the household alone, and the ever present menace of British troops all combined to take their toll after several weeks. Letters from John kept her going, but he continued to trust his letters only to personal messengers, which severely curtailed his opportunities to write. When five weeks went by with no letters, Abigail wrote, "I had rather give a dollar for a letter by the post, tho the consequence should be that I Eat but one meal a day for these 3 weeks to come." Instead, she had to be content with the information about John and the doings of Congress provided by the newspapers.

By mid-October, when John had been gone more than two months, she wrote, "my Much Loved Friend, . . . I dare not express to you at 300 miles distance how ardently I long for your return. . . . The Idea plays about my Heart, unnerves my hand whilst I write, awakens all the tender sentiments that years have encreased and matured, . . . The whole collected stock of ten weeks absence knows not how to brook any longer restraint, but will break forth and flow thro my pen." At times like these, when she felt her fortitude giving way, Abigail became pessimistic about the future and about the outcome of the conflict with Britain. Instead of praising the virtue of Americans and trusting that God would come to their aid, she found a lack of virtue; there was no serious effort to cut down on material display at a time when Americans should be returning to the "Simplicity of Manners" of their forefathers. "We have too many high sounding words, and too few actions that correspond with them." Instead of ultimate triumph, she saw "a Scourge and heavy punishment from heaven for our numerous offences, and for the misimprovement of our great advantages."

Like most radicals, Abigail could discern no easy resolution to the conflict between Britain and America; as one prone to strong views and exaggeration, she tended to see events in the worst possible light. Her solitude exacerbated her fears. It is hardly surprising that she, often alone with small children, close enough to Boston to feel threatened by the British presence yet far enough away to be forced to depend on rumor and secondhand information, tended to fear the worst. With no one close at hand to share her forebodings, it was easy for her imagination to run rampant.

Her constant concern about John's health and safety added to her fears. There was always the threat that English officials would round up the principal radicals and pack them off to England for trial, where neither sympathetic local juries nor sympathetic mobs could help them. In fact, Governor Gage had a list of men who might be subject to arrest if the orders came, although British attention at that time was focused largely on Sam Adams and John Hancock. Mercy voiced a mutual fear when she commented to Abigail that their husbands would be "Marked out as Early Victims to successful Tyrany" but reminded her that they must never interfere with their husbands' patriotic work. She and Abigail should look to the example of Portia to give them courage. Portia, wife of Brutus, was a favorite example of womanly virtue in classical times. Some months later Abigail, who had dropped the pen name "Diana" when she married, adopted "Portia" as her new pen name.

In December, after four months away, John finally came home. Just having him home did a great deal to calm Abigail's fears. Once again she had someone to talk to about politics and the colonies' fate; being able to air her fears made them seem less formidable.

Abigail's early forebodings may have been exaggerated, but the fact remains that in the end she was right. The next April saw war break out between British and American troops in Massachusetts. In June there were more battles, and it became clear to New Englanders that there was no turning back. Congress, however, which reconvened in May, spent the summer debating conciliatory petitions to the King. More than a year would pass after the war began in New England before it would declare independence.

The first battle of the Revolution was unexpected and rather haphazard. Militia companies had been drilling intensively for months and stockpiling ammunition against the possibility of attack. But when Governor Gage ordered a raiding party to march to Concord to confiscate American ammunition, he did not expect any serious resistance.

On the evening of April 18, under cover of darkness, the soldiers slipped out of Boston. A handful of Boston patriots had been watching the British soldiers closely and planning a warning system in the event of some such action. The raiding party had not even left Boston when Paul Revere and William Dawes saddled their horses and raced to warn Minutemen in the surrounding towns. When the redcoats reached Lexington, about 12 miles west of Boston, the town militia were waiting for them. No one knows who fired the first shot, but it set off a volley of fire that left eight Americans dead.

The redcoats then moved on to the neighboring town of Concord. Militiamen there dispersed without violence. The British troops seized the ammunition and began their march back to Boston. At a bridge just outside the town, however, they found between three hundred and four hundred Minutemen blocking their retreat. Two more Americans and three British soldiers fell in a skirmish lasting only a matter of minutes. The Americans were not proving very skillful in open battle. But as the redcoats marched back to Boston, Americans—Minutemen and anyone else who could lay hands on a gun—fired on them from behind trees, fences, and houses. Several hundred more troops marched from Boston to the rescue, but by the time the shooting was over seventy British were dead and more than twice as many wounded.

Abigail's worst fears had become reality, and yet now she felt calmer than she had for months. John's presence helped, although he was getting ready to leave for Philadelphia again. Knowing that the crisis she had been expecting for months had finally happened also contributed to her calm acceptance of events. Action was better than waiting. She refused to panic or to budge from home until actually threatened.

As yet the fighting did not affect the Adams household directly. Lexington and Concord were a good 20 miles from Braintree, the battles had been brief, the casualties relatively light, and both sides had retreated—the militia back to their farms and the redcoats back to Boston. Outside New England the battles, while ominous, could be viewed as minor skirmishes. But for Abigail, and for anyone else living anywhere around Boston, there were now two sources of concern. One was Boston, which became in effect a British camp, closed off from the rest of New England. The second concern, much more serious for people living in coastal towns like Braintree and Weymouth, was the possibility that they might any day be subjected to a direct British attack.

After Lexington and Concord, American militiamen laid siege to Boston. Camped in the neighboring towns of Charlestown, Cambridge and Roxbury, they kept the redcoats bottled up on the peninsula. The British retaliated by closing off the city and prohibiting anyone from entering or leaving. Abigail tried to sneak someone into town to take care of some business matters for John, but he failed in the attempt. Later, a few people were allowed to leave each day, but they could take very few of their possessions with them. According to Abigail, the rules about what they could take out changed daily. British officials drew up a blacklist of men involved in the Tea Party and would not allow them to leave, although Benjamin Edes, printer of the radical *Boston Gazette*, managed to escape to Braintree.

Braintree was not actually threatened at the moment, but

no one's life was quite the same. Refugees from Boston needed a place to go, and residents of outlying towns took in friends and relatives. Abigail housed as many people as she could. Some stayed overnight on their way to other destinations. Some stayed a week, some longer. She often provided meals for soldiers too. The house, she reported to John, was "a Scene of Confusion . . . you can hardly imagine how we live." One night she housed an entire company of militia on their way to join the encampments outside Boston. Some of the soldiers slept in the attic and the rest in the barn. The next morning they drilled in the field behind the house, with Johnny proudly marching up and down in their midst.

British troops periodically raided offshore islands for food and hay to feed their horses, adding to everyone's fears of an imminent attack. The redcoats could not move west out of Boston without tangling with American troops, so it seemed logical that they might move out by sea to coastal towns like Weymouth and Braintree. The local militia stepped up their drills and posted regular guards.

In the back of everyone's minds was the realization that they might have to pull up stakes and flee at any moment in the event of an actual attack. Eunice Paine, now living some miles south of Braintree in Taunton, wrote of her fears about an invasion there; Mercy Warren urged Abigail to pay one more visit to Plymouth before the war cut them off. Mary Nicholson wanted to visit Braintree, but her family would not let her travel because of fear of attack. Mary also tried to write Eunice but reported that it was harder to send a letter to Taunton than to England. John's brother, who lived in a remote inland section of Braintree, invited Abigail to go there with the children if the coast were attacked. John, meanwhile, urged Abigail to stay calm and not do anything rash. If an attack actually came, she should "fly to the Woods with our Children."

But when the next major battle came, it was not Braintree or Weymouth but Charlestown, just north of Boston, that suffered. Abigail awoke early to the sound of cannon fire on June 17. A haze of smoke from the guns was visible across the horizon. With Johnny, she climbed to the top of Penn's Hill for a better view. From there she could see that Boston—or some place very near it—was under attack, and that this was no mere skirmish like the fighting at Lexington and Concord.

The distant roar of guns continued all day. No one in Braintree had any reliable information about what was happening. Anxious, restless, unable to concentrate on mundane chores, Abigail sat down to write to John. "The constant roar of the Cannon is so [distre]ssing that we cannot Eat, Drink, or Sleep," she told him. More than ever, she believed that America was on the road to war with Britain. "The Day: perhaps the decisive Day is come on which the fate of America depends," she wrote. "The race is not to the swift, nor the battle to the strong, but the God of Israel is he that giveth strenth and power unto his people . . . God is a refuge for us."

Two days later she still had no clear information about the battle. Only one tragic piece of news was definite: Joseph Warren was dead. The handsome young physician had been one of their most intimate friends and, with John, one of the earliest advocates of American rights. Now he was one of America's first casualties. Abigail reported the news to John with a heavy heart. It had not taken long for the reality of the war to affect them personally.

The battle that Abigail watched from the top of Penn's Hill was fought over two other hills—Breed's Hill and Bunker Hill in Charlestown. After Lexington and Concord, American troops had fortified the two hills as part of their siege of Boston. Gage ordered his troops to capture Breed's Hill. The British soldiers storming up the hill were easy prey for Americans ensconced behind makeshift fortifications at the top, just as they had been for the militiamen hiding behind trees and fences in Lexington. In the end, however, the Americans had to surrender their fortifications there and on neighboring Bunker Hill. The Battle of Bunker Hill was a defeat for the Americans, but at the cost of extraordinarily heavy casualties for their British attackers with minimal losses among their own forces. Such results made it clear that defending Boston would not be easy.

The Battle of Bunker Hill intensified feelings of crisis in the towns south of Boston. British troops continued their petty harassment in the area: "They delight in molesting us upon the Sabbath," Abigail noted. She and many others feared that the British army would soon march south across the neck from Boston toward Braintree; two companies of the Continental Army were stationed in town to protect against that contingency. Other rumors circulated that troops from New York were marching north to join the army in Boston, but Abigail paid little attention to these stories. "We have got to that pass that a whole legion of them would not intimidate us," she told John.

Throughout the tense months of May and June John reported Congress's support for the beleaguered people of Massachusetts. He constantly tried to reassure Abigail, urging her to pay no attention to false alarms. In June he reported the selection of George Washington as Commander-in-Chief of the Continental Army, a move he thought would help unite the colonies. More companies of troops were on their way to Boston, and Washington himself would soon follow. Still, miracles were not to be expected. Unification took time, and Congress worked slowly. "America . . . is like a large Fleet sailing under convoy. The fleetest Sailors must wait for the dullest and slowest," he wrote Abigail.

John was concerned with philosophical unity, with charting the political course of America in broad terms. Abigail lived with the reality of war, and slow-moving fleets were not to her liking. "I want you to be more perticuliar," she wrote to John with a touch of asperity. "Does every Member [of Congress] feel for us? Can they realize what we suffer? And can they believe with what patience and fortitude we endure the conflict—nor do we even tremble at the frowns of power." Bostonians were "the most abject slaves under the most cruel and despotick of Tyrants," she reported. Inhabitants were forbidden to leave their homes. They had no fresh vegetables of fish. "A Lady who lived opposite says she saw raw meat cut and hacked upon her Mahagona Tables, and her superb damask curtain and cushings exposed to the rain as if they were of no value." Desperate to escape, some people paid as much as forty dollars for passes out of the city, and it was widely believed that several Americans had been jailed.

Abigail continued to take in as many of the homeless as she could and to help others find temporary lodgings. One such act of kindness involved her in conflict with one of her tenant farmers and produced the only situation during the entire war when she felt helpless without John's presence.

A friend of John's had left Boston with his family and stayed briefly with John's brother, who did not really have enough room for them. Their situation was complicated by the fact that the wife was pregnant. Abigail offered the use of the house next door to her, but the tenant who occupied it, a man named

Hayden, refused to move. As a compromise, she asked him to share the house, since he lived alone. Complaining that he was being put out for "Boston folks," he refused to make room for the refugees. Abigail was incensed at his heartlessness, especially considering the others in town who took in two or three families when they barely had room for their own. She was even more annoyed because Hayden had not paid any rent or done any work on the farm all spring, and his sons, who were supposed to help, were all in the army. But Hayden would not budge. Nastily, he told Abigail that John wouldn't force him to give up the house and that he would take his orders from him, not her. Angry at her powerlessness, she finally had to appeal to John. He backed her up in no uncertain terms and enclosed a letter ordering Hayden to vacate the house at once. But the obstinate Hayden still refused to move. Months later, in total exasperation, Abigail considered sending the sheriff after him.

By the summer of 1775 Abigail and her neighbors were used to living with rumors of British attacks, and the presence of more American troops inspired confidence. Moreover, the arrival of Washington and one of his generals, Charles Lee, could be taken as a sign that Congress was serious about their problems. In July she visited the army camp at Cambridge and met the two generals. Washington made a very striking impression. "You had prepared me to entertain a favorable opinion of him," she told John, "but I thought the one half was not told me. Dignity with ease, and complacency, the Gentleman and Soldier look agreably blended in him."

With Washington at the helm, organizing hundreds of local militia units into an army, war fever continued to mount in towns around Boston. In Braintree Abigail managed to maintain some semblance of a normal existence despite the skirmishes and the dangers of attack. As Mercy Warren observed, it was so far an odd kind of war. They lived in the midst of constant hostilities yet were not directly threatened. Despite the fighting, they managed to live their lives almost normally.

Most New Englanders would have agreed with Mercy's observation in the summer of 1775. Battles had been fought, and skirmishes continued from time to time, but the colonies still were not officially at war with England. Nor was independence by any means a foregone conclusion. Troops occupied Boston, and the people who remained there lived under military rule, but the British presence weakened the farther one got from Boston. Fear and rumor pervaded the countryside; militia companies drilled with the understanding that any day they might be called to service. But most towns were in no actual danger of attack, and most people spent most of their time worrying about the things they had always worried about—their farms, their houses, their children. Even the young men who joined the army did so only for short periods.

Like everyone else, Abigail lived this kind of divided existence. One day she was helping refugees find shelter; another day she was supervising the mowing of hay or trying to keep caterpillars out of the fruit trees. The summer of 1775 was unusually hot and dry, and she worried that the drought would damage the crops. She often concluded letters to John reporting the gravest events with requests that he send her pins or such other scarce necessities as coffee, sugar, and pepper.

The duality of her existence was clear to Abigail herself. It surprised her that she could be in such good spirits most of the time despite the dangers and hardships around her. "I . . . fear least a degree of stupidity or insensibility should possess my mind in these calamitous times or I could not feel so tranquil amidst such scenes, and yet I cannot charge myself with an unfeeling Heart. I pitty, comisirate and as far as my ability reaches fell ready and desirous to releave my fellow creatures under their distresses. But I am not naturally . . . of that restless and anxious disposition," she wrote John.

As always, John's absence was the greatest hardship for her. Her distress at his absence intensified during periods of quiet, when she had leisure to reflect on the happenings around her. John's work left him little time to write long letters, and she knew it. But still, at times she felt neglected. "I have received a good deal of paper from you; I wish it had been more covered," she complained in July. Soon afterwards she told him that not only were his letters too short, but they had no feeling. "I want some sentimental Effusions of the Heart," she wrote. "I am sure you are not destitute of them or are they all absorbed in the great publick. . . . I lay claim to a Larger share than I have had."

Abigail made such statements only rarely, however, despite the fact that John's involvement in politics and his sense of duty to his country undeniably took precedence over her and the children at many times during their life together. She did not complain more often because she felt the same sense of duty that he did and believed that a woman could best show her patriotism by encouraging and supporting her husband in his work for the public.

She also understood that John was genuinely torn between his public and private lives. He needed the sense of importance that went with public service, but he also loved his family intensely and suffered all the time that he was forced to be away from them. He was never really able to reconcile these two sides of his life. Abigail never asked him to choose between them, although there would be times later when she would be sorely tempted.

Finally, in mid-August, John came home on an all too brief leave of absence. He stayed barely three weeks in Braintree before returning to Philadelphia. Such a short time together after so many months apart, and the prospect of an equally long separation ahead, did little to improve Abigail's state of mind. She confided to Mercy: "I find I am obliged to summon all my patriotism to feel willing to part with him again. You will readily believe me when I say that I make no small sacrifice to the public."

For the moment, however, Abigail had no time to lament over John's absence. An epidemic of dysentery struck Braintree and the surrounding towns, and this new crisis consumed all her attention. Nearly everyone in the Adams household was sick. First Isaac, one of the hired hands, fell ill, then Abigail. Fortunately she recovered in a matter of days, because soon Tommy and two of the servants became ill. So many people in the town were sick that it was difficult to get any assistance, and Abigail, still weak herself, had to care for all the ill members of her household. For a few weeks the suffering of war was forgotten in the face of a more immediate danger. Tommy was extremely ill for several days.

Then Abigail's mother, who had come every day to help nurse Abigail and Tommy, caught the disease and declined quickly. It was apparent that she could not live more than a few days. At the same time Patty, one of the servant girls, lingered for days close to death. Abigail traveled back and forth between her house and her parents', trying to look after both patients. She was constantly afraid, as she approached each house, that she would be greeted with the news of her mother or Patty's death.

On October 1 Elizabeth Smith died. Abigail, consumed with grief, tried to follow her father's example of "patience and submission" but found it impossible, especially without John there to console her. "At times," she wrote him, "I almost am ready to faint under this severe and heavy Stroke, seperated from *thee* who used to be a comfortar towards me in affliction."

Patty died a week later after a particularly gruesome five-week illness. Abigail had not thought it possible that she could survive so long. Her suffering during the last weeks was extraordinary. Patty would have no one but Abigail care for her; still reeling from the blow of her mother's death, she continued to spend hours by her servant's sickbed.

Toward the end of October the epidemic gradually ran its course. Abigail and her neighbors tried to resume normal lives—or as normal as they could manage given the loss of life and the continued dangers of war.

Grieving over the death of her mother, Abigail felt little inclination to be social. "I have been like a nun in a cloister ever since you went away," she told John. She rarely visited anyone except her father and sisters. Running the farm took all her time and energy. In the evenings she sat alone by the fire, exhausted and unhappy, thinking about him and about her mother. For weeks after her mother's death, she could think of little else. "I . . . ruminate upon all her care and tenderness, and am sometimes lost, and absorb'd in a flood of tenderness." Without John to console her, it seemed impossible to conquer her grief.

New England was relatively quiet as 1775 drew to a close, and fears of British attack died down for the moment. Sobered by the battles of the summer and the personal tragedies of the early fall, Abigail pondered the future of the conflict. What had been accomplished at Lexington, Concord, and Bunker Hill? Would the rest of the colonies continue their support of New England? Americans were faced with a war that had begun almost spontaneously, and they as yet had no clear idea of their ultimate goal. For Abigail, John, and their fellow radicals, the goal by now was clear: independence. But could the rest of the country be made to see that?

Both Abigail and John had concluded, reluctantly, that a complete break with England had become necessary. Congress, however, was still working on petitions for reconciliation. Abigail objected to these efforts. She contended that England was no

longer a "parent State" but a "tyrant State." "Let us renounce
them," she argued, "and instead of supplications as formorly for
their prosperity and happiness, Let us beseach the almighty to
blast their cousels and bring to nought all their devices."

New England, for all practical purposes, was in a state of
independence already, and the problem of establishing some
form of government to take the place of the old royal governments had become serious. Almost all the colonies, including
Massachusetts, had set up extralegal governing assemblies, but
Congress hedged in the matter of formally authorizing the colonies to write constitutions and set up new permanent governments. Massachusetts simply reverted to its old charter; New
Hampshire asked Congress for formal instructions. Congress
sent back instructions authorizing New Hampshire to call a provincial convention to form a new government. Abigail took ex-
ception to the instructions, which referred to New Hampshire as
a "colony." Such instructions, she thought, were damaging because they only reinforced people's already great reluctance to
think of themselves as separate from Britain. On this point she
disagreed with John, who thought the instructions were good.
Their difference of opinion on this point was not unusual; although their political views were always very similar, Abigail
often took a more extreme position than John.

She also pondered the problem of the eventual establishment of a government for all of America and anxiously asked
John if Congress was considering the question. She understood
that getting Americans to agree on the form of a new government would be even more difficult than getting them to agree to
resist British rule. Contemplating the prospect brought out all
her fears about the corruptness of power and the weakness of
human nature. "I am more and more convinced that Man is a
dangerous creature, and that power whether vested in many or a
few is ever grasping," she wrote. "The great fish swallow up the
small, and he who is most strenuous for the Rights of the people,
when vested with power, is as eager after the prerogatives of
Government." They could break with England and eliminate
the monarchy, but still not achieve liberty because of the inher-
ent corrupting tendencies of power. The form of government, no
matter how perfect, would make no difference unless a high
level of popular virtue were maintained. The problem of establishing and maintaining a good government was complicated by

people's tendency to cling to old customs and their inability to agree on anything. Contemplating the problems, she told John, "I soon get lost in a labyrinth of perplexities."

The broad outlines of a new government were complicated enough, but there were also innumerable details to be considered. Abigail listened to opinions expressed around her and passed them on to John. Excise taxes should somehow be equalized, particularly on liquor, so that all the colonies followed the same policy and none had an undue advantage over others. Some effort had to be made to keep so much gold and silver from being shipped out of America to the West Indies. Expansion of native manufactures would be a better way to pay for imported goods. And something should be done about inflation, which was creating serious hardships in New England.

Through her correspondence with John during the many months they were apart, and through her discussions with friends, especially Mercy Warren, Abigail developed her political ideas and became more confident in expressing them. Popular opinion held that women had no business meddling in politics, but John praised his wife's talents and encouraged her to continue writing on political subjects, just as he had always encouraged Mercy Warren in her more public political writings. While noting with approval that John Hancock's wife, who had accompanied her husband to Philadelphia, did not talk about politics (or anything else, for that matter) in mixed company, he nevertheless added with pride, "but whether her Eyes are so penetrating and her Attention so quick, to the Words, Looks, Gestures, sentiments, &c. of the Company, as yours would be, saucy as you are this way, I wont say."

As a practical matter, John depended on Abigail's political observations. Throughout the battles and skirmishes of 1775, he relied on her letters to provide the most complete and accurate information, no small consideration in days of limited communication. He not only appreciated her diligence in reporting events but admired her skill in characterizing people she met and, in general, her facility in expressing herself. "If I could write as well as you, my sorrows would be as eloquent as yours, but upon my Word I cannot," he told her. Once he used a quotation included in one of her letters in a speech before Congress; on another occasion he told her friend Polly Palmer, "commend me to the Ladies for Historiographers. . . . There is a Lady at the Foot

of Pens Hill, who obliges me . . . with clearer and fuller Intelligence, than I can get from a whole Committee of Gentlemen."
John sometimes showed her letters to fellow delegates so they
could share the information. That practice distressed Abigail,
because she still felt self-conscious about her intellectual abilities. She often asked him to burn her letters. He never did.

Abigail's confidence in herself grew with her increasing opportunities to meet and converse with important political figures. She had dined with George Washington, Charles Lee,
and—at a recent dinner party at her uncle's—Benjamin Franklin.
Whenever acquaintances from Philadelphia traveled to New England, John gave them letters of introduction to Abigail, asking
her to show them every hospitality and introduce them to important men of the neighborhood. Abigail enjoyed these contacts, because they gave her firsthand word of John and the activities of Congress; the men, in turn, were impressed by this
woman of fiery political principles. John told her that one of his
friends, upon returning to Philadelphia, had pronounced her
"the most accomplished Lady, he had seen since he left England. . . . Dont you be proud," he added.

As Christmas approached and Congress showed no signs of
adjourning, Abigail began to find the separation unbearable.
Since Congress had first convened in August 1774 John had
spent only about five months at home. When Franklin visited in
October, he urged her to spend the winter in Philadelphia, and
she was sorely tempted. Her uncle, Norton Quincy, joked that if
John didn't come home soon, she should get a new husband.
John talked about getting another delegate to take his place. If he
was to return to Philadelphia, he too wanted Abigail to go with
him. "Whom God has joined together ought not to be put asun-
der so long with their own consent," he wrote. Finally he decided to leave for home without waiting for Congress to adjourn.
On December 21, he arrived unexpectedly in Braintree.

This time John stayed only slightly longer than he had in
August—a month. He seriously considered resigning as a delegate but left it up to Abigail to decide whether he should or not.
She could not bring herself to ask him to stay. "I found his honour and reputation much dearer to me, than my own present
pleasure and happiness, and I could by no means consent to his
resigning at present, as I was fully convinced he must suffer if he
quitted," she explained to Mercy. She knew John would regret

being out of Congress at the point when it was finally moving toward independence. And she also shared his belief that public service was a duty that at times superseded duty to one's own family. Mercy, whose husband was also away from home often as an officer of the Continental Army, sympathized. Coping with loneliness became an increasingly frequent theme in their correspondence, and their understanding of each other's feelings strengthened their friendship.

Despite all the talk about Abigail's accompanying John to Philadelphia, she stayed home in Braintree once again. There were many reasons for their decision. It would be difficult to leave the farm entirely in the hands of servants. Renting it out was a possibility, but then the entire family would have to move to Philadelphia, where living costs would be prohibitively expensive. John talked about taking Abigail and Johnny with him and leaving the younger children in the care of relatives, but Abigail thought it was bad enough that her children should be without a father during their formative years. She did not want to leave them motherless too.

In making these decisions—that John would return to Congress and that Abigail would stay behind—they established a pattern that would continue throughout their lives. A very strong sense of public duty and a belief in the revolutionary cause lay behind their willingness to endure personal unhappiness for the sake of John's political work, but they had more personal motives as well. John cherished the recognition that went with public service, and Abigail enjoyed a kind of vicarious importance as the wife of a public figure. They also both believed in the importance of maintaining their farm and family, and both had a deep-seated fear of debt. As a result, they were reluctant to turn over the farm to strangers or to separate the children from each other. Besides, the expense of moving them all to Philadelphia loomed as an overwhelming obstacle.

While John plunged back into the debate over the future of America, Abigail found politics in New England exceedingly dull. After months of worry about an attack, everything was quiet in January and February. And yet no one could be truly calm; it was like being in the eye of the storm, waiting for the next round of disasters. Impatient with Congress's foot-dragging on the question of independence, Abigail wrote John that there would be no difficulty getting the colonial assemblies in New

England to instruct their delegates to vote for independence. But moderates in Congress held out for one last attempt at compromise. As John explained, the crux of the problem was that issues long decided in New England were still subjects of debate in other colonies. He would have welcomed reconciliation but believed it impossible. He thought people who expected peace were being hopelessly naive.

In the midst of all this discussion of independence, Thomas Paine published his famous pamphlet *Common Sense*. Unlike any previous political tract, it openly advocated independence and argued that Americans should adopt a republican form of government. Paine's pamphlet could not have been better timed to aid the proponents of American independence. Brief and forcefully written, it appealed to the ordinary man in a way that the more abstract political writings of the 1760s and early 1770s had not. It was also cheaply priced and widely distributed.

Common Sense quickly became an eighteenth-century version of a bestseller and, by finally bringing the independence debate into the open, did more to influence public opinion on the issue than any previous writings.

John sent Abigail a copy of *Common Sense* in February, soon after it was published. She agreed with Paine's arguments and reported that they were well received in New England. She also hoped that the pamphlet would exert some influence over Congress and wondered how "one who wishes the welfare of their country . . . can hesitate one moment" in taking to heart Paine's proposals. John, who would later disagree bitterly with Paine's ideas, agreed with his arguments for independence but thought that his discussion of establishing a new government was inadequate. But he correctly predicted that *Common Sense* would have an impact on the deliberations over independence, although it would be months yet before Congress would come to a final agreement.

By early March the calm appeared to be over. Cannon could be heard from Boston harbor; all militiamen were ordered to report for duty; Braintree was devoid of men except for a small group guarding the town. Every day for a week the cannon kept up their roar. The combination of noise and worry at not knowing what was really happening kept Abigail from sleeping most of the time. One day she spent several hours on top of Penn's Hill watching the battle; from there she could not only hear the cannon but see the shell bursts. "The sound," she told John, "I think is one of the Grandest in Nature and is of the true Speicies of the Sublime. Tis now an incessant Roar. But O the fatal Ideas which are connected with the sound. How many of our dear country men must fall?"

Finally the roar ceased and the militia returned, after taking possession of Dorchester Hill just south of Boston. It seemed a very minor triumph to Abigail. "I would not have sufferd all I have to two such Hills," she told John. What she did not realize, however, was that the Continental Army now occupied a position where they were fortified against British guns but could fire on the city and on the British fleet in the harbor at will. The cannon used to fortify the hill had been dragged all the way from Fort Ticonderoga in New York. Within a few days, the Americans captured nearby Nook Hill. It became clear to the British generals, who remembered the lessons of Bunker Hill, that they could not dislodge the Americans without severe casualties, and that any attempt to do so would probably result in serious damage to Boston and to the fleet. So they struck a bargain with General Washington: The troops would evacuate Boston if allowed to go in peace.

On March 16, from atop her observation point on Penn's Hill, Abigail saw seventy to eighty ships, all apparently loaded and ready to leave, though no one could believe that the troops were actually leaving. Militia guarded the seacoast around the clock, fearing that the British preparations signaled a new attack. Still, the next day she watched as "the largest Fleet ever seen in America" prepared to sail out of Boston harbor. "You may count upwards of 100 & 70 Sail," she wrote John. "They look like a Forrest." Rumors spread that the troops had taken everything from Boston that they could carry with them and had destroyed the rest. This was one rumor that Abigail believed, as battered pieces of furniture—"Lids of Desks, mahagona chairs, tables &c—washed up on the shores of Weymouth and Braintree for the next several days.

For people who had been living with redcoats since 1768 and existing in a state of war for nearly a year, the sight of the British fleet leaving Boston harbor was a cause for rejoicing. Abigail, however, was more pessimistic. The British might leave Boston, but they would turn up somewhere else to plague another colony. But she was always prepared to see lessons in any event, and thought perhaps "providence" decreed that "the Seat of War should be changed from this to the Southern colonies that each may have a proper sympathy for the other, and unite in a separation." She understood well enough the effect that the presence of troops had in pushing New Englanders toward independence. She also understood that, however much sympathy for New England might be expressed in Congress, men who had not lived with the spectacle of British troops drilling in their cities and the sounds of cannon disturbing their sleep could not fully comprehend the seriousness of the American cause.

Chapter 6

Independence

With the departure of British troops from Boston, New Englanders were able to sleep more easily, although they lived with the knowledge that the war was only beginning. For the first time in nearly a year, travel into and out of Boston was unrestricted. Abigail and John still owned a house there, and only the threat of smallpox kept her from going immediately to inspect the damage to their property. A friend in town assured her that the house was not structurally damaged, although it was very dirty, and the few possessions they had left there were gone. For Abigail, who had never expected to see their house in one piece again, that was good news. "I look upon it as a new acquisition of property," she wrote John, "a property which one month ago I did not value at a single Shilling, and could with pleasure have seen it in flames."

Abigail had believed for some time that American independence was both inevitable and desirable. Now she made her views more explicit and began to think about some of the implications of independence. "I long to hear that you have declared an independancy," she wrote John at the end of March. Following the widely accepted political doctrine of the day, she argued that the King had betrayed his trust to his people and that he therefore no longer deserved to rule them. The Americans should "proclaim to the World in decisive terms" their separation from the King.

Assuming boldly that independence was only a matter of time, Abigail turned her thoughts to the form of government that would follow the colonies' separation from Britain. Like many Americans, she favored a republic rather than the English system of constitutional monarchy. But it was by no means a foregone conclusion at the time that Americans would in fact establish a republic. There were few precedents for republicanism and many arguments against it. The classic examples of republican governments were the Greek city-states and ancient Rome, all very small, homogeneous areas. There were no important European republics at the time, and most people believed that republican forms of government would not work in large nations. Advocates of republican government for America, while enjoying considerable popular support, still had to contend with the influence of centuries-old traditions of monarchy and aristocracy and with prevailing political theory, which stressed the instability of republics.

The form of a new American government was not the only political matter to engage Abigail's attention during the spring and summer of 1776. The anomaly of slavery in a nation dedicated to liberty continued to bother her, as it had for some time. But she was interested most of all in what the future status of women might be under a republican government.

She had grown up in a household with two black slaves, but by the time of the Revolution she was prepared to argue that people struggling for their own freedom could not morally enslave others. She suspected Southerners of being less enthusiastic than New Englanders in pressing for independence and questioned whether they would put up spirited resistance to British attack. Her doubts about Southern patriotism, which were not borne out, were inspired by her conviction that "the passion for Liberty cannot be Eaquelly Strong in the Breasts of those who have been accustomed to deprive their fellow Creatures of theirs."

She was not being quite fair, because New Englanders owned slaves too. But slavery was much less common there, and the economy much less dependent on it. By the time of the Revolution antislavery sentiment was widespread in New England and other Northern colonies, and all Northern states abolished slavery within a few years after the end of the war.

Revolutionary principles also inspired at least some Americans to give thought to the position of women. But because their inferior status was much more ambiguous, it drew much less attention. For Abigail, however, this was one of the most pressing issues. She had always argued that women should be better educated and continued to do so frequently. As one of the few practical steps available to her in that regard, she saw to it that her daughter studied Latin, a major omission in Abigail's own education. When John learned about this, he commended Nabby on her efforts but warned her "you must not tell many people of it, for it is scarcely reputable for young ladies to understand Latin and Greek."

More significantly, Abigail began to question the legal and political position of women in American society. In a letter to John discussing the question of independence, she wrote, "I desire you would Remember the Ladies, and be more generous and favourable to them than your ancestors. Do not put such unlimited power into the hands of the Husbands. Remember all Men would be tyrants if they could. If perticuliar care and attention is not paid to the Laidies we are determined to foment a Rebelion, and will not hold ourselves bound by any Laws in which we have no voice, or Representation." This is Abigail Adams's most famous and often-quoted statement and has given her a reputation as an early feminist. It is important, however, not merely for its feminism but for the way she linked the cause of women to the cause of the Revolution.

America was suffering from British tyranny, but all men were potential tyrants if their base instincts were not held in check by reason and virtue. This essentially pessimistic view of human nature lay behind Abigail's discussion of the proper form of an American government, and she believed that it applied equally to domestic government. In her view the forces governing human relationships were the same, whether the parties involved were nations or families. Her argument was similar to the one that she and others used to press for an end to slavery: "Whilst you are proclaiming peace and good will to Men, Emancipating all Nations, you insist upon retaining an absolute power over Wives," she told John. Abigail wanted Congress, in adopting new laws for America, to revise or eliminate those English laws that gave men absolute power over their wives.

On the issue of women's participation in the new government she was more ambiguous. She told John that women would not be "bound by any Laws in which we have no voice, or Representation," which might imply that she thought women should have the right to vote. But women's suffrage was such an unthinkably radical idea in the eighteenth century that such an interpretation of her words is risky. While Abigail was a revolutionary in the sense of favoring independence, she was not politically or temperamentally inclined to favor social revolution. On other occasions she voiced a more conventional view of women's potential political influence: that they could exert power by influencing their husbands.

She was not prepared to advocate a radically different position for women in society, for all her rhetoric about fomenting rebellion. In her eyes, improved legal and social status for women was not inconsistent with their essentially domestic role. She told John that the Republic ought to have "learned women" as well as "Heroes, Statesmen, and Philosophers" and then, to justify her statement, added: "If much depends as is allowed on the early Education of youth . . . great benefit must arise from literary accomplishments in women." Women's status should be improved, she believed, in ways that would enhance their work as wives and mothers.

It was an unusually cold spring in 1775, but despite the weather and the shortage of labor as more and more men enlisted in the army, Abigail was ready to plant by the middle of May. Good rains promised an abundant crop. "The barley look[s] charmingly," she told John. "I shall be quite a Farmeriss an other year." The high cost of labor, rising taxes, and inflation made it increasingly difficult for Abigail to make ends meet. John sent her fifteen pounds, John Thaxter paid twelve for his board, and she scraped together a little more than twenty from some other sources. The total of forty-seven pounds-plus had to stretch to pay for the hired horses to take John to Philadelphia, the wages of two laborers, an installment on the house in Boston, and two years' taxes. "Besides this," she told John, "[I] have supported the family which is no small one you know and paid all little charges which had occurd in the farming way."

In late June another smallpox epidemic broke out in Boston. This time Abigail decided to take no more risks and to have herself and the children inoculated. She made the decision without consulting John, partly because there was no time to consult him but also because she knew he would approve and did not want him to worry about them.

The process had changed little since John's inoculation more than a decade earlier. The family isolated themselves for several weeks, endured debilitating preparations for inoculation, and then subjected themselves to a mild form of the disease. Abigail and the children did not lack for company during their ordeal. Mary and Richard Cranch and their family, Abigail's younger sister Betsey, and John Thaxter all went together to Boston to be inoculated. They discovered that nearly every house in the city was filled with people immunizing themselves against smallpox.

The day after they had settled in Boston, Abigail received letters from John announcing that the Declaration of Independence had finally been approved. For the moment it seemed that her sacrifices had been rewarded. She looked forward to "the future happiness and glory of our Country" and felt proud that "a person so nearly connected with me has had the Honour of being a principal actor, in laying a foundation for its future Greatness."

Offical announcements of independence reached Boston about the same time as John's letters, and on July 18 the whole city turned out for a public reading of the Declaration. Abigail was not far enough along in the preparations for inoculation to be prevented from attending. The army with its guns and artillery and all the inhabitants of Boston gathered in front of the Town House. The crowd was quiet and attentive to every word of the Declaration, she reported to John, but as soon as the reading ended they broke into cheers. "The Bells rang, the privateers fired, the forts and Batteries, the cannon were discharged, the platoons followed and every face appeard joyfull." Later in the day the King's arms were removed from the Town House and burned in the middle of King Street. "Thus ends royall Authority in this State, and all the people shall say Amen."

Even the momentous news of independence could not distract her for long from the ordeal at hand, however. Inoculation turned out to be a lengthier and more unpleasant experience than Abigail had expected. Johnny and Tommy got through it with relative ease, but Nabby and Charley had to be inoculated a second time when the first attempt failed to produce results. Two weeks later, Nabby broke out and was much sicker than was normal; Charley remained unaffected and had to be inoculated a third time. When he finally broke out, it was not in the mild form usually associated with inoculation but in the "Natural way," as Abigail explained it. After more than a month of being exposed to a large household undergoing inoculation, he caught smallpox without benefit of any effective immunization.

Abigail warned John about Charley's illness. He seemed to be improving, she wrote, but it was too early to tell whether he would survive the disease. From Abigail's description of Charley's symptoms, John assumed the worst. He waited for further news, afraid to open each letter: "Yours . . . has fixed an Arrow in my Heart, which will not be drawn out, until the next Post arrives, and then, perhaps, instead of being withdrawn, it will be driven deeper." By the time his letter reached Boston, Charley was recovering. "I feel quite light," John responded to the good news. "I did not know what fast Hold that little Pratler Charles had upon me before."

The whole experience had lasted nearly two months and had been fraught with worry for Abigail. Yet, having successfully undergone inoculation herself, she was at least free to travel around the city at will while she was waiting for her children to recover. She was able to absorb the latest information about politics and had the leisure to correspond with John about the problems of forming a new government for the states.

Another virtue of her prolonged stay in Boston was a certain measure of privacy. While she and the children recovered they stayed with Abigail's aunt and uncle, where she had the luxury of a "pretty closet" to herself in which she could sit quietly to read, write letters, and daydream. "I do not covet my Neighbours Goods," she wrote John, "but . . . I always had a fancy for a closet with a window which I could more peculiarly call my own." Mostly she thought about John and imagined what it would be like when he returned. "I have spent the 3 days past almost intirely with you," she told him after sitting alone and reading over all his letters to her. "I have amused myself in reading and thinking of my absent Friend, sometimes with a mixture of paine, sometimes with pleasure, sometimes anticipating a joyfull and happy meeting; whilst my Heart would bound and palpitate with the pleasing Idea, and with the purest affection I have held you to my Bosom till my whole Soul has dissolved in Tenderness and my pen fallen from my Hand . . .

Forgive this Revere, this Delusion, and since I am debared real, suffer me, to enjoy, and indulge in Ideal pleasures—and tell me they are not inconsistent with the stern virtue of a senator and a Patriot."

Usually Abigail tried to avoid daydreaming about John and contemplating his return, because it made his absence seem even more painful. This time she let her thoughts wander where they would, because she knew he would be on his way home soon; she had been making arrangements for a servant with a horse to ride to Philadelphia and bring John home. Within a few weeks, perhaps sooner, he would be back in Braintree.

As he prepared to go home, John once again talked about staying there for good. As early as mid-July he had considered resigning from Congress and asking the Massachusetts legislature to appoint a replacement delegate. In August, although no replacement had yet been appointed, he began to make definite plans to come home. But September stretched into October, and still he wrote cryptic notes to the effect that the press of business required him to stay on a bit longer. Finally, around mid-October he returned to Braintree notwithstanding the fact that the Massachusetts assembly still had not appointed his replacement.

John came home thinking he had seen the last of the Continental Congress, but the Massachusetts legislature reconvened in November and chose him as a delegate once more. Again, he found it difficult to say no, although he had spent the better part of two and a half years attending Congress and was very tired and homesick. He and Abigail once more went through their discussion of his public duty versus his private happiness. It was a discussion they had had many times before and would continue to have many times in the future. Once again, public duty won out.

And once again Abigail concurred. In a letter to Mercy Warren she explained, "I had it in my Heart to disswade him from going and I know I could have prevaild, but our publick affairs at that time wore so gloomy an aspect that I thought if ever his assistance was wanted, it must be at such a time. I therefore resignd myself to suffer much anxiety and many Melancholy hours for this year to come." In short, Abigail had the same highly developed sense of public duty that John had. His sacrifice was to separate himself from family, farm, and everything else he loved; hers was to let him go, even to encourage him to go. For John, however, there were rewards—fame, a sense of power, the excitement of creating history. Abigail absorbed something of those rewards vicariously, but for her the sacrifice had far less to recommend it. She took pride in her ability to keep family and farm running smoothly under difficult conditions, but that task offered few of the rewards of public service, no matter how much it might be glorified as woman's great contribution.

John left Braintree in January 1777 after less than three months at home. Far from getting used to their frequent partings, they both found it more difficult than before to say goodbye. This time Abigail was pregnant for the first time in six years. She and John wanted the baby very much. They had planned to have another child, apparently on the assumption that John would return from Congress by the time of its birth and that his service there was almost ended. By the time he actually left Braintree, however, those assumptions were badly shaken, and Abigail faced the prospect of bringing another child into the world alone.

Couples, particularly among the middle and upper classes, commonly tried to limit their families in the late eighteenth century, even though birth control methods were limited to continence, withdrawal, and various folk devices of dubious efficacy. In the early years of her marriage, Abigail bore children in rapid succession—two years between Nabby and Johnny, then about a year and a half before each of her other births. Even by eighteenth-century standards her children were closely spaced: Two to two and a half years was closer to average. After Tommy, she and John had clearly decided to have no more children for the time being, perhaps because of the uncertainty of the times or perhaps because Abigail's rather delicate health needed a rest. After 1774, of course, John's long absences made birth control easier.

Now they wanted another child, despite the difficulties of the times and the uncertainty of the future. At thirty-two, Abigail had many childbearing years left—most women bore their last child at about forty—but she may well have felt that time was running out for her. She had every reason to want more children. Large families were prized, and a family with four children was considered small. She especially wanted another daughter, for the memory of little Susanna had not been erased by time.

It was hard enough to let John go, but it was still worse this time because he was going farther away. Congress had decided to convene in Baltimore, since Philadelphia was considered a likely target of British troops. It was not so much the distance that bothered Abigail as the possible danger to him and the probability that letters would take even longer to reach her. As long as the British army had occupied itself in New England, she drew some consolation from the thought that Philadelphia was safe from attack. Now, it was anyone's guess where the British would strike next. They might very well choose the seat of Congress in the hope of taking some distinguished prisoners.

The cumulative effect of long separations, pregnancy, and uncertainty about John's safety severely depressed Abigail's spirits. The dangerous but exciting days of Lexington, Concord, and Bunker Hill were over. There was little military activity in New England; the scene of action had shifted south. New Englanders were left to cope with shortages of goods, extreme inflation, ineffective price controls, and a general atmosphere in which greed seemed to have supplanted patriotism. Under such conditions it became more difficult for Abigail not only to manage the farm and support her family in their reduced financial circumstances but also to justify her own and John's personal hardships in the cause of liberty.

The reasons for the economic problems of the Revolutionary years were complex. They stemmed largely from the army's constant demands for men and supplies and the difficulty of establishing a coherent monetary policy for thirteen independent states with little sense of nationhood. The army's need for soldiers reduced the supply of laborers, driving up wages. Its need for food and clothing for its soldiers created increased demands for farm products, and many farmers discovered that it was more lucrative to sell to the army than to supply civilians in nearby towns. Shortages and higher prices were the result. At the same time the British blockade of American shipping sharply reduced supplies of imported commodities, which included such everyday items as tea, coffee, and spices.

A shortage of currency was another problem. Many of the states and eventually Congress itself tried to remedy it by issuing paper money. Paper money was not a new concept during the Revolutionary years; several colonies, Massachusetts included, had issued it earlier in the eighteenth century. In theory, it was viewed as a short-term expedient backed by future tax revenues. During the war, however, states issued paper money with no backing of any kind, and it quickly depreciated.

Individual towns and states tried to cope with high prices and high wages by establishing price ceilings for goods and services. Price controls were largely ignored, however. Rampant inflation continued through the spring, and paper money continued its downward slide. The price of goods paid for in paper was often three times their price in silver. But silver was scarce, so most people resorted to barter. Abigail described the situation to John: "You shall have wool for flax or flax for wool, you shall have veal, Beaf, or pork for salt . . . But money we will not take, is the daily language. I will work for you for Corn, for flax or wool, but if I work for money you must give a cart load of it be sure." Given the combination of cost and scarcity, there were many things that the family simply did without: sugar, molasses, coffee, tea. By June, she reported, prices were four times what they had been two years before and were rising daily.

Abigail never really understood why prices rose and paper money depreciated so rapidly. In her view, the ever increasing demands of merchants and laborers spelled moral weakness. The conflict between merchants and consumers and the willingness of many people to put private gain ahead of the public good distressed her deeply. "The Town of Boston has lost its leaders, and the respectable figure it once made is exchanged for party squables, for Avarice, venality, Animosity, contention, pride, weakness, and dissapation," she complained. Americans were "a most ungrateful people . . . With the best opportunities for becomeing a happy people, and all the materials in our power, yet we have neither skill nor wisdom to put them together."

In short, New Englanders seemed to be losing their revolutionary spirit. As far as she was concerned, maintaining fair prices was just as much a moral imperative as resistance to King George. What she could not understand was how much more difficult it was to inspire people to moral actions when their daily bread was at stake than when the issues were unfair taxes or the depredations of British troops.

Occasionally, however, New Englanders showed that they

had not forgotten their tradition of resistance to tyranny. On at least one occasion resentment at merchants hoarding supplies broke out in a Tea Party–style mob scene. This time irate housewives formed the mob. Abigail reported that "an eminent, wealthy, stingy Merchant (who is a Batchelor)" had coffee in his Boston warehouse that he refused to sell except at an exhorbitant price. A large group of women (estimates ran to 100 or more) marched upon the warehouse and demanded the keys; when the merchant refused, they seized him and threw him into their cart. Finally he relented, handed over the keys, and was dumped unceremoniously out of the cart while the women took the coffee from his warehouse. Meanwhile, as Abigail noted, "A large concourse of Men stood amazd silent Spectators of the whole transaction."

Despite her hardships Abigail took a certain pleasure in managing to keep the family fed, clothed, and out of debt. Her biggest problem was keeping the farm going with a minimum of help. On the whole, she succeeded; James Warren told John in the spring of 1777 that the farm had never looked better and that Abigail "was like to outshine all the Farmers." And John himself noted in mock jealousy that the neighbors would think his affairs were conducted better when he was away than when he was home.

Abigail tried to keep the household expenses down by weaving her own cloth and making all the family's clothes. Such efforts were partly a matter of necessity, for imported dry goods were no longer to be had. But domestic self-sufficiency also had become a matter of patriotism. Every step taken to reduce dependence on foreign imports was hailed as a contribution to American success in the war.

She and other women in the area joined forces to produce the cloth that they had always bought from Boston merchants in the past. Mercy Warren spun wool, which Abigail and other Braintree women wove into cloth. Mercy attached great significance to their efforts. It was important, she thought, that women take a leading role in encouraging domestic manufactures and simpler styles of clothing; ". . . the Lindsey Woolsey of their own Country, and the simplicity and puritanism of New England" were vastly preferable to the "Modes of Paris, and the Frenchefyed airs of Mademoisel from Varssailles." In Abigail she found a receptive audience for such sentiments, for they touched on many of her most fundamental beliefs—the equation of simplicity with virtue, the need for frugality, and the importance of women's efforts on the domestic front in ensuring the ultimate success of the American cause.

Being pregnant (or "in circumstances," as she described it) did nothing to ease Abigail's responsibilities during the winter and spring of 1977. Fortunately her health was better than it had been during any of her previous pregnancies. She was not upset about her condition, for, as she told John, "tis a constant remembrancer of an absent Friend, and excites sensations of tenderness which are better felt than expressed." Yet as the months passed her apprehensions mounted, particularly as it became obvious that John would not be able to return for the birth. When an acquaintance died in childbirth in April, Abigail became morbid, lamented John's absence, and, for the only time, hinted that she might demand his return in July. But she knew that she could not expect it, and so "I must summon all the Phylosophy I am mistress of since what cannot be help'd must be endured." It was the one moment when she admitted to John that she feared death; she was worried about what would happen to the children if she died.

It was the separation, however, more than the risks of childbirth, that made her melancholy during these weeks. In June she wrote, "I look forward to the middle of july with more anxiety than I can describe, and the Thoughts of 3 hundreds miles distance are as Greivous as the perils I have to pass through. I am cut of from the privilidge which some of the Brute creation enjoy, that of having their mate sit by them with ancious care during all their Solitary confinement." The combination of the months of separation and her apprehensions about childbirth upset her to the point that she contemplated John's death: "I . . . some times . . . immagine these separations as preparatory to a still more painfull one in which even hope the anchor of the Soul is lost." To make matters worse, in June, after months of tranquility, rumors of a British attack on Boston cropped up again. In her last weeks of pregnancy, when it was difficult for her to walk more than a short distance, Abigail did not know how they would manage to escape in the event of serious danger.

The second week in July she woke up in a "shaking fit". When it was over she could tell that her unborn baby was dead. Her doctor tried to reassure her, but she was convinced that she was right. A week later her fears were confirmed when she delivered a stillborn daughter. It was a difficult birth and showed that Abigail's apprehensions about death had not been idle worry. "It appeard to be a very fine Babe," she told John; it was perfectly formed and looked as though it were merely asleep. The tragedy was all the more poignant for both of them because they had hoped so much for another daughter. "My heart was much set upon a daughter," she wrote him. "I had a strong perswasion that my desire would be granted me. It was—but to shew me the uncertainty of all sublinary enjoyments cut of e'er I could call it mine."

She recovered quickly despite the difficult delivery and her grief over her dead child; if anything, John took the news harder than she did. Perhaps it was his frustration at being away from his family at such a time or a bitter reminder of the time lost from his other children that made him feel so strongly. He wrote to Abigail, "Is it not unaccountable, that one should feel so strong an Affection for an Infant, that one has never seen, nor shall see? Yet I must confess to you, the Loss of this sweet little Girl, has most tenderly and sensibly affected me." Even young Nabby was grief-stricken. She cried for hours at the loss of her infant sister.

Abigail's first venture out of the house after her confinement was a visit to John's brother and his wife, who had just had a baby. Seeing the child brought forth all her feelings of loss again. She, like John, was surprised at the intensity of her feelings for a child that had never lived, who had not been "endeared to me by its smiles and its graces." But the tragedy also made her draw even closer to her other children and to John, and once again she lamented the suffering they had endured in their years apart.

In the months after the loss of their daughter Abigail and John once again devoted considerable time and energy to that perennial pastime, observing and commenting on military actions. Hostilities between American and British troops had been relatively subdued during the early months of 1777, but by the end of July the pace of war quickened. Word came at that time that the enemy fleet was sailing to an as yet unknown destination. John worried about Abigail, fearing that the fleet might attack Rhode Island, while she, convinced that it would head for Philadelphia, worried about John. General Howe's fleet appeared to be headed for Philadelphia, but his intentions were a matter of conjecture. Congress, which had moved back to Philadelphia from Baltimore in March, made no immediate plans to move again. There was talk that the Revolution might turn into a general European war, with France and perhaps even Spain declaring war on England. John reported that the Americans had some hopes of getting military aid from France and financial assistance from the Dutch. Serious rumors of an invasion of Boston surfaced in August. Residents began to flee the city, and at one point Abigail, never one to panic, started packing a cartload of the family's possessions. For nearly a month no one could figure out exactly where Howe was going or what he intended to do. John became convinced that he was just plain stupid and moralized to Abigail about the importance of great women behind great men. After a discourse on notable women of ancient times, he concluded that Howe must lack such essential domestic support. "A smart Wife would have put Howe in possession of Philadelphia, a long Time ago."

On August 21 the fleet was sighted in Chesapeake Bay, obviously headed for Philadelphia. On August 26 the British troops landed. Washington's army marched through the streets of Philadelphia, and John was optimistic about a favorable outcome of the invasion. Then for days nothing happened.

Congress made no plans to move. John fired off letters to Abigail several times a week, keeping her posted on the latest developments; she thanked him for the detailed information on "the Movements of How, and his Banditti." Finally, at the end of September, a month after he had first landed at Philadelphia, Howe took the city with no resistance. Shortly before the surrender, Congress had moved north to Yorktown, Pennsylvania.

The capture of Philadelphia angered Abigail. "If Men will not fight and defend their own perticuliar spot, if they will not drive the Enemy from their Doors, they deserve the slavery and subjection which awaits them," she declared. But encouraging news from the north cushioned the impact of the capture of Philadelphia.

American and British forces had been engaging in a series of battles in northern New York since early September. On September 24 Abigail reported to John the news of the defeat of General Burgoyne at Bemis Heights on the Hudson River, comparing the bravery of the Americans to the courage of the men of ancient Sparta and Carthage. Barely a month later the campaign along the Hudson ended in the complete surrender of Burgoyne at Saratoga. It was the most decisive American victory yet, and it proved to be the turning point of the war.

As John had mentioned only briefly to Abigail, Americans sought military aid from France and the French, traditional enemies of Britain, wanted to promote an American victory. But they knew that aid to America would mean war with Britain, and they were not prepared to take that risk without firmer assurance that the Americans could ultimately win their war. The Battle of Saratoga was the first proof that the Americans were building a strong fighting force capable of defeating the highly disciplined British troops. The victory there helped American diplomats in negotiations with the French more than any amount of verbal persuasion could have. Finally French money, supplies, and men were on their way to help the American cause.

Although they could not know the extent of the consequences of Saratoga, Americans at the time understood its importance. Abigail was so excited about the victory that she took Nabby to Boston for the celebrations. Ironically, it was their thirteenth wedding anniversary, which made her think once again of the years she and John had been separated in the cause of the Revolution. "I have patiently as I could endured it with the Belief that you were serving your Country," she wrote John, "and rendering your fellow creatures essential Benefits. May future Generations rise up and call you Blessed, and the present behave worthy of the blessings you are Labouring to secure to them, and I shall have less reason to regreat the deprivation of my own perticuliar felicity."

But Abigail was about to be called upon to make her greatest sacrifice yet, and the victory at Saratoga indirectly had something to do with it. Within a few weeks of the battle, Congress granted John leave of absence to visit his family. This was to be an extended visit. Perhaps it would finally be the time that he would stay home for good. He even took on a legal case, the first since his election to Congress three years before. It was a maritime case, which required him to spend a couple of weeks in Portsmouth, New Hampshire, but such a trip was nothing compared to the travels and separations of recent years.

Shortly after John left for home, Congress elected him Commissioner to France to replace Silas Deane, one of three Commissioners already in Paris. He was to join Benjamin Franklin in Paris to negotiate a French alliance with America, a task made more promising and more urgent by the recent success at Saratoga. It was obviously a position of great prestige and importance, but it would require an even longer absence from home and a potentially dangerous ocean crossing in an American ship subject to British attack—and in the stormy seas of winter, at that.

Letters announcing John's appointment reached Braintree while he was in Portsmouth. Thinking that the letters might contain some important information that should be forwarded to John, Abigail opened them. Stunned at this new assault on her happiness, she had several days to brood over another impending separation before John came home. She did not brood entirely in silence, however. Instead she wrote letters, among the most anguished of her life, lamenting the prospect of this new longer separation.

The men in the Continental Congress by no means assumed that John would automatically accept the appointment. Several of his friends wrote urging him to take up his patriotic duty once more. Abigail, of course, knew better than anyone the strength of John's sense of duty and of his need to feel influential. Without even consulting him, she sensed that he would be unable to turn down this appointment. And she knew just as well that she could not bring herself to persuade him to stay home.

The news of the appointment came in a letter from James Lovell, another Massachusetts delegate. Abigail answered it, acting in John's absence, and took the opportunity to excoriate Lovell and Elbridge Gerry for having nominated John for the position. She understood the honor of the appointment but wished that John could now confine his activities to private life. He was tired of politics; his children needed a father; and she herself could hardly bear any more separation. "Can I Sir consent to be seperated from him whom my Heart esteems above all earthly things, and for an unlimited time?" she asked Lovell. "My life will be one continued scene of anxiety and apprehension, and must I cheerfully comply with the Demand of my Country?"

It was the most difficult moment of her life, and she tried to use John's absence to prepare herself to accept the inevitable. She hardly ate or slept while he was away. When he returned, she was still not reconciled to the prospect of his going to France.

As always, John told Abigail he would stay if she wanted him to. Of course she wanted him to stay, but she also had her own deeply felt sense of public duty. As she often did in such situations, she confided in Mercy Warren. Mercy urged her to let John go because the country needed his services. But she knew that her advice had a hollow ring, for not too long before she herself had asked her husband to give up an assignment in the army that would have required his traveling outside New England. Abigail would have every right to accuse Mercy of not practicing what she preached, but, Mercy argued, "we may profit by the advice Though we despise the Weakness of the Adviser." She also exercised the prerogative of the older woman when she told Abigail that she and John were still young and would have many years together after the war ended. Such thoughts were cold comfort to Abigail as she watched her children grow up without a father and wondered whether she would even see her husband alive at the end of the war.

In the end, of course, Abigail did let him go. Mercy had always thought she would and, indeed, thought all her own advice was superfluous. Some of John's colleagues in Philadelphia assumed that Abigail would accompany him. But if it was complicated and expensive to take her to Philadelphia, it would have been infinitely more difficult to take her to France, and so it was that she stayed behind once again. Instead, it was John Quincy who accompanied his father to France. Ten years old, the younger Adams was to have the opportunity to see some of the world, learn French firsthand, and help his father with clerical work as much as possible. For a New England farm boy, it was an unheard-of chance; for his father, it was the first step in training his son to be a statesman.

On February 13, 1778, the two Adamses went to Mount

Wollaston—now the home of Abigail's uncle, Norton Quincy— and walked with him to a secluded stretch of shoreline. There they waited while a small boat rowed in from their ship, the *Boston*, riding at anchor just offshore. By leaving quietly, almost furtively, they hoped to avoid attracting the attention of spies or enemy ships. After a hasty farewell to Uncle Quincy, father and son wrapped themselves in their cloaks against the winter wind and embarked for their new assignment in France.

Abigail did not go down to the shore to see them off. It had been difficult enough to say goodbye to them at home, and only the greatest effort of will kept her from breaking down in front of all her children. She knew that she could not bear to watch as their tiny boat bounced over the waves to meet the ship that would carry them so far away from her.

Chapter 7

A Woman's Sacrifice

All through the last few hectic days of preparations, Abigail had tried not to think about what it would be like when John and John Quincy left. Now they were gone. There were no more crates to pack, no more bundles of food to prepare to sustain them on their journey. There was nothing left to take her mind from the cold, hard fact of their absence.

She sat down at her kitchen table, a knot in her stomach, filled with despair. "Cannot you immagine me seated by my fire side Bereft of my better Half, and added to that a Limb lopt of to heighten the anguish," she lamented. Who could tell how long they might be gone?—months, surely, maybe even years. Who could tell if they would even see each other again? She tried not to think such thoughts, but she knew they were not altogether idle. Crossing the Atlantic in winter was hazardous enough in the best of times. In wartime the risks were far greater.

Despite the dangers, Abigail had wanted to accompany John to France. She could hardly bear the thought of any further separation, much less one of this magnitude. If John would not give up politics—and she knew in her heart that he would not—at least she could share his trials. But John thought that the expense would be too high, the logistics too complicated, and, above all, the perils of the journey too great for a woman. Reluctantly she acquiesced in his judgment and agreed to stay home.

She often regretted later that she had not insisted on having her way. "I wish a thousand times I had gone with him," she wrote six months after John's departure. Again she told herself that, in times like these, it was a woman's duty to support her husband in his public work and to sacrifice her own happiness for the common good. After four years of almost constant separation, however, it was becoming more and more burdensome for her to set aside her own happiness in the name of patriotism.

She wrote at length to her sister Elizabeth and to her cousins John Thaxter and Hannah Quincy Storer about her sorrow at having let John go alone and about the feelings of duty that had made her agree to it—as if she had to convince herself that what she had done was right. "I resign my own personal felicity and look for my satisfaction in the Consciousness of having discharged my duty to the public," she wrote Thaxter, who replied in the best patriotic style that her "sacrifice to the glorious American Cause" should ease her pain at parting from John. Hannah Storer wrote more candidly, and more sympathetically, that she believed her own patriotism would not stand up to the test of giving up her husband as Abigail had done.

John Quincy's absence compounded her loneliness, but it was easier to part with him. Children, after all, had to grow up and leave home sometime. In the eighteenth century apprenticeships and boarding schools often took them away at tender ages. Abigail had worried about John Quincy's having to grow up without his father. He had reached the age, she believed, when his father's advice and example were more essential than hers. Like John, she also believed that he would benefit from this unique opportunity to see something of the world. The dangers would be great, and the temptations to a young child perhaps difficult to resist, but the drawbacks would be outweighed by the advantages. She had to learn not to overprotect him. "To exclude him from temptation would be to exclude him from the World in which he is to live, and the only method which can be persued with advantage is to fix the padlock upon the mind," she observed. So she let him go and buried her feelings of loss in caring for her other three children.

John, for his part, never doubted the wisdom of refusing to allow Abigail to go with him. The voyage to France, which turned out to be even worse than he had expected, convinced him of it.

Two or three days out of Boston their ship hit a spell of stormy weather that made all the passengers seasick. They were still recovering when three ships, suspected to be British frigates, appeared on the horizon. The captain and crew of the *Boston*, anxious not to let slip an opportunity to capture a British merchant ship as a prize, sailed closer to make sure. Upon discovering that they were in fact closing in on warships rather than merchantmen, the Americans sailed off in the opposite direction, only to be chased for the better part of a day. The *Boston* finally eluded its pursuers but ran headlong into another storm.

After the first two weeks the storms subsided, and life on board ship became more tolerable. But the ship was unpleasantly crowded, and boredom afflicted all the passengers. When they were just a few days away from the coast of France, the *Boston* came perilously close to being captured again. Two large and heavily armed British frigates suddenly appeared on the horizon one moonlit night. Miraculously, the two ships failed to spot the *Boston* and glided on into the night.

On March 30, six weeks after leaving Boston, the Adamses' vessel pulled safely into the harbor at Bordeaux. Grateful to have land beneath their feet once more, John and John Quincy stayed in Bordeaux for a few days to recover from their travels and enjoy the hospitality of the friendly, inquisitive French. Then they set out for Paris, 500 miles away. They arrived on April 8 and moved in with Benjamin Franklin at his lodgings at Passy, a suburb of Paris, the next day. Finally, on April 12, both John and John Quincy got around to writing Abigail to tell her of their safe arrival. She did not receive their letters until the end of June.

Abigail, meanwhile, worried constantly about their safety, especially after several weeks went by with not a word about their arrival. A report that Benjamin Franklin had been assassinated, printed in the *Boston Gazette* at the beginning of March, further unsettled her peace of mind. Dangers from the sea and the British navy were bad enough without adding to them the threat of politically motivated murder. The report was not discredited until a month after its publication.

Then word came that the *Boston* had been captured and taken to Plymouth, England. Some reports said that the ship had arrived safely in France first and was captured on its return, but

Abigail did not know what to believe. John Thaxter tried to reassure her, but Abigail began anxiously writing to friends and asking what would happen if John were captured by the British.

She finally learned that John and John Quincy had arrived safely from a London newspaper taken from a captured English ship. Uncle Isaac Smith wrote in mid-June to say that a prize ship taken into Salem with the latest London newspapers on board reported that John had reached France. On June 30, almost five months after he had left Braintree, she received his April letter.

She had nearly given up hope of his safety. Not knowing where to find him, she even gave up writing letters. "My Heart so much misgave me that I knew not how to hold my pen, and the distracting thought of not knowing where to find you withheld my Hand," she wrote. Her life had been filled with "fear and anxiety," but the sight of familiar handwriting revived her spirits, at least for the moment. John, meanwhile, as late as June had no word of Abigail either, despite the many letters she had written since the beginning of March.

The long silences they endured that spring were only an indication of things to come, as the hazards of enemy ships made normally slow communications even worse. Abigail and John would each endure stretches of weeks and even months with no word of the other. The long silences were only one of the things that made this separation more difficult to bear than the others. The shortage of money and rising prices, which had plagued Abigail for months past, continued and even worsened. Uncertainty about the direction of the war and the future of the United States intensified. For months after the climactic battle of Saratoga American and British forces seemed to be at a stalemate. Taxes levied to finance the war rose sharply, adding to the financial hardships of ordinary Americans even while it seemed that nothing was being accomplished on the military front. On top of her financial worries, Abigail became more and more concerned about the children's education and about the effects of their father's prolonged absence. To compound her anxieties, the totally unreliable communications with Europe meant that she had to make all domestic decisions without advice from John.

For his part, John too faced new trials. The long-winded debates and petulant behavior of Congressmen were nothing compared to the intrigues of foreign courts. His lack of proficiency in

French, his difficulties in getting along with the other American Ministers, and the long delays in getting instructions from Congress made life as a diplomat frustrating and difficult. Though their experiences through the next few years could hardly have been more different, both John and Abigail were forced to cope with increasingly complicated and difficult problems just at a time when they were deprived of virtually all emotional support from each other.

John had little inkling of the difficulties that lay ahead of him when he arrived in France. At first he was overwhelmed by the beauty and elegance of everything about France—the countryside, the buildings, the art, the food, the wine, even the women. "This is a delicious Country," he wrote Abigail. "Every Thing that can sooth, charm and bewitch is here." Rarely at a loss for words, he eventually gave up trying to describe the charms of France.

Words failed him because France presented many contradictions for John. He was steeped in the ideology of New World simplicity and virtue versus Old World decadence and corruption, and he found decadence and corruption aplenty in France. But he wasn't prepared for his own positive reactions to the country. Its age and its feeling of stability and order impressed him and made him feel very much the provincial. The youth of the United States, according to popular ideology, freed it from the vices of Europe, but John was made acutely aware of the potentially disruptive effects of his country's lack of history and traditions. He hated the political and social system of France but was attracted to the sense of order that it created. Even more disturbing, however, was the delight he took in the beauty and sensuous pleasures of this strange country—a delight he could not quite suppress. Benjamin Franklin solved these contradictions by dressing and acting the part of country bumpkin while savoring the pleasures of Paris. John, characteristically, tried to solve the contradictions by denying them. His efforts to describe the beauty of France in letters home were almost always accompanied by assertions that such beauty had no effect on him. He had no time for pleasure, he often said, for he had to devote himself to public business.

John's reactions to French women illustrate some of his conflicting feelings. French women fascinated him; he found them handsome, charming, and better educated than American or English women. They were also openly affectionate, which startled the staid New Englander but pleased him nevertheless. The ladies were especially free with their kisses and embraces for Franklin, as John noted with some asperity.

John could not forbear to praise French women to Abigail, adding "Dont be jealous." Abigail, far from being jealous, was delighted with his observations on women and wanted to know more. Comments about their greater accomplishments only fueled her contention that education for American women had to be improved. "I can hear of the Brilliant accomplishment[s] of any of my Sex with pleasure and rejoice in that Liberality of Sentiment which acknowledges them. At the same time I regret the trifling narrow contracted Education of the Females of my own Country," she wrote John. Nevertheless, she added, she hoped he would not imitate Franklin in his "adventures" with the ladies.

While John explored France, Abigail too learned something about French hospitality. An immediate result of the French–American alliance was military assistance from the French navy. In late summer part of the French fleet dropped anchor in Boston harbor, which it planned to make its base of operations for an attack against British troops at Newport. As wife of one of the American Ministers to France, Abigail received courtesy calls from the principal French officers.

It was always a bit difficult for her to think of herself as the wife of a statesman, especially living as she did in a modest house on a farm far removed from centers of political and social activity. For the French officers, however, it would have been unthinkable not to call on the Minister's lady. Abigail relished their visits for the news they brought her of the political world.

The Comte d'Estaing, chief officer of the French fleet in Boston, invited her to dine on his ship with as many of her friends as she liked. He sent his barge to pick them up and prepared "An entertainment fit for a princiss." Several of the officers stayed at Uncle Quincy's house in Braintree, where she often socialized with them, and she also entertained them herself. Like John, Abigail was impressed with the polished manners and social graces of the French and she was forced to revise some of her stereotypical notions about the French people. "If I ever had any national prejudices they are done away and I am ashamed to own I was ever possessed of so narrow a spirit," she confessed to John. She also deplored the prejudices of other Americans against the French.

In early November the fleet left Boston, bound on an unsuccessful mission to liberate Newport. Its presence, brief though it was, made an entertaining diversion for Abigail and gave her the sense of being once again in the middle of political activity. Through the winter there was little to engage her attention. New England was no longer a battleground. It was certainly easier to live without the constant fear of attack, but it was also much less interesting. The sense of danger, of being part of a great cause, was gone—without any of the compensations of victory or peace. Military action was now concentrated in the South, and news of battles reached New England slowly. Without John as her regular correspondent in Congress, even political news reached her only sporadically. For Abigail, accustomed to feeling in the thick of political and military action, the slow pace of life was frustrating.

Even her domestic affairs required less of her time. Soon after John left, she decided it would be more profitable to rent their farm than to run it herself. She finally managed to evict Hayden, the difficult tenant who had refused to share his quarters with refugees from the city in 1775, and rented the neighboring house and farm to two young men. They took complete responsibility for farming the land and paying taxes on it.

The children also demanded less attention. Most of the time she had only Charley and Tommy at home. Nabby went to school in Boston in the fall. She came home around Christmas but then went off to spend several weeks with Mercy Warren early in 1779. Abigail was lonely without her daughter but had encouraged her to go first to Boston and then to the Warrens' home to broaden her experience. A long stay with Mercy, she believed, could not help but have a beneficial effect on Nabby.

She knew she would have to part with Charley before long, too. Now eight years old, he was ready to begin grammar school. Abigail faced the same worries about his education that she had with Johnny's. There was still neither an adequate school in Braintree nor a qualified tutor, so she planned to send Charley (and eventually Tommy, too) to stay with her sister Elizabeth in

Haverhill. Betsey's husband, John Shaw, could tutor them. She delayed sending them, however, ostensibly to wait for their father's approval but also because she was reluctant to part with her children so quickly.

It was some consolation to Abigail when her two-year-old niece Louisa came to live with her. Louisa was the daughter of her brother William, who lived on a small farm in Lincoln, several miles west of Boston. William, the black sheep of the family, had resisted his father's efforts to get him to attend Harvard, had failed in trying to establish himself as a merchant in Boston, and was now scratching out an existence on his small farm. He had a sickly wife, a brood of children, and very little money to support them. Abigail tried to relieve some of the burden by taking Louisa. The circumstances were unfortunate, but the solution worked out happily. Abigail had always wanted another daughter and was delighted to have a small child to look after. Louisa thrived under her care.

Abigail tried to stay informed about political affairs by corresponding with friends serving in Congress, although there was no substitute for John's regular letters. John Thaxter now served as a secretary to Congress and could be counted on as a regular correspondent; she also began writing to James Lovell, a casual acquaintance recently elected as a delegate from Massachusetts. She relied on both men not only to keep her informed about happenings in Congress but also to pass along news about military affairs and whatever shreds of information they received from Paris.

John Thaxter was an ideal correspondent. He had lived with the family while working as one of John's law clerks and, later, as the boys' tutor. He wrote diligently to Abigail, telling her news of the war, asking her opinions on political issues, and sending her books published in Philadelphia—much as John had done. She came to depend on his letters not only to satisfy her curiosity but also to relieve her loneliness. "I love to know what is passing in the world," she told him, "tho excluded from it."

Thaxter's youth, his family relationship to Abigail, and his long acquaintance with the Adams family all encouraged a candid and intimate correspondence. With James Lovell the situation was entirely different. She had first corresponded with him to complain about John's appointment to France; at that time he encouraged her to continue writing by complimenting her and taking seriously her requests for information. But Lovell was unlike any man Abigail had encountered before. His polite compliments and professions of concern for her well-being, appropriate enough for the wife of a former colleague in Congress, gave way to more effusive compliments that bordered on impropriety. Abigail chided Lovell for his "flattery" and "gallantry," but in tones that only encouraged him.

Her candid manner and the freedom with which she expressed feelings encouraged him to reply in a more familiar way than Abigail expected. In the weeks before she heard about John's safe arrival, she wrote to Lovell confessing her fears and asking for any news of John that might reach Congress. She appealed to his sympathies as a man who had also suffered from war—Lovell had been a prisoner of the British for a time—and had endured long separations from his family. She told him of her hope that "you will communicate to me some share of that hidden strength, . . . that I may endure this misfortune with becomeing fortitude." Such language was intended as a compliment to Lovell and as a way of forging a common bond between them. But Lovell took it as an invitation to a correspondence of greater intimacy. "Call me not a Savage," he noted in one letter, "when I inform you that your 'Allarms and Distress' have afforded me *Delight*!" If she wanted pity for her misfortunes, she should not send them in "the most elegant Dresses of Sentiment and Language."

It was not the kind of response Abigail had anticipated. She initiated the correspondence to learn about John and his possible fate, with the further hope that Lovell might supply her with political and military news as the correspondence continued. Instead, his letters talked about her. Such attention was indeed flattering, and yet to her way of thinking improper. Her subsequent letters to Lovell reflected her ambivalence. In reply to her protests at his excessive familiarity, he complained: "Must I only write to you in the Language of Gazettes, . . . Must I suppress Opinion, Sentiment and just Encomium upon the Gracefulness of a lovely suffering Wife or Mother? It seems I must or be taxed as a Flatterer." Somewhat petulantly, he resolved to confine himself to "*secret* Admiration." Lovell continued to write flattering phrases, however, and Abigail continued to scold him for it. "I know not whether I ought to reply to your favour of April the first," she noted, "for inded Sir I begin to look upon you as a very dangerous man."

But reply she did, and so their flirtation by mail continued. In one of his more startling missives, he described the effect one of her letters had on him as he opened it during a session of Congress: "Did it add to my former great *respect* for the Writer of it? No, Portia, not at the *first* Reading; but it forced from me, almost audibly, in a grave Assembly where I broke the Seal, 'gin ye were mine ain Thing how dearly I would *love* thee'!"

Their correspondence continued, notwithstanding Abigail's objections to Lovell's language, during most the time John spent in Europe. Not all of Lovell's letters were openly seductive, but even the more formal ones were sprinkled with compliments to "lovely Portia," and nothing that Abigail said could prevent occasional more flowerly outbursts. On the contrary, her protests enouraged him.

In reality, she did not try too hard to stop Lovell's attentions. Had she found his letters truly offensive, she could have simply stopped writing him; there were other men in Congress—Elbridge Gerry or Sam Adams, for example—who could have given her the news she craved after John Thaxter left his position in Congress the next summer. But Abigail secretly enjoyed the flattery and attention. And who could blame her? She was thirty-four years old, still young, but a wife of fourteen years with children entering their teens. She had been deprived of the company of her husband for the better part of four years. She did not get many letters from John, and those few that did make it were short and cryptic, devoid of the expression of love that had kept her going through the months he spent in Philadelphia. She felt deprived of companionship, of attention, of affection. James Lovell, flatterer though he might be, added some excitement to her otherwise dull life.

As the months went by, feelings of loneliness and depression began to overwhelm Abigail. She was normally a cheerful person and had learned to cope with being alone after four years of prolonged separations; but the distance, the infrequent letters, and the reduction in her household responsibilities all combined to sap her spirits. With the approach of winter, cold and snow isolated her and increased her depression. When February came it marked a year since John had left Braintree. Still there was no indication when he might return.

Abigail began to think of herself as a widow, "the most Forlorn and Dismal of all states." In a moment of bitterness, she wondered why she had to be the one to suffer, wishing "the wisdom of the continent had made choise of some person whose seperation from his partner would have little or no pain, or mortification—many such might have been found I dare say."

The only antidotes for her depression were letters from John, and those were rare. A substantial proportion of the letters they wrote to each other were lost when the ships carrying them were captured. While fully aware of this, Abigail nevertheless could hardly keep from being vexed when months went by without word from John. And John could not always fall back on the dangers of the seas as his excuse. The truth of the matter was that he didn't write very often. He was deeply troubled by the problems he encountered in France, which absorbed all his attention. It was typical of him that, when beset by political and personal difficulties, he found very little time to write to his family. Abigail, having unfortunately little inkling of his problems in France, could only interpret his silence as neglect.

John's difficulties were real enough, and his own inflexibility and feelings of self-doubt served only to aggravate them. Adjusting to a different culture, a new language, the protocol of the French court, and the intricacies of diplomatic negotiation would have been difficult for anyone in his position. On top of all that, he had to contend with the quarrels and backbiting of other American representatives in Paris. These quarrels, John believed, severely restricted the effectiveness of American negotiations. Although John was determined at first not to get involved in them, he finally found it impossible to remain neutral.

John could see instantly that Benjamin Franklin was the lynchpin in American dealings with the French. Franklin was enormously popular with French political officials and the French people; a skilled negotiator, he had the confidence of virtually everyone in the Continental Congress. It was clear from the beginning that John Adams, or anyone else for that matter, would play a decidedly secondary role to Franklin. John respected Franklin's skill as a diplomat but thought his intellectual abilities were overrated. He also thought Franklin was lazy, extravagant in his personal habits, and inclined to trust French officials too much. The longer John stayed in Paris, moreover, the more he deplored Franklin's morals. So John found himself not only playing second fiddle to another man, but to a man he felt to be in many ways his inferior. It was a particularly uncomfortable situation for one who had always been inclined to feel his own talents were not sufficiently recognized..

To complicate matters, Franklin and Arthur Lee, the second American Commissioner, were bitter enemies. Each tried to win John over to his side. Much of their animosity concerned the behavior of a third Commissioner, Silas Deane, whom John had replaced. Deane, in addition to his diplomatic work, had purchased military supplies in Europe for the United States government and had come under heavy criticism at home for alleged profiteering. Lee, one of Deane's most outspoken critics, was convinced that Deane was out to undermine his reputation. Franklin supported Deane and didn't trust Lee, even questioning his loyalty. John, thrown into the middle of this situation, found himself an "Umpire between two bitter and inveterate Parties." Added to the American delegation's disharmony was the further complication that all the Commissioners' secretaries were British spies. Consequently all the deliberations between the French and Americans were soon known in London.

In the midst of these problems, word arrived from Congress in February 1779 that it had appointed Franklin sole Minister to negotiate with the French, relieving Adams and Lee of their duties. Lee was named Minister to Spain, and Adams was neither provided with a new assignment nor instructed to come home. John had in fact written to Congress some months earlier suggesting that Franklin be named sole Minister. He had thought such a change would avoid many of the conflicts he witnessed, but when his advice was taken he was not so pleased with the results. Apparently Congress expected John to remain in Europe for the time being and continue his efforts to raise money for the United States until he received further instructions. But John took his lack of instructions as a personal affront, an indication that Congress did not care whether he stayed in Europe or came home.

Abigail knew very little about the situation in Paris. John's infrequent letters, when they reached her at all, rarely contained any details about either the negotiations or his problems with the other diplomats, for the straightforward reason that his letters might be read by spies or captured by enemy ships. What little news she heard from France usually came from the newspapers or from her correspondents in Congress. For example, she learned about Silas Deane's shady activities when he returned to Philadelphia and laid his case before Congress. Unhappy with its treatment of him, Deane made a public statement in the newspapers justifying his conduct. Abigail realized that the whole affair must have affected John, but she did not know exactly how. She herself believed that Deane had gone too far in publicly criticizing Congress. She feared that his actions weakened Congress and encouraged the public to feel suspicious of its elected representatives. While people should not obey their rulers blindly, in her opinion, they should show "proper respect" to the men to whom they delegated authority.

It was, she felt, bad enough that John told her nothing about what he was doing, but on top of that he seldom expressed any feelings of affection for her either. This too was a sign of John's troubled state of mind, but to Abigail it was unforgivable. She was struggling along by herself, after all, trying to be both mother and father to her children and trying to keep loneliness from overwhelming her. Instead of the weekly informative, affectionate letters that had sustained her when John was in Philadelphia, she got a few short, unemotional notes and months of silence. Finally, almost overcome by unhappiness, she lashed out at John and accused him of neglecting her. It was the first time in fourteen years of marriage that they had exchanged harsh words on paper. She complained not only that she sent him more letters than he sent her but also that hers were longer and more affectionate. Perhaps it was imprudent to write so freely, "but I cannot take my pen with my Heart overflowing and not give utterance to some of the abundance which is in it. Could you after a thousand fears and anxieties, long expectation and painfull suspences be satisfied with my telling you that I was well, that I wished you were with me, that my daughter sent her duty, that I had ordered some articles for you . . . &c. &c. —By Heaven if you could you have changed Hearts with some frozen Laplander or made a voyage to a region that has chilld every Drop of your Blood."

She understood full well that John's letters ran the risk of falling into unfriendly hands but thought he was being overly cautious. It was one thing to be careful about writing on political subjects, but what harm could be done by expressions of love? "The affection I feel for my Friend is of the tenderest kind," she told him, "matured by years, sanctified by choise and approved by Heaven. Angles can witness to its purity, what care I then for the Ridicule of Britain should this testimony of it fall into their Hands?"

It so happened that several days after this outburst she received three letters from John all at once; she was mortified to learn that he had received only one of her many letters. She had not yet sent her angry letter, but instead of tearing it up she sent it anyway as a statement of her feelings, apologizing "for harboring an Idea so unjust, to your affection." "Were you not dearer to me than all this universe contains beside, I could not have sufferd as I have done," she added.

John did not seem to feel the same need for frequent reassurances of Abigail's love for him and did not understand why she needed reassurance from him. He never wavered in his love for her, and she must know that; why did she need reminding? He never completely understood the extent of Abigail's depression and her feelings of being utterly cut off while he was in Europe. "For Heavens Sake, my dear dont indulge a Thought that it is possible for me to neglect, or forget all that is dear to me in his world," he told her. But he could not write anything "that one is not willing should go into all the Newspapers of the World," and regardless of Abigail's feelings on the subject, he did not want his innermost emotions broadcast to the world.

By December 1779, when Abigail's melancholy letters of the fall began to arrive, he already had some inkling that he would be removed from his position as Commissioner and was afraid that his efforts would go unappreciated. Feeling insecure about his position and his future, he was especially sensitive about his public image. To have his personal correspondence with his wife read or, worse, published might make him look weak. After receiving Abigail's third letter in "this complaining style," he told her that he had written several answers but could not send any of them. "One was angry, another was full of Greif, and the third with Melancholy, so that I burnt them all. —If you write me in this style I shall leave of writing intirely, it kills me. Can Professions of Esteem be Wanting from me to you? Can Protestation of affection be necessary? can tokens of remembrance be desir'd? The very Idea of this sickens me. Am I not wretched Enough, in this Banishment, without this. . . . I beg you would never more write to me in such a strain for it really makes me unhappy."

In February 1779 John finally decided to go home without waiting any longer for Congressional instructions. Going home, however, proved easier said then done. He and John Quincy went to Nantes in March, intending to take passage on the U.S. frigate *Alliance*. They arrived in Nantes only to discover that the *Alliance* had been diverted to Brest, where an exchange of prisoners was being negotiated with the British. Not one to remain idle, John went off to Brest to help with the negotiations and to try to speed up the *Alliance*'s departure for America. He returned to Nantes, and the two Adamses stayed there until the end of April, when they learned that the *Alliance*'s mission had been changed. It would no longer be sailing directly to the United States. John was advised to move himself, his son, and his baggage once again, this time to Lorient, where he could take passage in the *Sensible*, a French frigate assigned to take the Chevalier de la Luzerne, the new French Minister, to the United States.

The first week in May found John and John Quincy in Lorient waiting for a French ship and a French Minister. John was annoyed and frustrated to be waiting for a ship at a time when he had expected to be home. More than a month passed before they finally set sail on June 18.

Meanwhile Abigail was confused by the conflicting reports she had heard. By summer she had received no letters from John dated later than February. She knew from his earlier letters that Franklin had been appointed sole Minister and that John was left without a specific assignment. Not one to wait passively for information, she wrote to Lovell demanding to know what Congress intended to do about John. Why wasn't he recalled when the changes were made in the French delegation? Had he been specifically requested to stay in France? Had his conduct been impeached in any way? Lovell avoided her questions about Congress's intentions but said he thought it likely that John would be returning aboard the *Alliance*. Mercy and James Warren, however, had heard rumors that Congress was planning a new European assignment for him.

On August 2 Abigail was still trying to discover John's whereabouts when the *Sensible* dropped anchor in Nantasket

Roads. A crew member rowed John and John Quincy ashore and deposited them on the beach at Braintree near the point where they had embarked on a cold February day a year and a half before. Their arrival, of course, took Abigail completely by surprise.

Days later, a letter from James Lovell brought her the good news that, finally, he had learned that John was definitely on his way home from France.

Chapter 8

The Long Separation

August and September were happy months for Abigail and John. After eighteen months apart they were like honeymooners again. They took long walks in the late summer sunshine and rode over to Weymouth and Mount Wollaston for family suppers with Abigail's relatives. Abigail harvested the last of her vegetable crop while John, relishing the simplicity of being a farmer once more, inspected his fields and fences. She let herself hope that they would not have to endure any more long separations.

In September John went to Cambridge to attend the state constitutional convention, and Abigail was alone again. This time she didn't mind, however, because John was close by and came home on weekends. When he was home, he told her all the details about the delegates and the convention's deliberations. He had been chosen for the committee assigned to draft the constitution and then delegated by the committee to write the first draft. Abigail listened to him as he outlined the points that would go into the document and read every page as he wrote it. Once again she felt that she was part of the important events around her, so she didn't begrudge the days John spent away from home.

But in October a letter from Congress put an end to her happiness. Congress had designated John as Minister Plenipotentiary to negotiate treaties of peace and commerce with Great Britain. He would have to return to France as soon as possible, even though there was no immediate hope of peace. It would be important for him to be on the scene to negotiate whenever conditions were appropriate.

It was a cruel blow for Abigail. The pleasures of the last three months suddenly seemed like an illusion, a vision of happiness that tantalized her but was then snatched away. She relived all the same anxieties about John's crossing the ocean in winter under threat of enemy capture and all her days of loneliness and depression as she waited for letters that rarely came. But there was no question of John's refusing this appointment. He wanted it badly. It was balm for his injured pride. The loss of his earlier commission and the months he had spent in Europe feeling useless had left him with a sense of failure. When he came home, he had let Congress know in one of his long and detailed dispatches that he would like another European appointment. Now he had a commission even more important than the last, one that was his alone. He, not the overrated Benjamin Franklin, would be responsible for negotiating peace.

This time Abigail and John did not even discuss her going with him, even though the dangers of capture were much less now that the French navy was on their side. John had experienced one winter crossing and had found it more harrowing than anything he could have imagined. He refused to expose Abigail to such an ordeal. "There is nothing so odious as a lady at sea," he told her. Seasickness, crowded quarters, and poor food made it impossible for a woman to preserve any sense of "delicacy." John did not, however, feel any qualms about taking children across the ocean again. He decided to take only not only John Quincy but also Charles, who was only nine years old—even younger than Johnny had been when he made his first trip. John thought it was never too early to introduce his sons to the ways of the world.

Abigail raised no objections; seeing a foreign country and learning a new language firsthand were opportunities of such importance that a mother's heart should not stand in the way. She was also concerned that John's long absences would weaken his influence over his sons, and she urged John Quincy to make the second trip with his father when he initially expressed some reluctance. He needed his father's advice and attention more than ever now, she believed.

One cannot help but wonder why Abigail and John continued to subject themselves to such long separations. Certainly the practical obstacles to Abigail's accompanying John to Europe, or even to Philadelphia, were great. The Adamses were not wealthy by any means, and the expense of maintaining both the Braintree home and a household in a distant city would have posed a serious financial strain. John and the two boys could live at lodgings or move in with Benjamin Franklin, as they had on the first trip, but they would have been compelled to rent a house if Abigail and the other children went along too. Managing their farm from a distance, even with the help of tenants or relatives, would have been difficult but not impossible. Many other men and women suffered similar separations during the Revolution. Congressmen had no choice but to stay in Philadelphia for the duration of the legislative sessions; travel was too slow for them to go home frequently. Few could afford to bring their families. What made John and Abigail unusual was not the fact of their separation but the length of it. Other Congressmen served a term or two and then went home, relinquishing their places to someone else. If they were selected again, they declined. Many of the men who served long stretches in Europe either had no families or cared little for them. Benjamin Franklin preferred living apart from his wife; Thomas Jefferson, who went to France after the war, was a widower. Even soldiers usually enlisted for short hitches and went home when their time was up. Mercy Warren's husband, James, an army officer, resigned his commission rather than leave Massachusetts.

But John accepted position after position, and Abigail again and again refused to exercise her powerful influence to make him stay home. In consequence, they spent the better part of ten years living miserably apart. And there is absolutely no doubt that these separations made both of them miserable. It could never be said of John Adams, as it could of Benjamin Franklin, that he enjoyed Paris more for having left his wife behind. John and Abigail remained unquestionably devoted to each other and suffered severely from their prolonged separations.

They both believed that they endured their personal misery for the sake of their country's cause, that their own happiness was less important than the public good. Yet many other Americans who felt the same patriotic sentiments set some limits on their self-sacrifice. John, more than most men, felt driven to serve his country. He felt even more strongly driven to achieve public recognition for his contributions. A combination of his own ambition and a heightened sense of patriotism kept him pursuing a political career.

He felt honored by his appointment as Minister Plenipotentiary, even though dismayed by the dangers it involved, the difficulties of the task, and the prospect of separation from his family again. He professed to yearn for retirement from politics and a return to the simple life of country lawyer and farmer, yet given the chance he could not stay out of the limelight. He explained his acceptance of the appointment as his public duty but was clearly motivated by his craving for recognition as well.

John's sense of duty was at times a positive motivating force, but it could also be a negative one. Fully aware of his own ambition and brought up to believe in self-denial, he accepted unpopular commissions both to fulfill his sense of duty and to deny his personal ambition. If an assignment promised to make him unpopular and curtail his chances for glory, he could reassure himself that ambition was not getting the better of him. This was as true of his diplomatic assignments in Europe as it had been of his first important political role: defender of the British soldiers in the Boston Massacre case.

Self-denial and a sense of duty, in other words, could put the brakes on potentially dangerous personal ambition. John's denial of any personal pleasure or comfort while on public assignments enhanced his efforts to blot out his own ambition in favor of disinterested virtue. While in Congress he made constant mention of his efforts to minimize his living expenses in order to save tax dollars, all the while complaining that his frugality would go unappreciated. On his first trip to Paris he moved in with Franklin rather than establish separate lodgings and declined to maintain his own carriage, secretary, or servants. The denial of pleasure or comfort gave testimony in his own mind that duty and not ambition was what motivated him.

Abigail's motivations were even more complex, because she shared John's heightened sense of public duty and self-sacrifice without gaining any of the personal glory he achieved as a public figure. She believed that a woman served her country by supporting her husband in his public work, although by now she had reached a point where that line of reasoning was wearing thin. But she too had her more subtle reasons for agreeing to prolonged separations. She basked in John's glory to a considerable extent and enjoyed the attention she received as the wife of a public figure. Most of the time he shared the details of his work with her and sought her advice. She relished this involvement, for she was as fascinated by politics as he.

Most important, she understood John very well and loved him as deeply as any woman ever loved a man. She realized his need for political involvement and recognition, and could not bring herself to stand in his way. She could have persuaded him not to go to Congress and not to go to France but to stay home, practice law, and farm his land. But she understood how unhappy he would be if she did. Miserable when he was gone, she would have been equally miserable if he had stayed unwillingly and lived out a life of thwarted ambition. Either way she lost. But this way at least she had hope for the future.

Barely three months after he had come home, John was to set sail again on the *Sensible*. In addition to his two sons, his entourage included John Thaxter, who was to be his private secretary; Francis Dana, a young Boston lawyer appointed as secretary to the delegation; and one servant. The party boarded ship in Boston on November 13.

It had been an especially difficult parting from Abigail in Braintree; their repeated separations made goodbyes more painful than ever. He tried to comfort her in a hastily written letter just before the ship sailed. "We shall yet be happy, I hope and pray," he told her, "and I dont doubt it. I shall have vexations enough, as usual. You will have Anxiety and Tenderness enough as usual. Pray strive, not to have too much. . . Yours, ever, ever yours . . ."

The *Sensible* sailed two days later. Abigail was tempted to go to Boston to see John and the children one more time before they left, even though she would suffer the pain of parting again. Practicality got the better of emotion, however, as she told herself the ship would probably have sailed already. At least John's expression of confidence in their future happiness cheered her a bit, although she was prone to fits of pessimism and was depressed at the sight of her once again empty house. "My habitation, how disconsolate it looks!" she lamented. "My table I set down to it but cannot swallow my food. O Why was I born with so much Sensibility and why possessing it have I so often been call'd to struggle with it?"

Abigail had been struggling with her "sensibility" and with the strength of her love for her husband, which made separation so painful, for more than five years. Now, at the point when she could hardly bear any more time apart, she was to be called upon to struggle alone with her feelings for almost five years more. Mercifully, she had little inkling of how long this longest separation would last, for the war was winding down and John thought a treaty could probably be concluded in a year or so. But as the months turned into years and it seemed as if peace would never come, both Abigail and John became more and more depressed and disillusioned over the sacrifices they had felt compelled to make in the name of the national good.

For the first few months, however, Abigail adopted a philosophical, almost cheerful view of her situation. She did not have moments of regretting that she had stayed behind, as she had when John made his first trip to France; his descriptions of his first voyage had removed much of the allure from the idea of travel. She was also more resigned to receiving infrequent and out-of-date letters than she had been during John's first journey to Europe. In their short time together they had discussed the angry letters sent back and forth across the Atlantic during the preceeding months and had tried to explain to each other the feelings that lay behind them. As a result Abigail forced heself to be patient about waiting for letters, and John made more efforts to reassure her of his love.

With only two children to care for and the farm still rented to tenants, Abigail's day-to-day household chores did not consume all her time. Increasingly she began to enlarge her role as household manager by looking after John's accounts, investing in real estate, and even dabbling a bit in European trade. She undertook these activities at first out of necessity, to keep John's accounts in order and to balance the family budget as inflation raged in war-torn New England. Gradually she broadened her sights to make investments that she hoped would guarantee her family's future financial security.

It was clear to Abigail by now that politics was John's first love and that he would never make much money from it. It was equally clear that he did not want to be bothered about keeping up the farm or worrying about his family's future income. He might wax eloquent about riding over the Blue Hills and enjoying the humble life of a farmer, but negotiating for land or seeing that workers were hired to plow the fields attracted him far less than negotiating treaties and writing discourses on political theory. Abigail, on the other hand, had a head for business and was perfectly capable of driving a hard bargain to get what she wanted. She also discovered that she enjoyed such business dealings. Eventually she took over the family financial management altogether.

John had left Abigail with a small stash of silver coins, which she exchanged for paper currency from time to time to make small purchases of necessities. She exchanged only enough coin for a week or two at a time, because the paper depreciated so rapidly that it was foolish to keep too large a supply on hand. She relied on friends of John's in Boston to exchange her silver for her. Soon after he left, she wrote them inquiring about current exchange rates. "There are so many persons disposed to take advantage of me," she remarked to John Lowell, that she depended on a trustworthy friend to handle these transactions for her. But it was unlikely that anyone would succeed in cheating her. Even in dealing with trusted acquaintances, she wrote two men—Lowell and Oliver Wendell—to ask about rates. When Wendell quoted her a lower exchange rate than Lowell had, she politely but firmly informed him of the discrepancy.

Winter settled in with a vengeance, and for several weeks Abigail and the children were cooped up in the house with little news from outside, even from Boston. The snow was so deep that she didn't even get out to see Mary or her father. Days of sub-zero temperatures froze Boston Harbor for the first time in memory. Nabby, on a lark, went with friends across the ice from Braintree to Boston. Uncle Isaac Smith was astonished to see her at his front door on one of the coldest days of the winter. Abigail, however, decided that such sport was not for her. Instead she stayed close to her fireside, reading and writing letters. She sent letters to John by every ship headed to Europe.

At the end of February she finally heard that he and the boys had arrived safely but, to her surprise, in Spain rather than France. Their ship had sprung a leak off the coast of Spain, and the captain had decided to put into the tiny port of Ferrol rather than risk sailing on to Bordeaux. There John learned that it might take two months or more to repair the ship, and the chances of another ship coming into port bound for France were remote. Unable to bear the thought of waiting, perhaps indefinitely, in that dusty little town, he decided to rent carriages and travel to France by land. Abigail was relieved to hear of his decision. "I grow more and more apprehensive of the dangers of the sea," she observed, "tho I have really no Right to Quarrel with old Neptune, since he has 3 times safely transported my Friend." Once she knew he was safe on land, she didn't want to have to worry about him on another voyage.

Little did she know, as she wrote these words, what dangers and hardships her loved ones were enduring as they made their way, very slowly and tediously, to France. Equipped with coaches, mules, and guides, they set out to scale the mountains in one of the remotest parts of Spain in the dead of winter. John did not undertake the trip lightly, for he knew something of the difficulty of the terrain. Everyone advised them to wait for a ship, but he would not be deterred.

They traveled on roads so narrow and steep that they were often forced to get out of the carriages and walk long stretches. They stayed in inns worse than anything John could have imagined. The whole experience made a profound impression on John Quincy, who noted in his journal that they had stayed in rooms that one might think had housed half a dozen hogs for six months. "The People are Lazy, dirty, Nasty and in short I can compare them to nothing but a parcel of hogs, their cloaths are commonly of a dirt colour and their Breeches are big enough for to put a bushel of Corn in besides themselves," he observed uncharitably.

John too was appalled by the dirt floors of the houses; the absence of chimneys, which made the rooms very smoky; and the sharing of quarters by people and animals. It was with relief that they reached French soil and made their way to the familiar scenes and old friends of Bordeaux and Paris. John admitted to Abigail that had he known how difficult the trip would be, he would have waited for a passage by sea. He was thankful that she had not come along and even had some misgivings about having brought the children. "My affections I fear got the better of my Judgment in bringing my Boys," he confided. "They behave very well however."

John returned to Paris as a seasoned traveler to a favorite city. Because his mission was negotiating peace with Britain, and there were no signs that the British were prepared to negotiate in the near future, he had time on his hands. But because he had a definite commission, he had none of the feelings of uselessness that had plagued him on his previous trip. For the first few months he was able to enjoy seeing the sights of Paris. He wrote long letters to Abigail in the spring of 1780 describing his sightseeing, a far cry from the brief letters of a year earlier, when he had ridiculed such travelogues as the occupation of frivolous young men.

As soon as he arrived in Europe, John began sending Abigail small shipments of European goods: cloth, handkerchiefs, ribbons, laces, and tea ordered from merchants in Spain and France. Such goods, which he could buy relatively cheaply, commanded high prices at home. Abigail kept some of them for her personal use but sold most of them to help meet her expenses. People in and around Braintree were happy enough to pay for them, because imported goods were almost impossible to find and exorbitantly expensive when they were available. John had occasionally sent such shipments during his first stay in France, but too many ships had been captured for the practice to be profitable. Now the seas were far safer, and Abigail came to depend on the shipments as a way of supplementing her meager income.

She received the first shipment in the spring of 1780 and found all the goods "very acceptable." Handkerchiefs were the most useful, she told John, because they could be readily sold for hard money. Her only criticism of his choices concerned the glassware; he had sent only tumblers, and all of the same size, whereas wine glasses would have been more easily sold. But she assured him that anything he sent could be turned to profit. She urged him in the future to send handkerchiefs and calico, which were always in demand. Silk handkerchiefs would command double the price of linen ones, although they did not cost that much more in Europe.

Abigail did not always think of profit alone. She asked John to send a pair of silk gloves and cloth for dresses for herself and Nabby. Even in time of war and tight money, an occasional luxury seemed harmless enough. "A little of what you call frippery is very necessary towards looking like the rest of the world," she wrote him. Nabby, knowing that her father had no use for merely ornamental dress, prompted her mother to add that "she has no passion for dress further than he would approve of or to appear when she goes from home a little like those of her own age."

Eventually they became quite systematic in their little foreign trade. Abigail told John exactly what she wanted, and he sent her requests on to merchants, who shipped the goods to her directly. In July she told him to stop sending handkerchiefs because the market was glutted. Instead she wanted "15 yards of thin black mode [a type of silk] ditto white, ditto red, ditto blew, some black sattin proper for cloaks and low price black lace, calico and Irish linen, which is not higher priced than dutch, but sells much better, the best Hyson tea." By November, she branched out a bit, asking for "26 yards of Dutch bed tick, 2 Gray muffs and tippets, 2 bundles of english pins, 2 sets of House Brushes, 1 doz. of blew and white china tea cups and sausers, half a doz. pint china Bowls, half a doz. diaper table cloths . . . one Scotch carpet 4 yards square of 6 Ells, half a doz. white gauze handerchifs the same size that the black were." She also reminded John that "an Ell in Holland is but 3 quarters of our yard."

Finally John suggested that she simply write to the merchants herself. This she readily did, and for as long as John remained in Europe she ordered goods from merchants in Holland, Spain and France. She sold most of the goods herself but worked through others when necessary. Mercy Warren sold some things for her, and she could always rely on Uncle Isaac in Boston to find buyers if she couldn't.

As prices and taxes continued to rise and paper money continued to depreciate, Abigail depended on her trading ventures to make ends meet. A severe drought in the summer and early fall caused more trouble by forcing her and other farmers to dip into their supplies of stored hay to feed livestock. Paper money had depreciated so far that every silver dollar was worth seventy or seventy-five in paper; lamb cost $10 a pound, veal $7, and rye $110 a bushel. Every few months Braintree residents had to conscript more men and pay more taxes to support the army. Her tenants threatened to leave, complaining that they could no longer afford to pay the taxes. "They say two Cows would formerly pay the taxes upon this place, and that it would now take ten," she told John. "The burden is greater I fear than the people will bear."

At the same time that she began trading to meet current expenses, Abigail took steps to improve the Adamses' long-term financial security. In the spring one of their neighbors died and his farm came up for sale. Knowing that John had long been interested in the property, she immediately began negotiating for the purchase without waiting for his advice. During the next several years she continued to acquire land when it became available, ating with the advice and assistance of Cotton Tufts but relying mostly on her own judgment.

Abigail tried to keep up with developments in Congress and on the battlefields, but newspapers were scarce and the mails, as usual, were slow and unreliable. James Lovell did his part by sending her the journals of Congress, which she read and then sent on to John. Lovell's letters remained short on news and long on flattery, however. It hardly seemed possible, but his letters were even more outrageous than they had been during John's last absence. She did little to discourage him but asked him to continue writing and even occasionally engaged in a bit of flirting herself. "You will greatly oblige me by a continuation of your favours to your—I will not Scruple to say—*affectionate* Portia," she wrote after a stretch when his letters had been confined mostly to business. Lovell instantly obliged with another of his flowery communications. The truth of the matter was, as Abigail told Lovell, that his letters "amuse me in my retirement."

Because of Lovell's flirtatiousness, Abigail turned to Elbridge Gerry, the second Massachusetts representative to Congress, when she had serious business to discuss. Increasingly her business involved defending John's reputation. When a Philadelphia newspaper published an article identifying John as a "late member of Congress" and John Jay as Minister to Spain, she indignantly inquired of Gerry why Jay's current title had been included in the article and John's hadn't. Was John's commission not just as important as Jay's? And had he not been a Minister before Jay? She went on in a manner that showed she had picked up much of John's paranoia about people out to destroy his reputation.

Gerry, who recognized that the newspaper's failure to include John's current title was probably an unintended journalistic lapse and that demanding a correction would only turn a trifle into an issue, nevertheless took Abigail's letter seriously and tactfully suggested that the matter would be best left alone. And he continued to write to her, courteously and in detail, when she had bones to pick about the way John was being treated.

Defending John against slights, real and imagined, became a

growing preoccupation with Abigail during his time in France. It was one of the many ways that her view of her role in life began to change, probably without her quite realizing it. For many years her main tasks had been raising the children and managing the farm. As the children grew up, however, at the same time as John's political career advanced, she turned her attention more to him. The children still absorbed much of her energy, but she was never one to cling to them after it was time for them to be on their own, as her willingness to part with John Quincy and Charley showed. More and more, she concentrated on managing the family finances and shielding John from mundane cares and, as much as she could, from the criticism of his political foes.

Throughout 1780 and the early part of 1781 the war was not going well for Americans. Peace seemed distant. As long as the war continued, John would remain in Europe waiting to negotiate peace, and so there seemed to be no end in sight to Abigail and John's separation.

It had been a long time since New England saw any serious fighting. The British had evacuated Newport in late 1779, leaving the region free of enemy troops. They continued to raid other seaports occasionally, including New Bedford, New London, and New Haven, but for most New Englanders the periodic quotas of troops to be recruited and the ever increasing taxes were the only reminders that they were still at war.

By the beginning of 1780 the scene of heavy fighting had shifted to the deep South. Georgia was already firmly under British control, the only colony to be returned to the rule of a royal governor during the war. A French fleet under the Comte d'Estaing, the same officer who had entertained Abigail in 1778, laid siege to Savannah but failed to wrest the city from the British. French military assistance, in fact, had so far done little or nothing to improve the Americans' position. Estaing's departure from Southern waters encouraged the British fleet to mount an attack on Charleston, which was defended by an army under the direction of a Massachusetts general, Benjamin Lincoln. On May 12, 1780, after a siege of several days, Lincoln surrendered with five thousand men, three hundred cannon, and the rest of his arms—one of the worst American losses of the war.

It was summer before the devastating news reached New England. Abigail called the defeat "disagreeable" and "alarming" but took a philosophical view of the situation. Just as victories were God's rewards to a virtuous people, so defeats were His means of shaking the country out of its complacency and spurring it on to greater efforts. The victories and defeats always seemed to be mixed in such a way that no one could ever despair completely, nor could they ever feel completely confident of ultimate victory.

Despite the recent military defeats, Abigail was much encouraged by continued signs of women's efforts to do their part for the cause. Pennsylvania women's donations of their jewelry to raise money and of their time to make shirts for American soldiers drew her praise. Women, at least, "are not dismayed by defeats or misfortunes." She couldn't resist a bit of moralizing to John Thaxter on the importance of feminine patriotism and virtue: "America will not wear chains while her daughters are virtuous, but corrupt their morals by a general depravity, and believe me sir a state or nation is undone. Was not Adam safe whilst Eve was Innocent?"

In midsummer the French fleet established a garrison at Newport. The presence of a friendly force of six thousand helped boost morale in New England, but as far as Abigail was concerned the display of force came too late. She could never quite get over the Americans' failure to resist British invasion of Newport back in 1776 or the French failure to recapture that city in the summer of 1778. Even the defeat at Charleston didn't rankle as much as the memory of the capture of Newport.

The rest of the summer dragged on with little activity of interest, either political or military. American militia in North and South Carolina carried on a campaign of harassment—a kind of guerrilla warfare—against British troops based in Charleston. Their actions cast doubt on the British ability to carry out the plan of subjugating the entire South, but it was not the sort of dramatic fighting that reached the newspapers of New England.

The news that did reach New England in early fall was all bad. American forces under Horatio Gates, the hero of Saratoga, suffered another disastrous defeat in South Carolina in August. This defeat was almost forgotten, however, in the wake of even worse news: Benedict Arnold, a respected American officer, was a traitor. The commander of a garrison at West Point, New York, he had been corresponding for months with General Clinton, commander of British forces, and had agreed to turn over West Point to the British. The plot was discovered in September, shortly before Arnold's plan was to go into effect, when one of Clinton's aides, Major John André, was captured while carrying messages from Arnold. André was executed as a spy, but Arnold escaped to British lines, where he took command of a British force dispatched to Virginia.

Arnold's treason came as a devastating blow to Americans, including Abigail, not because of any real harm done—he was caught in time—but because it was so hard for them to comprehend that a supposedly loyal American could be guilty of such an act. That he was a man in a position of power and trust made it even worse. It severely shook the faith of a people accustomed to think of themselves as unusually principled and virtuous.

Abigail attributed Arnold's treason to a lack of religious principles. "How ineffectual is the tye of Honour to bind the Humane Mind, unless accompanied by more permanent and Efficacious principals?" she wrote in describing the incident to John. "Will he who laughs at a future state of Retribution, and holds himself accountable only to his fellow Mortals disdain the venal Bribe, or spurn the Ignoble hand that proffers it?" This was not mere rationalization on Abigail's part, for she believed absolutely that religious principles and moral behavior were inseparable. She also believed that there were too many Americans like Arnold, although perhaps not quite so depraved as he, and that their behavior was responsible for American failures in the war. "Unprincipled wretches," as she called them, sapped the virtue of the American people, drew the wrath of God, and stood in the way of victory.

She continually alternated between praising American virtues and condemning American vices, which always seemed to her to be increasing. But however pessimistic she became at times, Abigail never gave up the idea that God was on the American side. If Americans were too often falling victim to evil ways, they were still more virtuous than their enemies. "I trust we shall not be delivered over to the vengeance of a Nation more wicked and perverse than our own," she wrote John. She was aware that her belief in divine Providence was becoming a bit old-fashioned in the Age of Reason, but she still contended that "however this Belief of a particular Providence may be exploded by the Modern Wits, . . . yet the virtuous Mind will look up and acknowledge the great first cause, without whose notice not even a sparrow falls to the ground."

The disasters of 1780 were followed by a series of small but important successes in early 1781. Nathanael Greene, another New England general took command of American forces in North Carolina at the end of 1780 and with several other American officers undertook a guerrilla campaign of sporadic attacks and retreats against forces commanded by General Charles Cornwallis. Greene never really won a major battle, but his strategy thwarted Cornwallis's plan of capturing North Carolina. For the first several months of 1781 these two generals played cat and mouse. "The Fate of the Southern States is balanceing between Greene and Cornwallis," Abigail remarked. By March, as she told John, American forces had made substantial progress in recapturing South Carolina, and Cornwallis had moved the bulk of his troops to the North Carolina coast. From there he marched to Virginia. It was a fatal mistake, for he left conquered territory in South Carolina without adequate military support and chose to concentrate the bulk of his army at Yorktown, Virginia, a peninsula in Chesapeake Bay.

No one could predict, when Cornwallis marched into Virginia in May, that his actions would bring the end of the war. But during August Washington and the French general Rochambeau marched south to Virginia with seven thousand men while two French fleets—one from the West Indies, the other from Newport—moved into Chesapeake Bay, trapping Cornwallis. After a seige of several weeks, on October 19 Cornwallis surrendered with all his troops. It was the largest single British loss of the war.

After Yorktown, the fighting stopped. Even though the British still controlled New York and parts of the South, the loss of several thousand soldiers, the impossibility of subjugating the South after months of fighting, and the British government's increasing unwillingness to pursue the war indefinitely spelled the end to six years of war.

The victory at Yorktown was welcome news for Abigail and John, but it was overshadowed by their understanding that a peace treaty—and a permanent end to the war—were still far in the future. Abigail reported Cornwallis's surrender to John with little enthusiasm. John was not convinced that even so decisive a victory would force the British to the peace table, especially as long as they held New York.

They were correct in their misgivings. Although John was mistaken when he said that the British would never negotiate until the last redcoat had left American soil, nearly a year and a half passed after the fighting stopped before the definitive peace treaty was signed in January 1783. Those months were a time of deepening depression for both Abigail and John. Their separation stretched out interminably, and they both felt themselves growing older without the comfort of each other.

Throughout most of 1781 Abigail heard not a word from John and her two sons. News of a ship docking at Boston in January raised her hopes, but she was bitterly disappointed to learn that the captain had been chased by a man-of-war and had thrown all his letters overboard to prevent the interception of any important messages. It was the end of September before she finally received a letter from John, the first in ten months.

John was having a difficult time of it in Europe, with the usual result that he neglected to write to Abigail. He and the French Foreign Minister, the Comte de Vergennes, did not get along at all, partly because John was suspicious of French motives in helping the United States and partly because the two men simply did not like each other. John feared, quite correctly, that the French government wished to control the emerging new nation for its own ends.

Vergennes knew about John's suspicions and was dismayed that he alone had been appointed by the United States to deal with the British. He did everything in his power to delay any negotiations between John and British envoys while working to get Congress to recall him and replace him with someone more pliant. In this effort he enjoyed the full cooperation of Benjamin Franklin, who didn't like John any more than Vergennes did. Franklin disagreed with John about the United States' relationship with France. He thought the Americans should follow French advice in all their negotiations. When Vergennes wrote a detailed letter to Franklin complaining about John and announcing that he would have nothing more to do with him, Franklin sent a copy of the letter to Congress.

The hostility of Vergennes and Franklin made Paris unbearable for John, and in July 1780 he decided to leave. With John Quincy, Charley, and Thaxter, he set off for Holland, where he hoped to win Dutch recognition of American independence and negotiate loans from Amsterdam banks. Political recognition and financial assistance from Holland, he believed, would reduce American dependence on France and would be a further signal to Britain that the United States would not give up its independence.

While he stayed in Amsterdam, the boys studied at the University of Leyden. When Abigail learned that her sons were in Holland, the birthplace of such learned men as Erasmus and Grotius, she told them to send their impressions of the country. "You must not be a superficial observer," she told John Quincy, "but study Men and Manners that you may be Skilfull in both. . . . Youth is the proper season for observation and attention—a mind unincumberd with cares may seek instruction and draw improvement from all the objects which surround it." Despite her urging, however, neither of her sons found time to write her often.

Most of what Abigail learned about John came from the newspapers and her correspondents in Congress, and she didn't like what she heard. In June 1781, as a result of Vergennes's and Franklin's efforts, Congress appointed four additional Ministers to join John in treating for peace—Franklin, John Jay, Thomas Jefferson, and Henry Laurens—and revoked his commission to negotiate a treaty of commerce.

She first became suspicious that something was afoot from some rather vague comments in a letter from Lovell. Finally she learned the truth in an unfortunate way, when a letter from Alice Lee Shippen of Philadelphia to Sam Adams's wife came to her by mistake. She read the letter, whether by mistake (as she claimed) or out of curiosity. Among other things it stated quite clearly that Franklin was "blackening" John's character. The letter confirmed Abigail's fears and convinced her that Lovell had been something less than candid with her. She immediately dispatched a letter to him. "You will send me by the first opportunity the whole of this dark prosess," she demanded. He replied promptly with a sketchy but straightforward account of what had happened and promised to send more details in code to Sam Adams, who would transmit them to her.

This news produced in Abigail exactly the same reaction that it produced in John. There were sinister forces in Europe out to tarnish John's reputation in order to serve their own private interests; virtue and unflagging public service were never appreciated; good men could never expect anything but abuse. She set about defending John to Lovell, to Elbridge Gerry, and even to Mrs. Shippen.

Abigail engaged in her private campaign of support for John for one reason: "when he is wounded I bleed. I give up my domestick pleasure and resign the prospect I once had of an independent fortune, . . . Nor should I grudge the sacrifice, only let not the slanderous arrow, the calumniating stabs of Malice rend in peices an honest character which is all his Ambition." She knew, from long experience with publc life and John's sensitive temperament, just how angry and disappointed he would be when the news reached Europe. "I am pained when I reflect upon the anxiety it will give him," she wrote Gerry. He would refuse to continue serving in a position he found dishonorable, she thought; he would resign his position and come home; the country would lose a devoted, honest public servant, which it could ill afford at this critical time.

She was right about John's reaction to the news; she was right that he spent many anxious hours debating whether he should immediately resign and go home. But she was wrong if she thought he would return within six months, as she told Lovell. No doubt Abigail knew deep in her heart that John would not quit and come home as he had threatened to do so many times before when he thought his integrity was called into question. Somehow public duty always won out despite assaults on his honor, real or imagined.

While Congress deliberated about changes in the peace commission, John traveled back to France. Shortly after he left for Paris in early July, John Quincy, now age fourteen, left for Russia with Francis Dana. Dana had been appointed Minister to the court of Catherine the Great, but Congress neglected to authorize a secretary for him. He asked that John Quincy be allowed to accompany him as secretary and translator, since he was by now fluent in French, the official language of the Russian court, and Dana was not.

Russia in 1781 seemed like the end of the world. It was the frontier of civilization as Americans and Europeans viewed it then. Its government was even more dictatorial than the most autocratic of West European countries; much of its population still lived in serfdom centuries after feudalism had dissolved in Western Europe; its religion was different. Little was known about the country. It was difficult to reach—John Quincy and Francis Dana spent two months traveling to Saint Petersburg over routes at times even more difficult than the road through northern Spain.

Traveling to Saint Petersburg was a monumental undertaking for anyone, let alone a fourteen-year-old in the company of a young, inexperienced would-be diplomat who spoke no language but English. But John let him go, moved by the same reasoning that had caused him to bring his son to Europe in the first place: It would be good experience for a future statesman. He justified the decision to Abigail by saying, "He will be satiated with travel in his Childhood, and care nothing about it, I hope in his riper Years." He was wrong, of course; John Quincy built a political career as a diplomat and spent many years in European capitals. He even returned to Russia, as American Ambassador, almost thirty years later.

For Charles, who was homesick and in poor health, Johnny's departure made life unbearable. He was still a child, for all his travels and his standing as a university student, and he missed his mother. Finally he asked to go home. John agreed and sent him on board the *South Carolina* in the care of two American friends. It should have been a simple four- to six-week trip across the Atlantic. Summer was the safest and most pleasant time to sail, and Charles should have been reunited with Abigail, Nabby, and Tommy almost before they had word that he was coming home. Unfortunately, it didn't work out that way, and Charles's journey rivaled his brother's for length and adventure.

The *South Carolina* left Holland surreptitiously in August with a load of military supplies for the budding American navy. The captain proved to be incompetent and quarrelsome; after wandering around the North Sea and making a complete circuit of the British Isles, the ship no longer had enough water or provisions to make it across the Atlantic. Toward the end of September, therefore, it put into the Spanish port of La Corunna, near Ferrol, where the Adamses had made their premature landing almost two years before. Charles and one of his guardians left the ship to seek passage elsewhere.

They spent weeks in La Corunna waiting for another ship. Finally they took passage on the *Cicero*, a privateer registered in Beverly, Massachusetts. But again there were complications. A dead calm stalled the ship for three weeks. Then the crew spotted what they supposed to be British warships just off the coast near Bilboa. The *Cicero*, as a privateer, was equipped with guns and authorized to capture enemy ships; so the crew opened fire, only to discover later that they had attacked friendly Spanish ships. Each side had mistaken the other for British vessls. There were no casualties, and the misunderstanding was patched up amicably, but the net result was still more delay. The *Cicero* finally left the coast of Spain in the second week in December and sailed into Beverly harbor on January 21, 1782—more than five months after Charles had left Amsterdam.

It was September before Abigail learned about her sons' travels, and then she heard not from them or from John, but indirectly through other friends in the United States. At that point it had been ten months since she had received letters from John and the boys. Her loneliness at times was overwhelming. She reread old letters to comfort herself when no fresh ones arrived; sometimes she dreamed that they had returned, only to awake in anguish to her solitude. "O that I could realize the agreable reverie of the last Night when my dear Friend presented himself and two Son[s] safely returned to the Arms of the affectionate wife and Mother," she wrote John. "Should I name my dear Boys a tear will flow with the Ink—not a line have I received from them for more than a Year."

She approved of John Quincy's travels to Russia, even though she knew it would mean hearing from him even less frequently. As for Charles, her pleasure at the thought of his return was tempered by her concern about his traveling alone. Undoubtedly John had entrusted him to reliable friends, but still, she told him, she would have been happier if he had consulted her first. From September, when she first heard that Charles had left Europe, until his arrival in January, his safety was always a nagging concern in her mind. Her worries were needlessly intensified by the fact that she continued to assume that he was on board the *South Carolina*, which was working its way to New England by a very tortuous route via the West Indies. In December there were rumors that the ship had been lost at sea. When she eventually received word that Charles had gotten off the *South Carolina* in La Corunna, she still didn't know if and when he had sailed for the United States.

By the end of 1781 she had gone more than a year with nothing but a few short letters from John. Even John Thaxter, always her faithful correspondent, had sent nothing by the last four ships to Boston. Of John Quincy, she knew only that he was somewhere between Amsterdam and Saint Petersburg. And Charles might be in Spain or on some unknown ship somewhere in the middle of the Atlantic. Another winter was approaching with no prospect of a family reunion. Even Cornwallis's surrender did not seem to bring the country any closer to peace. "Alass my dear," she wrote John, "I am much afflicted with a disorder call'd the *Heartach*, nor can any remedy be found in America, it must be collected from Holland, Petersburg, and Bilboa."

Charles's arrival in January cheered Abigail considerably. She found her young adventurer in good health, undaunted by his journey, and most important, uncorrupted by "the facinating allurements of vice, decked in Foreign garbs," which might have tempted him during his stay in Europe. He was, moreover, still "perfectly attached to the modest republican Stile of Life, as tho he had never experienced any other."

Her joy in Charles's return was clouded, however, by news reaching her in the next few weeks that John was seriously ill. When he returned to Amsterdam in August 1781 after his brief trip to Paris, he fell ill with a debilitating fever that made him delirious for hours at a time and totally incapacitated him for more than a month. By the time Abigail heard about it the following February, he was completely recovered; but that was no help to her, as she was given to worrying about John's health anyway and was convinced that overwork, separation from his family, and the damp Dutch climate would prove his undoing.

His illness jolted her into realizing that John might die in Europe, that she might never see him again. The realization prompted her to reaffirm her still-strong love for him. "The age of romance has long ago past," she wrote, "but the affection of almost Infant years has matured and strengthened untill it has become a vital principle, nor has the world any thing to bestow which could in the smallest degree compensate for the loss." It was women's lot, she thought, to feel such affections more strongly, "to experience more exquisite Sensations than is the Lot of your Sex. . . . I never wonderd at the philosopher who thanked the Gods that he was created a Man rather than a Woman."

The years of separation, the worry about John's health and reputation, the concern about her children—all took their toll on Abigail, and by the winter of 1781–1782 she suffered "from a dejection of spirits which I cannot overcome." The news of the revocation of John's commission, distressing as it was, at least let her hope that he would resign in disgust and come home. By March, when she heard nothing about a resignation and had received only reports of John's suffering health, she became impatient about the sacrifices they had made and felt unwilling to endure more.

For years they had given up their personal happiness and their personal fortune to the service of the country. Now the war appeared to be over; John's honor was being questioned in Congress; and she saw people around her living in high style, making profits from the hardships of war while she suffered. She was tired of it all, and she wanted John home and out of politics. "I have been in daily expectation for months past, that Letters would arrive from you requesting leave to resign . . . and return again to your Native Land," she informed him, "assured at least of finding one Friend in the Bosom of *Portia*, who is sick, sick of a world in which selfishness predominates."

In the spring she began negotiating to buy land in Vermont, partly as a desperate effort to remove herself from the world around her that she found so depressing. She talked about her purchase as an investment, as something they could pass on to their children, but she also harbored a fantasy that she and John could retire to a secluded farm far from the scenes of politics. She must have known that John would never move to Vermont, even if he could be persuaded to give up politics. Abigail herself would have been reluctant to move so far away from her childhood home and family. But at a time when her loneliness seemed beyond endurance, Vermont became a dream, a hope, for a future free from war and politics.

She had first contemplated buying land in Vermont a year earlier, in the spring of 1781, when the area was first opened to public purchase. The high cost of land in eastern Massachusetts and the enormous increase in taxes encouraged many people to sell their land and move to the frontier. She started putting a little money aside to buy Vermont land, and by March 1782 she began to make serious arrangements, although the sale did not actually go through until July. The maximum purchase for any individual was 300 acres, so Abigail bought 300 in the name of each of their children in a township where several of her friends were also buying land. She became so determined to have this land that, when an unexpected expense came up—payment for Charles's passage home—she asked John to pay it so she wouldn't have to dip into her Vermont money.

John did not approve of Abigail's latest project. "Don't meddle any more with Vermont," was his cryptic response to her enthusiasm. To his friend James Warren he confided the reason for his opposition: "God willing, I wont go to Vermont. I must be within the Scent of the sea."

About a year later Abigail contemplated buying a farm closer to home, one she knew John would like to own. She hesitated, however, because the purchase would involve going into debt, and the future seemed too uncertain for her to do that with confidence. She told John she would buy the farm only if he would promise to come home and work it himself instead of running off to foreign courts, "leaving me half my Life to mourn in widowhood."

For years Abigail had sustained herself by thinking that it was her patriotic duty, a woman's particular contribution to the war, to part with her husband and struggle alone. The longer the war lasted, however, the more she saw people around her placing their own interests ahead of the common good. Merchants profited from the sale of scarce goods; anyone with money could lend it as exorbitant interest rates. Soldiers had to be bribed to join the army. Hoarding was rampant as inflation worsened. She struggled daily to make ends meet. Both she and John knew that he could make much more money as a lawyer than as a public servant. In 1774 and 1775, as a young, financially insecure family inspired by zeal for American rights, it was not so difficult to give up the promise of future fortune to make a revolution. In 1782, approaching middle age with children preparing for college, a time when most people of their class could expect to live comfortably, the Adams family was if anything in worse financial straits than it had been six years earlier. And although Abigail preached frugality, her definition of frugality did not extend to giving up the middle-class comforts to which she had long been accustomed. With the war winding down, with people all around her apparently throwing patriotism to the winds, it became more and more difficult to endure financial hardships and long separations.

It was particularly galling when she saw people who had been below her in social status or family connections make money and put on airs. "The whole of your Sallery would be inadequate to the expence in which some live now, in furniture, equipage, cloathing and feasting, who were not worth ten Spanish milld Dollors when the war commenced," she commented bitterly to John. She began to wonder whether John's career in public service, no matter how important to the country, was worth the financial sacrifice, particularly when the public seemed not to appreciate his efforts. "You are loosing all opportunities for helping yourself, for those who are daily becomeing more and more unworthy of your Labours and who will neither care for you or your family when their own turn is served—so selfish are mankind," she complained. "I know this is a language you are unwilling to hear. I wish it was not a truth which I daily experience."

She complained that "The Manners of our Country are so intirely changed from what they were in those days of simplicity when you knew it, that it has nothing of a Republick but the Name." But what really upset her was not so much the decline in manners as the fact that upstarts were getting rich, and money rather than breeding seemed to be the key to social status. Only people rich enough to maintain a "publick table & Equipage" received any attention. Worst of all, young men who were mere clerks when John was a successful lawyer were now earning money hand over fist and displaying their new wealth with carriages and country houses. Abigail, still living in the tiny house where she and John had lived when they were first married, thought they deserved something better for their years of sacrifice and public service.

Chapter 9

Years of Decision

By the fall of 1782 Abigail's depression over her prolonged separation from John became acute. They had been apart three years, twice as long as John's previous trip to Europe, with no end in sight. Peace still seemed remote. Every occasion reminded Abigail of the sadness of their years apart, and she became increasingly impatient at the continuation of their separation. The next year and a half, a time of deepening depression, would be the worst months of her life.

On their eighteenth wedding anniversary Abigail sat down late at night to write to John and let herself give in to her emotions. Her love for him, undiminished by years, helped comfort her lonely hours, but she could not help thinking about the precious time together that was lost forever. More and more over the next months she brooded about their lost youth. She had been thirty when John first went to Congress. Now she was nearing forty; John was approaching fifty; the children were growing up; and still there was no prospect of their being together again. Justifiably, Abigail felt that the best years of their lives had been lost in miserable separation.

Sometimes she wished that John had never become prominent and they they could go back to living the way they had in the early years of their marriage. "I recollect the untitled Man to whom I gave my Heart, and in the agony of recollection when time and distance present themselves together—wish he had never been any other," she lamented. "Who shall give me back Time? who shall compensate to me those *years* I cannot recall?

How dearly have I paid for a titled Husband; should I wish you less wise that I might enjoy more happiness!"

As if it were not enough to be miserable and lonely, some local gossips began speculating about John's attachment to Abigail, wondering a bit too publicly about how a man who really loved his wife could stay away from her so long. Such comments cut her all the more deeply because the combination of John's long absences and the infrequency of his letters sometimes produced nagging doubts of her own. In her rational moments she knew he loved her just as passionately as she loved him, but it was hard to stay rational in the face of years apart.

John too was tiring of their separation, tiring of public life, and feeling pessimistic about whether peace would ever be accomplished. Even Dutch recognition of American independence in April 1782, with prospects of financial aid for the United States, did little to cheer him. His diplomatic efforts in Holland, undertaken against the better judgment of Franklin and Congress, had been a stunning success and proved the correctness of his judgment. But he believed that his work in Holland would never get the recognition it deserved.

John's thoughts during these months paralleled Abigail's to a remarkable degree. He joked, as she frequently did, about their spirits flying back and forth across the ocean: "What a fine Affair it would be if We could flit across the Atlantic as they say the Angels do from Planet to Planet. I would dart to Pens hill and bring you over on my Wings." He too brooded over his advancing age and the time together that was lost forever. Like Abigail, he remembered the third anniversary of his leaving home with a cryptic note in his diary: "Oh when shall I return?"

Homesickness made John and Abigail both think, independently of each other, about her joining him in Europe. John at first suggested it half-jokingly, but in May he he declared, "I must go to you or you must come to me. I cannot live, in this horrid Solitude, which it is to me, amidst Courts, Camps and Crowds." As always, John was caught in a dilemma created partly by circumstances and partly by himself. It was true that as long as peace negotiations were up in the air it was uncertain how long he would have to remain in Europe. But it was equally true that he could resign at any time and go home, particularly since he was now only one of five peace Commissioners. He did not really want to resign, however, despite his professed wishes to fly to the foot of Penn's Hill, nor did he wish to stay in Europe two or three years longer—and the peace negotiations could easily last that long. The obvious solution was to send for Abigail, but, as he put it, "this is opening a scaene of Risque and Trouble for you that I shudder at."

In Braintree, it was Nabby who first broached the subject of going to Europe, by herself, to keep house for her father. "Could you make a Bridge she would certainly present herself to you," Abigail reported, "nor would she make an ungraceful appearance at the Head of your table." Perhaps she, like the boys, could benefit from a stay in Europe. Abigail worried that Nabby was too quiet, almost unsociable, although she admitted to John that "She would please you the better" for her reserve. John, touched by his daughter's devotion, nevertheless rejected the idea as too dangerous.

About the same time, in July, Abigail thought seriously of making the trip to Europe herself. Her thoughts went to the extent of considering arrangements for caring for the two boys and the farm in her absence. She mentioned her plans to John hesitantly, however, "fearing a rejection of my proposal and it is of so tender a Nature I could scarcely bear a refusal." By October Abigail was ready to put aside her fear of rejection. She made up her mind that she definitely wanted to go to Europe if John intended to stay much longer. For her, unlike John, there was no equivocating. She feared the ocean crossing and would prefer that he come home, but she could not stand any more separation. To try to win his assent, she presented her plan as a matter of wifely duty, a way to help care for John and make his life easier. "I Hardly think of Enemies of terrors & Storms," she wrote, "But I resolve with myself—to do as you wish—if I can add to your Happiness—is it not my duty— if I can soften your Cares—is it not my duty? —if I can by a tender attention and assiduity prolong your most valuable Life—is it not my duty?"

But she would not go without a clear request from John, and he could not bring himself to make such a request. The closest he came was in November, when the British government finally authorized a representative to treat for peace with the Americans. John was convinced that his hands would be tied in dealing with Franklin and Vergennes and that he would therefore be compelled to resign. But he told Abigail to make inquiries about whether Congress planned to extend his commission in Europe for at least another year. If the answer was yes, she and Nabby should begin preparations for a trip to Europe the next spring.

Barely a month later he changed his mind. The unpleasantness of an ocean crossing for Abigail and Nabby, his own uncertain position in Europe, and his homesickness made John decide to resign and go home. Two weeks later, in mid-December, the preliminary articles of peace between Britain and the United States were signed, strengthening John's resolve to leave. John Quincy was on his way back from Russia, and the two would come home together in the spring or early summer. John would be a "good domestic husband" for the rest of his life, he assured Abigail.

John had talked of resigning, going home, and getting out of politics many times before. Abigail was no doubt skeptical of his promises of future domesticity. She never fooled herself about John's devotion to politics, no matter what he might say. But she did think that he had been in Europe long enough, and she much preferred his coming home to her going to Europe. When she received his letters promising resignation, she gave up all thought of going to join him. John's resignation proved as illusory as his past ones, however, and by January he was equivocating about whether he would stay or go.

Two substantial difficulties stood in the way of resigning, in John's mind. First, although the preliminary peace treaty had been signed, it was not at all clear that the negotiations were over. The treaty had to be approved by both Parliament and Congress, and there was some question as to whether Parliament would approve it. Second, and more important to John, was the lingering question of his original commission to negotiate a treaty of commerce with Britain as well as a peace treaty. That commission had been revoked when the peace commission was expanded. John had said little at the time about the loss of his commission, but the more he thought about it now the more it rankled. Increasingly during the early months of 1783 his lost commission became an obsession. His honor, Congress's honor, and the country's good all demanded that his commission be restored to him.

The first inkling that John might not resign after all came at the end of January, when he wrote Abigail that there was a slight possibility that Congress would accept his resignation but then renew his commission to negotiate a commercial treaty. He hoped that would not happen, he said, because he wanted to come home, but if it did happen then she should join him in Europe. Refusing a new commission was not a possibility John considered.

Two weeks later he reversed himself, telling Abigail that he planned to resign regardless of what Congress did and that she should not plan to come to Europe. In emotional turmoil over his resignation, his commission, and his political future, he wrote weekly, sometimes daily, to Abigail. His letters were filled with conflict. Sometimes he said she should come; sometimes he said she shouldn't. Always he brooded over the question of his honor. Officially, he asserted that he did not really want to stay in Europe, that life there was onerous; he tried to convince Abigail, who was quite prepared to believe him, that she would hate Europe. But a question of honor was involved, he said, as well as the good of the country. Congress should live up to its commitments and he should serve his country regardless of personal hardship. The United States needed a commercial treaty with Britain. He was the person best qualified to negotiate it.

John was concerned about what he would do next, notwithstanding his professed desire to return to the quiet life and scenic beauty of his farm. The war was over, a provisional government had been formed, and the most exciting and challenging chapter of American history was about to begin. John did not want to retire now; he wanted to help shape the future of his country. And the job he wanted was more than a commission to negotiate a treaty of commerce with Britain—he wanted to be the first American Ambassador to the British court. It was just the sort of post that appealed to John's Puritan sense of duty. It would be one of the most important positions in the new republic, and also one of the least recognized. The first Minister to the late mother country could expect to be ignored at best and reviled at worst. No one could possibly accuse a man of coveting such a thankless job. And yet for John Adams, the old radical, the man once considered a dangerous traitor by the British government, there would be a certain wry pleasure in appearing at the Court of St. James's as the official ambassador from an independent nation.

It is unlikely that John admitted, even to himself, how much he wanted an appointment as Ambassador to Britain. He certainly didn't admit it to Abigail. Instead he continued to write her about his frustration over the time wasted waiting for approval of the preliminary treaty, about the gossip in Paris regarding who would be appointed Ambassador, and about his desire to come home. But as winter turned into spring, it became increasingly clear that John had no intention of going home until the definitive treaty was completed and the question of his political future decided.

April dragged into May, the summer months arrived, and still there was neither progress on the treaty nor instructions from Congress. John's plans to go home in the spring were postponed until fall and finally until the following spring. It was approaching four years since he had left home. "I wonder whether any body but you would believe me Sincere if I were to say how much I love you, and wish to be with you never to be Seperated more?" he wrote Abigail in July. But he still did not send for her nor set a firm deadline for departing from Europe.

Abigail, not surprisingly, was rather confused about whether or not to prepare for a trip to Europe. Her inclinations ran against going, so when John wrote several times during the winter and early spring about coming home, she dropped her travel plans and set her heart on seeing him in the summer. Her hopes were soon dashed, however, because June brought news that Congress had renewed John's commission to negotiate a commercial treaty with Britain—long before the news reached John—and the first of John's letters discussing the possibility of his becoming Ambassador to England. Aware that the commission would probably detain him in Europe, she did not try to talk him out of staying. But the thought of his becoming Ambassador to Britain was another story. She did not want him to accept the position if offered, because she did not relish the thought of becoming an Ambassador's wife. "I beg you not to accept it," she said of the prospect; "Call me not to any further trials of the kind!" She wanted nothing more than a quiet life at home with her family. Living in a European capital, playing hostess to statesmen and courtiers, did not appeal to her.

She decided that she had sacrificed long enough. Abigail had the same exalted sense of public duty as John, but unlike his, her sense of duty had limits. Over the past several months she had gradually come to believe that she and John had done their share and deserved to look after their own interests for a change. John did not have to give up his career as a public servant. She knew, despite his protestations to the contrary, that he would not give up politics. But a career in politics did not have to mean a difficult, unrewarding job far from home.

Although Abigail was prepared to go to Europe if necessary to end her prolonged separation from John, she would much prefer their reunion to take place on her side of the Atlantic. John's indecision over whether to remain in Europe or go home left her in a state of sustained anxiety; first he led her to believe that he would soon be home, then dashed her hopes with his next letter.

Now that the children were growing into adults, it would be easier for her to make the trip to Europe. And yet, ironically, the very fact that they were no longer children intensified her desire for a reunion in Braintree. She had been deprived of the pleasure of raising her children in company with her husband. Now, acutely aware of her advancing age and their growing maturity, she hoped that they might enjoy a normal family life, however briefly.

When John first went to Congress, Nabby was nine and Tommy only two. Now Nabby was eighteen and receiving suitors, Charley and Tommy were preparing for college, and John Quincy—"my wanderer," Abigail called him—was seeing the world and hobnobbing with foreign kings and diplomats.

Nabby's growing up affected Abigail more than her other children's. She was especially close to her only daughter and through her was reminded of her own adolescence and first love. Nabby was actually very different from her mother, however. They did not look at all alike. She had blond hair; Abigail's was dark brown. Nabby was taller and thinner than her mother, who was inclined to plumpness. Her personality was different, too. She was shy and reserved, in contrast to her mother's volubility. She was not so intellectual and much less interested in politics. Abigail worried that her daughter was too quiet, that her reserve might be taken for haughtiness. She also believed Nabby to be less emotional than herself, a thought which inspired mixed feelings. Abigail had suffered from her great "sensibility," as she called it, but at times it also contributed to her happiness. She approved of her daughter's reserve and seriousness but also wanted her to experience the joy and excitement of an intense, romantic love. A "tender passion," she told John, would make Nabby less reserved and more attractive.

John disagreed and told Abigail to stop criticizing Nabby for her quiet manners. They were her most attractive quality, he said. If she spoke little in company, so much the better, "and I would have this observed as a Rule by the Mother as well as the Daughter." Sometimes, John thought, Abigail stepped too far outside the bounds of acceptable female behavior. Nabby was more conventional, but he counseled Abigail not to try to change her.

Nabby in fact was endowed with more "sensibility" than her mother knew. She missed her father almost as desperately as Abigail did but tried not to show it, because she didn't want to make her mother even more unhappy than she already was.

Just when Nabby felt most depressed, a new young man arrived in town. Eventually he provided the "tender passion" that Abigail wanted for her daughter. Royall Tyler, an attractive young lawyer from a well-to-do Boston family, came to Braintree to establish a practice in the spring of 1782. Because he boarded with the Cranches, Abigail and Nabby quickly became acquainted with him. He brought with him a reputation for being a something of a dandy. Rumor (reasonably well substantiated) had it that he had squandered a fortune left him by his father and had paid more attention to Boston ladies than to his law books.

Abigail forbade Nabby to have anything to do with Tyler. But, with frequent calls at the Adams home, he soon won Abigail over completely. From forbidding Nabby to have anything to do with him, she reached the point of actively encouraging their romance.

Nabby was less interested in Tyler than her mother was. Worse still, she began to wonder whether she was even capable of loving a man. "Your Amelia is the same cold indifferent Girl she ever was," she confided to Betsey Cranch. ". . . I long to be in Love." By spring, however, the combination of Tyler's persistance, Nabby's own craving for love, and Abigail's urging produced a full-blown romance.

Abigail later had cause to regret that she had encouraged Nabby's romance. She was torn by conflicting feelings about Tyler. On the one hand, she found him attractive, witty, and an interesting conversationalist. His presence brightened otherwise dull evenings. But she was bothered by the stories about his background. His reputation as a dandy and a spendthrift—so contrary to Abigail's values—disturbed and interested her at the same time. She wrote a series of letters to John in December and January in which she managed to portray Tyler's character in the worst possible light while trying to convince him that the young man had reformed. He had "dissipated" two or three years of his life and much of his money, but now he was building a successful practice in Braintree, she told John. He regretted his past and was working hard to rebuild the fortune he had lost.

It was the kind of description bound to arouse John's strongest negative reaction. It almost seemed that Abigail, loath to try to break up her daughter's romance and herself captivated by the young man, wanted John to intervene and declare him an unsuitable match for Nabby. She confessed to him that she did not know quite how to handle the situation. Viewing the situation rationally, she knew that it was a bad match and that John would disapprove. But she was reluctant to try to break off the romance completely. "I feel too powerfull a pleader within my own heart & too well recollect the Love I bore to the object of my early affections to forbid him to hope," she explained. Lonely, unhappy, starved for affection from her long-absent husband, she was captivated by Tyler and began to relive, through the young couple, her own youthful romance. The young Tyler reminded her all too much of the young John Adams—and she never forgot what it felt like to be young and in love.

John reacted predictably, horrified that his daughter should take up with a "reformed Rake." Nor was he mollified by Abigail's description of Tyler's good qualities—his charm, his ease in conversation, his interest in literature. Nabby should marry a lawyer, to be sure, but a lawyer who spent his evenings at work rather than in conversation with ladies; nor was John enthusiastic about a poet or a "Professor of belle Letters."

The thought of Nabby's marriage to an undesirable man—or indeed, of Nabby's marriage to anyone—disturbed him deeply, and he dwelled on the subject in letter after letter to Abigail. "My 'Princess,' take care how you dispose of your Heart," he admonished his daughter. She should not marry a man of "Gaiety and Superficial Accomplishments" but a "thinking Being . . . It must be one who can ride 500 miles upon a trotting Horse and cross the Gulph Stream with a steady Heart. One may dance or Sing, play or ride, without being good for much." In other words, she should find a man like her father. The thought of Nabby's marriage only reminded him of how long he had been away from home. He had hoped to be home by now and to choose a husband for her, or at least advise her. But now it was too late.

John was also disturbed by Abigail's complicity in Tyler's courtship of Nabby. He saw through her expressions of concern about the romance and perceived that Tyler had won over Abigail too. "I dont like this method of Courting Mothers. There is something too fantastical and affected in all this Business for me," he told her; had she kept out of the whole affair, perhaps it would have died a natural death.

John's fears came to nothing, however, for by spring the romance appeared to be cooling off. Abigail used her influence to persuade the couple to delay their marriage. She urged them to wait until John returned and could give his consent in person. Nabby and Tyler both expressed a willingness to wait for his approval. But she would not go so far as to forbid the match absolutely, believing realistically that "voilent opposition never yet served a cause of this nature—Whilst they believe me their best Friend, and see that their Interest is near my Heart, and that my opposition is founded upon rational principals, they submit to my prohibition." To help Nabby get her mind of Tyler, Abigail sent her to Boston for an extended visit. When she returned in the spring, Tyler renewed his calls but, Abigail assured John, Nabby viewed him only as a friend and would not encourage him unless John consented to the match.

About the time Nabby returned from Boston, Charles and Tommy left to pursue their studies with their uncle, John Shaw. The husband of Abigail's younger sister Elizabeth, Shaw was minister to the congregation in Haverhill, north of Boston. Like many ministers, he took private students to help supplement his meager salary. Abigail was reluctant to send her youngest children so far away—Haverhill was a long day's journey from Braintree—but she finally concluded that there was no other way for them to get an adequate education. Charles, at thirteen, had to begin his preparation for Harvard in earnest, for it was customary for boys to enter at about the age of fifteen. Tommy was not that far behind his brother, particularly since Charles's education had been erratic in Europe and had been interrupted for several months by his trip home. Both boys had to be prepared extensively in Latin and Greek, and it required a scholar to train them properly.

Abigail had never liked John Shaw much, but there was no

Abigail's father, William Smith. Portrait by John Singleton Copley. *Courtesy Mrs. Lewis Greenleaf, Nantucket, Massachusetts.*

Abigail Adams at age twenty-two. Portrait by Benjamin Blyth, 1766. *Courtesy Massachusetts Historical Society.*

The Adams home in Braintree. Except for brief periods in Boston, Abigail lived here from the time of her marriage to John in 1764 until she joined him in Europe in 1784.

A view of Boston in 1768. Engraved and printed by Paul Revere. *Courtesy Boston Atheneum.*

Mercy Otis Warren. Portrait by John Singleton Copley. *Courtesy Museum of Fine Arts, Boston. Bequest of Winslow Warren.*

The Adams residence at Auteuil, France. From Fernand Girardin, *Maisons de Plaisances Françaises.*

Grosvenor Square, London, in 1789. The Adamses lived in one of these townhouses during their stay in London from 1785 to 1788. Watercolor by Edward Dayes. *Courtesy British Museum.*

Peacefield, the "wren's house" in Quincy that Abigail and John bought toward the end of their stay in Europe. It was their home for the rest of their lives. The original façade was about half the length of the house as it appears today. Photograph by George Dow. *Courtesy Adams National Historic Site.*

Philadelphia's High Street, near the point where Abigail and John lived. Engraving by W. Birch, 1799. *Courtesy Library of Congress.*

Washington in 1800 as seen from the Capitol.

John Quincy Adams at twenty-nine. Copley painted this portrait in London in 1796, at his wife's request; she and Abigail had become close friends during the Adamses' years in London. John Quincy had the portrait framed, and he and Mrs. Copley sent it as a surprise gift to Abigail. *Courtesy Museum of Fine Arts, Boston. Gift of Mrs. Charles Francis Adams.*

Thomas Boylston Adams at twenty-three, by Parker. Thomas had this miniature painted at his mother's request. She had it made into a bracelet as a reminder of him during the years they were separated while he lived in Europe. *Courtesy Massachusetts Historical Society.*

Abigail Adams in her fifties, by Gilbert Stuart. According to Abigail's nephew, Stuart said while painting this portrait, "he wishes to god, he could have taken Mrs. Adams when she was young, he believes he should have had a perfect Venus." John Adams's reply was "so he would." It took Stuart years to finish the portrait, however; he began it in the 1790s and did not complete it until after 1800. *Courtesy National Gallery. Gift of Mrs. Robert Homans.*

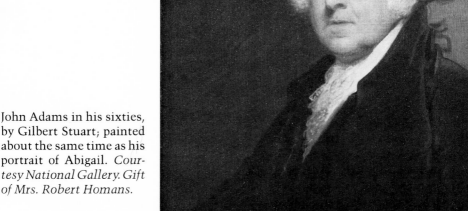

John Adams in his sixties, by Gilbert Stuart; painted about the same time as his portrait of Abigail. *Courtesy National Gallery. Gift of Mrs. Robert Homans.*

Abigail's sister, Elizabeth Smith Shaw Peabody, by Gilbert Stuart. *Courtesy University Art Collections, Arizona State University.*

A view of the town of Quincy as it looked in the years just after Abigail's death. Watercolor by Eliza Susan Quincy. *Courtesy Massachusetts Historical Society.*

denying his erudition, and he had successfully prepared several other students for Harvard. Even more important, the boys would be living with her sister rather than boarding with a family of strangers. Elizabeth, she knew, would care for the boys as if they were her own.

During the winter and spring, as Nabby fell in love and the younger boys prepared for their move to Haverhill, John Quincy traveled across Europe—alone this time, as Francis Dana remained at his post in Russia. Johnny left Saint Petersburg in October and traveled across the northernmost countries of Europe in the coldest months of the year. His progress was slow, with long interruptions by bad weather. There were stretches of weeks when no letters got through to Dana or to John, and both men became increasingly frantic at the lack of news from the intrepid fifteen-year-old. John occasionally saw newspaper notices of his son's arrival in one capital or another, but Dana was left completely in the dark. By January, thinking John Quincy must be back in Holland, he couldn't understand why he had no letters from either father or son.

But in January John Quincy was still far from Holland. Winter storms delayed him two weeks in a small town in Sweden. Then he went to Stockholm, where he was introduced to the King, and to Gothenburg, the country's major port, where he conversed with merchants about developing trade with America. From Sweden he crossed to Copenhagen, where he called on the French Minister and received the first reliable news about his father in weeks. By now it was late February, but he delayed his journey several days to wait for a favorable wind to sail to Hamburg. The trip by sea would be much shorter than going by land. He waited too long, however; the harbor froze and he had to travel by land anyway, which cost him at least two extra weeks. In Hamburg he was delayed even more—almost a month—waiting for some gentlemen who were supposed to accompany him on the remainder of his trip. He made good use of his time, however, by talking with more merchants interested in trade with America. One of these men found the young American so remarkable that he wrote a letter to compliment John on the talents of his precocious son.

John Quincy finally left Hamburg on April 5 and made it to The Hague in just over two weeks, only to discover that his father was still in Paris. Not knowing how long he would be in

Paris, John instructed his son to stay in Holland in the care of friends at The Hague.

Comfortably settled into his new routine, John Quincy finally wrote to his mother—for the first time in nearly two years. He apologized for being so deficient as a correspondent but offered as his excuse that he had been "almost at the world's end." Abigail could hardly contain her joy when she received the first of his letters after a two-year silence. She was filled with advice for her son, still urging him to guard his moral character, for she could never quite overcome her fear that Europe would corrupt him.

When a trunk of his books and papers arrived in Boston, she took heart at seeing the evidence of his good habits. It was neatly packed; the books were well chosen; a pile of translations attested to his efforts to continue his studies; the poems he chose to transcribe showed excellent taste. Her worries about her oldest son stemmed from the opposite reason to her worries about her daughter: He was too temperamental, too emotional. If Nabby was too different from her mother, John Quincy was too much like her, and like his father too. As a child he had always been more unruly than the other children, full of a "great flow of Spirits and Quick passions," but now it seemed that he had developed the reason and judgment to guide them.

In September 1783 John finally received word from Congress that he, Franklin, and Jay had been appointed Commissioners to negotiate a treaty of commerce with Great Britain. The news ended his doubts and vacillations, and he wrote immediately to ask Abigail to come to Europe with Nabby as quickly as possible. She could sail in November or December; they would spend the rest of the winter together and return home the following spring.

Unfortunately, his decision came too late. Abigail was apprehensive enough about crossing the Atlantic under any circumstances, and she absolutely refused to consider a winter voyage. "I am too much of a coward," she told John. More important, after months of John's telling her about the dangers of ocean travel and the difficulties of living in Europe, she had set her heart on his coming home. Now she had to change her thinking again, to prepare herself emotionally for pulling up roots and going to Europe. Abigail tried very hard to persuade John to decline the position. She reminded him about all the arguments he had used in the past to dissuade her from traveling to Europe—arguments that he now seemed eager to forget in his urgency to have her join him. She pointed out that neither of them was in particularly good health; he needed a long rest at home, and she would certainly suffer from an arduous journey. She reminded him that the prestige of his position would be more than offset by its difficulties. She argued that his self-sacrifice was no longer so important now that the war was over. She really did not want to come to Europe; his return was "the object my Heart pants for."

Her arguments were not mere talk. Abigail had lived for years in an unsettled state, separated from her husband and sometimes from her children, coping with the hardships of a wartime economy. She had sustained herself with the thought that eventually the war would end and they would all be reunited to live a happy, normal life. Now the war had finally ended, and it looked as though her dream of domestic tranquility was going to be snatched away from her again. She was acutely aware of advancing age, even though she was only thirty-nine. She worried about John's health and her own; she was convinced that they would not live to see old age and that their remaining time together was therefore short. She already felt cheated out of some of the best years of her life, and didn't want to lose of any more of them.

Abigail had been willing to set aside her fears and brave the trip to Europe to join him during the war, at a time when his services seemed desperately needed. But now, she thought, it was time to set all that aside and pick up the threads of their shattered life. Deep in her heart, however, she knew that no amount of argument about the need for his services at home would keep John from staying in Europe. And she began to wonder if indeed he did not love politics better than he loved her: "I know not whether I shall believe myself how well you Love me," she told him, "unless I can prevail upon you to return in the Spring."

It was not that she wanted him out of politics altogether. She knew that was impossible, despite John's periodic resolutions to return to private life. But she wanted him to continue his political career at home. "I have no reason to think that my Friend would be permitted to retire from publick life, whilst his active powers can be of any service to his Country, a state of inactivity was never meant for man," she wrote John Thaxter. In one of her more revealing comments about the appeal of politics, she added, "Love and the desire of glory as they are the most natural, are capable of being refined into the most delicate & rational passions."

Abigail was in a very precarious state emotionally during the last weeks of 1783. Her father died in September, and once again she grieved alone, without benefit of John's comforting presence. She expected every day to hear news that John had accepted his new commission, which would end all hope of his coming home. She knew this would precipitate a critical decision of her own—the decision finally to go to Europe.

In mid-December she went to Boston to visit her aunt and uncle, Isaac and Elizabeth Smith. While she was there, her uncle encountered Francis Dana, just off his ship from Russia and on his way home to Cambridge. Isaac insisted that Dana come home with him to see Abigail, who had no idea that he was returning from Europe. When Abigail saw him walk through the door, she burst into tears. "My Heart swelled with grief, and the Idea that I—I only was left alone, it recalld all the tender scenes of seperation, and overcame all my fortitude," she wrote. "I retired and reasoned myself into composure sufficient; to see him without a childish emotion." When she returned home, she discovered John Thaxter waiting for her, also fresh from Europe. Delighted as she was to see her cousin Thaxter, and happy as she tried to feel for Elizabeth Dana, these reunions only reminded her of her own unhappiness.

John continued to importune Abigail to come to Europe. He would understand if she did not want to make a winter crossing, but she must definitely come in the spring. And so the New Year found Abigail making preparations to cross the Atlantic.

She knew she could force the issue and get him to decline his commission and come home, but she had never been willing to do such a thing. Besides, she still harbored a sense of adventure, buried under her conviction that all she wanted was a quiet life at home with her family. The youthful Abigail who had wanted to see the world had not been entirely lost in the matronly woman absorbed in family duties.

One of the many ways that Abigail resembled John was her ambivalence about public life and recognition. She was much more attached to domestic life and family than he; his eloquence about his humble farm and the beauty of the Blue Hills was mostly rhetorical. On the other hand, she had her share of ambition and desire to be at the center of activity, even if hers was less pronounced than John's. She might worry about what sort of figure she would cut in the courts of Europe; her fears about crossing the ocean, and about becoming a public figure, were real. But there was a side of her that was bored with her simple domestic life and was ready for the adventure. As she got older she, like John, continued to wax nostalgic over the simple life left behind, but she also learned to enjoy being in the limelight. Eventually her talk about humble cottages and domestic tranquility became just as rhetorical as his.

For the moment, there was yet another impetus for going to Europe. Nabby's romance with Royall Tyler had not died a natural death as Abigail expected, and getting her away from him for an extended period seemed a way either to break off the affair or at least to subject it to the test of time and separation. John had suggested as much back in October and had pledged that if Nabby still wanted to marry Tyler when she returned he would not stand in the way. Abigail contemplated going to Europe alone, but her daughter's companionship was one of the few things that would make the trip bearable. Nabby, dutiful daughter that she was, said that she did not particularly want to go but would if her mother wanted her to.

She and Tyler resigned themselves to the separation, but Tyler wrote a formal letter to John requesting permission to marry Nabby when she returned. John, who was never able to deny his daughter anything, swallowed his stern comments about Tyler's unsuitability and gave his consent. Even before he received the letter, he had softened enough to tell Abigail that if she approved of the match, she should allow the pair to marry and live in the Adams house. By that time, however, both Abigail and Nabby had decided that mother and daughter would go to Europe.

In January Abigail began making her travel plans. She bought several additional tracts of land and arranged with Cotton Tufts to look after their holdings and keep an eye out for additional parcels they might want to buy. He would take care of all the family's financial affairs in her absence. Charles and Tommy would stay with the Shaws, and Mary Cranch would look after John's aging mother. Pheby, who had been freed by Abigail's father in his will, would stay in the house. Abigail turned over John's old accounts receivable to Tyler, who would try to collect the old debts before more bankruptcies rendered them worthless.

The most difficult task was making arrangements for her niece Louisa. Abigail had no choice but to send her back to her mother, but Louisa was reluctant to go. She had lived with her aunt for as long as she could remember. Louisa had waited throughout the fall for news of John as if her life depended on it, Abigail reported, and would be reassured only when Abigail promised that she could come back to live with them when they returned from Europe.

Even as she began making her final arrangements—hiring servants to accompany them and inquiring about sailing dates for various ships—Abigail still wished that somehow the plans could be changed and John would come home. "You invite me to you, you call me to follow you, the most earnest wish of my soul is to be with you," she wrote John, "but you can scarcely form an Idea of the conflict of my mind. It appears to me such an enterprize, the ocean so formidable, the quitting my habitation and my country, leaving my Children, my Friends, with the Idea that perhaps I may never see them again, without my Husband to console and comfort me under these apprehensions—indeed my dear Friend there are hours when I feel unequal to the trial." She consoled herself by thinking of their reunion, "but . . . my fears, and anxieties, are present; my hopes, and expectations, distant."

At the beginning of April, when the time approached for their ship to sail, she worried at not receiving any recent letters from John. Perhaps she remembered the many times before that he had changed his mind, the letters that said "come" closely followed by letters that said "don't come." Perhaps she hoped that something would change his mind and the next ship would bring news of his own departure. In any case, she and Nabby decided not to sail in mid-April, even though the ship's captain, John Callahan, agreed to wait several days for them to complete their arrangements.

She and Nabby waited six weeks, and still no further instructions came; so Abigail booked passage on the *Active*, scheduled to sail from Boston around the middle of June. She knew nothing about the captain or any of the other passengers. She never dreamed she would travel such a distance without a male escort, in the company of total strangers, she told John, "but let no person say what they would or would not do, since we are not judges for ourselves until circumstances call us to act."

John, meanwhile, was getting impatient to see them. He expected them to arrive sometime in May, so he sent John Quincy to London to wait for them, and incidentally to improve himself by listening to debates in Parliament. John Quincy was disappointed when Captain Callahan arrived on June 1 without his mother and sister, carrying instead letters from them saying that they awaited further instructions. John was surprised and upset that they weren't in Callahan's ship. How could they be expecting letters from him, when he was expecting *them* any day? There was nothing to do but call John Quincy back to Holland and wait until they heard definitely of Abigail's and Nabby's arrival.

Once Abigail had made up her mind to go and finally had booked her passage, nothing would stop her. Thomas Jefferson, who had been appointed by Congress to join the Commissioners in Paris, rushed to Boston in mid-June with the idea that the Adams women could accompany him to Europe. He was planning to sail from New York in a ship bound directly for France, and he urged Abigail to change her plans and go with him. He arrived only a day before the *Active* was due to sail, but there was still time for Abigail to change her mind. A more congenial male escort for the journey could hardly be found. But Abigail had finally prepared herself to go. She had said all her heart-wrenching goodbyes, and she would not be dissuaded from her plans. On June 20 the two women boarded the *Active* and set sail for "that once great Nation" that Abigail had long ago dreamed of visiting.

Chapter 10

Europe

~~~~

Abigail and Nabby embarked for London with two servants, John Briesler and Esther Field; a cow to provide milk for the voyage; and several trunks packed with clothes, dishes, and books. There was one other woman passenger, coincidentally also named Adams. The four woman found themselves the objects of considerable curiosity and chivalrous respect. As Abigail reported to her sister Mary, they could not cross the ship's cabin without a gentleman jumping up to assist them.

Prepared to expect the worst from an ocean voyage, Abigail found that the accommodations and food fell below even her most pessimistic expectations. The *Active* was a relatively small ship, carrying only about a dozen passengers in addition to the crew. Their quarters consisted of a large cabin where they took meals and spent most of their day except for short stretches on deck. Two small cabins off the main room were given to the ladies for their sleeping quarters. Abigail shared one with Esther Field, and Nabby and Mrs. Adams had the other. The men slept in the main cabin. Unfortunately, the private cabins were suffocating when the doors were closed, so the women were forced to keep their doors open except when they dressed. Abigail was mortified by the lack of privacy. "What should I have thought on shore," she wrote Mary, "to have layed myself down to sleep, in common with half a dozen Gentlemen?" It was, she noted, a "sweet situation for a delicate Lady, but necessity has no law."

Even more trying for a "delicate lady" were the dirt, the smell, and the nearly inedible food. The ship's cargo consisted largely of oil and potash—"the most odorifferous kind," Abigail commented. The oil leaked and the potash fermented. The crew did nothing to keep the ship clean, and the cook was lazy, dirty, and unskilled at his art. The captain, a perfect gentleman in Abigail's estimation, nevertheless seemed incapable of seeing to the cleanliness of his ship.

For the first several days at sea neither Abigail or anyone else could do much about their surroundings, because they all became violently seasick. "To those who have never been at Sea or experienced this disspiriting malady tis impossible to discribe it," Abigail noted in her diary; "when once it seazes a person it levels Sex and condition."

The whole experience made her reflect often on John's comment that there was nothing so disagreeable as a lady at sea. A casual comment, made years earlier, Abigail had never forgotten it; now she felt disagreeable indeed. The only justification for a woman to go to sea, she decided, was "going to a Good Husband and kind parent."

Finally the sea calmed, the ship stopped its violent rolling, and Abigail felt well enough to go up on deck, where she "beheld the vast and boundless ocean before us with astonishment, and wonder." She lost no time in contemplation, however, but proceeded to take over the ship and clean it up. "As I found I might reign mistress on Board without any offence I soon exerted my Authority with scrapers mops Brushes, infusions of viniger, &c. and in a few hours you would have thought yourself in a different ship." Briesler took charge of a group of crewmen to accomplish the seemingly impossible task. The passenger quarters became tolerable, and the gentlemen, she noted, were well pleased with her efforts.

Not satisfied with merely cleaning the ship, she then ventured into the galley, where she taught the cook how to "dress his victuals" and made a few puddings herself, "the only thing I have seen fit to eat." She also unpacked some of her own dishes, there being not enough in the galley to serve all the passengers, then supervised the daily cleaning of the cabins and of the milk pail, "which had been enough to poison anybody."

With the worst bout of seasickness over and the ship in tolerable shape, Abigail, Nabby and the other passengers settled down to the dull routine of an ocean voyage. They could expect to be at sea a minimum of four weeks. The expanse of ocean, so impressive at first sight, became tiresome after several days of the same endless view. The passengers spent only about an hour a day on deck to get some fresh air and what little exercise could be had by pacing up and down a small ship. The rest of their waking hours they spent in the main cabin reading, writing, talking, or playing cards.

Abigail started a diary, partly as a self-conscious way of recording her impressions but partly also to occupy her time and keep track of the passage of the days. "If I did not write I should lose the Days of the Weeks," she noted. When she tired of reading and writing, she followed the captain around the ship, learning the names and functions of the various masts and sails, until he gallantly assured her that she was ready to take her turn at the helm.

Several days out of port a storm broke the monotony of the voyage. The passengers had to brace their feet against tables tied down with ropes; at night they could stay in bed only by holding the sides of their bunks with both hands. Abigail described the ship as a "great cradle rocking with amaizing force from side, to side . . . not a wink of Sleep to be had, bottles, mugs, plates, every thing crashing to peices." Apparently it was not a bad storm as storms went. "The Sailors call it as Breize only," she noted, "But if it was only of that kind; good heaven defend me from a storm."

Far worse than the storm was the dead calm they encountered several days later, during which the ship idled motionless with not a breath of wind to fill the sails. The enforced stillness made Abigail philosophical. "I begin to think that a Calm is not desireable in any situation in life," she wrote. Every object is most Beautifull in motion, a ship under sail trees gently agitated with the wind, & a fine woman danceing . . . man was made for action." The ship became a "partial prison," especially when the weather was cold or rainy and the passengers were confined to the cabin.

Inevitably, some of passengers began to get on each other's nerves. One man in particular annoyed Abigail. He was Scottish, the only non-American on board, a "high monarchacal man" with "inflamibility enough to furnish a Waggon load of Baloons." She often felt like taking issue with him on political questions but tried to restrain herself. Once, however, she could not resist telling him that Americans believed in recognizing merit rather than titles, and that it must be "mortifying" to British noblemen to be beaten in battle by "mechanicks & mere husbandmen." Moreover, they "esteemed it our glory to draw such characters not only into the field, but into the Senate." The other passengers, she told Mary, enjoyed this conversation immensely.

Exactly four weeks after leaving Boston the travelers caught their first sight of land. The seasickness of the early days now seemed far behind as they sailed up the English Channel. Two days' sail up the Channel brought them to Deal, where the passengers were rowed ashore in small boats. The surf was high, and they were all soaking wet by the time they reached shore. Then they had to trudge through wet sand to reach an inn where they could change clothes before the stagecoach journey to London.

Abigail and Nabby reached London on July 21, two days after landing at Deal. Their traveling companions left them at a hotel recommended by the ship captain and went off to look for Abigail's cousin, Isaac Smith, Jr. London, even in the eighteenth century, was an enormous, sprawling city, but within thirty minutes Smith and another cousin, Charles Storer, appeared at the hotel, ready to search for lodgings for the two women.

Abigail immediately wrote to John at The Hague. "Your Letter of the 23rd has made me the happiest Man upon Earth," he replied. "I am twenty years younger than I was yesterday." The pressure of business kept him from coming to London to meet them, but John Quincy set out immediately. He would buy a carriage for their use and bring them back to The Hague, where they would stay a short time before going to Paris.

Abigail and Nabby were impatient to see them, but in the meantime they were fully occupied with sightseeing and social engagements. It seemed as if every American living in London came to call. Among the visitors was Richard Cranch's cousin John, who traveled all the way from the west of England to pay his respects. Abigail was so swamped with callers, unfortunately, that they had only a short time to talk. "But do you know that I paid a visit to the ambassadress?" he exclaimed to Abigail's old friend Eunice Paine. "I have, & am mad to think of it: How so? Why I staid but half an hour; and some impertinent man of rank interrupted the preface, to one of the finest tete a tetes that was *going to begin* in the world." Nabby impressed him too: She was a great beauty, he assured Miss Paine.

John Quincy arrived in London on July 30. Abigail hardly recognized her son. He towered over his mother and sister, tall, slim, and full of energy. His fine blond hair was pulled back at the neck in the fashion of the day; he was still too young to adopt the affectation of a powdered wig. He had his mother's dark, twinkling eyes, although she thought he had grown to look more like his father. His travels had left him with a certain polish that made him look older than his seventeen years, but he greeted his mother and sister with all the boyish enthusiasm of a child. "He is the same good humord Lad he formerly was," his mother observed.

They planned to return to The Hague as quickly as possible, but then word came that Jefferson had landed in France and was on his way to Paris. Because his presence was all that was needed for the treaty negotiations in Paris to begin, both Abigail and John Quincy wondered whether it wouldn't make more sense to travel to Brussels and meet John there. Their questions were answered when a letter arrived from John telling them to stay put until he could meet them in London; then they would all travel to Paris together. He would be there in a week at the latest.

It was one of the constant features of eighteenth-century travel that no one could ever predict exactly when he would arrive anywhere. Weather conditions—be they stormy seas or muddy roads—delayed departures and added days to travel time. Letters moved slowly, and of course there was no form of instant communication to announce one's arrival. Consequently John's and Abigail's reunions always had a quality of surprise about them. It was no different on August 7 when the packet from The Hague docked and John hastened to Abigail's lodgings at the Adelphi Hotel. Without warning, he was there, looking a bit older and considerably plumper—but Abigail hardly noticed. Five years of loneliness and unhappiness dissolved in a moment.

Nabby returned a few minutes later to find subtle, almost intangible changes in their quarters. "I saw upon the table a hat with two books in it; everything around appeared altered, without my knowing in what particular. I went into my own room, the things were moved; I looked around—'Has mamma received letters, that have determined her departure? —When does she go? —Why are these things moved?' All in a breath to Esther.

"'No ma'am, she has received no letter, but goes to-morrow morning.'

"'Why is all this appearance of strangeness? —Whose hat is that in the other room? —Whose trunk is this? —Whose sword and cane? —It is my father's,' said I. 'Where is he?'

"'In the room above.'

"Up I flew, and to his chamber, where he was lying down, he raised himself upon my knocking softly at the door, and received me with all the tenderness of an affectionate parent after so long an absence. Sure I am, I never felt more agitation of spirits in my life; it will not do to describe."

Abigail told Mary several months later, "poets and painters wisely draw a veil over those Scenes which surpass the pen of the one and the pencil of the other; we were indeed a very happy family once more met together after a Seperation of 4 years." They had little time to relax and reflect on the months past, however, for John was anxious to press on to Paris. John Quincy had already procured a carriage, and they set out the next day for France.

Abigail had spent just three weeks in London, but in that short time she met many of the Americans living there and formed her crucial first impressions of life in Europe.

London was totally unlike any place she had ever seen. Her idea of a city was Boston, where one could walk from one end of the town to the other in less than an hour. London had about 800,000 residents sprawled across an area so large that Abigail couldn't possibly take in all of it during her short stay. Within a few blocks of her hotel were public buildings more magnificent than anything she could have imagined—St. James's Palace, home of the royal family, with its ornately uniformed guards and elaborate gardens; the ancient, cavernous Westminster Abbey with its beautiful stained glass; and the much newer St. Paul's Cathedral, almost austere by comparison, designed by Christopher Wren and built after the great fire of 1660.

She took note of the elegant residential districts around the palace and just beyond it, to the west and north. Georgian-style townhouses of brick or stone lined the tree-shaded streets and perfectly proportioned squares—a sharp contrast to the narrow, crooked lanes and mixture of house styles in Boston. These houses, too, had been built after the fire on land that had been open fields fifty or a hundred years earlier.

These elegant homes, the ornate public buildings, even the carriages and the dress of the people she observed in London's streets and parks all indicated to Abigail the great wealth of England's upper class. The United States had its wealthy merchants and landowners, to be sure, but here the degree of wealth surpassed anything she had seen at home.

The attention Europeans paid to fashion struck her especially forcefully; the number of servants required to transform one into a lady of fashion was appalling. "There is a rage of fashion which prevails here with despotick sway," she observed. "The couleur & kind of silk must be attended to; & the day for putting it on & of, no fancy to be exercised, but *it* is the *fashion* & that is argument sufficient."

For all their effort, she thought the London ladies were less attractive than American women. "The softness peculiarly characteristick of our sex & which is so pleasing to the Gentlemen, is wholy laid aside here; for the masculine attire and manners of Amazonians," she asserted. Prepared to find the Old World decadent, corrupt, and wallowing in luxury, Abigail found what she was looking for in the manners of English women, even though she had to admit that London was pleasanter than she had expected. This contrast between Old World and New was to become a constant theme as she traveled to Paris and eventually back to London.

As much as she might profess to dislike the customs of Europe, she could not avoid them altogether. The wife of a public figure could not wholly eschew fashion. She and Nabby shopped for clothes in London, fretting over the expense. Finally they decided not to buy anything until they reached Paris, where the fashions might well be different. Abigail did break down and have her hair dressed in the style of London ladies, however. Sending a servant to hire a barber, she soon discovered one of the differences between American English and its parent language. "The fellow staird, was loth to ask for what purpose I wanted him, at last he said you mean a Hair dresser Mam, I believe, aya says I, I want my Hair drest, why Barbars Madam in this country do nothing but shave."

Despite her many negative impressions, in general Abigail liked England. In three weeks she had made several friends, whom she left with regret for a country where she expected to find fewer Americans and would have difficulty speaking the language.

Paris, by contrast, proved to be a disappointment. It was somewhat smaller than London, with slightly more than 500,000 inhabitants, but to Abigail it seemed much more crowded. Paris had not expanded physically in the last hundred years as London had; it had experienced no devastating fire to encourage planned new construction. Where the newer sections of London boasted wide streets with gutters and pedestrian walkways on each side, Paris streets were narrow, with the old-fashioned gutters running down the middle, fed by improvised drains from each house. The difference in sanitation was not lost on Abigail. Upon being told that she had not really seen all of Paris yet, she observed, "One thing I know, & that is, that I have smelt it. It is the very dirtyest place I ever saw."

Paris lacked London's newer town houses and neatly laid out squares. The houses, to her mind, were ugly and the streets impossibly cluttered with refuse. It did have some impressive public buildings and gardens—the cathedral of Notre Dame and the Palais de Justice, sitting opposite each other on the Ile de la Cité in the middle of the Seine River, for example. The gardens of the Tuilleries were beautiful but not so expansive as Hyde Park in London. And there was nothing to compare with the Palace of St. James's, for the French royal family maintained its headquarters serveral miles outside of Paris, at Versailles. "Boston cannot Boast so elegant publick Buildings," she admitted, "but in every other respect, it is much superior in my Eyes to Paris, as London is to Boston."

They decided not to live in Paris, so Abigail was spared the noise and the smells. Instead they rented an enormous barn of a house in Auteuil, a suburb about 4 miles outside the city. Auteuil was a small town with all the charm of a rural village, and yet it was very convenient for John's business. Franklin lived at Passy, the neighboring town. It was a short ride to his lodgings, where the Commissioners would conduct most of their meetings. Just beyond Auteuil—not more than half a mile from their house—was the Bois de Boulogne, a huge park with tree-shaded paths, ponds, and broad meadows. John's walks there were one of the few pleasures he remembered from his earlier trips to France; its proximity was one of the reasons he wanted to rent that particular house. Here, he and Abigail could insulate themselves from the unpleasantness of Paris and try to recreate their quiet family life in a rural setting.

In London Abigail had been horrified at the number of servants needed to create a fashionable lady. In France, where she had to establish a household, she was even more horrified to discover the number of servants needed to run a house. Accustomed to functioning with only two or three servants for the past several years, she now found that she would have to hire at least eight in addition to John Briesler and Esther Field. Each servant had a specific task and would do nothing else, she discovered to her dismay. It took more people to accomplish less, and it took all her skill to manage the staff to see that anything at all got done. Ridiculing what she called the "Etiquet" of the servants, she called them "a pack of Lazy wretches . . . saddled upon you to support and maintain for the purpose of plundering you . . . I have been so vexd sometimes, that I have been ready to send them all packing at once." None of them did as much work in a day as an American servant would, she claimed. If John and Esther didn't do double duty, even eight French servants would not have been enough.

Abigail's tirades about servants expressed the outrage of a thrifty Yankee and her concern about the expense of living in Europe on the salary that Congress paid its representatives. But her concern about their expenses also reflected her anxiety about a new way of life. John had been living in the public eye and learning to live with European customs for years, but it was all new to Abigail. Suddenly, after living most of her adult life in a seven-room cottage, she was mistress of a thirty-room mansion. She traveled in a gilt carriage and shopped for a wardrobe of Paris fashions. The expense of this new life was frightening—the more so because it seemed uncontrollable. It was not their own wishes that led them into these extravagances, but the demands of their position as public figures. For Abigail, the most difficult part of her new position was knowing that she lived in the public eye and that her standard of living would be constantly scrutinized by others.

Their house certainly befitted the status of an Ambassador. It was an enormous structure with a beautiful garden, but Abigail thought the house was much too big and badly arranged. It was drafty and in poor repair, hard to keep clean, and hard to heat. Most of the floors were tile, which was difficult to care for, and there were no carpets. Abigail had to hire a servant expressly to wash the floors, a process he accomplished by strapping brushes to his feet and skating around the rooms. In general, she had the same complaint about the house that she did about Paris and, indeed, much of Europe: It was dirty. With thirty rooms, hard-to-clean floors, and lazy servants, it was a constant struggle to keep it up to her standards of cleanliness.

Still, there were parts of the house that delighted Abigail. Her own bedroom, with an adjoining "appartment" overlooking the garden, was a perfect place to read and write letters, just the sort of private space that she had often coveted. The garden, with plants of every imaginable description, covered five acres. There were orange trees, grape vines, and china vases filled with flowers. Paths led to hidden alcoves filled with exotic plants; a tiny summer house was tucked away in a thicket of trees. In the temperate climate of France, the Adamses could enjoy their garden at all seasons, and it went a long way to make up for the strangeness, the difficulties, and the loneliness of living in France.

New impressions bombarded Abigail during the first few weeks at Auteuil. If London had seemed utterly different from America, France was even more different from London. The overly masculine, unfashionable women of London contrasted with the excessively feminine and fashionable French. Like John on his first trip, she could not help but be attracted to the sociability of the French people at the same time that she deplored their sensuous approach to life. Unlike John, however, she was much quicker to condemn their customs, especially the behavior of their women.

Her introduction to French women came as a shock. Benjamin Franklin invited the Adamses to dinner with a group that included Madame Helvetius, one of his dearest friends in Paris. She appeared sloppy and dirty to Abigail. She entered the room and immediately kissed Franklin exuberantly on both cheeks, a custom common enough in France but shocking to Abigail. Worse still, she sat at the dinner table with her arm around Franklin's neck; after dinner she threw herself down on a chair, "where she shew more than her feet." She brought her dog along—"her favorite this she kisst & when he wet the floor, she wiped it up with her chimise. I own I was highly disgusted." It was hard for her to believe that this woman was one of Franklin's best friends and a constant visitor to his house. "You see that manners differ exceedingly in different Countries," she told her niece. "I hope however to find amongst the French Ladies manners more consistent with my ideas of decency or I shall be a mere recluse."

On the whole Abigail found the manners of the French people not at all to her liking. The business of life in France was pleasure, she told all her friends, and she could not figure out when anyone did any work. The people who constantly crowded the streets, theaters, and places of amusement must live on bread and water, since they obviously were not earning a living. Not only the throngs of people in themselves, but their dress, their manner, and their expressions bespoke their search for enjoyment. The streets of London were no less crowded, she remembered, but there "every appearence indicates buisness," unlike gay and carefree Paris.

The Puritan in her was especially appalled at the Parisian sabbath. It was a day not of worship and reflection but of recreation. The Bois de Boulogne rang with music and laughter; booths were set up to sell cake and wine. The most amazing thing was that the French never seemed to tire of their amusements. Everything in her culture taught her that amusement for the sake of amusement must eventually become tiresome, however enjoyable it might be in small doses. Clearly the French attitude was entirely different, and beyond her comprehension.

Abigail never felt any of John's ambivalence about French culture. Unlike him, she was not attracted by the pleasures of French society but felt only disapproval for their pursuit of the pleasures of the senses. But she tried to be tolerant and eventually learned not to be shocked at French manners. After several months she was no longer upset when a man sniffed the food at a dinner party before passing it to a lady; he was only making sure it was fit to eat. She even got over her distress at seeing women kiss men on both cheeks.

Some things, however, were beyond acceptance. Abigail never understood French sexual morality. The French did not seem to take marriage seriously. Both men and women openly kept lovers; prostitution was rampant; and illegitimate children were a major social problem. She was horrified that thousands of women in Paris were registered as prostitutes and that hundreds of them died of poverty and disease each year. She visited the foundling hospital, where abandoned children were cared for, and was impressed by the quality of care and the compassion of the women who worked there; but she was distressed at the conditions that made such an institution necessary—conditions that she ascribed solely to prostitution and immorality.

Even among the upper classes, marriage was not sacred. In most families she saw "seperate appartments; seperate pleasures & amusements shew the world that nothing but the Name is united." She attributed this situation partly to the perpetual pursuit of pleasure, which released all restraints on the "Appetites & passions," but partly also to French marriage customs, which encouraged early betrothal of children. By the time couples married, their interests had often totally diverged, and both husbands and wives freely sought lovers. It also bothered Abigail that most French couples wanted only two or three children, in contrast to the large families commonly sought in America.

Beyond French marriage customs themselves, it was the cause of the customs that Abigail faulted: the desire to perpetuate hereditary distinctions of class that led parents to create matches for their children. Once again she saw a lesson for Americans: They must avoid all distinctions of rank and family and permit only distinctions of merit. She dwelled on the immorality of French marriage customs at length because she deeply believed that marriage was the basis of a well-ordered society, along with religion, education, and hard work. In France all these props seemed weak. The pursuit of pleasure, loose sexual morality, the ignorance of the mass of the people, and the apparent disrespect for religion all made her wonder how French society could survive. In her simple contrast between New World virtue and Old World corruption, all the weaknesses of French society could be attributed to a loss of innocence; France was a country "grown old in Debauchery and baseness." But always there was the concern that America, too, might be going the way of France.

For the most part, the Adamses lived a retired life at Auteuil. Abigail claimed to be even more immersed in domestic pleasures than she had been in Braintree, although her household responsibilities were far different. Here servants did many of the things she was used to doing herself. In Boston she had done most of her own marketing; in Braintree much of their food had come from their garden, and she spent hours canning and pickling fruits and vegetables to tide them through the winters. In Auteuil their garden was strictly ornamental, and servants made the trips into Paris to the markets. Every detail of their household, from making the beds to keeping their clothes cleaned and pressed, was handled by servants. But Abigail discovered that she could consume almost as many hours supervising the servants as she had doing her own work at home. And she still did almost all her own sewing, for she trusted no one to do it as well as she.

Her social life was restricted. Abigail's limited knowledge of French—she could read tolerably well but had difficulty speaking—on top of her mixed feelings about French society discouraged her from visiting with French women, and there were few Americans living in Paris. John's rather unusual position also limited their social contacts. He was not considered a regular member of the diplomatic corps and therefore was not invited to court functions or to the constant round of parties given by people connected with the court. Jefferson described the American Commissioners as "the lowest and most obscure of the whole diplomatic tribe." Abigail was just as glad of that. The pleasure of having the family together again more than made up for the lack of outside amusements.

They soon settled into a comfortable routine. Abigail spent her mornings supervising her servants' work or sewing, while John Quincy and Nabby studied. Promptly at noon, John went for his daily walk while she and Nabby had their hair dressed. At two they ate dinner, followed by an afternoon of reading. John often spent the morning or afternoon at Passy, meeting with Franklin and Jefferson. They persisted in the American custom of afternoon tea; when that was over, John taught John Quincy mathematics until around nine, when the whole family gathered around the table for a game of whist.

There were few friends to interrupt their solitude. They occasionally had dinner with Franklin, but no more often than propriety dictated. He and John remained cool toward each other, and neither Franklin's manners nor his other guests were much to Abigail's liking. Thomas Jefferson was their most frequent visitor. He and John made an odd-looking pair. The lanky Virginian stood a good 6 inches taller than John, who had grown plumper with age. But they had been fond of each other ever since they had worked together on the Declaration of Independence. Despite their different backgrounds, they had much in common. Both were passionately fond of books, and both preferred a quiet family life to the sort of continuous social life that Franklin enjoyed.

Abigail took to Jefferson quickly. He was young—just a year older than she—handsome, and gracious in manner. His unaffected charm and his attentiveness to her and the children won her over completely. "He is one of the choice ones of the Earth," was her judgment. She felt a particular sympathy for him, because his life had been tinged with tragedy; his wife had died not long before, leaving him with three daughters. The oldest, Martha, just twelve years old, had accompanied him to France. A lonely man, he all but adopted the Adams family. Abigail, Nabby, and John Quincy became his companions nearly as much as John did.

Jefferson visited weekly if not more often. He was the only person in France with whom they enjoyed the kind of casual, intimate social life that they were used to at home. They often went sightseeing together. Jefferson lived in Paris itself and was much more favorably disposed toward French society than the Adamses; he often prodded them into doing things they would not have done on their own.

Abigail's curiosity would not allow her to stay at home all the time. Like any tourist, she visited the great cathedrals of Paris. Despite their splendor, she found in them little more than confirmation of her anti-Catholicism. The churches, she thought, "seem rather calculated to damp devotion than excite it." The custom of confession seemed designed to encourage sin by granting ready forgiveness.

The theater pleased her much more. She was an avid reader of plays, but there were no theaters in New England. Here she could indulge her taste for drama as often as she liked. They also went to the opera, which was less pleasing; the latest Italian opera, all the rage in Paris, was in Nabby's words "a good representation of the ridiculous." But with the fashionable Parisians, who "had rather be amused than instructed," according to Abigail, the opera was much more popular than the theater.

The opera provided every possible sensual amusement with its elaborate scenery, rich costumes, and elegant music. For one whose experience of music had been limited to hearing an occasional harpsichord or flute, it was a heady experience. "O! the Musick vocal and instrumental, it has a soft persuasive power and a dying dying sound," she explained to Mary. "Conceive a highly decorated building filled with Youth Beauty, Grace, ease, clad in all the most pleasing and various ornaments of Dress which fancy can form; these objects singing like Cherubs to the best tuned instruments most skilfully handled, think you that this city can fail of becoming a Cytherea and this House the temple of Venus?"

Of all forms of stage entertainment, dancing astonished Abigail most. The first time she saw dancing on stage, she was instantly caught up in the beauty of the performers and their costumes; but when they actually started dancing, "I felt my delicacy wounded, and I was ashamed to bee seen to look at them, girls cloathed in the thinest silk & gauze, . . . springing two feet from the floor poising themselves in the air, with their feet flying, and as perfectly shewing their Garters & draws, as tho no peticoat had been worn . . . their motions are as light as air and as quick as lightning. They balance themselves to astonishment." She had to admit that several performances wore off her "disgust" and she actually enjoyed the spectacle, yet she could never stop reflecting on the deleterious effects of a life on the stage for a young girl's moral character.

Other forms of entertainment were harmless but totally frivolous. Hot air balloons were all the rage that fall, and the Adamses could not resist going with the curious to watch a balloon launching. Nearly 10,000 people gathered in the Tuilleries one September afternoon to watch an enormous balloon rise slowly into the air. Such spectacles seemed silly, yet irresistible just the same. As Nabby commented, "This people are more attentive to their amusements than anything else; however, as we were upon the same errand, it is unjust to reflect upon others, whose curiosity was undoubtedly as well founded."

Neither Abigail nor any member of her family ever wavered in their preference for life in America over life in Europe. In France they lived in a far grander style than they ever had in Braintree, despite Abigail's constant worries that they didn't have enough money to support their way of life. In her mind, however, the fancy house, the lavish entertaining, the elegant dresses, and the many servants were all part of a mode of living that had been forced on them by John's public position. She was happy about the opportunity to see Europe, but after a few weeks of it, her curiosity satisfied, she would just as soon have gone home. "I turn my thoughts to my lowly cottage to my rough hewn garden as objects more pleasing than the gay & really beautifull one which now presents itself to my view," she wrote Royall Tyler. "My taste is too riggedly fixed to be warped by the gay sunshine & splendour of parisian attractions."

Abigail's preference for her "lowly cottage" was part of her unshakable belief that America was superior to Europe—a superiority based on its simplicity, its supposed lack of extreme wealth and class distinctions, its religion, and its emphasis on family. She had come to Europe convinced that she would not be taken in by its splendors, and she interpreted everything she saw in light of her "riggedly fixed" taste. The simple cottage in Braintree became a metaphor for the superiority of American life.

In other ways, however, Abigail's longing for her simple life at home was real, and not just so much chauvinistic rhetoric. After the excitement of seeing new places wore off, she was often homesick. She missed her sisters, her two younger sons, and all the friends and relatives who had been part of her life for as long as she could remember. Because she loved to talk, she found the language barrier in France a constant source of frustration, notwithstanding her efforts to learn French. Even when she could understand conversations or talked with English speakers, the trivial, polite conversation at elegant social gatherings hardly satisfied her craving for serious discourse. Indeed, all the trappings of European social gatherings struck her as false and affected, from the way she had to dress to attend them, to the triviality of the conversation, to the waste of money apparent in extravagant food, drink and dress. Quiet gatherings with friends and family were much more appealing to her. "I had rather dine in my little room at Braintree with your family and a set of Chosen Friends, than with the Marquisses Counts & Countesses Abbes & Great folks who dine with us today," she told Mary.

The difficulty they had making ends meet and the relatively poor showing they made compared with diplomats from other countries only made the situation worse. The United States, a new country without much money and without any sense of the importance of maintaining proper diplomatic relations with foreign nations, provided rather stingy salaries for its representatives abroad. In the eyes of other Europeans, unfortunately, the frugal Americans looked merely ridiculous. Abigail thought it extravagent to employ eight servants and had difficulty paying their wages; but the British Ambassador had no fewer than fifty servants, and the Spanish Ambassador had seventy. The Adamses could not hope to match the expensive entertainment of the European diplomats, and Abigail was torn between her scorn for such displays of extravagance and her mortification at appearing to disadvantage in diplomatic circles.

As the months went by, she felt more and more alone and homesick for New England. "What a sad misfortune it is to have the Body in one place & the soul in another," she told Mary. The mild winter of France was hard to get used to. Even the beautiful Paris spring failed to lift her spirits. The garden that had so delighted her when they first moved to Auteuil no longer held the same attraction. The flowers were beautiful, but they were not her flowers, and she could not take much interest in them.

For the first time in her life, she bought a pet—a tiny songbird—and soon felt more attached to it than to anyone outside her family. She compared herself to the poverty-stricken man with a dog, who bought food for his dog when he had barely enough food for himself. When asked why, he replied, if he didn't have his dog, who would love him? "You can never feel the force of this replie," she confided in Mary, "unless you were to go into a foreign Country without being able to speak the language of it—I could not have believed if I had not experienced it, how strong the Love of Country is in the humane mind."

Throughout the months in France, Abigail kept close tabs on their affairs at home. Charles and Tommy progressed well in their studies through the winter; Charles would be ready to enter Harvard the next summer. She and John decided that it was time John Quincy went home to enter Harvard too; for all his considerable schooling and experience in Europe, they had long felt that he should finish his education in his own country. The difficulty was that John Quincy was much older than boys entering Harvard, and his learning presumably surpassed theirs too. So John asked Cotton Tufts to request that the overseers of the college admit him as an advanced student, to either the third- or the fourth-year class. This was accomplished by Christmas, and they began to make plans for John Quincy's return in the spring.

Cotton Tufts also continued to look after their financial affairs, and Abigail was as avid as ever to have him buy more land for them. She and John disagreed over what to buy, however. John was interested in a particular farm near theirs, but she did not want it. Tufts agreed; the land was wearing out and would not produce good crops. Abigail wanted a larger farm, one with a spacious house that they could move into when they returned. She had heard of its availabiity from Royall Tyler and persuaded John to consider buying it. "It is a bold stroke for a wife," she told Tufts. But John, on further reflection, hesitated at such a large purchase; they could not buy it without going into debt, and, as he put it, "I love to feel free." Abigail reluctantly agreed but told Tufts to continue making inquiries about the farm anyway.

In fact, John was quite happy to leave the direction of affairs at home to Abigail. For the first few months that she was in Europe, Cotton Tufts wrote long letters to both of them about their financial affairs and the expenses of their children. After a while, however, he wrote to John about politics and to Abigail about finances. She told him that it was impossible to get John to think about anything domestic; he wanted everything to run smoothly but could not be bothered with details himself. "He chuses I should write & think about them & give directions," she explained. "Tho I am very willing to relieve him from every care in my power, yet I think it has too much the appearence of weilding instead of sharing the scepter." After their years apart, when Abigail had been forced to take care of all domestic and financial affairs, there seemed no reason to revert to the more conventional way of doing things. The one domestic detail that John did pay attention to was his sons' education. But buying land, finding tenants for their farms, and having the house repainted—all those things were best left to Abigail.

By the beginning of May, John Quincy began preparing to go home, while John and Abigail once more faced a decision about where they would live. The commercial treaties were almost completed, and they could contemplate going home the following spring. Abigail, homesick and tired of French society, wanted very badly to go home. But the question of the ambassadorship to London still loomed on the horizon. Abigail was no longer so strongly opposed to the prospect of being America's first official emissaries to Britain; now that she and John were reunited and she knew she could survive life in European society, the thought did not frighten her. But she worried about the cost of living in London, which was even more expensive than France, and about the hostility they might expect from their recent enemies.

Before she had much time to to dwell on whether or not they would remain in Europe, the word came from Congress that John had been appointed Minister Plenipotentiary to Great Britain. He would be the United States' first official diplomatic representative to its old mother country. Of course, there was never any question of his declining the assignment, so by mid-May it was not just John Quincy but the whole family who began preparing for a journey.

Despite her criticism of France and her feelings of being out of place there, Abigail felt sad as she left Auteuil, knowing she would probably never return. "I think I have somewhere met with the observation that nobody ever leaves Paris without a degree of tristeness," she told Jefferson. England would feel more familiar, and she would see many more Americans there, but she would miss her quiet country retreat, and she didn't expect to find any new companions so congenial as Jefferson. The letters that they later exchanged across the Channel were but a poor substitute for his constant companionship.

Even parting with the servants—the lazy wretches who had given Abigail such trouble—filled her with sadness. As the Adamses got into their carriage to leave Auteuil for the last time, the servants surrounded them to wave a tearful goodbye. At the last moment Abigail's little bird, distracted by the commotion, refused to stay in the carriage, so she gave it to Pauline, the adolescent girl who had been her hairdresser and personal maid. Then, with a last look at their garden, they left their rambling mansion behind.

Chapter 11

"The Ambassadress"

When Abigail, John and Nabby arrived in London it seemed as if everyone else in England was there too. It was the King's birthday, always a time of celebration; a new Parliamentary session had just opened; and a festival of music by Handel was under way. Accommodations were scarcely to be had at any price. The Adamses finally found lodgings at the Bath Hotel, where Abigail discovered to her dismay that four rooms cost more than their entire house at Auteuil. Located in Piccadilly, the hotel was much too "publick & noisy" for her taste, but until they could find a suitable house they had little choice.

Abigail instantly decided that she preferred England to France, just as she had expected. Aside from the noise, which took some getting used to after the suburban quiet of Auteuil, she found London a much grander and more prosperous city than Paris. Jefferson teased Abigail about her partiality for England, which, after all, had been America's mortal enemy only recently. "I consider your boasts of the splendour of your city . . . as a flout, and declaring that I would not give the polite, self-denying, goodhumoured people of this country . . . for ten such races of rich, proud, hectoring, swearing squibbing, carnivorous animals as those among whom you are," he told her. It became a recurrent half-serious, half-joking topic with them—a sign of their differences of temperament and a hint of the more serious differences that would later divide Jefferson from both Abigail and John. Although England had been an enemy and France a crucial ally, John had never trusted the French politically and had never been entirely comfortable with their culture. Abigail agreed. She felt much more at home in England, which shared with America a common language, religion, legal system, and many of the same customs.

After several days of house-hunting, Abigail and John rented a townhouse in Grosvenor Square, one of the newest and most fashionable sections in London. The house was not nearly so large as their mansion at Auteuil, but, with three floors of living quarters, a kitchen in the basement, and servants' rooms on the fourth floor, it had ample space for their small family. It overlooked the square, a five-acre plot of land laid out in formal walkways lined with trees and shrubs. The neighborhood was a popular residence for government officials and diplomats, including Lord North, the former British Prime Minister, who lived just across the square. The thought of having their former enemies for neighbors amused Abigail. "We have not taken *a side with* Lord North but are still *opposite* to him," she joked.

The cost of living in London was higher than in Paris, as Abigail had expected, and the frustrations of hiring servants were just as annoying. As in Paris, each servant had his or her own well-defined tasks and refused to do anything else. But the division of labor was not quite the same, so she had to learn an entirely new system. Her staff included a personal maid for Nabby and herself, who dressed their hair, took care of personal linen, and did some sewing; a butler, who directed all the servants, kept accounts, and took care of wine, table linen, dishes, and silver; a housemaid who cleaned and made beds; two footmen who stood behind their carriage, waited at table, and answered the door; a coachman; a cook; and a kitchen maid. The servants expected her to hire in addition a housekeeper, laundry maid, and a porter, but she absolutely refused. As it was, she remained convinced that three Americans could do the work of the eight servants she hired.

Once settled in their new home, the first order of business for the entire family was their official presentation to the King and Queen. It was the first of many official functions. In London they would all be expected to play a more public role than they had in France. Facing George III as representatives of the newly sovereign United States of America was a daunting prospect. John worked for days on a speech that would be both firm and conciliatory. He was carefully coached on the proper method of approaching the King, addressing him, and leaving his presence. To John's surprise, George turned out to be friendly and respectful, and the audience went off without incident.

Abigail and Nabby did not have to go through a private audience but had their introduction to court at one of the royal family's regular receptions or "drawing rooms." They chose their gowns with great care. Abigail was determined to retain as much of her American simplicity as possible while conforming to accepted fashions in court dress. She insisted to her dressmaker that she would have no "foil or tincel about me." Her gown was a relatively simple one of white silk trimmed with white crepe, lilac ribbon, and mock point lace, with a three-yard train. Her one concession to fashion was the skirt, which was arranged over a hoop of "enormous extent." Ruffled cuffs, a lace cap with two white plumes, a lace handkerchief, and two pearl pins for her hair completed her "rigging," as she called it.

She and Nabby spent the better part of a morning dressing for the afternoon reception, although Abigail snatched a few minutes to write Mary about all the preparations. "My Head is drest for St. James and in my opinion looks very tasty," she wrote while waiting for Nabby's hair to be arranged. Finally, with skirts carefully draped over their hoops and every curl in place, they stepped gingerly into their carriage to ride the few blocks to the palace. Their wide hoops barely cleared the narrow carriage doors, and the feathers in their hair brushed the ceiling. Abigail felt ridiculous but reminded herself that the ordeal would soon be over.

At the palace, they walked past lines of guards into the ornate building and were ushered into an enormous reception room. At least two hundred people crowded around the walls of the room in a vast, misshapen circle. After a few minutes' wait, the King, Queen, and Princesses entered and slowly made their way around the circle, shaking hands and making polite conversation with each guest in turn.

The whole process seemed interminable. She and Nabby waited four hours for their turn, meanwhile, like everyone else, ogling the others in the crowd and their finery. The King was surprisingly friendly to them. He politely asked Abigail if she had taken a walk that day. She resisted the urge to tell him that she had spent the entire morning dressing for his reception. The Queen, on the other hand, seemed embarrassed by their pres-

ence, and the Princesses were barely civil. Abigail noted criti-
cally that the King had a red face. Nor did she find the royal
women any more attractive. As for the ladies of the court, they
might boast high rank, but she found them "in general very
plain ill shaped and ugly."

When she finally got home, exhausted, Abigail reflected,
"What a fool do I look like to be thus accutored & stand here for
4 hours together, only for to be spoken to by 'royalty.'" But she
found the experience instructive nevertheless. She had had four
hours to observe the kind of people who frequented royal receptions and to measure herself against them. "I found the Court
like the rest of mankind mere Men & women & not of the most
personable kind neither; I had vanity enough to come a way
quite self satisfied," she confided to John Quincy. "I saw many
who were vastly richer drest . . . but I will venture to say that I
saw none neater or more elegant."

The whole experience carried her a long way toward over-
coming her shyness at being thrust into public life. It also made
an excellent tale for the friends and relatives back home. The
Cranch family had a good laugh when they relayed the story of
the court reception to another friend in Braintree, who declared
herself shocked at the bad manners of the King and Queen—to
keep people waiting four hours without asking them to sit down
or offering them food and drink!

The Adamses' presentation at court was only one of the
things that made their life in London very different. Abigail's
social life consumed much more of her time now than it had in
France, partly because they lived right in the city, partly because
there was no language barrier, but mostly because of John's position. As the official representatives of the United States in England, they were expected to receive and make official visits,
attend royal receptions regularly, and occasionally entertain
other members of the diplomatic corps. Worst of all, their lives
were constantly exposed to public scrutiny, even more than in
France, and public opinion in many quarters of England was still
hostile to Americans.

They had scarcely landed in London when attacks directed
against them began appearing in the press. This too was a new
experience. Here John was important enough to draw the fire of
anti-American newspapers. Some of his attackers were English,
but others were American expatriates who had fled to England

during the Revolution rather than fight for independence. "The Tory venom has begun to spit itself forth in the publick papers as I expected," Abigail wrote Mary, "bursting with envy that an American Minister should be received here with the same marks of attention politeness & civility which is shewn to the ministers of any other power." Indeed, the King and high-ranking government officials could hardly have been more polite. It was all the others, the nameless voices behind the newspaper articles, who made them feel unwelcome.

Knowing beforehand that they would be exposed to hostile attacks in the press did not make the nasty stories and snide comments any easier to take. Abigail was particularly upset at pundits who made fun of the rather austere financial circumstances of the American Minister. Diplomats were expected to live elegantly and entertain lavishly. Most of them were independently wealthy, with private fortunes to supplement generous salaries from their governments. The Adamses, however, were not wealthy and received a much smaller salary. Abigail had bemoaned the difficulty of living on a Minister's salary in France, but in London the higher cost of living and their official position made for a still greater strain.

It made not so much difference to Abigail that she herself could not live more lavishly or entertain more often; in fact she was living more extravagantly than she had ever dreamed she would. The implied insult to the United States was what bothered her. Being unable to conform to the expected standard of living for a public official made the United States look ridiculous. The impression presented to others was that their country didn't know enough or care enough about foreign affairs to support its Ministers adequately. "Let them use at home oeconomy where it is a virtue, but do not let them disgrace themselves abroad by narrowness," she argued.

It was customary for a newly-accredited Minister to give a dinner for the entire diplomatic corps. By the end of the summer the newspapers were making fun of the Adamses for their failure to meet this traditional obligation. Abigail worried that, if they gave such a dinner, they would be reduced to a meager standard of living for the rest of the year. In September they decided that the diplomatic dinner could be put off no longer, and fate helped them along a bit. Just days before the dinner, an American ship captain who was friendly with the Adamses arrived from the

West Indies with a "noble Turtle" as a present. At 114 pounds, it was more than adequate to make a fine turtle soup for the assembled company.

The negative remarks in the press did not stop after the Adamses fulfilled their social obligations to the diplomatic corps. In fact, they were to be a constant feature of their life in London. Abigail could take scant solace in the fact that the attacks generally were not directed at them personally but rather at their position as representatives of an upstart nation.

Her experience in London instilled in Abigail a distrust of the press that never left her and, if anything, heightened with time. Equally important, she became convinced that Congress was not adequately supporting them and that the situation would not change. Throughout John's later public career she harped on the inadequacy of his salary for his position.

In many ways Abigail's complaints were justified. The salaries of public officials in the early republic were indeed low, certainly compared to those of European officials, and the loose libel laws of the eighteenth century permitted newspapers to print just about anything they wanted to, true or not. But regardless of the reality of the situation, Abigail's conviction—shared by John—that they were underpaid and unfairly slandered fitted neatly into her belief that public service was at best a thankless job. For years they had suffered from long periods of separation while John served his country; now they suffered from the barbs of scurrilous newspaper editors and the contempt of hostile Britons. Never was John adequately rewarded for his services—not with money and not with praise from a grateful nation. But, for Abigail and John, putting up with this situation was just one more in the long series of sacrifices they had made in the name of public service. Given their determination not to allow the pleasures of living elegantly in London to corrupt their American simplicity, it was just as well that they had to endure some unpleasantness. The hostility they encountered helped them keep their distance from a way of life that otherwise could become all too attractive.

London, like Paris, was filled with amusements of every description, and Abigail, against her better judgment, went to see many of them during her first months in London. "The Learned pig dancing dogs, and the little Hare that Beats the drum, it is incredible what sums of money are nightly lavished upon these kinds of amusements, many of them fit only to please children," she wrote to her aunt, Lucy Tufts.

Londoners, like Parisians, had raised the pursuit of pleasure to a fine art. Vauxhall Gardens and Ranelagh, on the edges of the city, were enormous "pleasure gardens" with elaborately landscaped promenades where the fashionable could stroll in order to see and be seen in their most elegant clothes. Singers and actors provided entertainment for the patrons, or they might simply sit at a table, sip coffee or tea, and watch the crowds go by.

The theaters too were a never ending source of entertainment. They offered everything from Shakespeare to the latest raucous comedy, from Italian opera to musical variety shows. Most incredible of all to Abigail were the displays of tumbling and tightrope dancing. They were worth seeing at least once, she rationalized, as a demonstration of the agility of the human body. She was dismayed, however, to see that women as well as men engaged in such acrobatic feats as somersaults, cartwheels, and headstands. "All this is wonderfull for a man," she told Aunt Tufts, "but what will you say, when I assure you I have seen a most Beautifull girl perform the same feats! . . . why say you what could she do with her peticoats? It is true that she had a short silk skirt, but she was well clad under that, with draws, and so are all the female dancers upon the stage." But no effort at modesty could convince Abigail that women could engage in such activities without losing their femininity.

While she scorned the more frivolous entertainments, Abigail looked forward to serious theater with great expectations. When the famous actress Sarah Siddons made one of her rare appearances in September, Abigail was as excited as any London theatergoer. Tickets were hard to come by, but a well-placed bribe could secure box seats with little trouble. "It would be difficult to find the things in this Country which money will not purchase," she commented.

They went to see Mrs. Siddons in several of Shakespeare's plays including *Othello* and *Macbeth*. Long a devotee of Shakespeare, Abigail had never seen his plays performed. When she finally had her chance, she could not overcome her moral convictions enough to appreciate the plays themselves as works of art. Mrs. Siddons' performance as Lady Macbeth was unparalled, but she was too good a woman to be playing such an evil character,

Abigail thought. Worse yet was seeing her as Desdemona in *Othello*. "I lost much of the pleasure of the play," she told her sister Elizabeth, "from the sooty appearance of the Moor. Perhaps it may be early prejudice, but I could not seperate the affrican coulour from the man, nor prevent that disgust & horrour which filld my mind every time I saw him touch the gentle desdemona." In reading the play, of course, the "sooty appearance" could be imagined away.

In fact, Abigail was generally disillusioned with performances of Shakespeare's plays. Much of his langauge, she thought, "is so uncoath that it sounds very harsh. He has beauties which are not equald, but I should suppose they might be renderd much more agreeable for the stage by alterations." She had nothing but praise, however, for Mrs. Siddons's private character as well as her abilities as an actress. She was a woman of great virtue, married with five children. Luckily her brother was an actor too, and they often played opposite each other, "so that both her Husband, and the virtuous part of the audience can see them in the tenderest scenes without once fearing for their reputation." Mrs. Siddons escaped the fate of the French opera girls through her close attention to private virtue.

Despite her doubts about the moral character of anyone associated with the stage (Mrs. Siddons excepted), Abigail enjoyed the theater. She was also fascinated by the sights of the city, from the tightrope dancers to the Tower of London. The social life of which the Adamses were necessarily a part palled quickly, however, and the constant round of visits and parties became a chore rather than a pleasure. After her official presentation to the royal family, she would have preferred never again to set foot in the Palace of St. James's. In fact, she went only as often as etiquette demanded.

Diplomatic receptions were no more interesting. Gambling and card-playing, the favorite pastime at all such parties, seemed to Abigail a consummate waste of time, and she avoided them whenever she could. On one occasion, at a party given by the Swedish Ambassador, she not could avoid being trapped at a card table and, to her astonishment, won four games in a row. Another woman at the table, who had set the betting at a high half-guinea per round, got disgusted and left their table "to attack others, which she did at 3 other tables where she amply made up her loss." The gambling bothered her even more than the time wasted at cards—it seemed especially unfit for women. "But such a set of Gamblers as the Ladies here are!!" she wrote Mary. "& such a Life as they lead. good Heavens were reasonable Beings made for this?"

"Dissipation" was Abigail's favorite word for such time-wasting, unproductive amusements. It was an all-purpose term for any activity designed only to amuse without serious purpose. Mindless small talk, card-playing, gambling, frivolous comedies and stage shows—Europe abounded in such pastimes, and to her dismay the Europeans could absorb endless quantities without tiring of then. Surely this was one of the clearest examples of Old World corruption, and there were signs that it was encroaching upon American society too. Abigail was often torn between her belief that Americans were above European-style dissipation and her fear that it was only a matter of time before they would follow in the path of Europe.

Another thing that bothered her about London society was the dominance of the court and the royal family. Everyone, it seemed, vied for attention and favors at court. In the London social pecking order, upstart Americans came last, and Abigail discovered that many Americans in London tried to hide their nationality in order to avoid the snubs of people whose favor they wanted to gain. Both Abigail and John, hostile to royalty and the privileges of rank, flaunted their Americanness and refused to curry favor with people of rank. As she explained to Mary, "I know I am lookd down upon with a sovereign pride, and the smile of Royalty is bestowed as a mighty Boon. As such however I cannot receive it, you may be sure my countenance will never wear that suppliant appearence which begs for notice, consequently I never expect to be a Court favourite." The sort of social climbing that went on at court, like the "dissipation" so favored by wealthy Londoners, confirmed Abigail's convictions about the virtues of America.

London society did have its pleasures for the Adamses, however, for not all Englishmen kowtowed to royalty, and not all Americans were ashamed of their nationality. Unlike their situation in France, where they had felt socially isolated except for Jefferson's company, in London they found no shortage of new friends. They made warm friendships among that small group of Englishmen who had supported American independence and continued to work for reform in English government. Most of them were "dissenters" or members of congregations outside the Church of England, the spiritual descendants of the Puritans who had settled New England. Their religious views, as much as their political convictions, endeared them to the Adamses.

Richard Price, minister to a congregation just outside London, was one of the most prominent of these pro-American Englishmen. He became the Adamses' closest English friend. They attended his services nearly every Sunday—a welcome change from France, where the best option they had been able to find was to attend Dutch services, which had been too Calvinist for Abigail's taste. Price and other dissenters filled not only a spiritual gap but a social one as well. A simple dinner and conversation with these men was the closest approximation to those gatherings of family and friends back home that they missed so sorely in England. "I am . . . so old fashioned as to prefer the society of dr. price, dr. jebb, and a few others like them to the midnight Gamblers & the titled Gamesters," Abigail told Elizabeth.

She also got a chance to meet her old heroine, Catharine Macaulay. By then Mrs. Macaulay, long a widow, had scandalized London by marrying a man young enough to be her son. The marriage tarnished her image in Abigail's eyes but not enough to prevent her from inviting the couple to dinner when the opportunity arose. She was pleasantly surprised to find that the former Mrs. Macaulay, now Mrs. Graham, was more feminine than she had expected. As much as Abigail admired women who could succeed in a man's world, she expected them to lose some of their womanliness in the process. She could not quite overlook Mrs. Graham's ill-considered remarriage, however; Mr. Graham appeared even too young to be the husband of a woman half her age. But, she told Mary, there is "frailty in all humane characters."

Nabby's cynicism regarding London society and her lack of interest in the city's amusements more than matched Abigail's. Without her mother's official duties and household responsibilities, separated from her fiance and friends, she was often bored and unhappy. She chafed at the restraints that fashionable society placed on young ladies and quickly tired of the endless round of polite visits that were supposed to occupy her time. And Nabby had her own special reasons for being upset in the summer and fall of 1785. After several months abroad, letters from Royall Tyler came less and less frequently, with no explanation. Finally she began to wonder if he had forgotten her.

When John Quincy went home, Nabby instructed him to seek out Royall Tyler and learn the reasons for his silence, but even then she was thinking about breaking her engagement. After she reached London, she thought more and more seriously about it. The presence of the attractive Colonel William Smith, secretary to the American legation and a constant visitor at the Adams house, did nothing to change her mind. Colonel Smith was handsome, polite, attentive, and present; Royall Tyler was far away and indifferent.

William Smith fell in love with Nabby almost as soon as he met her. Ever perceptive, Abigail sensed his interest and took it upon herself to warn Smith that Nabby was already attached. She would have liked nothing better than to see Nabby break off with Royall Tyler and become engaged to Smith, who was fast becoming a favorite with all the family; but it would not do for Nabby to appear to end her engagement merely because someone more attractive happened on the scene. The engagement to Tyler had to end independently, because of his faithlessness. Then, after a suitable interval, a romance with Smith might be encouraged.

John and Abigail decided that William would be relieved of his duties for several weeks and sent to Prussia to observe military demonstrations there. It seemed an appropriate task for a gentleman of military background—Smith had been George Washington's aide-de-damp during the Revolution—and would get him out of way and absolved of any complicity while the engagement with Tyler was concluded.

Smith left London in August with Abigail's blessings. "Time I dare say will extricate those I love from any unapproved step into which inexperience & youth may have involved them," she wrote him, "but untill that period may arrive Honour, Honour, is at stake—a word to the wise is sufficient." Smith took the hint and wrote only official dispatches and innocuous travelogues addressed to the family.

Meanwhile, in August, Nabby finally made the break with Tyler. With great deliberation, she told him that she did not

wish to see him again and returned his letters and the miniature
he had given her on her departure for Europe. She wanted it to be
over quickly, with no discussion; she asked that friends and
members of the family never mention Tyler to her again.

Abigail, however, wanted to know exactly what people at
home said about the broken engagement. She was afraid their
friends would accuse Nabby of fickleness, she told Mary, and
wanted to make it very clear that Tyler had brought his troubles
on himself. In fact, everyone at home commended Nabby for
having the courage to end what was clearly an unhappy affair.
Tyler's behavior had become more and more erratic after she
left. He kept letters written by the Adamses to other people and
sent to him for delivery; he spent less and less time at the Cranches', appearing only to eat and sleep; and when Nabby's final
letter arrived, he responded by wearing her miniature promi-
nently around his neck and declaring that he would take the
next ship to England to try to clear up their misunderstanding.

William, meanwhile, stayed in Europe long past the conclusion of the Prussian military demonstrations. He traveled extensively, stopping in Paris to visit Jefferson. In November he had
still not returned to London, and no letters had been received
from him in weeks. As work piled up, John pressed Nabby into
service as his secretary.

William's long absence and his silence distressed Nabby and
exasperated John. When he finally returned the first week in December, however, he exercised all his charm on the Adams family and was back in their good graces in short order. He also lost
no time in making his attentions to Nabby official. At the end of
December he asked Abigail's permission to marry Nabby. It was,
of course, customary to ask the father rather than the mother for
a daughter's hand, and Smith acknowledged as much; but he felt
timid about approaching John. He wanted to be sure of Abigail's
support first.

By February William and Nabby were officially engaged. Abigail thought their actions a bit hasty but observed philosophically, paraphrasing Shakespeare, that "a Heart agitated with the
remains of a former passion is most susceptable of a new one."
They set a June wedding date.

As pleased as she was with the match, Abigail could not
banish anxiety as the wedding date approached. Nabby, her oldest child and the first to marry, was also her only daughter. For

the first time she had to face the prospect of seeing her children leave home permanently. Somehow it was harder to part with Nabby than it was to see John Quincy sail to Europe or to leave Charles and Thomas behind in America studying for college. Perhaps it was because she was the only daughter; but perhaps it was also because Nabby would be starting her own family and separating herself from Abigail more conclusively than the boys did when they were away at school.

By now all three boys were at Harvard. John Quincy had entered with advanced standing in April, joining Charles, who was then in his second year. Tommy entered just after commencement in July; John Shaw and Cotton Tufts had debated whether he should wait another year before starting college. But neither Abigail nor John wanted him held back if he was intellectually ready for college.

John Quincy had found it difficult to settle down to the life of a student after his years in Europe. He didn't think much of his fellow students—"a confused medley of good, bad, and indifferent"—or of the faculty. The tutors, he told his mother, were too young and inexperienced for their positions. Abigail responded by cautioning him against a tendency to be overly critical. She urged him to be careful that his knowledge and his experience of the world didn't make him "assumeing, and too tenacious of your own opinions," and reminded him that his teachers were to be respected regardless of his private opinion of their qualifications. And if he thought he had greater knowledge than his peers, she admonished, "reflect that you have had greater opportunities of seeing the world . . . that you have never wanted a Book, but that it has been supplied you, that your whole time has been spent in the company of men of Literature & science. How unpardonable would it have been in you, to have been a Blockhead."

It was a substantial relief, of course, that Elizabeth and Mary, her two sisters, were near the boys in Massachusetts, for she had confidence in her sisters' care. Their reports eased her worries. Elizabeth assured her, for instance, that John Quincy had thrown himself into his studies with single-minded determination: "Indeed he searches out knowledge as if it was his Meat, & Drink, & considered it as more precious than choice Gold." As to Charles, he was quite different. He was the most socially accomplished, "the favorite of the *Muses*, & the

Graces—as well as of the Ladies—." Tommy was the solid, practical one. In him his aunt saw "a more martial, & intrepid spirit.
A fine natural Capacity, & love of Business, & an excellent faculty in despatching it."

Mary's reports to Abigail agreed closely with Elizabeth's.
John Quincy studied so hard that Mary was afraid he would ruin
his health. She asked Cotton Tufts to talk to him about the need
for exercise and a bit of diversion. Charles, she observed, was
really *too* handsome. He would soon steal the heart of every girl
he met.

Now that the boys were in college, Mary took over from
Elizabeth the role of surrogate mother. She lived much closer to
Cambridge, and her own son Billy was also at Harvard. All four
boys spent their vacations at the Cranch home. Mary, with the
help of her two daughters, made and mended their clothes and
saw that they were properly provisioned when they returned to
Cambridge. Abigail often sent fabric from London for her sons'
clothes, but Mary was also adept at cutting down the outgrown
jackets and breeches of one boy for the next in line.

Abigail paid her sisters for her sons' room and board, but she
understood that no price could be placed on the love and care
that the boys received from their aunts. Far away and unable to
reciprocate by helping out with family cares, she tried to show
her appreciation by sending presents—little luxuries that she
knew her sisters and nieces could not buy in Boston and couldn't
afford even if they could find them. Silk for dresses, the latest
fashionable sandals, bonnets, and ribbons crossed the Atlantic to
brighten the wardrobes of the Cranch and Shaw women. Mary
Cranch, who had some notion of what such things cost, felt herself forever in Abigail's debt, but Abigail knew that no amount
of largess could repay her sisters for their attention to her children.

Chapter 12

A Homesick American

As the novelty of London began to wear off, Abigail's thoughts often turned to home. She missed the boys, her sisters, and all her friends and relatives. She also felt cut off from political events as the thirteen independent states struggled to form themselves into a nation. So starved was she for news of home that she invited every American ship captain in port to dinner, whether she knew him or not. Some of them were bashful about dining with the American Ambassador in his grand townhouse on Grosvenor Square, but Abigail was insistent. She pumped every one of them for the latest information about the United States.

In the autumn of 1786 the news from home was disturbing. The United States was in the grip of a depression, commerce was at a standstill, bankruptcies were on the rise, and farmers were losing their land through foreclosure. Congress seemed incapable of doing anything to relieve the problems, mostly because the states fought among themselves about what ought to be done. The nation desperately needed to raise revenue and adopt uniform measures for regulating commerce, but the states were so jealous of their own powers that they would not delegate any authority to Congress, which appeared to be on the verge of collapse.

Worst of all was the news from Massachusetts. Disgruntled

farmers in the western part of the state, deeply in debt and in danger of losing their land through foreclosure, had banded together to close down the courts by force. Reports indicated that the rebellion was spreading throughout the western part of the state and that hundreds—if not thousands—of men were up in arms, protesting the currency shortages and economic depression that threatened their livelihoods.

Shays Rebellion, so named for its leader, Daniel Shays, began in Northampton when several dozen farmers armed with muskets barricaded the entrance to the Hampshire County Court House. They demanded a moratorium on suits for debt and a temporary halt to all court sessions so that no more farmers would lose their land until the state's economic situation improved. Their petitions for relief had fallen on deaf ears; now, using tactics reminiscent of the Revolutionary mobs of the 1760s, they took matters into their own hands and forced the courts to halt.

Abigail was horrified that Americans, so lately released from war with Britain, would now turn against each other. "For what have we been contending against the tyranny of Britain," she asked, "to become the sacrifice of a lawless Banditti? . . . Will my countrymen, justify the maxim of tyrants, that mankind are not made for freedom?" Mobs and conventions had been justified when used against British oppression, but now, used against a new government struggling to gain stability, to Abigail they smacked of treason.

Abigail's reaction to Shays Rebellion and to the problems of the United States in general was one of the first signs of her transformation from a revolutionary to a conservative upholder of order and stability. Her interpretation of the American Revolution was very limited: Americans had fought to throw off British tyranny and nothing more. Now they should unite in forming a strong government, elect good men to office, and let them run the country. She did not believe that any change in the basic structure of American society was necessary; on the contrary, she feared any such change as destructive of order. And she was shocked at the suggestion that political change might be a continuing process.

In a letter to Thomas Jefferson about Shays Rebellion she described the rebels as "Ignorant, wrestless desperadoes, without conscience or principals" who "have led a deluded multitude to follow their standard, under pretence of grievances which had no existence but in their immaginations." She was horrified when Jefferson replied that he hoped the captured rebels would be pardoned. "The spirit of resistance to government is so valuable on certain occasions, that I wish it to be always kept alive," he told her. "It will often be exercised when wrong, but better so than not to be exercised at all. I like a little rebellion now and then. It is like a storm in the Atmosphere." She was so upset at Jefferson's attitude that she could not bring herself to write to him again for months.

For the first time since the early days of resistance to Britain, Abigail had to face the fact that not all Americans agreed with her on the direction the country ought to take. She had always believed that there was only one right path to follow in politics and that people who took opposing views were either misguided or corrupt. It was easy to feel that way when the enemy was clearly defined. The Americans who had sided with Britain during the Revolution were either corrupted by Crown patronage or too timid to face the prospect of war. But how could she explain the heresy of a man like Thomas Jefferson, a brilliant statesman, author of the Declaration of Independence, a man who had supported the Revolution against Britain as ardently as she had? In the years to come she would discover that many other former allies disagreed with her on basic political issues. She had no way of explaining their behavior, so she persisted in thinking that they were deluded, although she granted that men like Jefferson had the best of intentions.

Abigail's political conservatism was not entirely new, although it was influenced by her years in Europe. She, like John, was of conservative temperament and had always viewed the Revolution as a political rebellion only. She believed that society was inevitably hierarchical and that distinctions of social class were essential to order and stability—even though she objected to the rigidity of those distinctions in European countries. "A *levelling* principal," she believed, was "very unfavourable to the existance of civil Liberty." She thought that only men of property and talent should hold positions in government and that once elected, they should be allowed to rule with a minimum of popular interference.

Abigail had showed signs of this social conservatism long before she ever went to Europe, but her years there intensified it.

She became even more conscious of social distinctions and of the power of tradition in maintaining social and political stability. Even more important, she lost touch with events in America, despite her strenuous efforts to keep informed, while being constantly bombarded by English skepticism about the future of the American experiment. She was influenced, in spite of herself, by European perceptions of the United States and came to look at American problems through European eyes.

She understood little about the economic depression that plagued America, for example. She constantly heard the complaints of London merchants who had extended credit to American merchants and were unable to collect. The Londoners, in a mad rush to reopen trade with the United States after the war, had shipped enormous quantities of goods to American ports and had extended generous—too generous—terms of credit to American merchants. The Americans, equally eager to restore their damaged businesses, accepted the terms. The imports glutted American markets; the merchants were unable to sell them and consequently were unable to pay their creditors.

To make matters worse, the British refused to allow Americans to trade with the colonies in the West Indies, a trade that had always been the mainstay of American commerce. They also levied heavy taxes on many American goods, making them prohibitively expensive in British markets. These two policies effectively destroyed American merchants' capacity to pay for British imports with products of their own. They had to pay cash instead, and cash was exceedingly scarce. Currency exported to pay for British goods only compounded a general shortage of money, which hurt everyone—farmers as well as merchants.

Abigail knew about the British commercial policies, because John was trying, unsuccessfully, to negotiate a commercial treaty that would end them. But she did not connect them with the economic distress that afflicted so many Americans. Instead, she blamed the Americans themselves. By importing such quantities of English goods, they had moved away from the habits of self-sufficiency and frugality that they had learned during the war.

The rebels in Massachusetts were not, in her view, victims of economic circumstances but people who had grown rich during the war and now refused to pay their debts. "The lower class of people who can least bear wealth grew indolent & overbearing. They could live easier upon less labour & in reality they felt little of the publick burden," she observed. "Now they are oblig'd to labour more gain less & pay more, they are exclaiming on all hands & foolishly think that the fault lies with their rulers." They had cast off their old habits of frugality and tried to rise above their social position as well—a double sin. Abigail's analysis of the rebels' motivation showed a complete lack of understanding not only of current economic conditions in Massachusetts but also of the economic troubles of the war years. She was also influenced by the belief, widespread in England, that the United States would never survive as a nation. The present situation in America, viewed from her perspective, seemed to justify British beliefs. Americans were so divided among themselves that they could not begin to defend themselves as a nation; Shays Rebellion was only the worst example of their internal dissension. Abigail began to wish more and more that she were at home and able to see for herself the troubles of her country.

By the end of 1786 brighter news filtered across the Atlantic. As awareness of the need to strengthen the faltering American government grew, a national convention was organized to discuss revising the Articles of Confederation—or perhaps even to write an entirely new constitution. John had clear ideas on the sort of government needed, and merely patching up the Articles would not be good enough. The convention ought to write a constitution that would provide for a much stronger federal government, one that would have clear authority over and above any state government and would be headed by a strong executive—a provision that was sadly lacking in the Confederation government. Unable to be part of the convention, he did the next best thing; he pushed aside all other business and set to work writing a definitive treatise on the nature of government. It turned into a massive project. He bought every book he could get his hands on about European governments and attempted a comparison and analysis of them all. He wrote hastily, feeling an urgent sense of the importance of his work; he wanted copies of his book to be in the hands of the delegates when they met in Philadelphia in May.

The result was his *Defense of Constitutions*, published in London early in 1787 and quickly reprinted in the United States. It was one of John's most famous works, and also one of his least popular. Abigail, who agreed with his theories, warned him that he would be accused of advocating monarchy. John thought not; but she turned out to be right.

John was working so single-mindedly on his book around Christmas that Abigail decided to take a trip and see some of the English countryside. She, Nabby, William, and a group of Americans living in London went to Bath to take in some of the festivities of the winter season.

This beautiful town, site of ancient Roman baths and showplace of Georgian architecture, was a fashionable spa for London's wealthy, who went in droves to Bath in the winter. "I spent a fortnight in Amusement & dissipation," she wrote Mary—and she enjoyed herself thoroughly despite her usual negative reactions to such wasteful play.

Abigail and John wrote to each other nearly every day. She worried about his health in the damp London cold, but he urged her to enjoy herself and not worry about him. If extra blankets didn't keep him warm at night, he would take a "Virgin" to bed with him. "Ay a Virgin," he teased, explaining that he had in mind a stone bottle filled with hot water placed between the sheets to warm a bed, popularly referred to by that term. "An old Man you see may comfort himself with such a Virgin, . . . and not give the least Jealousy even to his Wife." Abigail replied that although she missed her "bedfellow," she would not resort to an "Abbe." 'You recollect in France that they are so polite to the Ladies as to accomodate them with an *Abbe*," she teased, "when they give the gentleman a Nun."

Abigail enjoyed her trip but was happy to return to London and her own home. The trip made her reflect on the different kinds of pleasures in life and on their meaning. On many occasions during her years in Europe she railed against "dissipation," or pleasure for pleasure's sake, until it became a litany repeated almost too often to be believed. She began to sound like the prim Puritan who found any sort of pleasure sinful. But her views were more complicated than that, and nowhere were they more clearly expressed than in her long letter to Mary describing the fashionable life at Bath.

"To derive a proper improvement from company," she wrote, "it ought to be select, & to consist of persons respectable both for their Morals, and their understandings." But unfortunately, "such is the prevailing taste, that provided you can be in a crowd, with here & there a Glittering star, it is considerd of little importance what the Character of the person is, who wears it." Too many people failed to realize that they must look for happiness "in their own Hearts," not in outside amusements.

Her experiences at Bath moved her to ask, "What is the Chief end of Man?" Every "rational Being," she believed, must have some purpose in life beyond mere pleasure for pleasure's sake. "Enjoyments without settled principals, laudable purposes, mental exertions and internal comfort" were meaningless; "and how are these to be acquired in the hurry & tumult of the world? My visit to Bath and the scenes which I mixed in, instead of exciting a gayety of disposition, led me to a train of moral reflections."

If the gay crowd at Bath, the fashionable court in London, and the pleasure-seeking French had inner values and a sense of purpose in life, she did not see it—but then, she was not really looking very hard. Abigail never probed deeply into the minds and souls of the people she met in Europe. She was a keen observer of the external characteristics of her surroundings: buildings, monuments, trees, flowers, dress, even behavior; but she had little comprehension of people's beliefs or motivations. The external qualities of life in Europe were so different from what she had been used to in America that she reacted quickly and negatively, fitting her observations into preconceived notions of Old World decadence. In her continuing criticism of European life, she also tried to convince herself that she remained uncorrupted by her surroundings—that she would return to America unspoiled by the luxury and pleasures of Europe.

Back in London Abigail was caught up in yet more "dissipation." The Queen's birthday celebration was coming up, an annual gala that Abigail detested as a "prodigious expence from which I derive neither pleasure or satisfaction." She had more serious things on her mind, too—reading over John's book before it went to the printers, sorting through the welcome accounts that Shays Rebellion had been crushed, and planning for new family responsibilities.

Nabby gave birth in late April to a son, christened William after his father. Abigail teased her sister Elizabeth about being a great-aunt: "you may put up with that since your sister is forced to with the Epithet of Grandmama." Soon after the birth of his son, William Smith left London on an assignment to Portugal, and Nabby and the baby stayed with her parents. At forty-three, Abigail might not have felt old enough to be a "grandmama," but in fact she loved her new role, and having Nabby and little William with her was a welcome diversion. It was fortunate that Nabby had a good nurse to help care for her and the baby, because Abigail was sick during much of the early spring. She was less upset by her illness than by the fact that it forced her to miss most of a series of scientific lectures to which she had subscribed. She was especially disappointed because it was a rare opportunity for her to learn about a subject usually closed to women.

In her disappointment, she pondered one of her favorite subjects, the narrow scope of women's education. "The study of the Household" might be the most appropriate subject for women, but why, she asked, shouldn't they study more intellectual subjects as well? "Surely as Rational beings their reason may properly receive the highest possible cultivation," she wrote to her young niece Lucy Cranch. "Knowledge will teach candour & she who aims at the attainment of it will find her countenance improved as her mind is informed & her looks enobled as her Heart is elevated, & thus may she become a pleasing companion to the man of science & of sensibility, enabled to form the minds of her children to virtue & to knowledge & not less capable or willing to superintend the domestick oeconomy of her family for having wanderd beyond the limits of the dressing room & the kitchen."

In fact, education for women in America was vastly improved after the Revolution, justified by some of the same arguments that Abigail expounded in her letter to Lucy—arguments that better education, far from destroying women's femininity or threatening family harmony, would make them better wives and mothers. Abigail, however, went a step farther. Women's minds were just as capable of absorbing knowledge as men's, she believed, and they too had a right to be educated.

In June she added another child to her family for a few days. Thomas Jefferson's younger daughter, Polly, arrived in London en route to join her father in Paris. She had had a long, tiring, and bewildering voyage from Virginia, accompanied only by her maid, a slave named Sally Hemings, herself only fifteen or sixteen.

While Abigail looked after Polly Jefferson in London, her sister Mary was busy preparing for John Quincy's commencement in Massachusetts. The Harvard commencement was the most festive occasion of the year around Boston. Graduates provided food and drink for their friends and relatives, and Mary, whose son was also graduating, began planning and consulting Abigail months ahead of time. For Commencement Day Mary cooked two shoulders of beef, four hams, and six tongues, and baked biscuits enough for an army and a cake that required 28 pounds of flour. Richard Cranch had portable tables constructed. They carried the tables, the food, and gallons of cider and wine by wagon to Cambridge.

After the festivities John Quincy went home with the Cranches to relax for a few weeks before traveling to Newburyport where he would study law with Theophilus Parsons. There had never been any question that John Quincy would follow his father into the legal profession. John and Abigail had never expressed any doubts about the matter, nor had John Quincy himself.

By the summer of 1787 John decided that he did not want to stay in Europe any longer. His commission as Minister to England would expire the following spring, and he wrote to Congress asking that it not be renewed. A year earlier, when John had talked of going home, Nabby made light of it: "My Pappa has talkd of the next Spring for his return every season since I have been in Europe." But this time he meant it. He and Abigail would leave London in the spring of 1788.

Just about the time that John began to think seriously about going home, Cotton Tufts wrote saying that a large house and farm in Braintree had come up for sale. Abigail had been in the house many years before and remembered it as an elegant, spacious home. Both she and John instructed Tufts to buy it for them. They would certainly need a bigger home, Abigail told him, if only to house the books John had acquired in Europe.

In September Tufts wrote back to say that he had succeeded in purchasing the house and farm for them. Abigail immediately began to make plans to redecorate the house to suit their tastes. She sent off instructions to Tufts to have the rooms painted and papered to go with the furniture they would be bringing back from Europe. They would want to add a room to accommodate

John's library, but that would have to wait a while; at the moment they couldn't afford it. Abigail remembered too well how unsettled she had felt in Paris and London, living in lodgings, looking for houses, and waiting for them to be ready. When they went home, she wanted to move into her own house immediately.

In July and August, while they were making their initial plans to go home, they also decided to take a trip through western England. With Nabby and little William, they spent a month visiting cathedrals, villages, seaside resorts, and castles.

One of the first stops was Winchester, where the Adamses attended services at the famous cathedral. Abigail noted caustically that she was "much more entertained with the venerable and Majestic appearence of the Ancient pile, than with the modern flimsy discourse of the preacher." In Winchester she also did a little investigating of her family tree. The first Earl of Winchester had been the Saar de Quincy, a signer of Magna Carta. She remembered that her grandfather had once showed her a parchment document tracing the family tree back to William the Conqueror, and her trip to Winchester inspired her to write Mary asking her to find out who had the parchment now.

"You will smile at my zeal," she said, "but can it be wonderd at, that I should wish to Trace an Ancestor amongst the signers of Magna Carta." She had another motive too. Americans cared so little about genealogy that they rarely bothered tracing their families beyond the generation that emigrated to the colonies; and so the English "twit us of being descended from the refuse of their Goals and from transported convicts." Sensitive to English slights and increasingly aware of the importance attached to ancestry in Europe, she would prove that her ancestry, at least, was unimpeachable.

From Winchester they went on to Southampton, a popular seaside resort. Abigail, who had lived practically within sight of the ocean all her life, had never been swimming in it. Beach resorts did not exist in America. Determined not to miss anything, she went to one of the beachfront dressing rooms, where she was given an ankle-length flannel gown, socks, and an oil-cloth cap—what the well-dressed lady wore for bathing in 1787. She was delighted by the "experiment" and wrote enthusiastically to Mary that such bathing places should be established at Boston, Braintree, and Weymouth. Later, however, after seeing several more resorts, she began to put them in the same class with all the other English amusements of which she disapproved. The "rage" for watering places was turning into a "national evil as it promotes and encourages dissipation, mixes all characters promiscuously, is the resort of the most unprincipald female characters."

From Southampton they passed through Dorchester, which Abigail thought looked very much like Dorchester, Massachusetts. Then they went a few miles out of their way to visit Weymouth, for which her home town had been named.

Here, and throughout her trip, Abigail was appalled by the evidence of poverty and extreme social stratification that she saw around her. A widow owned the entire town of Weymouth, and all its residents were tenant farmers. The thought that so much land was owned by so few people and that so many ordinary people could never hope to own their own land seemed to her the most damning characteristic of the Old World. "Thus is the landed property of this Country vested in Lordships, and in the Hands of the Rich altogether," she wrote. "The peasantry are but slaves to the Lord, notwithstanding the mighty boast they make of Liberty." It was the existence of poverty in the midst of plenty that upset her most. "Poverty hunger & nakedness is the lot & portion of the needy peasantry," she told Elizabeth, ". . . their mud cottages, & misierable Huts astonish'd me, & yet to look around them, . . . plenty smild on every side, but not an inch of land for them."

Her travels made her feel grateful that she had been born an American. She praised "the ease with which property is obtained, the plenty which is so equally distributed," ignoring the poverty that did exist in America, the wretchedness of some of the Massachusetts farmers who had rebelled the year before, and even her own observations about lower orders of people. Neither law nor the prerogatives of a hereditary aristocracy prevented Americans from buying land; the fact that poverty did, especially in the postwar years, seemed unimportant to her. Nor did she understand the reasons for the poverty she witnessed in England. She blamed moral vices that weakened the whole society and worried that Americans were heading in the same direction. "Deprecate that restless spirit," she urged, "and that banefull pride ambition and thirst for power which will finally make us as wretched as our Neighbours."

Throughout the fall and winter Abigail thought mostly about going home. They would not leave until March, but innumerable preparations had to be made. She sent off her instructions to Cotton Tufts about fixing up the house, began to think about which furniture to take and which to leave behind, and made inquiries about ships to America. By January she had struck a bargain with John Callahan, a Boston ship captain with whom she had been long acquainted, on the terms of their passage.

Sometimes they speculated about what John would do when they got back home. Important political changes were taking place. A new constitution had been written and would soon be ratified. Already there was talk, both at home and in London, about what role John Adams might play in the new government. Rumor had it that he would be Vice President. Abigail assured Cotton Tufts, however, that John was returning to America as a "private man." No one need fear him as a competitor for office; his independent views over the years had made him far too unpopular to win high public position.

Toward the end of their stay, to escape the frenzy of packing, Abigail moved into a hotel. Nabby and William were also getting ready to leave; they would sail shortly after her parents in a ship bound for New York. These were hard days for Abigail, for on top of the pressure of getting ready to leave, she was going to have to say goodbye to Nabby, William, and her adored little grandson. This younger generation was going to live in New York, William's home, and so the time of daily visits between mother and daughter was nearly at an end.

On March 30 John and Abigail finally left London for Portsmouth, where they expected to board their ship. Unfortunately, they arrived ahead of the ship, which had been delayed by adverse winds. After a week they received word from Captain Callahan that they would sail instead from Cowes. They hired chaises, went to Cowes, and put up at a pleasant inn with a view of the harbor. For a day or two Abigail enjoyed the lovely view from their hotel, but she quickly became bored. She read all the books and finished all the sewing she had brought to occupy herself until the ship sailed; she went for walks; she visited nearby Carisbrook Castle. Finally, on April 20, their ship sailed, only to be blown into another port to escape a storm. There they sat another week. It was the beginning of May before they were out of sight of England.

Abigail felt no regrets at leaving Europe. She told Jefferson, "I have lived long enough, and seen enough of the world, to check expectations, and to bring my mind to my circumstances, and retiring to our own little farm feeding my poultry and improveing my garden has more charms for my fancy, than residing at the court of Saint James's where I seldom meet with characters so inofensive as my Hens and chickings, or minds so well improved as my garden." She felt that the past four years had not been her happiest. "Tis Domestick happiness and Rural felicity in the Bosom of my Native land, that has charms for me. Yet I do not regret that I made this excursion since it has only more attached me to America."

Chapter 13

The Vice President's Lady

The voyage home was long but uneventful. To her great relief, Abigail suffered very little from seasickness. Her feelings now were very different from the ones she had had on her first sea voyage. This time she set out with few apprehensions about the future but instead with joy at the prospect of being home again after four long years away.

She left Europe feeling confident that her years there had not changed her at all. "Believe me I am not in the least alterd," she wrote Mary, "except that I wear my Hair drest and powderd, and am two years older, & somewhat fatter which you may be sure is no addition to my looks, but the Heart and mind are the same." Reflecting on the riches, the power, and the ceremony she had seen in Europe, she declared that none of that had changed her preference for the simplicity of America: "I feel that I can return to my little cottage and be happier than here," she observed. Being an Ambassador's wife, moving in royal social circles, living in an elegant house with a large staff of servants—she would give up all that with pleasure to become an ordinary citizen again.

Abigail and John reached Boston at the beginning of July. At the wharf crowds of well-wishers greeted them, and John Hancock, now Governor of the state, met them with his carriage.

They stayed for several days at the Hancock mansion on the edge of Beacon Hill, where they were lavishly entertained as befitted a returning Ambassador. Tommy and Charley came down from Haverhill, and John Quincy from Newburyport, for a joyful reunion with their parents. Letters from New York reported Nabby's safe arrival there.

The pomp and ceremony of their reception was flattering indeed, but it made Abigail and John feel a bit uneasy. They had not expected to be feted so enthusiastically, and both were impatient to get home to Braintree and pick up the threads of their old life. When they discovered that Hancock intended to escort them home in his coach-and-four and that the citizens of Braintree planned to march part of the way to Boston to meet them, they were dismayed. To avoid such an embarassingly unrepublican spectacle, John borrowed a horse and rode home unannounced. Abigail and the children followed a day or two later. They planned to stay with John's brother Peter until their furniture's arrival from London.

Despite Abigail's many instructions of the previous months, the new house was not even close to being ready. The "Garden was a wilderness & the House a mere Barrack," she complained to Nabby, and for the first several weeks they shared it with a "swarm" of carpenters and masons until Abigail almost regretted the day they had ever decided to buy a larger house. To make matters worse, their furniture, shipped from London at such effort and expense, arrived damaged.

It was not only the condition of the house that discouraged Abigail. From London she had remembered the forty-year-old house as elegant and spacious, and indeed, compared to their old cottage, it was. But its seven rooms seemed cramped after the mansion at Auteuil and the townhouse in London. For all her talk about longing for her humble cottage in Braintree, Abigail's expectations had been raised by her years in Europe. By New England standards, the new house was no humble cottage but a substantial home, much larger than most. Abigail, however, confessed to Nabby that "in height and breadth, it feels like a wren's house." If she and William visited, Nabby should take care not to wear any feathers in her hat and William shouldn't wear shoes with heels, or else they wouldn't be able to stand up straight.

Without being fully aware of it, Abigail had changed. She

did not come home putting on airs, something she feared people would accuse her of doing; but in more subtle ways she had changed markedly. Her friends, her family, a sense of domestic tranquility were just as precious as ever, but no matter how much she might talk about the virtues of a simple life, four years of luxury were not easily forgotten. She set about converting their "wren's house" into an impressive home, doubling its size during the next few years, and furnishing it with fine pieces bought in Europe.

The years in Europe also helped change her attitude about John's political career. During the war she had spent many years alone, wishing that John would forsake politics and return to his law practice. She went to Europe wishing that she could have persuaded him to come home instead. Both she and John had always pretended that his political career was temporary and would end when the crisis of the Revolution passed. By now, however, it was obvious that John was in politics to stay; the only question was what his next role would be. Abigail, after four years of living with him in the political limelight, accepted this fact.

Abigail had always enjoyed political debate. What she hated was not politics itself but the disruption to her family life caused by John's involvement in politics. After four years together, she could take a much more positive view of his career and enjoy her own involvement in political activity. Over the next few years she would continue to dislike the traveling, the time away from her children and her home, and the frivolous socializing that were inevitably part of a politician's life. But as long as she and John were together—and she was part of his political career, rather than excluded from it—she enjoyed being a politician's wife.

In early 1788 John's future political position remained unclear. He had been away from home, and from all the domestic political debates and factions, for ten years. One thing was certain: Everyone expected him to play a prominent role in the new government, and no one believed his mumblings about retiring from politics. The first elections for President and Vice President were scheduled for November. The Presidency was clearly beyond John's grasp, because everyone expected George Washington to fill the top position, but many political observers believed John had a good chance for the Vice Presidency. John wanted the job but complained as usual that his talents would not be recognized and that his unpopularity would keep him out of office.

Through the late summer and early fall, Abigail and John worked to get their house and farm in order. Relishing the quiet of Braintree after his years in Europe, John named their new home "Peacefield." Abigail unpacked the furniture and had the damaged items repaired. She supervised the workmen who painted and papered the walls. One small room completely paneled in mahogany seemed too dark, so she had it whitewashed. John had fences built and bought quantities of livestock. Because they had no barn, Abigail wondered exactly where to put the animals. John assiduously avoided speculating about the coming elections, although reports came in from friends around the country assessing his chances for collecting votes in their states.

As the elections drew near, Abigail became the principal source of political information in the household. Early in November she went to New York to be with Nabby, who was expecting her second child. As the nation's capital, New York was the center for political gossip. John decided not to accompany her, mostly because his exaggerated sense of propriety dictated that he stay out of the political limelight while the election was being decided. It would not do to look too eager for office.

Abigail arrived too late to help Nabby during her labor and delivery—baby John was born several days before her arrival—but in plenty of time to observe the political scene. "I suppose you will tell me I have no Buisness" with politics, she wrote John; "I design to be vastly prudent I assure you hear all & say little!"

The November election was only the first stage in the long, complicated process of choosing a President and Vice President, however. Voters at that time chose only their representatives to Congress and a group of electors, who met later to select the chief executives. Electors were pledged to specific candidates but were not bound by those pledges; so the choice of the President and Vice President would not be definite until the electors met in February. And in fact it was the end of March before they learned for sure that John had been elected Vice President to serve with George Washington. The news was hardly a surprise; for all his complaints about being unappreciated, John knew that he was the favorite for the office. And despite his continued ambivalence about political life, he was pleased to be chosen. Abigail was also pleased, even though his election meant, for her, another difficult move and adjustment to yet another city. Once again she would be torn from her family and friends, only months after being reunited with them.

John left almost immediately for New York, for it was imperative that the new government begin functioning immediately to establish its legitimacy. Abigail stayed behind, because the living arrangements and even the salaries of the newly elected executive officials still had not been established. When he arrived in New York, John found that Congress did not plan to make any specific housing arrangements for the chief executives but rather expected them to provide for themselves out of their salaries—which had not yet been determined.

House-hunting proved to be enormously difficult and time-consuming, and John quickly decided that he needed Abigail in New York immediately. It was obvious that they would be unable to rent a furnished house, so he told her to bring tables, linen, silverware, and beds. She could send them by cart to Providence and from there by ship to New York.

Abigail, meanwhile, had her hands full getting fences built, barley planted, stones carted away, and manure spread on the farm. Surplus livestock had to be sold and hay ordered. The quantity of work to be done overwhelmed her, everything seemed to go wrong, and she was losing sleep for worrying about it. Worst of all, she had been counting on John's brother to take over the farm when she went to New York, and now he was saying that he would not be able to make enough money from the farm to pay the taxes. She was so busy she didn't even have time to make a long-planned trip to Haverhill to see her sister. At this point moving furniture to New York was very low on her list of tasks to be accomplished.

Abigail and John worked at cross purposes through much of May. John wanted her to come to New York to help him find a house. He felt he needed her advice. Abigail, however, didn't want to begin the arduous process of packing and moving until she knew that they had a house to move into. In addition, the problems of the Braintree farm were immediate and pressing to her. John, far away and engaged in more exalted business, no longer took much interest in the farm.

Finally, with William Smith's help, John rented a house about a mile outside New York, complete with stable, coach house, garden, and 30 acres of land. He still didn't know what his salary would be, but he told Abigail that this house was much cheaper than smaller houses in the city itself. It was, however, totally unfurnished. William advised Abigail to bring as much furniture as possible, since it would be very expensive to buy the things they would need in New York. John, who missed Abigail terribly after a month apart, told her to forget the problems of the farm and come to New York immediately.

Abigail was still uneasy about going to New York before she had the farm organized to her satisfaction, and before they knew exactly what John's salary would be. She hated to move their furniture to New York so soon after they had shipped it from Europe; she also expected that they would return to Braintree during Congressional recesses and would need their furniture then. In effect, they needed to furnish two entire houses, and Abigail didn't see how they could manage to do it on the salary that Congress was likely to vote John. But she began packing boxes and shipping furniture anyway, a task that consumed most of her time during May and early June.

Meanwhile, John became increasingly impatient. He missed her, he didn't feel well, he was tired of living with friends; he wanted her to come immediately. Her long absence had been a mistake, he thought; but he didn't seem to understand how long it took to move a household.

Finally, around the middle of June, Abigail finished packing and sealing the more than one hundred boxes to be shipped to New York. Having written one last anxious letter to John Quincy, admonishing him to keep an eye on his younger brothers lest they stray into some moral pitfalls in Cambridge, she said goodbye to her sister and friends and set out with her niece, Louisa, for New York.

They went by stage to Providence and then by ship to New York, where Abigail was pleasantly surprised to discover the lovely house that John had rented for them. A country estate called Richmond Hill, it was about a mile north of the city, which was then confined to the southern tip of Manhattan Island. The house stood on land that is today the heart of Greenwich Village. Perched on a high hill and partly hidden by trees, it commanded a spectacular view of the city and Long Island on one side and New Jersey on the other. The distance from town had a few disadvantages. Abigail found that the number of trips back and forth into town to get supplies—as many as four a day—required keeping an extra servant, and in winter travel to and from town became difficult. But despite the problems she was so delighted with the view and the rural setting that, as she told Mary, "I would not change this situation for any I know of in Town."

Abigail found that hiring servants and setting up her household were just as difficult in New York as in Auteuil and London. In fact, English servants, about whom she had always complained mightily, suddenly looked good compared to the help she hired for Richmond Hill. Almost all of them, it seemed, had an unfortunate tendency to get drunk. Even the young woman that Abigail imported from Braintree proved troublesome. John Briesler, who had been working for the Adamses since he accompanied Abigail to Europe, became indispensable. "I can no more do without Mr. Brisler," Abigail told Mary, "than a coach could go without wheels or Horse to draw it."

Servant problems were not the only similarity between life in New York and life in Europe. Abigail quickly found that all her time could be consumed with visits and official entertaining if she didn't plan her days carefully to save some time for herself and her family. Here as in Europe, etiquette demanded that visits be made and returned, but it was not necessary actually to *see* the person visited. Leaving a calling card to show one's polite attentions was sufficient. So Abigail made a rule for herself: She made no visits in the morning, when most women were likely to be home. Instead she paid her calls after 6 P.M., when she rarely found anyone at home and could get fifteen to twenty calls out of the way in an hour or two. She also made it a rule to receive no company on Sundays, setting aside that day entirely for her family.

More formal social obligations could not be avoided so easily, however. Abigail, as well as Martha Washington, was expected to play hostess at a weekly "levee," an open house to which the local residents came and paid their respects to the first families. Abigail took her cue from Mrs. Washington, observing carefully the style she followed at her levees as a model for her own. In many ways these affairs resembled the royal "drawing rooms" in London on a smaller scale. The formalities

observed were similar. Every visitor was announced by a servant; ladies curtseyed to Mrs. Washington; the President went
around the room and spoke to each visitor. His manner displayed "a grace dignity & ease, that leaves Royal George far behind him," Abigail noted.

In addition to her weekly levees, Abigail invited every Senator and Congressman to dinner. Her dining room seated twenty-
four, and at that rate it took a month to entertain everyone. She
was just as glad that most of the legislators left their families
behind and lived in boarding houses; besides having fewer people to invite to dinner, the bachelor Congressmen could not reciprocate, so the Adamses' social calendar was less crowded
than it would have been otherwise.

Despite Abigail's preference for a quiet family life, being in
the limelight was a heady experience. Although she was accustomed to the role of political wife by now, there was an important difference about her life in New York. In Europe she and
John had been one couple among many in the diplomatic corps;
now they were second only to the Washingtons in importance.
In Europe Abigail had attended levees and state dinners; now she
was giving them herself. Once again, she was determined that
her new status would not change her. "I have a favour to request
of all my near and intimate Friends," she wrote Mary. "It is to
desire them to watch over my conduct and if at any time they
perceive any alteration in me with respect to them, arising as
they may suppose from my situation in Life, I beg they would
with the utmost freedom acquaint me with it." She did not actually believe that her manner toward her friends had changed but
"mankind are prone to deceive themselves."

Inevitably, Abigail found that her relations with some old
friends were strained by her years in Europe, her new position,
and her increasing conservatism on political issues. She was
hardly alone on this score, however, for the 1780s and 1790s
were years of political turmoil as Americans debated the future
of their young nation. Former partners in the Revolutionary
cause differed bitterly in their views about the government that
should replace British rule. The debate over the new Constitution had been so acrimonious that many people feared that its
opponents would try to undermine the new federal government.
There were constant disputes about exactly how the provisions
of the Constitution should be implemented.

Abigail and John lined up firmly on the side of strong central government, and that alone caused them to part company with some of their old friends and compatriots of the 1760s and 1770s.

For Abigail, the most difficult pill to swallow was the behavior of her old friend Mercy Warren. Both Mercy and her husband, James, were staunch antifederalists. They opposed ratification of the federal Constitution as a dangerous encroachment on local initiative and popular rights. Abigail, who was never able to accept the idea that differences of opinion could be legitimate, thought Mercy was "gravely misled." She took their disagreement much harder than John did. John, she noted, was still able to treat the Warrens as the good friends they had always been, whereas her reaction was to avoid any further contact with Mercy. "I feel it, and I cannot deceive," she told Mary regretfully. "They were my old and dear Friend's for whom I once entertaind the highest respect."

Their years in Europe had influenced Abigail's and John's view of American government; John's position as Vice President now confirmed many of the ideas they had picked up there. Seeing the problems of American foreign relations from the European side had convinced them of the importance of a strong national government, as well as the necessity of tradition and ceremony. They both believed, for example, that government officials, especially the President and Vice President, should have special titles and that they should live in a style befitting their high status. Such apparently trivial externalities were important in creating respect—and therefore encouraging stability—for the new government. Many Americans, however, opposed such ceremonial trappings as ill-suited to a republic. Some viewed them as insidious ways for an already too-powerful government to become even more powerful. The United States, they believed, should shun such decadent European practices, not copy them. To Abigail and John, such reasoning seemed hopelessly naïve.

John made himself unpopular in some quarters with his obsession about the question of titles for new government officials. How to address the President was a subject of great debate in the first session of the new Congress. John argued for a kingly title like "His Excellency." Others, who believed that a title was important but wanted something that sounded more republican, came up with various awkward-sounding appellations like "His elective majesty." Eventually the Senate came up with the even more awkward "His Highness the President of the United States and Protector of the Rights of the Same." But the title that got the most play in the newspapers was the descriptive one given John by his opponents: "His Rotundity."

Abigail was no less concerned with titles and other marks of respect for the new government. When the opposition newspapers criticized the Washingtons for living in a house furnished by the government at great cost and for riding about in a carriage pulled by six horses and attended by four servants, Abigail defended them. "This is no more state than is perfectly consistent with his Station," she observed to Mary. "I think he ought to have still more state, & time will convince our Country of the necessity, of it."

Congress adjourned at the end of September, after a remarkably active first session in which it established executive departments, laid the groundwork for the federal judicial system, and approved the Bill of Rights. Abigail had hoped throughout the summer that the Adamses could return to Braintree until the next session of Congress. But when the time came to make a decision about going home, the prospect of uprooting herself and her household seemed too formidable a task. With the bulk of their furniture in New York, she did not see how they could set up housekeeping temporarily in Braintree without going to great trouble and expense. Besides, the possibility that Congress might meet again earlier than they expected further diminished her enthusiasm for making the trip. John went home for a few weeks to rest and visit friends, but Abigail stayed in New York. In December John was back, bringing with him the butter and eggs Abigail had requested. The butter in New York, she firmly believed, was inferior to the local Braintree variety and was far more expensive.

Congress reconvened in January, and Abigail settled into her familiar pattern of visits and levees once again. What had been a novelty the previous spring was now merely dull routine. She received company every Monday; Mrs. Washington, every Friday; and other prominent women, the other days of the week. "If any person has so little to employ themselves in as to want an amusement five Evenings in a week, they may find it at one or other of these places," Abigail told Mary. For her part, she went to Mrs. Washington's about every other week and to the other gatherings less often.

Characteristically, she was more interested in attending Congressional sessions than in making the rounds of open houses and tea parties. In February she and several other politicians' wives attended the debates on funding the United States' war debts, the hottest issue of the current session. Most of the time, however, the debates seemed more subdued than they had been in the previous session. The new government, which had appeared so shaky and vulnerable at its creation, had survived its initial crisis. While few people—least of all Abigail—thought it yet safely established on a firm footing, there no longer seemed to be any danger of its immediate demise.

In June Congress passed legislation to move the capital city to Philadelphia, so Abigail had to think about plans for another move. All in all, it was to prove an eventful summer. In August Nabby had another baby, a boy. Thomas had graduated from Harvard in July, and John Quincy was admitted to the bar. Once again Mary Cranch had arranged a commencement entertainment.

Thomas didn't know exactly what he wanted to do next. The examples of his father and brothers pushed him toward the study of law, but he was clearly not enthusiastic about it. Both Abigail and John Quincy agreed that Thomas would do better in business than in law, but in the end he followed his brothers into the legal profession with very little discussion of the alternatives. It was determined that he would join his parents in Philadelphia in the fall and seek a tutor there.

Meanwhile, John Quincy set up a law office in Boston in a front room of the house his parents still owned. Because many ambitious young lawyers were competing for a limited amount of legal business, he could expect months, perhaps years, of continued financial dependence on his parents before becoming independent. John Quincy was also suffering the pangs of frustrated romance; he was in love with the beautiful and accomplished Mary Frazier of Boston. But a young lawyer with no clients and few prospects could not hope to support a family. Abigail did her best to break up the affair with repeated warnings about the dangers of early marriage. Eventually she accomplished her objective, and John Quincy remained an unwilling bachelor for several more years.

As for Nabby, it was becoming painfully apparent that not all was well with her and William. William's employment since their return from Europe had been erratic, and they depended on money from his mother for their support. Now he had a minor government post, but the salary was not sufficient to support Nabby in the style to which she had become accustomed. If William had acted on John's advice three years earlier, Abigail told John Quincy, they would not be having financial troubles now. John's advice had been to study law, which was always John's advice to young men looking for a career, but it was apparently contrary to William's inclinations. She was particularly distressed that William did not have "independent" means of support but depended on government jobs. A career in government service, to her way of thinking, was hardly better than no career at all.

Toward the end of September Abigail very reluctantly began to make serious plans for moving to Philadelphia. Despite her earlier misgivings about moving to New York, she had come to like the city and especially Richmond Hill. Now she would have to go through the process all over again. She would have to meet new people, she complained to Mary, and "make and receive a hundred ceremonious visits, not one of ten from which I shall derive any pleasure or satisfaction." Worse was the prospect of separation from her children again after a year of having both Charles and Nabby living with her. Leaving the grandchildren behind was no easier. She envied Mary her stable life with all her children nearby: "it is my destiny to have mine scatered, and scarcly to keep one with us." The prospect of having Thomas with her for the first time in many years was her only consolation.

Abigail hated the idea of moving so much that she finally made herself sick over it. Halfway through the packing, she became so weak that the least effort made her ill, and she was plagued by insomnia. On top of the packing chores and fretting over her children—Charles would move in with Nabby, which was at least some comfort—she had to worry about finding someone to look after the Braintree house. It would be difficult to rent, because she was determined that they would go home during the next Congressional recess. Nor did she want to rent it to a family who would bring its own furniture, for in that case Abigail would have to find a place to store their remaining possessions.

The problem of running the family's affairs at home provided an occasion for Abigail to complain again about how their financial position suffered from years of public service. No one, she sometimes thought, had property that yielded a lower return than theirs. In part, however, she blamed John, who always insisted on investing in land but was never at home to look after it. Cotton Tufts had been advising them for years to put more of their money in public securities, and Abigail agreed. "I have the vanity . . . to think that if Dr. Tufts and my Ladyship had been left to the sole management of our affairs, they would have been upon a much more profitable footing," she confided to Mary. "In the first place I never desired so much Land unless we could have lived upon it. The money paid for useless land I would have purchase[d] publick securities with. The interest of which, poorly as it is funded, would have been less troublesome to take charge of than Land and much more productive. But in these Ideas I have always been so unfortunate as to differ from my partner, who thinks he never saved any thing but what he vested in Land." Abigail was right, although she had conveniently forgotten her own investment in Vermont land, which had turned out to be unprofitable. One of the actions of the new government was to guarantee interest payments on public securities, and people who had bought them toward the end of the war, when the price was cheap, reaped a handsome return on their investment.

Despite her illness she managed to finish the packing, and in late October they moved to Philadelphia, once again choosing a house in a country setting a short distance outside the city. Her ill health had made the trip slow and tedious; she could stand to travel only about 20 miles a day, so it took them five days to go from New York to Philadelphia.

The journey, however, was only the beginning of her troubles. She expected the house to be ready to move into as soon as she arrived but found that their furniture had arrived only one day earlier. The painters had not finished painting, and since the house had been uninhabited for four years, there were many other repairs that needed to be made. Three days after they moved in, Louisa fell ill, followed shortly afterward by one of the servants.

They had barely recovered when Thomas came down with what Abigail called "acute rheumatism" (probably rheumatic fever), which virtually paralyzed him for three weeks. Fortunately, they had an able physician in Benjamin Rush, an old friend of

John's, but Abigail was convinced that the damp Philadelphia climate made their illnesses worse. Having described her woes to Mary, she added, "in the midst of all this, the Gentlemen and Ladies solicitious to manifest their respect were visiting us every day from 12 to 3 oclock in the midst of Rooms heepd up with Boxes, trunks, cases &c."

To make matters worse, Nabby wrote in December that William had suddenly decided to go to England to collect some debts owed to his family. This move only added to Abigail's concern about her daughter's financial situation, and she worried about Nabby's being left alone with a new baby. She wanted Nabby to come to Philadelphia to spend the winter with them, but the logistics seemed too complicated.

Once the repairs and painting were finished, Abigail was pleased with her new quarters, but it always seemed that every place they moved was more expensive than the last; and so it was with Philadelphia. It also seemed that the servants got progressively worse, and she began to think of importing more of her help from Braintree. She desperately wanted a *"decent woman* who understands plain cooking," she told Mary. "I firmly believe in the whole Number of servants—not a virtuous woman amongst them all: the most of them drunkards." Abigail now attributed the servant problem in New York and Philadelphia to the high number of foreigners in those cities compared with New England—the first indication of a nativist prejudice that was to become much more pronounced in the years of turbulent political conflict to come.

She found the Philadelphians friendly and quickly gained a favorable reputation among them. The routine of visits and levees was much the same as in New York, except that there were even more social gatherings to attend. Philadelphia was "one continued scene of Parties upon Parties, Balls and entertainments equal to any European city," she observed. She never liked Philadelphia as much as New York, and the social routine quickly became tiresome. Living outside the city freed her from constant callers, especially in the winter, but it had its disadvantages too. John had to make the trip into town every day, regardless of weather, and the servants consumed much of their time going back and forth to town for food and other supplies.

By the next winter, Abigail and John decided that the inconveniences of their country home outweighed the advantages, and they rented a house in the heart of the city. Their new house was much smaller than the one at Bush Hill—adequate for the family's needs, certainly, but cramped for official entertaining. Its dining room, for example, seated only sixteen to eighteen, compared with twenty-four at Bush Hill. As a result Abigail had to give even more dinners to get through the list of people who must be invited. The kitchen had no oven, and Abigail, who had a cook but liked to do much of her own baking, baked pastries in the ashes of the kitchen fireplace.

Living in the city in general increased her social obligations. To cope with the number of callers, Abigail held a levee every Monday night, open to everyone who wanted to come, and gave a formal dinner every Wednesday. She spent all day Tuesdays preparing for Wednesday's dinners, and all day Thursday cleaning up. Any time left over always seemed to be taken up with returning visits and attending other people's dinners. "I feel that day a happy one that I can say I have no engagement but to my Family," she told Mary. At least she had some decent servants, for once, including "a cleaver, sober, honest & neat black woman" as her cook.

For the remainder of John's term as Vice President, they settled into a comfortable if hectic routine. From late fall, when Congress convened, until sometime in the spring, when it adjourned, they lived in Philadelphia; the moment Congress completed its session, they went home to Braintree. After their year and a half in New York and Philadelphia with no time at home, they decided never again to spend a summer in the nation's capital. The complications of moving their household twice a year were more than outweighed by the restorative effects of a few months at home.

Neither one of them enjoyed their months in Philadelphia very much. Abigail hated the constant entertaining, although she learned to manage it systematically and efficiently, and as always she missed her family and friends at home. John found his job as Vice President increasingly boring and frustrating. His sole function was presiding over the Senate; he could not participate in debates, although he sometimes forgot himself and lectured to the Senators, and he could not vote except to break ties. The Vice Presidency, he once told Abigail, was the most "insignificant office . . . ever . . . contrived." His limited responsibilities at least permitted them to spend the minimum possible amount of time in Philadelphia. When Congress was not in session, John had nothing else to do.

Both Abigail and John felt an intense distaste for the growing partisan political debate that surrounded them in Philadelphia. The conflicts that divided Congress during its first two sessions were mild compared with the debates that erupted during the winter and spring of 1791. The issue was the establishing of a national monetary system, and it encompassed such touchy questions as federal assumption of state debts from the Revolutionary period, creation of a national bank, and the levying of import duties as the nation's primary source of income. Alexander Hamilton, Secretary of the Treasury, was the architect of this bold plan, which more than anything else would strengthen the federal government and reduce the autonomy of the individual states.

As proponents of strong central government, Abigail and John supported Hamilton's plan, and they were appalled at the intensity of opposition that it generated. Abigail was especially concerned at the divisions between Northern and Southern states. The commercial and fledgling manufacturing interests in the North supported duties on imports, while the primarily agricultural South objected to a measure that would, in their opinion, increase the cost of their purchases while doing nothing to enhance their own economic position. "I firmly believe if I live Ten years longer, I shall see a devision of the Southern & Northern States," Abigail observed, "unless more candour & less intrigue, of which I have no hopes, should prevail." Her one consolation was that Hamilton was taking much of the heat from the opposition that usually was directed at John. "The V President, they have permitted to sleep in peace this winter," she told Mary.

It was not merely the conflict over Hamilton's plan, but the increasingly vitriolic partisan conflict in general that bothered Abigail. She and John had been the victims of nasty attacks in the press often enough in England, but there they could attribute the hostility to lingering British resentment over American independence. Here every attack on the new government seemed to Abigail like an attempt to undermine the stability of the new nation. Americans, she believed, ought to be grateful for what the government was accomplishing, not critical of it. More and more she wondered if they were not fighting a losing battle against the forces of subversion and ingratitude.

Most of Hamilton's program was finally approved, Congress adjourned, and Abigail and John went home to Braintree in May 1791. It was the first time that Abigail had been home since she had joined John in New York two years earlier. Mary had the house ready for them—she had aired the rooms; unpacked carpets, linens, and dishes; hired servants; and had the garden planted. For Abigail, the tension of Philadelphia life quickly slipped away as she settled into the comfortable routine at home. She could not escape her worries about politics entirely, but at least she didn't have to listen to political gossip day in and day out. In the quiet and familiar surroundings of her own home no problem seemed so serious as it did in Philadelphia.

That summer at home persuaded Abigail and John never to stay the year round in Philadelphia again. Abigail, of course, didn't need much convincing. She had always considered the Philadelphia climate unhealthy; summers were particularly bad because of the punishing heat. She missed her New England friends terribly, and just knowing that she would have several months with them in the summer helped her get through the winters. And, of course, at home she lived among people of compatible political sentiments, people who loved and respected her and John. Here she could indulge in the sort of intellectual political discussions that she enjoyed and escape the seamier side of politics that seemed to have taken over Philadelphia.

When they returned to Philadelphia in the fall, they discovered one more good reason for their annual summer vacation. The city was struck with a deadly epidemic of yellow fever. Everyone who could possibly manage it had fled the city; rumor had it that more than two thousand refugees were in New York alone.

Yellow fever replaced smallpox as the most dreaded disease of the late eighteenth century. Inoculation had greatly reduced the mortality of smallpox, but there was neither prevention nor cure for yellow fever. No one at the time had the slightest notion that the disease was carried by mosquitoes; they knew only that it appeared in summer and ended with the first sign of cold weather. This epidemic, which killed about 10 percent of Philadelphia's population, was the city's first large-scale battle with yellow fever. For the next several years, it struck again nearly every summer.

By the spring of 1792 speculation about the November federal elections was already running rampant. Washington wanted to step down after one term but was persuaded to change his mind; clearly he would be reelected. The Vice Presidency, however, was another story. Opposition to the Federalist administration during its first three years had hardened into a distinct political party. Its members, headed by Thomas Jefferson and James Madison, called themselves Republicans. In 1792 they decided that it was time to try electing at least one of their own men to executive office. Washington was obviously unbeatable, and Hamilton, as Secretary of the Treasury, was an appointee and therefore beyond the electorate's reach. So the Republicans decided to concentrate their efforts on the Vice Presidency. For once John couldn't talk about retiring to the quiet life of a farmer; if Washington agreed to stay, duty demanded that he stay also. To be defeated when Washington was reelected would be humiliating. John was in the distasteful position of fighting for reelection to a job he despised.

As soon as possible after Congress adjourned, he and Abigail escaped to Braintree, or Quincy, as it was now called. The north parish of Braintree had split off to form a new town, which was named after Abigail's grandfather. Thomas, now well into his legal studies, stayed behind to look after their house. He and Charles, who was still in New York, also kept their parents informed about all the latest political rumors. As usual, John would not condescend to get involved directly in the political fight, but he would be well informed from behind the scenes.

Abigail was sick through much of the summer with malaria, or "intermittent fever," as she called it. She had first contracted this disease the summer they lived in New York, and she suffered recurrent attacks nearly every year. Like yellow fever, malaria was caused by mosquitoes, but it was much less deadly. It was rarely fatal but could never really be cured, and it attacked its victims at intervals of months or years with chills, fevers, and aches. Abigail was debilitated for several weeks with the disease. When it came time to return to Philadelphia in the fall, she had neither strength nor enthusiasm for the journey. If John lost the election, his weeks as a "lame duck" Vice President would be extremely unpleasant for both of them, so finally they decided that he would go alone. He would take lodgings, thereby avoiding any obligation to entertain or mix socially with his political opponents. If he lost the election, he could stay out of the public eye and return to Quincy as quickly as possible. As much as Abigail and John hated to be separated, it seemed to be the easiest way to handle a potentially unpleasant situation.

John himself was in no hurry to return to Philadelphia. Congress reconvened in October, but he remained in Quincy until late November, reaching Philadelphia only days before the electors were to meet and make their choices, on December 5.

Both Abigail and John interpreted the election as a test of the fate of their country. Like most Americans of the time, they were uncomfortable with the notion of party conflict or indeed of any opposition whatsoever to the elected government. But in their case it became a personal matter; they equated opposition to John's reelection with attacks on the very fabric of the nation. It was the opposition that was motivated by party spirit and played the politics of faction; they themselves were statesmen with only the interests of their country at heart.

On December 5, the day the electors met, John wrote Abigail, "This Day decides whether I shall be a Farmer or a Statesman after next March . . . how the result will be I neither know nor care." Abigail, on the other hand, while agreeing that the result was unimportant to them personally, wrote John on the eve of the election that "tomorrow will determine whether their Government shall stand four years longer—or Not." In fact, by the time the electors met, there was relatively little doubt of John's reelection as Vice President. Abigail took the results as a sign that the country knew where its best interests lay after all, despite the attempts of partisans to sway its mind.

John, however, took little pleasure in his reelection. He had no stomach for the party politics developing in the nation; he was not a good politician and had been happier in diplomatic jobs, where personal popularity did not count for much. Party spirit would eventually destroy his career, he told John Quincy; it was something he had expected from the beginning of his days in politics. He would stick out his second term and then retire. "Four years more will be as long as I shall have a Taste for public Life or Journeys to Philadelphia," he told Abigail. "I am determined in the meantime to be no longer the Dupe, and run into Debt to support a vain Post which has answered no other End than to make me unpopular." It was a familiar refrain, a promise that would once more be honored more in the breach than in the observance.

Chapter 14

An Interlude at Quincy

Abigail's life for the next four years harked back to her earliest years as a political wife, the years John spent as a delegate to the Continental Congress while she ran the farm in Braintree. Poor health, the heavy expense of maintaining two households, and the sheer disinclination to continue acting the role of the Vice President's lady kept her in Quincy for all of John's second term. For his part, John spent as little time as possible in Philadelphia, returning home for the long spring–summer Congressional recesses. He, too, had little appetite for life in the nation's capital, especially as partisan politics became even more heated in the next few years.

Years together had dulled the memory of their painful separations, and Abigail was surprised at how lonely she was when John left in November. As usual, she worried about him constantly and believed that no one could take care of him as well as she. "I hope Brisler minds to have a fire in your Bedroom and that your sheets are well aird and your Bed well cloathd," she wrote before John could have gotten a third of the way to Philadelphia. "I have the advantage of you," she joked later, "I have Louisa for a bedfellow but she is a cold comfort for the one I have lost."

John hated to be alone, even more than Abigail did; next

winter, he told her, she would have to come with him or he would resign and go home. But they both knew that he would never resign; and Abigail had had enough of Philadelphia.

Each fall, when John prepared to return to Philadelphia, they discussed Abigail's going with him, and each fall the same objections came up. Her health was not good, and the Philadelphia climate, she feared, would just make it worse. It was difficult to find someone trustworthy to care for the farm. John's salary as Vice President was not sufficient to maintain a household and entertain in a style appropriate to the Vice Presidency; at the end of John's first term, they were $2,000 in debt. The last reason was a particularly telling objection for Abigail, who continued to manage the family finances and fretted over the high cost of official entertaining in Philadelphia. Neither of them thought the Vice Presidency a rewarding enough job to justify financial sacrifice. When John lived alone in Philadelphia, they not only managed to stay out of debt but even saved some of his salary to put toward improvements on their Quincy farm.

Although she stayed home throughout John's second term, Abigail lost none of her interest in politics. She and John wrote to each other weekly, if not more often, to exchange views on politics as well as domestic news. John described the debates in Congress and sent her the Philadelphia and New York newspapers with their detailed accounts of government proceedings. She reported local political opinion and expounded at length on her own views of political events. Not since the Continental Congress years had they written to each other so fully and so frequently.

These were years of crisis for the new nation. European wars threatened the precarious neutrality of the United States, which was ill equipped to become involved in another war so soon. Americans disagreed sharply among themselves over foreign policy, and this conflict threatened the fragile stability of the young government. Abigail viewed these events with alarm. Over the next four years she became even more convinced of the necessity of strong central government and of the dangers of popular dissent. Her political conservatism strengthened and solidified; her letters to John were a principal means of developing and expressing her ideas.

As always, her ideas and John's were quite similar, although she continued to be more extreme and more strident in her language. He influenced her, to be sure, but she also had a great deal of time alone to develop her own thoughts. Often they came up with the same ideas at the same time and wrote them to each other in letters that crossed in the mail. Abigail called this "the Tellegraph of the mind." She exerted an influence on his thinking, just as he did on hers. Gradually the degree of mutual influence became almost imperceptible. By the time John became President, they thought virtually as one person, and Abigail's intellectual influence over John, always important, became absolutely critical.

The overriding political issue of the next several years involved American relations with France. The United States' benefactor during the Revolution, France was now engaged in a revolution of its own. Most Americans praised the French Revolution in its early stages, viewing it as a struggle for political liberty much like their own. Abigail was suspicious of it, however, at a time when most Americans had nothing but uncritical praise for the French. "However great the Blessings to be derived from a Revolution in government," she observed, "the scenes of anarchy cruelty and Blood which usually preceed it and the difficulty of uniting a majority in favour of any system, are sufficient to make every person who has been an Eye witness to the demolition of one Government recoil at the prospect of overturning Empires and kingdoms." Her comments reflected her own disillusionment with the results of the American Revolution; she had learned slowly and painfully that it was easier to overthrow a government than to create one. Her doubts also foreshadowed the growing conflict within the United States over the French Revolution.

By 1792 the Revolution had escalated into a war between France and England and threatened to erupt into a full-scale European war. The treaty of 1778, under which the French had provided military aid to the Americans, obligated the United States to reciprocate. There were strong moral pressures as well for Americans to help their fellow revolutionaries. But the United States could ill afford to tangle with Britain again so soon. Trade with Britain, renewed immediately after the Revolution, was crucial to the American economy, and ties of culture and sentiment still bound the United States to its old mother country.

Ideally, the United States should remain neutral in this conflict, but France and England each applied pressure to enlist the United States on its side.

The issue of support for the French Revolution quickly became part of the growing party conflict in the United States. Jefferson and the Republicans sympathized with France; the spirit of the new revolutionary government there was harmonious with their goal of making the United States government more egalitarian. The Republicans enjoyed substantial popular support, for most Americans sympathized with the French cause, at least so far. The Federalists, on the other hand, were concerned about the importance of British trade to the American economy and were, in general, more conservative in temperament.

More seriously, most Federalists believed that the French Revolution itself had gotten out of hand. What had started out as a laudable effort to establish a constitutional monarchy and ensure greater liberties for the ordinary French citizen now threatened to become a bloody civil war. The King and Queen were imprisoned; disputes raged about the type of government to be created; and political executions reached alarming proportions. It appeared that the French intended to create a popular democratic republic—a government even more radical for its times than that of the United States.

The actions of the French revolutionaries were frightening to conservatives like John and Abigail, but the spirit behind the actions was in some ways even more frightening. "Liberté, égalité, fraternité"—the French revolutionaries' slogan—went a good deal farther than the old American revolutionaries were prepared to follow. Liberty, yes—but equality of all men? The end of all distinctions of social class? Such thinking smacked of anarchy, and of the worst abuses of liberty.

In Abigail's view, the purpose of the American Revolution had been to change government, not to change society. But there was always the danger that a revolution might go too far and liberty might be translated into a new kind of tyranny. Shays Rebellion, she believed, had been an early example of the potential dangers generated by revolution; so, for that matter, was the antifederalist opposition to a strong central government. Now, just when it seemed that the new government had stabilized and moved out of its dangerous period, the French Revolution offered a potent example to those Americans who still believed the American Revolution had not gone far enough. To Abigail, the radicaliśm of the French, more than anything that had yet happened in America, exemplified the potential dangers of revolutions and republican governments. By completely abolishing the monarchy and aristocracy, the social underpinnings of French society, they risked subjecting themselves instead to the tyranny of the majority, of mob rule.

Many Americans, however, applauded the actions of the French revolutionaries. In the large cities up and down the Atlantic Seaboard men created political societies modeled on the "Jacobin clubs" of France. These societies—part social club, part political organization—formed an important popular base of support for the emerging Republican party. Very few of the clubs had explicit ties with France or advocated direct American aid to France, although they were generally sympathetic to the French Revolution and favored democratizing American government in rhetoric similar to that popular in France. Ironically, the French societies that inspired their American counterparts had themselves been modeled on the political organizations of the American Revolution, like the Sons of Liberty and the Committees of Correspondence. Now, however, to people like Abigail and John, these political societies seemed dangerous, if not downright subversive.

Abigail saw subversion in every pro-French political society and thought the Republican Party existed solely to give aid and comfort to the French. All opponents of the government, and of the Federalists in general, were "Jacobins" to her. Popular talk of "liberty" and "equality" frightened her, because she feared that such talk might incite the same kind of violence in America that now plagued France. Her political beliefs, her reading of history, and her temperament told her that social distinctions were not only compatible with political liberty but necessary to preserve it. The cry for equality was unjustified, in her opinion, because American society was totally unlike the French. Here there was no entrenched clergy or nobility to overthrow, so Americans had no cause for complaint.

Behind her growing conservatism was a profound distrust of the capacities of the ordinary man or woman. Such people, she believed, were incapable of thinking rationally about important issues but would follow a charismatic leader blindly and could easily be duped by propaganda. If not held in check by men of education and uderstanding, they would lead the country into the tyranny of democracy. It was exactly this sort of thing that was happening in France.

She went so far as to argue that "unless mankind were universally enlightened, which never can be, they are unfit for freedom, nor do I believe that our Creator designd it for them." History, she believed, demonstrated otherwise. If men were intended to be free, "all Ages and Nations from Adam to the present day would not have been one standing continued and universal proof to the contrary. Some were made for Rule others for submission." In a nation like the United States, the "enlightened" minority of the population were intended to rule, rather than a hereditary class as in the nations of Europe.

Both England and France engaged in tactics calculated to force Americans out of their neutrality. The British harassed American shipping and impressed American sailors to serve in the British Navy, accusing them of being British deserters. British ships also attacked French West Indian islands, inciting slaves to riot and sending French planters fleeing for their lives to the United States. The French also committed atrocities; in the fall, after encouraging American ships to trade at French ports, the French government seized American ships in port and sold their cargoes. At about the same time, word of the Jacobin bloodbath—the execution of thousands of political prisoners—reached the United States. Americans, who had managed to win a revolution and create a new government with no domestic bloodshed, were horrified at the reports coming from France. Support for the Revolution, once widespread, diminished quickly.

By the time Congress convened in December 1793, war seemed all but inevitable. John firmly believed that the Republicans' pro-French activities, aided by popular support, would inflame the British into declaring war against the United States, but there was nothing he as Vice President could do to stop it. It was not simply the French that the United States had to contend with, but the British, who continued to raid American shipping with impunity. For weeks Congress took no action as the sense of impending crisis deepended. Complaining of "eternal Indecision," John wrote Abigail: "I wish for the Times when Old Sam and Old John conducted with more wisdom and more success."

Finally, in April Congress appointed John Jay as special envoy to negotiate with England in an attempt to resolve the crisis. Both Abigail and John, who had a high regard for Jay's talents as a diplomat, were pleased with the appointment, but Abigail doubted that he would be able to do any good. "There are some evil spirits who would fault the measure of heaven & quarrel with the Angle Gabriel were he sent even to declare pease on Earth, and good will to men," she wrote.

Although Abigail thought and wrote a great deal about politics during the winter and spring, managing the expanded holdings of the Adams family was a more immediate concern. She had had years of practice running a farm alone, but since their return from Europe the amount of their property and the time required to manage it had multiplied. John Quincy looked after the house in Boston and collected rent from the tenants there, but Abigail had the sole responsibility for running their old farm at Penn's Hill plus the estate where they now lived. In March she negotiated the purchase of yet another farm and bought cows, along with equipment for a dairy. And there was the never ending problem of finding tenants and laborers.

She reported to John on her management of their lands and asked his advice, but there was little he could do from Philadelphia. So complete was his confidence in her decisions—she was "so valourous and noble a farmer," he told her—that he spent little time thinking about affairs in Quincy. By late spring, however, when it looked as if John would not get home until June, Abigail began to have increasing doubts about her ability to continue running the farms alone. It was not so much that she questioned her own ability as that the pressure of managing a substantial estate without any material help from John began to weigh heavily on her. To add to her worries, John's mother fell ill and appeared perilously close to death for days on end. Abigail took on the burden of caring for her, a task which fed her anxieties and sapped her strength.

The combination of politics, the farm, and family illnesses gave Abigail plenty to worry about through the spring. At such times she sorely missed John's company. "I want to hear every day from you," she wrote him. "I want to sit down and converse

with you, every evening I sit here alone and Brood over probabil-
ities and conjectures." As the months went by and still there
was no prospect of John's return, she tried to be patient. As she
had so many times in the past, she told herself that his service to
the country was more important than her happiness. "I check
every rising wish & suppress every anxious desire for your return," she told him, "when I see how necessary you are to the
welfare and protection of a Country which I love." At other
times, however, she wanted John to retire. The old dilemma—
public duty versus private happiness—was still with them, renewed once again by their months of separation.

At the end of May John finally began his preparations to go
home, even though Congress was still in session. Days before
his planned departure he learned that Washington intended to
appoint John Quincy as Minister to Holland. John had often said
that he hoped John Quincy would stay out of politics, but now
all such talk vanished as he saw his son following in his footsteps in a diplomatic career. Never doubting that John Quincy
would accept the position, he fired off letters full of advice during his last few days in Philadelphia.

Abigail frequently lamented that her family seemed des-
tined to be widely scattered. Now she had to part with John
Quincy, but like John she had no doubts that he should accept
the appointment. In a letter to Martha Washington, she noted
that "at a very early period of Life I devoted him to the publick."
His departure would be painful to her, but knowing that he was
serving his country would be compensation for her loss. Not
only did she encourage John Quincy to accept the post, but she
heartily approved his suggestion that he take Thomas with him
as his secretary.

John Quincy and Thomas sailed from Boston in September
1794. At the beginning of November John left for Philadelphia
again. This time he was certain that Congress would not sit more
than four months. He would be back early in March, he promised Abigail, "ardent for another Agricultural Campaign more
glorious but less fatiguing than the last."

John stopped in New York to visit their children. Nabby and
the grandchildren were all well, he reported, and Charles was
prospering in his law practice. In Philadelphia he took lodgings
at a hotel where several Congressmen lived. Most of them, he
told Abigail, differed with him politically, but that did not

bother him. He was pleased with his quarters, and Congress opened its session on a more positive note than the previous year. "Antifederalism, Jacobinism and Rebellion are drooping their heads, very much discouraged," he was pleased to report.

His optimism was borne out. Political tension had indeed quieted remarkably, and both France and England appeared less threatening. But John, far from enjoying this calm interlude, quickly became bored. "There is scarcely animation enough in either house, to excite attention," he wrote Abigail. "One may sleep in the midst of a Debate. I have not yet tried however." As always when he was bored with politics, John longed for home. Throughout his career, whenever he was busy with a political crisis or felt his actions were important to his country, he tolerated his separation from Abigail without grumbling—and often without writing to her. But whenever things were quiet, he wrote often, agonized over their separation, and took great interest in the affairs of his farm.

Now, unlike the previous year, he asked Abigail to write in great detail about the agricultural labors. To amuse herself and to keep him informed, she kept a detailed daily account of her work on the farm—a "Diary of Husbandry" as John called it. "I wish I had a farm here," he told her. "I would give you my Chronicles of Husbandry in return for yours." He talked again about either resigning or bringing her with him the next session. He became nostalgic about the past and found time to read books he had never read before. On the whole, it was the most "innocent" session of Congress he had ever known, and it left him feeling useless and lonely. "I know not what to write to you," he told Abigail, "unless I tell you I love you, and long to see you—But this will be no News."

Unlike John, Abigail had little time to be bored or lonely, but still she sometimes envied him his activities in the "Buisy world." She sympathized with his loneliness and told him he really ought to go out more, even though she understood his impatience with social "amusements." It was too bad he couldn't occupy himself with knitting and sewing, as she did. They were a "great relief in these long winter Evenings which you poor Gentlemen cannot use." She even teased him about missing her; he wanted his wife to be with him, she wrote, "but dont you know that you will prize her the more for feeling the want of her for a time?" In the past, John had often been totally absorbed in business, too busy to write, while Abigail chafed at her narrow, restricted world. Now her domestic responsibilities had vastly increased, while John's political responsibilities declined. It was a striking reverse of their former situation.

This winter Abigail had even more than her usual duties to worry about. Just before John left for Philadelphia, her brother-in-law John Shaw died suddenly, leaving her sister Elizabeth in straitened financial circumstances. Abigail went to Haverhill early in November to console her sister and to try to decide what to do about the farm in Medford that they owned jointly. Shaw had done most of the work of overseeing the farm and its tenants; now the experienced Abigail was to take over. The farm had been pretty much neglected for years, and the house needed major repairs. Financial responsibility was complicated by the joint ownership, and the sisters discussed the possibility that one might buy the other out. Abigail was willing to sell to her sister, but she would really prefer to buy Elizabeth's share, for the farm was the only part of her father's estate left to her. John agreed: "Paternal Acres are always good Land," he wrote.

When Abigail returned from Haverhill, she brought her niece Betsey Quincy with her. Elizabeth found her adolescent daughter difficult to manage and thought she needed a "new mother" for a while. Abigail, she was convinced, would set Betsey straight. A few months later, Elizabeth astonished the rest of her family by marrying Stephen Peabody, a minister from Atkinson, New Hampshire, just north of Haverhill. Elizabeth admitted that she remarried so hastily in part because of her desperate financial situation. She could no longer support herself entirely by taking in boarders, and the charity of the Haverhill parish would not last forever.

Abigail had one of her perennial bouts of fever in December and was sick most of the month. Forced to slow down her daily pace, she had more time for reading and reflection. She continued to brood about the situation in France, especially now that her sons were headed for Europe. She worried that France would invade Holland in its campaign of European conquest. She also spent a good deal of time thinking about one of her favorite topics: the status of women. Although she had become increasingly conservative on political issues, she continued to argue for an end to women's political and legal liabilities.

The 1790s had, in fact, seen substantial improvements, at

least in women's education, and a spate of books and pamphlets stirred up controversy on women's place in society. While Abigail was recovering from her illness she read "Bennett's Strictures on Female Education," "Louisa Bennett's Letters to a Young Lady," and "Lady Craven's Journey to Constantinople." She particularly liked "Bennett's Strictures," which advocated better education for women, long one of her favorite causes. "He is ingenious enough," she wrote John, "to acknowledge & point out the more than Egyptian bondage, to which the Female sex, have been subjugated, from the earliest ages."

Abigail acknowledged that great strides had been made in the improvement of women's education in the years after the Revolution, although she noted that "much yet remains to be done." Inspired by the belief that a free republic depended upon a broad base of educated citizens, including women, the first secondary schools for women were opened in several American cities in the 1790s. The most common specific justification for improving women's education was the argument that, as mothers, they were responsible for raising the next generation of citizens; they themselves needed to be well educated in order to teach their children. This was an argument that Abigail herself had made many times in the past. Now, amid all the turmoil and upheaval of the 1790s, she at least had the satisfaction of seeing her ideas prevail on a matter close to her heart.

There were other, more radical writings on the position of women circulating in the 1790s, and Abigail read them too. Most notable was Mary Wollstonecraft's "Vindication of the Rights of Women." Unlike the advocates of women's education, who merely wanted to improve women in their traditional role, Wollstonecraft argued that women's intellectual capacities were equal to men's and that reason demanded that they be educated equally. Her views were considered extreme at the time, but to Abigail they made a great deal of sense. Although she did not concur with all of Wollstonecraft's ideas, she agreed with enough of them for John to tease her about being a "disciple of Wollstonecraft," and in fact the natural rights theory behind the "Vindication" held a strong appeal for her.

She never believed, as many men of her time did, that women were innately inferior to men. She did concede, however, that they had different traits and talents, which fitted them for a social role different from men's. Such thinking led Abigail to a potentially radical view of women's rights, but that potential was blunted by her conservative views on society. Marriage and family were among the basic props of social order, and anything that undermined them threatened that order, she believed. Rich or poor, male or female, every person had his place in society and must fulfill his roles and duties, or chaos would result. She could argue that women were equal to men and still believe that their place was in the home, subject to their husbands—just as she could argue that all men were created equal while still maintaining the importance of social distinctions.

In the long run, although Abigail accepted many of Wollstonecraft's arguments, she was not prepared to argue that the place of women in society should be fundamentally altered. "However brilliant a woman's tallents may be, she ought never to shine at the expence of her Husband," Abigail wrote. "Government of States and Kingdoms, tho God knows badly enough managed, I am willing should be solely administerd by the Lords of the Creation." Women should confine themselves to "Domestick Government."

In January the first letters came from Thomas, reporting his and John Quincy's safe arrival in Holland. Early in February Nabby gave birth to a daughter. These two events cheered Abigail so much that she traveled to New York in late spring to visit Nabby and her family. While there she visited Charles too, and met the woman he would soon marry—Sally Smith, Nabby's sister-in-law. It was not until August, however, after both Abigail and John had separately returned to Quincy, that Charles announced that he and Sally were to marry. The Adamses had often worried that Charles, quite a ladies' man, would marry prematurely, and in fact they had tried to break up this romance just as they had broken up John Quincy's. At the age of twenty-five, Charles was young to marry by Adams family standards. But his law practice was prospering, and there was no reason for him not to consider starting a family. Nabby, who approved of his choice, informed John Quincy of the marriage by commenting, "after all the Hair Breadth scapes and iminent dangers he has run, he is at last Safe Landed."

Congress had ratified Jay's Treaty by a narrow margin during a brief summer session, and Abigail and John were both back in Quincy by the end of the summer. The treaty was controversial and fueled the fires of partisan battle. By the time John left for Philadelphia at the end of November, opposition to the treaty had reached substantial proportions, with several towns publishing resolutions against it. Abigail, alarmed at such displays of grass roots political opinion, attributed the widespread unrest in the land to "Jacobins" who were working "to allarm & terrify the people into measures disgracefull to the Country." Long distrustful of the press, she blamed newspapers for stirring up opposition to the treaty and the government. As the session progressed, however, it appeared that the crisis over the treaty would be overcome; while Abigail was ready to "humble all Jacobinical wretches in the dust," John reported from Philadelphia that the opponents of the government were weakening. By the end of December Abigail informed John that her pessimism about the future of her country had lessened somewhat, "tho I am not certain that it will Live to old Age."

The New Year brought continued debate over Jay's Treaty, more potential political crises, and, most important for John and Abigail, the news that George Washington was planning to retire when his term ended in another year. "You know the Consequence of this, to me and to yourself," John wrote Abigail. "Either we must enter upon ardours more trying than any ever yet experienced; or retire to Quincy Farmers for Life." At the moment Washington's proposed retirement was a secret known only to his closest associates, and it was still possible that he would change his mind, as he had four years earlier. But John, obviously one of the logical candidates to be his successor, could not help brooding over the prospect. Neither could Abigail. Their letters throughout January and February were frequent, and the presidency was almost always the main topic.

As usual when John contemplated a major step in his political career, he assumed that his unpopularity would deny him the office to which he thought himself entitled. He wavered between resolving to retire and admitting his ambition for the presidency, deliberations he characterized as a conflict between private desires and public duty. In short, he behaved at this juncture just as he had at every other time of decision in his political career. In January he told Abigail that he did not yet know what his "duty" would be. "It is no light thing to resolve upon Retirement," he added.

Despite his occasional doubts, John thought himself clearly entitled to the presidency. If Washington chose not to continue as President, it seemed logical to John that he, as Vice President, should succeed to the highest office. He said as much to Abigail in terms that made him sound like the monarchist he was often accused of being: "I am Heir Apparent you know," but the "French and the Demogogues intend I presume to set aside the Decent." Later, he predicted that Jefferson or Jay would be elected "If the succession should be passed over."

Abigail reacted no less predictably to the prospect of John's becoming President. She did not want him to continue in public life; she did not want a public role for herself; but she would not stand in the way of his duty. "My Ambition leads me not to be first in Rome, and the Event you request me to contemplate is of so serious a Nature that it requires much reflection & deliberation to determine upon it," she told him. If she thought only of herself, she would ask him to retire. But, she added, "I dare not influence you."

She felt all her usual qualms about John's continuing in politics. They would be exposed to the public eye and to public criticism more than ever before. No one could ever be as popular as Washington; his successor would come in for heavy criticism just because he was not the revered "Father of his Country." It had been difficult enough for Washington to hold the country together. How could a less popular man hope to maintain the precarious balance of opposing factions? Underlying her concerns was the fear, felt by many in America, that the fragile young government might not survive a transfer of power.

It was precisely these concerns, however, that convinced Abigail that John's duty would lead him into the presidency. A man of long experience in government and firm integrity, he was above party faction and had only the best interests of his country at heart, or so she reasoned. After brooding for a long time about the pitfalls of the highest office, she wrote John, "I think what is duty to others and what is duty to ourselves. I contemplate unpleasant concequences to our Country if your decision should be the same with the P—s for as you observe, whatever may be the views and designs of party, the Chief of the Electors will do their duty, or I know little of the Country in which I live." And, she admitted, being President would have its compensations. It would be a difficult job, but also a "flattering and Glorious Reward."

She also worried about her own role should John be elected President. Martha Washington had been an exemplary First Lady, quiet, charming, polite, and popular with everyone who knew her. Abigail was not certain whether she had "patience prudence discretion sufficient to fill a station so exceptionably" as Mrs. Washington. "I have been so used to a freedom of sentiment that I know not how to place so many gaurds about me, as will be indispensable, to look at every word before I utter it, and to impose a silence upon my self, when I long to talk."

John did not share Abigail's fears about herself. There was no doubt that she would carry off her role perfectly, he told her. As for himself, he would not openly seek the presidency, but he would not pull himself out of the race, either. "I am weary of the Game," he told Abigail. And yet, in a moment of unusual candor, he noted, "I don't know how I could live out of it." For all his talk of retirement, John preferred the rough-and-tumble life of politics. And Abigail knew it. She never had any doubts about what his decision would be on seeking the highest office.

As the Congressional session dragged on into March and it looked as if John would not get home until summer, Abigail's old resentment over her sacrifices to the public cause flared up. "No man even if he is sixty years of age ought to live more than three months at a Time from his Family," she complained to John. He missed Abigail too. "Oh that I had a Bosom to lean my Head upon!" he lamented. But he was outraged at the hint that he was getting old. "How dare you hint or Lisp a Word about Sixty Years of Age. If I were near, I would soon convince you that I am not above forty."

Finally, on the fourth of May Congress concluded its debates and adjourned. John immediately made plans to go home. By the end of May he and Abigail were reunited, watching from a distance the political machinations that would decide their future.

Abigail had more to worry about than farms and politics through the spring and summer. Charles was happily married and doing well in his legal practice, but John Quincy was more discouraged than ever about his personal and political future. William Smith was engaged in some shady business dealings that had both Abigail and John worried about Nabby's financial security.

William, whose financial future had looked bleak only a couple of years earlier, had speculated extensively in real estate and was building a substantial fortune as a result. Abigail and John, who had once criticized William for not having enough money to support their daughter, now criticized him for having too much. During the spring, however, some of William's business associates went bankrupt, leaving him liable for a substantial sum in bad debts. His losses were large, and he had to sell a considerable amount of land to cover them, although the Smiths were still left with a comfortable estate.

Abigail, who disapproved of fortunes made through speculation, thought the affair would have positive benefits. The Smiths had lived too extravagantly, and now they would have to change their ways. They were forced to stop building a country house that was too big anyway, and they would have to live a more "quiet and retired Life." Of course, as far as Abigail was concerned, William was the one responsible for their immoral, extravagant life-style. Nabby, she asserted, "has ever been averse to all kinds of extravagance and dissipation." She was confident that with less money they would be happier.

Letters from John Quincy convinced Abigail that there was a new woman in his life. He offered little more than hints about her identity or his true feelings—perhaps remembering his mother's stern disapproval of his last romance. Abigail teased him for more information and finally guessed that his new love was one of the daughters of Joshua Johnson, an American merchant living in London. True to form, she counseled caution. He shouldn't marry too early, and he should be careful about his choice. She and John both preferred that he come home to choose a wife, but they put up no direct opposition.

Abigail had guessed correctly. John Quincy had fallen in love with Louisa Catherine Johnson during the weeks he spent in London in connection with the negotiations over Jay's Treaty. Far from making him happy, however, his affection only made him feel more frustrated. His future as a diplomat seemed uncertain, especially with a change of administration imminent. He could not take on the obligations of a wife and family without more permanent prospects. He acknowledged the wisdom of his parents' advice against early marriage but noted that if he waited until all conditions were right, he would be single forever. Besides, he added, "Prudence is a sorry match maker."

In May he returned to The Hague, still a single man. Louisa was devastated by his departure, but John Quincy, with typical Adams stoicism, told her to prepare herself for a long separation. Unlike her, he had had ample models of separation as a test of love. His letters to Louisa bore more than a little resemblance to those of his parents many years earlier. But in June John Quincy unexpectedly received word that President Washington had appointed him Minister Plenipotentiary to Portugal. The new position meant a promotion in rank and a higher salary; at long last he could afford to marry. Within weeks he returned to London and married Louisa. Abigail was pleased at the news, because she knew how lonely her son had been. But she worried about his taking so young a wife to a foreign post. With no experience of the world, how would Louisa react to the luxuries of a royal court? And how would a woman brought up entirely in Europe react to America, especially after spending time at a foreign court? John Quincy responded to his mother's concerns now as he had to her earlier concerns about his choice of a wife—respectfully, but with assurances that he knew what he was about.

In September George Washington made his official announcement that he would not accept a third term as President. "The die is cast! All America is or ought to be in mourning," Abigail declared. The possibility that John would succeed Washington was now more than mere speculation, and Abigail and John had to think long and hard through the autumn about their future.

In 1796 American politics was still very much a gentleman's game. The Federalists nominated John Adams, and the Republicans Thomas Jefferson, without either man's having openly campaigned for himself. Their supporters, however, particularly those in the press, were not so gentlemanly. Republi-

can newspapers blasted John, accusing him of being a monarchist and a foe of republicanism. They criticized him for having
a son in high office, and made a virtue out of the fact that Jefferson had only daughters. These attacks only confirmed Abigail's
fears about the fate of Washington's successor; no one could
hope to equal his popularity or his ability to unify all factions.

In the midst of the electioneering John left for Philadelphia.
He arrived just days before the electors were due to meet and
cast their votes, which was to be on December 7. There was
some talk in Philadelphia that Thomas Pinckney of South Carolina, the Federalist candidate for Vice President, might be
elected instead of one of the two Presidential candidates. In fact,
Alexander Hamilton and other extreme Federalists were maneu-
vering to get Pinckney elected instead of John, whom they considered too moderate and too difficult to influence. Hamilton in
particular wanted Pinckney, because he thought he could control him and, in effect, rule the country from behind the scenes.
Such machinations were possible because electors did not spec-
ify their choices for President and Vice President. The man with
the highest number of electoral votes would be President, and
the one with the second highest, Vice President.

As they so often did, Abigail and John each wrote to the
other on the fateful day, December 7. But their thoughts on the
election were quite different. Abigail was, as usual, melodra-
matic about the consequences of the election for the country:
"on the decision of this day, hangs perhaps the destiny of America." John, on the other hand, reflected on his own feelings about
being elected President. More candid than usual, he admitted his
mixed feelings about politics, his desire for the glory of the office, and his dread of the humiliation of losing. "I laugh at myself twenty times a Day," he told Abigail, "for my feelings, and
meditations & speculations in which I find myself engaged . . . if
my Reason were to dictate I should wish to be left out. A P. with
half the Continent upon his Back besides all France & England
. . . to carry will have a devilish Load." He concluded by admitting his confusion. "It really seems to me as if I wished to be left
out. Let me see! do I know my own heart? I am not sure."

There would be a long delay between the vote of the electors
and the official counting of votes by Congress, which would not
take place until February. Rumor and speculation about the
result ran rampant in the intervening weeks. One of the more

persistent stories was that Pinckney would beat both Adams and Jefferson and that Hamilton was behind his election. John took the possibility of Pinckney's election seriously but scoffed at the stories about Hamilton.

Abigail took a different view of the situation. In many ways a more astute political observer than John, she had long distrusted Hamilton. She was entirely prepared to believe the stories about his influencing the election and declared that it was only what she expected from a man of such boundless ambition. "You may recollect," she told John, "that I have often said to you, H—n is a man ambitious as Julius Caesar, a subtle intriguer. His abilities would make him dangerous if he was to espouse a wrong side, his thirst for Fame is insatiable. I have ever kept my Eye upon him."

By the week before Christmas enough votes had been counted unofficially for people to start congratulating John on his election, though he remained skeptical for a week or two more. The Vice Presidency remained in doubt somewhat longer. He told Abigail, "a narrow squeak it is as the Boys say, whether he [Jefferson] or P. [Pinckney] shall be Daddy Vice: a Character that I shall soon relinquish. . . . I have been Dady Vice long enough." At the end of December John's election looked so certain that he began seriously thinking about the practical problems of assuming the highest office. For the moment, the perplexing problems of a house, carriage, horses, furniture, and linens took priority over the dangers of foreign entanglements and domestic factionalism. Such household details took up an enormous amount of time, especially because Abigail was not there to help—"Luckily for you," he told her.

Abigail, however, worried about all those things and more. She still harbored a wish that they might retire instead of taking on even greater responsibilities. "Retirement at Peace Field," she told John, "I think would be a much more eligible situation than to be fastned up Hand & foot & Tongue to be shot at as our Quincy Lads do at the poor Geese and Turkies." But retirement would have to be postponed again, for at least four years more.

Chapter 15

Mrs. President

❧ ❧

John's election to the Presidency renewed all of Abigail's ambivalence about political life. On New Year's Eve she dreamed that she was riding in her coach when suddenly she saw many black balls the size of 24-pound cannonshot coming straight at her. They burst and fell to the ground before they reached her, but at that moment two guns were fired next to her ear. When she described the dream in a troubled letter to John, he urged her not to let her anxieties get the best of her; but clearly the prospect ahead frightened her.

Abigail worried most about the responsibility of running the country at a difficult time without the massive public support that Washington had enjoyed. The United States was in imminent danger of being dragged into a major European war with neither the money nor the military resources to succeed. The country was bitterly divided over foreign policy issues, and the peaceful transfer of executive authority from one administration to the next had yet to be tested. It rested on John Adams, a catankerous, unpopular man of little flexibility, to resolve these problems. Abigail had total confidence in his integrity and judgment but knew as well as he did that his personal qualities would make a difficult job still more difficult.

Abigail had her own personal concerns as well. As abrasive in her own way as John, she would find it hard to emulate Martha Washington's gracious Southern hospitality. Her weak health was an added problem. No longer could she remain in Quincy while John spent four or five months a year in Philadelphia; as First Lady, she would not be able to escape social duties. Both she and John would have to spend the greater part of the year in the capital.

At least the election of Jefferson as Vice President made her optimistic about the potential for unity between the Federalists and Republicans. Although Abigail and John had fallen out with Jefferson since their days of friendship in Paris, they never completely lost the respect they felt for each other. "Tho wrong in politicks, . . . and tho frequently mistaken in men & measures," she noted, Jefferson was still a man of integrity and sincerity.

John was much less concerned with all these matters. He worried instead about the practical details of becoming President. They would have to rent a house suitable to their station, preferably the same one the Washingtons had lived in; they must buy a carriage and horses, furniture, and other equipment for the house; and they must think about official entertaining, something John had been spared while living in bachelor quarters as Vice President. All these expenses would have to be taken out of a salary that had remained unchanged for eight years (at $25,000) while inflation had drastically cut its value. Congress refused to raise the salaries of the President and Vice President, even though the rent had doubled on the house the Washingtons had lived in. Much of the furniture in the house that had been bought at public expense would have to be replaced, and the cost of horses had at least tripled in seven years. "We shall be put to great difficulty to live and that in not one third the style of Washington," John complained to Abigail. Washington had had a substantial private fortune to supplement his salary; John and Abigail did not. They would just have to cut out most of their entertaining, John decided, and live frugally. Abigail agreed but reognized that some public entertaining was necessary to maintain respect for the office.

They decided that John should stay in Philadelphia alone through the spring and go home to Quincy in the summer; then Abigail would return with him in the fall. But John quickly discovered how difficult it was to make domestic arrangements without her help. Accustomed to having such things as house, furniture, and servants handled efficiently by Abigail, he spent an inordinate amount of time fretting about them without accomplishing much. Abigail made some suggestions from Quincy, but there was relatively little she could do at such a distance. Nor was she inclined to do very much anyway. In her opinion, Congress ought to provide a suitable house and furniture for the President; if the Adamses rushed around trying to make their own arrangements, it would be easy for Congress to do nothing.

At the moment she was much more concerned about their farms in Quincy. As was his habit, once John became more heavily involved in public business he completely lost interest in affairs at Quincy. In January he lamented to Abigail that he would miss seeing his crops growing that spring but added, "I have however almost forgotten my Farm . . . My whole Time and Thoughts must be devoted to the Public." Abigail, however, disagreed with John's casual attitude toward their property. She considered the farm "our *dernier* resort, as our Ark of Safety. I think it ought not to be sufferd to fall into decay."

Abigail's biggest chore was finding someone to look after their home farm when she left for Philadelphia. Ideally, she wanted someone who would live in their house while the Adamses were in Philadelphia, then move out in the summers when they returned to Quincy. She had a particular family in mind but could not persuade them to take on the responsibility of the Adams farm. March turned into April, and still she had found no one to care for their home.

The leases on their other two farms were running out, and Abigail had to negotiate new terms with the tenants there. One of them, a man named French, was particularly reliable and a hard worker, and she was eager to keep him. Inflation, however, had also made life hard for the tenants, who paid their own laborers and taxes; French wanted several concessions, including a new team of oxen, before he would agree to stay another year. Abigail, who normally drove a hard bargain, assented to all his wishes, so valuable a tenant did she consider him.

She had more trouble hiring laborers to work on the home farm. One man, a "bird of passage," as she called him, would not stay on another year. Another was troublesome and drank too much, so she didn't want to keep him; he had spent all winter building a stone wall and still wasn't finished. Then she lost one of her best laborers because two other people outbid her for his services. Abigail, who was always complaining about the high cost of labor, had offered him "more than I dare tell," but it still was not as much as others were willing to pay.

Along with her hired help, Abigail employed two or three black indentured servants. One of them, a boy named James, inadvertently created a minor local crisis that she quickly squelched. When a man in town opened a night school for apprentices, charging nominal tuition, James asked permission to attend. Abigail, who had taught him to read and write herself, granted it with pleasure.

A few days later one of her neighbors came by and asked her to withdraw James from the school. If she did not, he said, the school would close because the other boys would refuse to go. Why? Abigail asked. The other boys refused to attend school with a black boy, the neighbor responded. Abigail, who was no advocate of racial equality but did believe in education for everyone, exercised some of her piercing logic on her neighbor. Why did the other boys not refuse to go to church, she asked, where blacks attended the same services? Why were they so eager to have James play his fiddle for their dances, when to do so he had to be in the same room with them? To deny James an education was "attacking the principle of Liberty and equality upon the only ground upon which it ought to be supported, an equality of Rights." If James could not go to school, how could he hope to equip himself to earn a living? She asked her neighbor to send the other boys to her, confident she could convince them of their error. "Tell them," she added, "... I hope we shall all go to Heaven together." And that was the end of the controversy.

Abigail continued to ask John's advice about running the farms, but she received little in return other than repeated assurances of his confidence in everything she did. Unfortunately, however, John not only ignored the little details but sometimes forgot to send money when Abigail needed it. When town taxes fell due in March, she had no cash to pay them. Twice she turned the tax collector away with a promise to pay him later in the month. If she couldn't pay, the man responded, he didn't know who could.

On March 4 John was inaugurated President of the United States. He was so nervous about the event that he could not sleep the night before. "I am a Being of too much Sensibility to act any Part well in such an Exhibition," he told Abigail. Although he played down the importance of the occasion, later he regretted that none of his family was with him at what he called "the most affecting and overpowering scene I ever acted in." Abigail read all the speeches and accounts of the inauguration and was so moved by them that she too couldn't sleep one night. She was especially pleased that Washington had delayed his trip home to Mount Vernon long enough to attend the ceremony. "It will not fail to add Luster to the transaction in the Eyes of all foreign Nations and be honorable to his successor," she wrote John.

Shortly after the inauguration John moved into the house that the Washingtons had occupied. To his dismay, it was a mess—chairs were broken, there were no dishes, the house-cleaning had not been finished. He felt more and more helpless without Abigail's advice and decided not to buy any more furniture until she came in the fall. Nor would he hire any female servants, but would wait instead for her to bring women with her from New England.

By the end of March John was finding it impossible to manage a household as well as the country. He decided that Abigail must change all her plans and come immediately. Abigail, of course, could not pull up stakes and leave instantly, but John showed little awareness of the many things she had to do before she could move to Philadelphia. Through the month of April he dashed off letters every few days exhorting her to drop everything and come. She replied that she would come as soon as possible, "but there are many arrangements to make, or deliver all up to destruction, at once." This she was not willing to do, no matter what John said.

On the whole, things were progressing smoothly on the farm. The interminable stone walls were almost finished, plowing was getting under way, a new cart was being constructed, and the necessary tools had been purchased. Abigail made arrangements to have someone look after John's aging mother and agreed with John's brother to board a laborer who had been living on their farm. The big problem still was finding someone to live in their house and look after their farm. Finally she decided to ask a family named Porter. If they declined, she told John, she would have to sell all their possessions at auction and rent the house and farm to anyone who would take it, a most unsatisfactory arrangement. "It seems as if all our own interest must be sacrificed," she lamented.

Fortunately the Porters agreed to take the farm. By the third week in April Abigail was just about ready to leave when a freak spring snowstorm brought all the farm work to a halt. Then, just two days before she was scheduled to leave Quincy, John's mother died. Her death came as no suprise; she was eighty-nine and had been ill for some time. Still, it deeply affected Abigail. It was some small consolation that she had died while Abigail was still there to arrange the funeral.

Finally, at the end of April, Abigail and Louisa left Quincy. They reached Nabby's home at East Chester on May 4. Abigail found the situation there upsetting. William's financial reverses were worse than originally assumed. He had left East Chester, ostensibly to look after some real estate interests, and Nabby didn't know exactly where he was. On top of financial failure, Nabby now had to cope with loneliness, living without her husband in a small, remote town where she had few friends. "My reflections upon prospects there, took from me all appetite to food, and depresst my spirits, before too low," Abigail wrote her sister. "I could not converse with her. I saw her Heart too full. Such is the folly and madness of speculation and extravagance. To her no blame is due. Educated in different Habits, she never enjoyed a life of dissipation." The grandchildren were fine, but Abigail worried about bad influences on them. "I wish they were at Hingham under your care," she told Mary. Fortunately Charles, who had married William's sister, was doing well, living "prettily but frugally." Sally Smith Adams, in her opinion, was "a discreet woman . . . quite different from many of the Family."

The trip from New York to Philadelphia, which should have been relatively simple, turned out to be one of the most unpleasant journeys of Abigail's life. Unusually heavy rains turned the clay roads into a sea of mud, and the stagecoaches that constantly traveled the route cut deep ruts. The road, she reported, "was like a ploughd feild, in furroughs of 2 feet in deepth, and was very dangerous." The trip was so bad that she spent two days in bed afterward. But then she plunged right into her social duties. On her first day "at home" she received calls from thirty-two ladies and almost as many gentlemen in two and a half hours. She would go through the same ordeal every day for a week. At least she would be spared hosting formal "drawing rooms" for a while; they were traditionally suspended during the summer. "Mrs. Tufts once stiled my situation, splendid misery," Abigail remarked after her first few days as First Lady. "She was not far from the Truth."

She quickly settled down into an organized routine, determined not to let her multitude of social obligations get the best of her. "I keep up my old Habit of rising at an early hour. If I did not I should have little comand of my Time," she reported to Mary. Her "early hour" was 5 A.M.; the hours between five and eight were hers alone. At eight the family breakfasted, and then Abigail spent most of the morning looking after household affairs. At eleven she dressed for the day's more formal activities, which began with receiving visitors from noon to two or sometimes three. At three the Adamses ate dinner, except on "company days," which were invariably Tuesdays and Thursdays. After dinner she went for a ride in her carriage or visited others. At seven she was back home to spend some time with the family before an early bedtime.

Company dinners were major productions, with as many as thirty or forty guests at a time. One evening shortly after Abigail arrived, they entertained the entire Senate and Cabinet, which at that time totaled thirty-eight men. The House of Representatives was too large to be entertained at one sitting, so she planned a series of dinners for them. In the midst of planning her fifth large dinner party she wrote wearily that, after one more such affair, "I shall have got through the whole of Congress, with their apendages."

She had barely finished her round of dinners by July 4, when the President's family traditionally staged a large entertainment. It was one of the few times that Abigail criticized George Washington. He had begun the annual affair, inviting all of Congress, the leading citizens of Philadelphia, and state officials. Those who would not fit in the house were seated at long tables in the yard. Cake, punch, and wine were served. Washington had spent close to five hundred dollars each year on this gathering, Abigail reported to Mary; the guests consumed 200 pounds of cake and two quarter-casks of wine and spirits. "You will not wonder that I dread it, or think President Washington to blame for introducing the custom, if he could have avoided it," she added.

Official entertaining was a more onerous chore than it had

been when she was merely the Vice President's wife, but at least Abigail's domestic staff functioned more smoothly than her previous one. She had brought all her female servants with her from Quincy, except one woman to assist the cook, and turned over the chore of hiring and firing male servants exclusively to John Briesler. For the first time, Abigail set up a new household without complaining bitterly about the servants.

Political problems overshadowed the frustrations of official entertaining, however, as the French situation grew increasingly grave through the spring and summer. France, now governed by a small band of dictators known as the Directory, had intensified its campaign against the United States. Incensed by the election of Adams, who was known to be generally unsympathetic to France, the Directory ordered that American ships captured while carrying any British goods whatsoever be summarily condemned and their cargoes confiscated. They also ordered the American Minister to France, Charles Cotesworth Pinckney, out of the country. In effect, the Directory did everything short of declaring war on the United States.

In an effort to avoid war John decided to appoint three special envoys to negotiate with the Directory. He chose Pinckney, the expelled Minister; John Marshall of Virginia, one of the few Federalist leaders from the South; and Francis Dana, his former companion in Europe from the Revolutionary years. Dana declined the appointment, and John chose another old friend, Elbridge Gerry, in his place.

The crisis over France kept Congress in session well into the summer and prevented Abigail and John from getting away to Quincy in June as they had hoped. Abigail believed that the United States' position was becoming more critical every day. The Directory, she believed, was so unprincipled and power-hungry that it might do anything; but she also continued to believe that the danger came as much from within the United States as from France. Once again she saw Jacobins behind every tree, ready to join French agents in overthrowing the United States. And once again she considered the "Jacobin" newspapers the worst offenders in undermining public unity and confidence.

Congress finally adjourned early in July, and Abigail and John decided to go home to Quincy for a few weeks. They stopped in East Chester and took Nabby and the grandchildren with them to Quincy for the rest of the summer. William, whose financial affairs were still in disorder, had gone off to inspect some land in upstate New York as part of his latest effort to recoup his lost fortune.

Abigail worried about her grandchildren's future. William and John were old enough to begin their formal education, but there were no schools in East Chester. She was afraid that the boys would "imbibe" the spendthrift habits of their father rather than the good old New England virtues of industry and frugality that she so prized. The best solution seemed to be to remove them from East Chester; at the end of the summer she sent them to her sister Elizabeth in Atkinson. The boys could be prepared for college in an academy there under the watchful eye of their greataunt. Nabby concurred in this arrangement, but it was Abigail who concocted the plan, worked out the details, and paid for the boys' tuition and board.

Abigail, John, and Nabby stayed in Quincy two months. By the beginning of October, when it was time for them to get back to Philadelphia, that city was in the throes of another yellow fever epidemic. They decided to go as far as East Chester and stay at Nabby's home until it was safe to continue south, but the epidemic dragged on longer than anyone expected. John and Abigail remained in East Chester for a month before they dared enter the stricken city.

Abigail had never spent more than a day or two in East Chester on her way to and from Philadelphia. Now, cooped up there for a month, she was appalled at the thought of Nabby's spending a winter there alone. "One might as well be out of America as in this village only 20 miles distant from N York," she wrote Mary, "for unless we send in on purpose we cannot even get a Newspaper out." Nabby had no friends there; with her husband and sons away, she had only her daughter for company. Letters from William were few and far between, and no one knew exactly where he was or when he was coming back. Unwilling to leave Nabby alone under these conditions, Abigail urged her to come along and spend the winter in Philadelphia. But Nabby, whose sense of domestic responsibility was just as strong as her mother's, refused to leave her home in case William should return unexpectedly. Abigail was convinced that Nabby would be waiting for him all winter.

She actually thought it would be better in some ways if William did not return. Abigail did not want Nabby to suffer, but she also thought William was a bad influence on the children. She had long been convinced that he was a good-for-nothing; his long absence and mysterious silence confirmed her judgment. Commenting on her decision to send her grandchildren to New Hampshire, she noted, "I was fully sensible that the Boys must be taken from all their connections to break them of habits which they had imbibed. There were a train of uncles and Aunts and servants to spoil them and very few examples such as I wisht to have them innured to, and I dread their Fathers return least he should take it into his Head to take them away." In short, it was not just William but his whole family who were corrupting her grandchildren, and there was a part of her that wanted to sever all connection with the Smith family, despite the lip service she paid to Nabby's conjugal duties.

Abigail also spent a good deal of time during the winter worrying about affairs in Quincy. Their house, she had decided that summer, was definitely too small, and she was scarcely on the road back to Philadelphia when she began corresponding with Cotton Tufts about a large addition. By the end of November Tufts was having plans drawn up for her approval, although work did not begin until late the next spring. He and Abigail decided to extend the rear of the building and knock out a wall to create a single room large enough to accommodate John's library.

These changes were completed the following summer, shortly before John and Abigail returned for their annual visit. All of the planning and most of the construction were accomplished without John's knowledge. Abigail preferred to surprise him. He would be happy with the additions when completed, but hearing about them while they were under construction would only cause him extra worry. It was her way of shielding him from any concerns except national business, which she had been doing for years, although never quite to such an extent. She kep her secret by making it clear to John that he was not to open her mail. She had scolded him once for opening a letter from Mary; after that, all correspondence with Mary was sacrosanct, so she instructed Tufts to enclose his letters in hers.

John had his little secrets with Tufts too. The President asked him to invest more money in land even though he knew that Abigail disapproved. But she was too clever for him; she wrote Tufts that she knew what John was up to. She preferred to invest in securities, and sent Tufts money for this purpose whenever she could scrape it together out of her household budget. Since she, in effect, controlled most of the family's money, that was not too difficult to do. She also managed to pay for most of the addition to the house in this manner, sending $100 here, $200 there, whenever she could manage it.

Abigail almost got away with her plot. For months she relished the prospect of watching John's reaction when he saw the changed appearance of their house. But a few weeks before they were to leave Philadelphia, a friend from home came to town and called on the Adamses. Not knowing that the construction was a secret, he spilled the beans. "The President had a hearty laugh & says he is sorry it was not carried clear along," Abigail told Mary.

Abigail could get away with ordering her grandchildren to New Hampshire and with ordering an addition to be built to the house without John's knowledge, because for years she had run the family without any significant interference from anyone. As she grew older she became more outspoken, more opinionated, and much more willing to assert her views on the way things ought to be done. John was only too happy to have all things domestic taken care of without his giving them a second thought, and the children had long since gotten used to deferring to Mamma's judgment.

She also became bolder about expressing her opinions on politics. Although she never presumed to press her ideas on John, she did offer her advice, and he came to depend on her as his closest confidante. She quietly sent letters and articles supporting John's policies to friendly newspaper editors with instructions to publish them. They always complied. Usually such items were taken from letters of John Quincy, who regularly sent his mother dire predictions about France's intentions toward the United States. Abigail was always specific in her instructions to the editors; she told them exactly which passages to publish and which words to change so the author's identity would be concealed.

Other people recognized her great influence over John. She received frequent letters from office-seekers asking her to intercede with the President, and she answered many of them. Some people thought she had too much influence; one Republican Senator observed sarcastically that "the President would not dare to make a nomination without her approbation." But in the political jungle of Philadelphia in the 1790s, John sometimes thought she was the only person he could trust completely. This was never more true than in the winter and spring of 1798.

The Congressional session opened quietly enough. Pro- and anti-French passions still ran high, and French depredations against American shipping were still the main topic of debate. But until the envoys arrived in Paris and sent back information, there was little that could be done. Abigail continued to rant and rave about French agents and Frenchified Americans, about the lies of "Jacobin" newspapers and the moral degradation of the French nation.

The Directory, she believed, was driving itself to destruction by its tyrannical actions and was trying to take the rest of Europe and America with it. She was afraid that the United States was not firm enough in its resistance to French aggression and invoked memories of the more glorious days of the American Revolution. "I am at a loss to know how the people who were formerly so much alive to the usurpation of one Nation can crouch so tamely to a much more dangerous and dareing one," she wrote. She was mortified that Massachusetts had elected three "Jacobin" Congressmen, but on the whole she found in the politics of the New England states her sole cause for optimism. Philadelphia was a hotbed of Jacobinism, and the South had been on the wrong political track since the end of the Revolution; but New Englanders, for the most part, showed a remarkable unity of purpose. She feared that the pro- and anti-French factions would tear the country apart. It was especially troublesome that the South tended to be pro-French and the North anti-French. "I hope we may be held together," she wrote to her sister Elizabeth, "but I know not how long, for oil & water are not more contrary in their natures, than North and South."

When she was fired up about the evils of the French, Abigail sounded very much like someone advocating war, which ran counter to all of John's efforts for peace. But in her calmer moments she too advocated peace and she understood perfectly well that nothing could be done until letters arrived from the envoys. In January the first news from them arrived indirectly in letters from the American Minister in Holland, and the news was enough to confirm Abigail's worst fears. The French had refused to receive the Americans. Still, no action against France could be taken until official dispatches arrived from the Ministers themselves.

January and February dragged on with no official news. Finally, at the beginning of March, the first official dispatches from the envoys confirmed the earlier indirect reports. Because John confided everything to Abigail, she knew immediately about the events that fulfilled all her predictions. Not only had the Directory refused to receive the envoys after insolently keeping them waiting for weeks, but the chief Minister, Talleyrand, had the gall to suggest that they might be received if the United States paid a bribe of $250,000. The Directory also wanted a loan of $12 million and a public apology for John's anti-French remarks made in a speech to Congress the previous spring. Acceding to these demands was a condition of their recognition by the French government. The Americans refused, and the prospect of peace negotiations collapsed.

John sent the dispatches to Congress with requests to appropriate money for expanding the army and navy and to permit merchant ships to arm. Congress voted to publish the dispatches; the result was an outpouring of public anger against France. The anti-French rhetoric of the Federalist party seemed vindicated at last. John and his party were never more popular than in the spring of 1798. "Millions for defense but not one cent for tribute" was the slogan coined by one newspaper editor. The three agents of Talleyrand who had demanded the bribe (called X, Y, and Z in the envoys' dispatches) became the villains of the day.

The XYZ Affair stifled pro-French opinion, briefly quieted the Republican press, and turned the tide of public sentiment from favoring peace at all costs to favoring preparedness for war. The town meetings that had earlier petitioned the President to preserve peace now sent addresses denouncing France and supporting his policies. Congress authorized money to construct more ships, purchase arms, fortify the harbors, and triple the size of the army. John Adams suddenly, to his great surprise, became the man of the hour. He and Abigail, instead of being lambasted in the press, were cheered wherever they went.

Abigail, not surprisingly, interpreted the sudden surge in the President's popularity and in anti-French opinion as a sign that "the people" were finally coming to their senses. Suddenly she changed her tune about public willingness to defend American liberties. "The people are daily becomeing more firmly decided, and united," she reported to John Quincy, "more disposed to repel insult with due energy, and having failed in attempts to negotiate, I think they will unite to defend our Country and protect our Commerce." This was a point she had often made before. The people, left to their own devices, were fundamentally just and would eventually do the right thing. They were easily duped by newspapers and unscrupulous politicians; they often acted painfully slowly; but sooner or later they would find the right path and follow it. The great rush of support for John's policies strengthened that belief more than anything ever before.

From Abigail's point of view, the XYZ Affair produced more positive than negative results. As she told Cotton Tufts, it seemed as if the envoys had sent back good news rather than bad. It was true that war looked imminent, but "war with union, war in defence of all we hold dear is not so allarming as the secret plots which were diging mines for our destruction." After all, in effect the country was already at war because of French attacks on American ships, but Americans to that point had not been able to defend themselves adequately. "I hope we shall have spirit and energy sufficient to arm, and defend ourselves," she wrote, "and if that obliges us to declare war, the sooner the better."

But neither John nor Congress was prepared to declare war just yet. Instead they concentrated on building up the United States' woefully inadequate military forces. The Navy launched three new ships in the summer, and Congress authorized construction of twenty-four more. To protect against the possibility of a direct French attack against the United States, Congress also ordered that an army of several thousand troops be raised, and John asked George Washington to come out of retirement and serve as its Commander-in-Chief.

There could be little opposition to strengthening the country's military defenses. But John, along with most Federalists, believed that measures also had to be taken to quell dissent within the country itself. For some time there had been talk of taking steps to control both the increasing numbers of foreigners in the United States and the totally unrestrained press. These two issues were linked in Abigail's mind. She maintained that the most unscrupulous journalists were invariably foreigners, who had come to America to stir up popular opposition to the government. In the present quasi-war conditions such measures seemed increasingly necessary. As a result, in June and July Congress passed the Alien and Sedition Acts—a series of laws that permitted the arrest of newspaper editors for publishing seditious statements against the government, increased the naturalization period for foreigners from five to fourteen years, and allowed the deportation of aliens accused of seditious activities.

No one was more strongly in favor of such laws than Abigail. She had argued their necessity for months end was much more adamant on the subject than John. Once the laws were passed, Abigail thought they were far too weak. In their final form they "were shaved and pared, to almost nothing," she complained to John Quincy. Nevertheless, she added, "they have had a salutary effect, weak as they are."

The Alien and Sedition Acts proved enormously unpopular and gave the Republicans a critical issue to use against John in the next election. They also had relatively little effect; all of them either lapsed or were repealed by 1801. But at the time Abigail and others of like mind were absolutely convinced that foreign subversives stalked the United States and that unscrupulous newspaper editors were their agents.

A story went around Philadelphia in May that French residents, with some American sympathizers, had conspired to set the city on fire and massacre the inhabitants. Abigail became even more agitated when she read a book by a Scotsman named John Robinson, who asserted that a European conspiracy was forming to overthrow all established religion and with it all the free governments of the world. She was absolutely convinced by the book, especially when John Quincy wrote her that a French agent, Dupont de Nemours, had been sent to the United States to form societies like those described by Robinson. She told everyone she knew about the book and about John Quincy's comments on it. There was never any evidence to support Robinson's preposterous theories, but such were the times in 1798 that conspiracies, foreign agents, and dangerous incendiaries seemed omnipresent.

By summer war appeared certain. Congress did everything to prepare for war with France short of actually declaring it. This omission, Abigail thought, was a great mistake. When Congress adjourned without declaring war, she criticized the members for their lack of courage. John, of course, had not recommended such a declaration and was himself eager to avoid war. But she disregarded all that and attributed Congress's inaction to her favorite whipping boy, foreign influence.

Abigail and John were eager to return to Quincy for their annual summer vacation, but the gravity of foreign affairs prolonged Congress's session and demanded John's presence even after Congress adjourned. It was August before they were able to get away for a few weeks' rest. The summer heat in Philadelphia had become unbearable, and the weather as they traveled through New York and New England was almost as bad. Abigail could not recall a more miserably unpleasant journey. By the time they reached Quincy, she was seriously ill. She took to her bed and stayed there for three months, prostrated with the intermittent fever that plagued her periodically.

She usually had one or two bouts of intermittent fever a year, but they seldom kept her in bed more than a few days. This attack was the most serious she had ever experienced. For days she believed herself near death. Nabby was at her side constantly, and John worried himself to distraction, sick with the thought that he would lose his "dearest friend." But Abigail was not yet ready to give up, and slowly she pulled out of the crisis. By early November she was well enough for John to leave her and return to Philadelphia. It was still out of the question for Abigail to risk her health by accompanying him. Instead he had for a companion his nephew, William Shaw, whom John had just hired as his personal secretary. Nabby left for home several days later.

When both John and Nabby had gone, Abigail was very lonely. She was still not fully recovered and remained confined to the house. Not until the end of November was she strong enough to go out for short rides in her carriage and visit her sister. As her health improved, she contemplated joining John in Philadelphia. But John was afraid that the journey, combined with the hectic social life of Philadelphia, would prove her undoing. "I know you have certain Ideas that you have a Part and that you ought to be at it. But these Duties are superceded by necessity," he wrote. He discouraged her from coming and consoled her with his certainty that the Congressional session would be short and that he would be home by March or April.

Over the next few months, both Abigail and John worried increasingly about their children. William Smith seemed no closer to a permanent solution to his financial troubles. Now Charles too showed signs of poor judgment and emotional instability. Charles, the charming boy who had captivated everyone around him, the promising young lawyer who had built a successful practice at a remarkably early age, had taken to drink and was neglecting his business and his family. John Quincy had left Charles in charge of his financial affairs, and he appeared to be making a mess of them as well. Abigail and John Quincy tried without success to get Charles to account for his investments with John Quincy's money. Abigail, in addition, lectured him by mail on his behavior. But she recognized that he was emotionally troubled and that there was little that a mother's letter could do. "The poor child is unhappy I am sure," she told John Quincy, "he is not at peace with himself, and his conduct does not meet my wishes. . . . I hope my Letters will in time have their effect. I have discharged my duty I hope faithfully but my dying Bed was embitterd (as I then thought it) with distress for the only child whose conduct ever caused me pain."

John despaired over Charles's problems. In a black mood one day, he wrote Abigail that children were nothing but trouble. George Washington was a happy man, he told her, because he had no children to give him pain. When he reflected on his children's problems, guilt gnawed at him—guilt about his devotion to public duty, his years away from home, the time not spent with his children. Shouldn't he have stayed home and looked after their interests? he asked Abigail. As a successful lawyer, he might have amassed the money that could bail out Nabby and her husband or set John Quincy up in practice instead of sending him overseas. But it was too late to change now. "I have done all for my children that I could," he wrote, "and meant all for the best. What have I not suffered? What have I ever enjoyed? All my Enjoyments have been upon my farm. Oh that my Children and Grandchildren were all Farmers!"

Abigail tried to console John. Her first loyalty was always to him, and she would never allow him to diminish the importance of his life's work. "With respect to what is past," she told him, "all was intended for the best, and you have the satisfaction of knowing that you have faithfully served your generation . . . at the expence of all private Considerations. . . . You do not know whether you would have been a happier Man in private, than you have been in publick Life." As for George Washington's fortunate lack of children, she noted, "if he has none to give him pain, he has none to give him pleasure." She herself never expressed any doubts about the way she had raised her children. She continued to believe that a mother's influence was paramount in her children's future development, but she also understood that no one was perfect, and she had done her best.

At least there was one bright spot on the horizon. Thomas was on his way home at last. Abigail and John expected him to arrive sometime in December, although they had no definite word about waht ship he had taken from Europe. The usual anxiety that Abigail felt whenever a member of her family went to sea was intensified as December drew to a close and she still had no word of Thomas. Finally, on January 13, John received a letter from Thomas announcing his arrival in New York after nearly two months at sea. He lost no time in getting to Philadelphia, arriving at the President's house two days later, just as one of John's levees was breaking up. Tears streamed down John's face as he greeted his youngest son for the first time in four and a half years.

Thomas stayed in Philadelphia three weeks before setting out to visit his mother, who was impatiently awaiting his arrival. Abigail rejoiced to see him, but the sight of her youngest son—handsome, robust, his manners refined, his wit sharpened, and his powers of observation heightened by his years in Europe—only reminded her of the failure of her other son, Charles. Her happiness at seeing Thomas was tempered by her constant worry about "one, of whose reformation I can flatter myself, with but faint hopes."

There was only one thing that Abigail regretted about not being in Philadelphia that winter—besides missing John's company, of course—and that was being away from the scene of political action. William Shaw wrote her regularly and sent all the Philadelphia newspapers, but John had little time to write, and his infrequent letters were brief. "I dont like the president as a correspondent half as well as *the vice* president," she told him.

On the whole, it was a quiet winter compared with the crisis of the year before. The American Navy did an effective job of keeping French ships out of American coastal waters. Losses among the merchant marine were vastly diminished. British forces had inflicted serious defeats on the French in European battles, and so the prospect of French invasion of the United States looked less and less likely. Elbridge Gerry returned from France in the fall, bringing the first indications that the French were prepared to negotiate. In February, encouraged by France's peace feelers, John appointed William Vans Murray, then minister to the Netherlands, as Minister Plenipotentiary to France.

The response was immediate and vociferous. The Republicans, of course, could be expected to criticize everything John did, but on this decision many Federalists criticized him also. Extreme Federalists like Alexander Hamilton hated the French and preferred war to a negotiated peace. They had a great deal invested in keeping alive the fear of an imminent French invasion, and peace negotiations ruined that illusion. Some moderate Federalists approved of John's action in principle but believed it would be more appropriate to send a peace commission composed of at least three Ministers rather than a single man.

Abigail was amused when Thomas returned from a trip to Boston where he had overheard some Federalists say that they "wisht the old woman had been there; they did not believe it would have taken place." They had good reason for such a statement, for Abigail was more warlike than John on the question of France, and her influence over him on political matters was well known. It had been Abigail, after all, who complained at length the previous spring when Congress adjourned without declaring war on France. But this time she agreed with John. "The old woman can tell them they are mistaken," she wrote him, "for she considers the measure as a master stroke of policy."

She had several reasons for approving of John's action. It showed that the United States, despite all its provocations, was still working for peace, and it challenged the Directory to prove its sincerity in professing an interest in peaceful negotiation. Nevertheless, she believed that war could not be ruled out. She argued that it would be a mistake to reduce military strength, as the House wanted to do, because "to ensure any kind of success to the negotiation, they should be prepared at all points for war, if it fails. Pray am I a good politician?" she concluded.

Nothing—not even the controversy over reopening diplomatic negotiations with France—was enough to keep John in

Philadelphia after Congress adjourned in March. He left so abruptly, in fact, that many Philadelphians complained that he was neglecting public business. A friend of Abigail's tried to write her tactfully on the subject, but she dismissed the warning without even discussing it with John. The post brought letters promptly from Philadelphia, and he spent much of his time in Quincy answering them, so where was any harm done? As far as Abigail and John were concerned, five months apart was more than enough.

By the time John arrived home, work was well under way on a new barn that he and Abigail had planned the previous summer. As it neared completion, they began thinking about an even more ambitious project, a large addition to the house that would virtually double its size. Plans had to be drawn up and lumber ordered, and so the addition did not actually get under way for many months. But eventually these changes substantially completed the transformation of "Peacefield" from a comfortable seven-room farmhouse to a gracious estate fit for a President and his lady.

In April Thomas returned to Philadelphia to establish a legal practice there. Abigail had hoped he would settle near Quincy, and she parted with him reluctantly. She worried about him, especially about the danger of yellow fever; she made him promise that he would flee the city at the first sign of disease. She also wrote to a close friend in Philadelphia, Mary Otis, asking that Thomas be permitted to board with them. She was concerned about his "delicate" health, she told Mrs. Otis, and would rest easier knowing that he lived under her "maternal care."

Thomas himself had other ideas, preferring to live in a boarding house recommended by his friends rather than board with the Otises. Thomas had a streak of independence that caused him to bridle at his mother's protectiveness. He chose to live in Philadelphia and to live on his own. He spent much of his time with Quakers, and preferred their simple dress to the ornate styles fashionable in the 1790s. He refused to wear a wig or dress his hair in the manner common among gentlemen, despite his parents' criticism. He wrote gleefully to Abigail of an encounter with a man who had known John twenty years earlier. The gentleman, he wrote, said that Thomas reminded him of his father as a young man; in particular, John had worn his hair the same way. "Did he, indeed, Sir?" Thomas responded. "The information is very acceptable to me and shall not be lost, for I have been somewhat persecuted since my return on account of the cut of my hair." The man replied that no doubt it was because the wigless Thomas appeared too "democratic."

Abigail's health improved steadily through the summer, and she decided definitely to return to Philadelphia in the fall. She had a special reason this winter, aside from her desire to be with John and fulfill her duties as First Lady; this would be the last season that the government would meet in Philadelphia before moving to the new capital city of Washington.

It was also the last time, presumably, that she would live in close proximity to Thomas, so she asked him to grant her one request—to live with his parents during the coming winter. He might keep his office elsewhere and come and go as he pleased, but at least she would have the pleasure of his frequent company. Somewhat reluctantly, Thomas agreed. Nabby and Caroline also spent most of the winter with them. William, who had accepted a commission in the newly organized Army, would spend the winter training troops at a camp in New Jersey.

As usual, Abigail stopped in New York on her way South. Charles's situation had not improved, but she was delighted with his two daughters. Susan, the older one, at three years of age showed remarkable intelligence. She "would stand all day to hear you read stories, which she will catch at a few times repeating, and has got all goody Goose stories by Heart," Abigail told Mary. "She tells me all her Letters and would read in a month if she had a good school." Abbe, the younger, was even prettier than her sister and appeared to be equally precocious. But Abigail worried about their future. With a drunkard father who neglected his business, how could they ever hope to have the education and care they deserved?

For Nabby's children she was slightly more hopeful. At least the boys were still in school and safely under Elizabeth's care. Abigail continued to pay close attention to their schooling; they should be particularly attentive to writing and mathematics, she told her sister. "I want to have them not smatterers intoxicated with superficial knowledge but hard students and deep thinkers.

Impress them with the Idea that they have not any dependence but upon their own exertions," she wrote. They too could not expect any help, either moral or financial, from a ne'er-do-well father.

It was a very social winter in Philadelphia. The next year was to see the seat of government move to the new federal city of Washington, and so Philadelphians were making the most of their last season as the nation's capital. The wives of Congressmen, who believed (correctly, for the most part) that there would be no living accommodations for them in Washington, were also taking advantage of their last winter in civilized society. In addition to the usual drawing rooms, Abigail entertained twice a week and received visits constantly. Despite the hectic pace, her health was better than it had been in years. In fact, she herself caught some of the spirit of the time and enjoyed the active social life more than she cared to admit.

As the nation's capital and largest city, Philadelphia was also America's fashion capital. Abigail did not particularly like the latest fashions, but she let her friends at home know what well-dressed ladies were wearing that winter. She sent the wife of one of her cousins a miniature gown as a model of the latest style, with detailed descriptions of the accessories and hair styles currently favored. She also took advantage of the First Lady's influence in matters of society and fashion to try to change styles she considered frivolous. In particular, she thought that fashionable ladies did not dress warmly enough in winter. "I wish any thing would persuade the Ladies that muslin is not a proper winter dress," she told Mary. "So far as example goes, I shall bring in the use of silks. At my Age I think I am priviledged to sit a fashion."

It was not merely the flimsy fabric but also the style of the new fashions that bothered Abigail. The "empire style" featured simple dresses with low necklines, short sleeves, raised waistlines, and loose, flowing skirts—a sharp contrast to the tight bodices, elaborate long sleeves, and heavy, full skirts that had been popular for decades. The empire dresses were intended to drape the body in folds of fabric in imitation of Greek and Roman statues. They were part of the renewed interest in classical styles that swept painting, sculpture, and architecture in the 1790s. But while most people applauded neoclassical styles in art, some questioned their appropriateness in women's dress. A

Philadelphia minister attacked the new fashions as indecent, and Abigail agreed. Not only were the necklines too low and the sleeves too short, but the drapery of the skirts revealed too much of the body's form. When a woman attired in such a dress was introduced at Abigail's drawing room and made her curtsey as etiquette demanded, "every Eye in the Room had been fixd upon her, and you might litterally see through her." Most women, she noted, did not dress quite so daringly, "but they most of them wear their Cloaths too scant upon the body and too full upon the Bosom for my fancy. Not content with the *show which* nature bestows, they borrow from art, and litterally look like Nursing Mothers."

Political debate was relatively subdued that winter compared to previous years. The disputes with France seemed to have been resolved, for the time being at least, and attention centered on domestic matters, specifically the coming Presidential election. A year before the election, parties and factions were already trying to carve out their places. The Federalists were seriously divided between the extreme wing of the party, which looked to Alexander Hamilton for leadership, and the moderates, who followed John Adams. The Republicans were gaining strength and were determined to put one of their men in the President's chair in 1800.

All this "electioneering," as Abigail called it, distressed her. The Presidency, in her opinion, was not supposed to be a subject of political debate and backroom deals. Once the people elected a President they ought to leave him there, she contended, until he either chose to retire or betrayed the public trust. But it was obvious that things were not going to work that way. It also became increasingly clear as the months went by that John might lose the election.

John expressed his usual ambivalence about continuing in public office and his usual conviction that his unpopularity would make the decision for him. But Abigail, despite her professed desire to spend the rest of her days quietly in Quincy, clearly believed that John should be reelected and should continue to serve. The prospect of his defeat made her doubt the wisdom of holding frequent elections. "One or two more Elections will be quite sufficient I believe to convince this people that no engine can be more fatally employd than frequent popular Elections, to corrupt and destroy the morals of the people," she wrote. For three years "we have enjoyd as much peace, quiet, Security and happiness as any people can boast of." But now, with an election just a few months away, all the old political venom was back in circulation.

The political attacks on John came from two sides—from Republicans and from some Federalists—but Abigail naturally thought the greater threat came from the Republicans or Jacobins, as she continued to call them. To Abigail, election of a "Jacobin" President was tantamount to overthrowing the government. "What ungratefull Beings must we be in America," she complained, "if we permit party annimosities, and private ambition to overturn the goodly fabrick of our National Government." The election of Republicans in several states at the same time looked suspiciously like conspiracy to her. She believed that the election of a Republican as President, even her old friend Jefferson, would threaten the stability of the country.

Abigail's last few weeks in Philadelphia were clouded by acrimonious political debate and by her fears—genuine if unfounded—that the country might not survive the next election. But nothing could dampen her spirits completely, as she enjoyed an unusually early and beautiful spring. Philadelphia, she had to admit, was a lovely city. She admired the streets laid out in an orderly grid plan—in such marked contrast to New England towns—the abundant trees, the brick-paved streets, and the elegant town houses, many of them built in the last few years. As she contemplated leaving, she felt sad, even though she had never expressed much love for the city before. She had always felt a twinge of regret when she left a place knowing she would probably never return; now she felt the same emotions as she had upon leaving Paris and London. "There is something always melancholy, in the Idea of leaving a place for the last time," she explained to Mary. "It is like burying a Friend."

Her sadness at leaving Philadelphia was heightened by her apprehensions about what lay ahead. Washington, by all reports, was as yet little more than a village in the wilderness, and she wished that the move could be put off at least until the beginning of the next Presidential term.

Abigail's three years as First Lady had substantially changed her attitudes about Philadelphia, about its society, and even about politics. She enjoyed the time she spent there during John's Presidency and stayed away one winter only when she was too sick to travel; during the Vice Presidential years, on the other hand, she had resented the time spent in Philadelphia and had eventually used her health as an excuse to stay home.

What changed Abigail's attitude was the importance of John's position as President and, by implication, hers as First Lady. They were still attacked in the press, they still thought John's salary was too low, they hated the rough-and-tumble of political life as much as ever, but no one could deny that John had achieved the public recognition he craved. After the XYZ Affair, he even enjoyed a good deal of unaccustomed popularity. Abigail had always established her own identity through her husband's achievements. When he thought he was unimportant, as he did when he was Vice President, she too thought of herself as unimportant. With John as President, she threw herself into the role of confidante to her husband and First Lady to the nation. She too felt that her work was important, and she forgot for the moment her desire to be at home among her family and her distaste for public life. Ironically, just as she began to enjoy being a political wife, John's public career—and hers with it—ended.

Chapter 16

"The Federal City"

Abigail left Philadelphia in May and stopped off at the army camp in New Jersey where Nabby and Caroline had gone to live with William. She had a grand time touring the camp and reviewing the troops. "I acted . . . as your proxy," she told John. Abigail had always been John's "proxy" in some ways; she was his closest confidante, a sounding board for his ideas, and an informal adviser. During his years as President, when they were almost constantly together, her role as political adviser became even more important. More and more she referred to herself and John collectively, almost as if they were one mind or one person. During the last few months of his presidency, as he came under increasing political fire and faced the very real possibility of losing his bid for reelection, Abigail's constant presence and support became more critical than ever.

Her visit to the army camp was a fascinating experience, but Abigail found little there to reassure her about Nabby's future. An army camp was no place to raise a daughter. Besides, the army was about to be disbanded by order of Congress, and William would become a private citizen again, his future prospects as uncertain as ever. Predictably, Abigail tried to persuade Nabby to spend the summer with them in Quincy.

On her way home she stopped to see Charles and his family. A few days' visit convinced her that Charles had not mended his ways. In fact, the situation there appeared so serious that she decided to take Susan, the older of Charles's daughters, home to

Quincy with her. Sally took Abbe, the younger daughter, with her to live with Sally's mother later in the summer.

Abigail and Susan arrived in Quincy on the last day of May to find that the addition to their house was progressing, "but not so fast as I wish." She was now able to supervise the last stages of building and finishing in person. When the job was completed later in the summer, Abigail finally felt that she had the house arranged to her satisfaction.

The new addition, along with those completed in previous years, doubled the size of the original house. It included a new entryway, a much-expanded kitchen, and a huge drawing room on the first floor. Abigail moved her finest European furniture and the family portraits to this spacious new room. With windows on three sides looking out over the grounds, the room was pleasantly cool in summer, although its large fireplace was not always effective against the drafts of winter. Upstairs above the drawing room was an equally large room for John's study. Outside, the addition blended remarkably well with the original house. The new windows and shutters were built to look like the old, and the front door was moved to maintain the symmetrical appearance of the house.

Abigail had a full house that summer, with Nabby and Caroline visiting in addition to little Susan. Supervising the completion of the addition was an extra burden. But the subject that was most often on her mind was the coming Presidential election. This campaign was even more acrimonious than the one four years earlier, largely because the Federalists were seriously divided and were slinging mud at each other as well as at the Republicans.

The whole affair disgusted Abigail. She had never been able to accept the idea of competing political parties, each with its own set of candidates to promote. To her there was one "correct" political position, and anyone who had the best interests of the country at heart followed it. All those with other opinions were misguided or pursued their own selfish ends. Nor could she accept the idea that a frequent rotation of elected officials might be beneficial. Stability was crucial, she believed, and elected officials ought to be continued in office as long as they were performing their jobs adequately. She remained convinced that the election of a new President with political views substantially different from John's would be a disaster for the country.

The split among the Federalists bothered Abigail even more than the machinations of the Republicans. In her opinion, the Federalists were not a political party at all, but simply the aggregate of all men who supported the government and the Constitution. For some of them to engage in the same kind of wheeling and dealing favored by the Republicans was a sorry state of affairs indeed. Alexander Hamilton, the acknowledged leader of those Federalists who had split with John over the issue of peace with France, was now up to the same sort of tricks he had practiced in the 1796 election—working behind the scenes to drum up support for a candidate whom he could control—but this time he was aided by widespread disaffection in Federalist ranks. This time he was also much more open about his politicking.

The "little General," as Abigail called him, used his position as commander of the army to build up political support. While traveling around the country ostensibly to review troops, he was really "Electioneering," she complained. Thomas in Philadelphia and friends in New York sent news that confirmed her conviction that Hamilton was trying to divide the Federalists and undermine the present administration. She believed— correctly, as it turned out—that his machinations would only hurt the Federalists and contribute to the election of Jefferson.

The Hamiltonian Federalists were united primarily by their hatred of France, a hatred so extreme that they preferred war to a negotiated peace. They believed that the United States' best interests lay with Britain and that the country should align itself with Britain against France. Abigail dubbed them the "Anglo-American faction" and was convinced that such extreme pro-British attitudes were just as dangerous as the Republicans' pro-French views. She firmly believed that the United States must maintain its independence from all foreign nations and that both the Hamiltonians and the Jeffersonians threatened that independence. "Brittania & Gallia, are the two rivals which have severed many Friends," she wrote. "One party is making Love to one, and an other party to an other—and they are ready to sacrifice some of their friends, and their chief into the Bargain because he insists upon it that he will not quarrel with either." Only if John were reelected could disaster be avoided. Then, she believed, "we may get on four years more should he live so long, with tolerable quiet."

It was not only her husband's political career but her son's that would be affected by the Federalists' behavior. A Republican President would almost certainly recall John Quincy, but Abigail thought it was time he came home anyway. He had been gone six years, and she and John missed his company. More to the point, it would be best for his career to come home now. In explaining her reasoning to him, she showed herself to be a shrewd political analyst, quite capable of considering her son's best interests as well as his country's despite all her disclaimers to the contrary. She was fond of telling John Quincy that the time had come when he could serve his country better at home than abroad, and she told him so again now. But the time had come when he could serve himself better at home too. "Services rendered to a Country in a diplomatic line can be known only to a few," she wrote him. "If they are important and become conspicuous they rather excite envy than gratitude."

Abigail's comments to John Quincy were one sign of her increasing tendency to run the lives of her children and grandchildren. She didn't advise John Quincy to come home, she told him. Like Thomas, however, John Quincy was capable of standing up to his mother while remaining deferential toward her. He decided that it would be most proper for him to wait to be recalled rather than submit his resignation; and he also made it clear that he was not particularly eager to leave Europe. He was finally beginning to feel that his presence there was important, and he had no desire to return to the bar. Clearly, if he could stay in politics, he would.

By the end of the summer John and Abigail were convinced he would not be reelected, and there was some indecision—characteristic indecision—about whether Abigail should accompany John to Washington in the fall for the last months of his term as President. Finally, however, they decided she should. John left Quincy on October 11, and Abigail followed several days later. John reached Washington November 1 and pronounced the President's house "habitable." Meanwhile Abigail stopped in New York to see Charles and learned that he was seriously ill and was unlikely to live more than a few weeks. His illness was a combination of ailments—a serious cough, a liver infection, and dropsy—and his doctors had given up any hope of curing him.

There was nothing Abigail could do. Her son, the child who had been the "darling of the neighborhood" and of his father's companions in Europe, the young man who had captured ladies' hearts with his handsome face and charming manners, was dying at the age of thirty-one. Abigail could only take leave of her son and try to hide her grief, knowing that it was the last time.

Charles died early in December, shortly after Abigail reached Washington. "Weep with me over the Grave of a poor unhappy child who cannot now add an other pang to those which have pierced my Heart for several years past," she wrote Mary. "He was no mans Enemy but his own—He was beloved, in spight of his Errors, and all spoke with grief and sorrow for his habits."

Charles's problems and his death remain shrouded in mystery. Abigail and John never discussed them much, apart from expressing their distress at his unstable habits. Abigail often described him as "unhappy," a man not at peace with himself. He abandoned his family and his business for varying stretches of time and indulged in drink. In a later century his problems would have been diagnosed as mental illness, but Abigail and John could see his decline only as a failure of moral will.

It was ironic that in some respects Charles appeared to be the most successful of the Adams sons. He had achieved enough success in his legal practice to support himself independently at an earlier age than either of his brothers; he married younger, in part because he could support a wife at an earlier age; and he had the greatest facility for getting along with other people. But he was also impetuous and capable of getting into scrapes as well. He had been mixed up in some student protest at Harvard, to his parents' chagrin. His early marriage (at twenty-five) seemed to his parents impetuous. He invested unwisely in speculative ventures, in part with John Quincy's money, which threatened his financial security. His financial problems probably triggered his final breakdown, but the pressures of living up to the exacting standards of the Adams family no doubt contributed to it.

It was some measure of the powerful force of the Adams family that, after Charles's death, Sally and her children spent most of their time with her dead husband's parents rather than with her own. Abigail continued to raise Susan as her own child. Sally and Abbe, after a few months with her mother, also went to live with the Adamses.

A brief visit in Philadelphia cheered Abigail's spirits somewhat, for Thomas was everything a mother could wish for in a
son. Then she set out for Washington through unfamiliar terrain over rutted, bumpy dirt roads. She encountered few difficulties between Philadelphia and Baltimore, but the country between Baltimore and Washington was a virtual wilderness. The
first inn where they could get a night's lodging was 36 miles
south of Baltimore, a long day's journey. Friends in Philadelphia
suggested that she and her companions stay instead with a family named Snowden, who had an estate 21 miles south of Baltimore. In the sparsely settled South, putting up with casual acquaintances or friends of friends was commonplace, but Abigail
refused to be a burden to anyone. So she left Baltimore early in
the morning, determined to make the 36 miles to the inn.

They might have managed it, but they took a wrong turn
and wandered about in the woods for two hours trying to find
their way. Finally they met a black man with a horse and cart
who led them back to the main road. The coachman drove the
horses at fast as he could to make up for lost time, but sundown
found them near the Snowdens' house and still many miles from
the inn. "I halted but could not get courage to go to his House
with ten Horses and nine persons. I therfore orderd the coach
man to proceed, and we drove rapidly on," she recalled.

They had scarcely gone a mile when Major Snowden gal-
loped up on his horse. He had heard that Abigail would be passing through and was watching for her party, with his horse saddled and ready to intercept them. He urged her to return to his
house and refused to take no for an answer. The roads were dangerous, the inn distant and hardly suitable for quartering the
First Lady in any case. The size of her party was of no consequence. A bit relieved at not having to travel further, Abigail
returned to the Snowden estate "where I was received with my
Family, with what we might term true English Hospitaility,
Friendship without ostentation, and kindness without painfull
ceremony."

The next day Abigail and company set out again and finally
reached Washington. Although she found much to praise in the
new capital, she was mildly contemptuous of its pretensions. As
she described it to Mary, "I arrived . . . at this place known by
the *name* of *the city*, and the Name is all that you can call so." It
was, as she expected, "a new country, with Houses scatterd over
a space of ten miles, and trees & stumps in plenty." Very few

houses had been completed to accommodate the influx of government officials, and most people lived in the older towns of Alexandria and Georgetown rather than in Washington itself. Alexandria was lovely, but Georgetown was in Abigail's opinion "the very dirtyest Hole I ever saw for a place of any trade. . . . It is only one mile from me but a quagmire after every rain."

The President's home, "a castle of a House," as she described it, was beatifully situated on a hill overlooking the Potomac with a superb view of Alexandria, but it was far from being finished. It was much too large and impossibly drafty; Abigail had to keep thirteen fires going all day to make it livable. It was a house built "for ages to come," she believed. Someday it would be finished, properly furnished, and adequately staffed. At the moment the Adamses could not afford to hire enough servants to run such a house, and the enormous public rooms had no plaster, paint, or furniture. Abigail used the great east room to hang her laundry. In its present condition it was good for little else.

All of Washington had the same raw, unfinished quality as the President's House. Planned by the French engineer Pierre L'Enfant, it was to be a city built from scratch as the nation's capital, an enduring monument to the American republic, a grand city of great marble buildings linked by wide boulevards. The Capitol and the President's House, each built on its own hill, would dominate the city. Although the area was sparsely populated at the time—Alexandria and Georgetown were hardly more than sleepy villages with an occasional ship passing through—it was expected that the government itself would attract people, commerce, and money to make the new federal city prosper. Unfortunately, the men who predicted rapid growth for the new city were wrong. Construction had begun in the mid-1790s, but when Abigail and John arrived in the fall of 1800 none of the public buildings had been completed, few houses had been constructed, and most of the lots remained unsold.

There were in the entire city only 109 "permanent" buildings (i.e., built of brick or stone) and 372 dwellings considered "habitable." Most of the latter were small wood houses, some little more than huts. Three hundred members of the government, many with their families, arrived in the fall of 1800 to try to squeeze into the little available housing along with the several hundred people already living there.

The Capitol, like the President's House, was incomplete.

Two wings had been constructed, but the middle section connecting them had not even been started. The whole area between the Capitol and the President's House was a virtual swamp, as was much of the rest of the city. There were no paved roads. Venturing out after a hard rain was often hazardous, as carriages easily got mired in several inches of mud. Diplomats arriving at the President's House to pay official calls often had to scrape mud from their boots before entering the mansion, which they reached by climbing a long flight of crude wooden stairs. Even the dirt roads followed no apparent system. People identified their places of residence by the nearest public building rather than by street or number.

It was easy to get lost, especially at night, there being no street lights. One story that went around concerned a group of gentlemen who got hopelessly lost after leaving a dinner party; they rode around Washington's "streets" until dawn, even though they were only a mile or so from the Capitol. The grounds of the President's House were just as bad as the rest of the city. They were cluttered with workmen's shanties, piles of bricks, old brick kilns, and pools of water, which were breeding grounds for mosquitoes.

Social life in Washington paled by comparison with Philadelphia. The permanent population was small. Most Senators and Congressmen lived in boarding houses clustered around the Capitol. Abigail still had plenty of official entertaining to do, but she missed the friends she had acquired over the years in Philadelphia. There were consolations: Her nephew William Cranch and his wife Nancy lived in Washington, and Abigail was able to renew her acquaintance with Catherine Johnson and her family. But even seeing the Johnsons could be difficult, since they lived about 3 miles away, a formidable distance given the state of roads in Washington.

Washington was not so far from Philadelphia, but the atmosphere was completely different. It was clearly part of the South. Abigail had long harbored a streak of anti-Southern prejudice, and her experiences in Washington only reinforced it. The slow pace of life distressed her—"the universal character of the inhabitants is want of punctuality," she complained.

What most upset her was the widespread use of slave labor. Much of the construction work and all of the menial labor in Washington was performed by blacks hired out by their owners.

Abigail quickly discovered what later historians have made much of: Enslaved workers have little incentive to perform their tasks efficiently. She told Cotton Tufts about watching twelve black workmen from the window of the President's House. They were assigned to carry away dirt from the road in front of the house. First they filled four carts, and then four men hauled them some distance away while the remaining eight leaned on their shovels and waited for the others to return. Then all twelve began filling the four carts again. "Two of our hardy N. England men would do as much work in a day as the whole 12," she exclaimed, "but it is *true Republicanism* that drives the slaves half fed, and destitute of cloathing, . . . to labour, whilst the owner walks about idle." Here she got in a dig at Republican political leaders, many of whom were wealthy Virginians who talked about equality for all men while their own lands were worked by slaves.

Abigail was also disgusted by the sense of superiority that slavery instilled in all whites, even the poorest. "The lower class of whites," she noted, "are a grade below the negroes in point of intelligence, and ten below them in point of civility. They look like the refuse of human nature." White men considered idleness a virtue even if they owned only one slave, or none. No white man would do work considered too menial for his race. As a result, Washingtonians had trouble getting enough wood to heat their homes despite its abundance. No white man would deign to cut it. John Briesler spent hours trying to procure the wood needed for the President's House but got only empty promises for his trouble. When the Adamses did manage to get wood, 6 feet was delivered when a cord was ordered, and the prices were exorbitant. But there was nothing that anyone could do about it, Abigail noted in disgust.

Abigail had scarcely arrived in Washington when the first election returns started coming in. Electors met in the various states at different times from October to December, so word of the progress of the Presidential election trickled in slowly. Despite John's conviction that he would not be reelected, up to the beginning of December he and Jefferson were running about even in electoral votes. But in the second week in December the returns from South Carolina were reported. The Federalists had counted on a strong showing in that state to carry the election; they were reasonably confident because of past Federalist strength there and because Charles C. Pinckney, John's running mate, was a South Carolinian. The electors split their vote, however, ensuring the election for Jefferson and the Republicans.

It was a very close election. Jefferson and Burr each received seventy-three votes, and Adams sixty-five. Given the growing popular strength of the Republican Party, it was remarkable that John Adams did as well as he did. But Abigail and John, typically, did not see it that way. To them the election meant a repudiation of John's principles, a slap in the face by an ungrateful public.

Personally, Abigail claimed, she was pleased enough with the outcome. "At my age and with my bodily infirmities I shall be happier at Quincy," she wrote Thomas. Her one personal regret about the loss of the Presidency was, ironically, the loss of the salary—after years of complaining about the low salary and declaring that public office was a precarious means of earning a living. In fact, however, the Adamses had managed to save a substantial portion of John's salary during most of his years in public office and had used it to improve their house and farm, buy more land, and invest in public securities. Now, without the salary, they would have to live on the interest from their securities and the proceeds of their farm, which were minimal. Despite their extensive holdings, the land they owned was not really productive enough to yield a sizable marketable surplus, and the rents they received from their various farms were barely enough to cover taxes and maintenance. They would have to curtail their standard of living, which annoyed Abigail even though she claimed not to care about it.

She even managed to argue that John's financial problems would have a more serious negative effect on the public than on themselves. "We will live in independence because we will live within our income," she asserted. "If that is mean & much below the rank we ought to move in, the fault is not ours . . . the country which called into service an active able & meritorious citizen . . . at advanced years can dismiss him to retirement (and poverty in the worlds sense) that country must bear the disgrace." Apparently she believed that a country's honor demanded that its ex-Presidents live in style, but she failed to see that the vast majority of Americans would have laughed to be told that John Adams would go home to Quincy to live in "poverty."

She professed to be much more concerned about the fate of the country than the fate of the Adams family. A Republican President, whether Jefferson or Burr, would be a disaster for the country, she believed. After twelve years of peace and prosperity under Washington and Adams, the country would now be threatened with war and internal strife. The Constitution would be overthrown, and an orderly society would give way to chaos in the name of equality for all men. European nations would lose confidence in the United States, and public credit would be undermined, by the very fact that Americans could make such a radical change in their government. The country would appear "unstable fluctuating and Revolutionary" in the eyes of others. And, most dangerous of all, by electing an "infidel" as President, they might forfeit their claim to God's protection. "If ever we saw a day of darkness, I fear this is one which will be visible untill kindled into flame's," she wrote.

Abigail was always prone to predict dire consequences from any events she disapproved. Now she consigned the United States to hellfire and brimstone as a result of the Republican victory. In her doom-and-gloom rhetoric she was not alone. Throughout the campaign both parties had predicted the direst consequences if the other side won. John Adams, said the Republicans, was a monarchist who wanted to rule for life, marry his son to a daughter of George III, reunite America and England, establish life tenure in the Senate, and squelch forever the freedom of the press. Thomas Jefferson, the Federalists contended, was an atheist, a puppet of the French Directory, and the tool of an unwashed multitude whose election would introduce strife and bloodshed in the manner of the French Revolution.

The language was overblown, but the fears behind it were real. In 1800 the Federalists and Republicans stood for substantially different points of view on almost every issue, unlike the rival political parties of a later era. The nation was young and the Constitution relatively untested. The extent of the federal government's power was still a subject of heated debate, and the principle of frequent changes in the executive branch was far from generally accepted. The Republicans and the Federalists actually were not quite as different from each other as they asserted at the time, but the election of a Republican administration did mean a substantial change in official policy, with a reduced role for the federal government and more emphasis on popular participation in government. Thomas Jefferson called the election of 1800 a revolution, and Abigail agreed. But for her, revolution was to be dreaded rather than applauded.

Despite Abigail's claims that she cared more about the good of the country than about her husband's feelings, she dwelled incessantly on the ingratitude of the voters who had turned him out of office. Again and again she ran through the litany about his devoted public service and his sacrifices of personal fortune and comfort. She painted John as a man ready to retire but kept in office only by his sense of patriotic duty, a man who preferred retirement but was needed in office to stave off disaster for a fledgling republic. None of this was true, and deep in her heart Abigail knew it. John had wanted very much to be reelected, for reasons that included a sincere belief that either a Republican or a Hamiltonian administration would be a disaster, his desire for popular acclaim, and his need for the salary that went with the office. Abigail realized this, and yet she perpetuated the myth that John cared nothing about politics for its own sake. All her life she helped create and preserve his image as the disinterested statesman who would really rather be back on his farm in Quincy. Now all her comments about public ingratitude revealed the truth that she didn't want to admit, even to herself. John Adams was indeed a patriotic statesman who always thought he acted in the best interests of his country. But he also loved politics and had self-consciously made a career of it. At sixty-five, he was not ready to retire.

Nor was Abigail ready to retire, despite her professed desire to settle down to a life of tranquility in Quincy. She had always been ambivalent about John's political career; the separations she endured during the Revolution and the long months she spent at Quincy during his Vice Presidency all attested to the fact. But over the years she had become more and more caught up in the game. By the time John was elected President, much of her ambivalence vanished. John depended on Abigail's constant advice, and she relished her involvement in public affairs. There was, of course, a side of her that was happy to go home. But she, like John, would have preferred to stay. And, like him, she felt the bitter sting of rejection and ingratitude.

After the election returns were tallied, life in Washington was painful for Abigail and John. From mid-December, when it was clear that he had lost the election, until March 4, when his successor would be inaugurated, John had to govern the country as a lame duck. Abigail could escape to Quincy a bit earlier, but the winter weather would keep her too a prisoner in Washington until sometime in February. But she was determined to hold her head high and show no signs of the injury she felt. She would not retire from society just because of the defeat, she told Mary. "I would strive to act my part well and Retire with that dignity which is unconscious of doing or wishing ill to any, with a temper disposed to forgive injuries."

Nevertheless, she began almost immediately to make preparations for her final journey to Quincy. With Louisa, Susan, and their personal servants she left Washington in mid-February. Just before they left, Jefferson paid a visit to say goodbye, a gesture of friendship that was unexpected and very touching to her.

Abigail had long since gotten used to traveling without a gentleman escort, but on this trip she was apprehensive. Winter journeys through the Northeastern part of the country were always difficult. The most serious obstacle was the Susquehanna River between Baltimore and Philadelphia. Unfortunately, when Abigail and her party arrived at the Susquehanna, ice still covered the river, but it was not thick enough to bear the weight of horses and carriages. The ice was solid enough for people to walk across the river, so Abigail sent a messenger to hire a carriage and horses on the other side. But demand had been brisk, and no carriages or horses were to be had. Luckily for Abigail, a gentleman acquaintance in Baltimore had offered to accompany her as far as the Susquehanna, and he now used his ingenuity to get the little group across the river.

First he sent one horse across the ice; it got safely to the other side. It appeared that horses individually, but not four of them pulling a carriage, might cross the river safely. So he sent the other horses across, one at a time, and then hired men to push the carriage over the ice. The same men then dragged Abigail and her companions across the river in a boat fitted with runners. Just as they approached the other side, the men fell through the ice into water deep enough to soak them above their boots. They had made the crossing just in time, she reported to

John. Within hours warmer weather had thawed the ice to the point where the river was unsafe to cross even on foot.

The roads between the Susquehanna and Philadelphia were in better shape than Abigail had expected, and she was soon reunited with Thomas. Convinced that Philadelphia would become "a hotbed of turbulence and sedition," she renewed her efforts to persuade Thomas to move to New England. The political climate in Pennsylvania was so unpleasant that he would soon feel compelled to move, she wrote, somewhat wishfully, to John Quincy. At the moment, however, Thomas had no intentions of bowing to her pressure.

The day before Abigail reached Quincy, she stepped out of her carriage a bit too quickly and caught her foot in a hole in the carriage floor. She bruised her foot so badly that she could not walk. When the travelers finally pulled up in front of the house after an exhausting journey, she had to be carried in.

Being home at last, for good this time, made up for much of the bitterness and disappointment of the last few weeks. John was still in Washington, but this last separation would be blessedly brief. Early in the morning on March 4, the day Jefferson was to be inaugurated, he and William Shaw quietly left Washington. John did not attend the inauguration, as Washington had attended his; he did not say goodbye to his old friend; he did not announce his departure. He left so quickly, a Republican newspaper joked, that he was seen rushing through New York on the same day. That, of course, was impossible. But he did travel as fast as he could until he was reunited with Abigail, there to settle down to be the "monarch of stoney field."

To Abigail, however, he remained forever "the President." For the rest of her life she never referred to him by any other title.

Chapter 17

The Matriarch of Peacefield

～ ～

Abigail adjusted to retirement much more quickly than her husband. John nursed his wounds for months, writing letters and essays in justification of his political decisions. Abigail declared that he "appears to enjoy a tranquility and a freedom from care which he never before experienced," and that he viewed political events "with a total indifference," but these statements expressed what she wanted to believe rather than the truth. John was in fact deeply hurt by his rejection at the hands of the nation. Abigail could not feel the rejection so strongly, however, for although she identified herself completely with John, there were limits to her absorption in him. She had always been of two minds about her own involvement in politics. She enjoyed her public role and yet regretted the time spent away from Quincy and her family. Now at last there would be no more agonizing decisions about whether to go with John or stay home, no more painful separations.

In some crucial ways, Abigail was luckier than John. For a woman there was no such thing as retirement. She had always enjoyed her role as wife, mother, and household manager; now she threw herself into that role with renewed energy. John, by contrast, for the first time in his life had no specific task in front of him. He would continue to write, of course, but the contemplative life never really appealed to him. He felt useless in a way that Abigail never could as long as she had the physical strength to run her household.

All that Abigail lacked to complete her return to domesticity was a house full of children. Her own were grown, but she found substitutes in her grandchildren. Susan, Charles's older daughter, lived permanently with them, and Nabby's sons, William and John, came during their school vacations. Sally and Abbe were there much of the time, and Nabby and Caroline visited for long stretches. And, over the next few years, many more grandchildren would be added to her brood.

Soon after settling in at Peacefield, Abigail decided that it was time both John Quincy and Thomas came home, and she set about using all her powers of motherly persuasion to induce them to settle near Quincy. John had recalled John Quincy from his post at Berlin just before his term ended, and Abigail assumed that he would resume his legal practice in Boston. She hoped he would renounce politics, or so she said; under a Republican administration, she believed, "the post of honour will be a private station."

In July John Quincy and Louisa started home with their infant son George Washington Adams, born the previous April. When their ship docked at Philadelphia in September, John Quincy set out immediately for his parents' home, with a brief stop in New York to see Nabby. It had been seven years since he had sailed for Europe, still hardly more than a child in his mother's eyes. Now he returned, a mature adult, seasoned diplomat, husband, and father. Abigail could scarcely contain her joy and pride at seeing him again.

She had to suppress her curiosity about her new daughter-in-law and grandchild, however. Louisa and George had gone to Washington to visit her parents. John Quincy expected them to travel north alone, but Louisa insisted that he come to Washington, spend some time with her parents, and then accompany her back to Quincy. After a month with Abigail and John he went to Washington. Eager to get home, he cut the visit there as short as he possibly could.

John Quincy's and Louisa's complicated travel arrangements were only the first sign of conflict between the demands of their two families. John Quincy would have saved himself a good deal of travel time by going first from Philadelphia to Washington with Louisa and later to Quincy, but he could not delay seeing his parents even two or three weeks. Louisa was no less eager to see her parents and sisters, but she had to struggle against her husband's determination to spend as little time as possible away from Quincy. He had endured seven years of separation from his family in the name of public service and had been perfectly willing to stay in Europe even longer, but now that he was home again he would not give even as much as seven weeks to Louisa's family. Like his father, John Quincy put duty to his country ahead of duty to his family—but he also showed signs of a tendency to put duty to his parents ahead of duty to his wife.

As they traveled north, Louisa's apprehensions mounted. She had never met any of her husband's family, nor had she ever been to New England. The reputation of the formidable Abigail Adams was well known, and Louisa was well aware of John Quincy's devotion to his mother. A shy, reserved woman, Louisa was afraid she would not measure up to her brilliant and outspoken mother-in-law.

Louisa's first weeks in Quincy fulfilled her worst expectations. Abigail and John received her warmly, but she had the distinct impression that they considered her a "fine Lady" who would never quite fit into their family circle. "The old gentleman took a fancy to me, and he was the only one," she recalled many years later. Louisa Smith was so jealous of the new Louisa in the household that, on the evening of their arrival, she left the dinner table crying and refused to eat.

Abigail expected Louisa to be a fragile, impractical "lady," since she had been raised in a wealthy London family. Her expectations became a self-fulfilling prophecy. The more Louisa tried to please her mother-in-law, the more insecure and tongue-tied she became, and her bashfulness was interpreted as pride. Louisa had in fact been raised as a lady and, by her own admission, had been spoiled and indulged by her parents. Her upbringing was altogether different from that of a New England child, and she found New England customs strange, to say the least. "Had I steped into Noahs Ark I do not think I could have been more utterly astonished," she wrote. Everything was different—the church (Louisa was raised in the Church of England), the style of dress, the time of eating dinner, even people's manners, which to her seemed very stiff and formal. The constant parade of friends and relatives who arrived to greet John Quincy and his family only bewildered her more. It was hardly surprising that she reacted by getting sick. Shortly after her arrival she developed a fever, took to her bed, and stayed there almost the entire time she spent in Quincy.

Louisa could hardly wait to get out of Abigail's and John's house and into the home that John Quincy had purchased for them in Boston. Even then her troubles pursued her. She had never been responsible for running a household; the two servants whom she and John Quincy had taken with them from London to Berlin and had now brought to Boston ran everything with perfect competence. As a young woman growing up in London, she had been accustomed to living in a household run almost totally by servants. In New England, however, a woman who did not take charge of her household more directly was considered deficient in her duty. She should be able to cook, milk cows, and tend a garden—even if she employed servants to do most of that work for her. As Louisa herself explained, "an accomplished Quincy lady" was a very different creature from an accomplished London lady. Abigail tried to instruct Louisa, but she was so nervous about being unfavorably compared with her mother-in-law that she seemed unable to grasp any of Abigail's advice.

To Abigail's dismay, John Quincy soon plunged back into politics. In April, after only a few months at home, he was elected state senator, and in November he ran for Congress. He lost his bid for Congress, and Abigail was glad of it. She hoped he would confine his political service to his native state; she hated the thought of his leaving Massachusetts, even for part of the year. John Quincy, Louisa, and George came to Quincy every weekend, arriving Saturday and staying through Monday or even Tuesday morning. Sometimes Louisa and George stayed through the week. Abigail, so long deprived of her children's company, came to depend on those weekly visits.

With John Quincy safely settled nearby, Abigail renewed her efforts to bring Thomas home from Philadelphia. His law practice showed no signs of improving, and he was often discouraged; he talked vaguely of giving up law and becoming a farmer in upstate New York, where land was cheap. Abigail tried to cheer him up with the thought that his lack of success was not his fault. She also sent him money, without telling John, to supplement his meager earnings.

She and John never stopped telling Thomas that he ought to

leave Philadelphia. When he talked about buying a farm in New York, they stepped up their urgings. Abigail agreed that New York was prosperous and had a bright future despite its wrong-headedness in politics, but she wanted Thomas to move back to Massachusetts, not out to the frontier. Thomas, finally tired of all this unwanted parental advice, wrote Abigail that she should stop worrying about him so much. He might not be making a fortune, but he was doing all right; he was not in debt, nor was he dependent on his parents. In short (although he didn't put it so bluntly) they had no right to dictate to him.

Abigail was somewhat chastened by his letter. She responded in a subdued and kindly tone that she and John sympathized with his problems and knew that he was doing his best. Then she played her trump card. Any time he wanted to be a farmer, he could come home and take over one of their farms. She had in mind the land that had belonged to her uncle, Norton Quincy. He had died not long before and had willed one-third of his estate to the Adamses. Their share included Mount Wollaston and several coastal islands—an excellent parcel of land. John was in the process of buying out the other heirs (including Cotton Tufts) and wanted very much to keep the farm in the family. But Abigail's campaign to lure Thomas back to Quincy suffered a serious setback the following spring. Cotton Tufts sold John his share of Norton Quincy's farm, which John intended to pay for with funds he had invested in Holland during his years in Europe. John Quincy had undertaken the management of those funds while he lived in Holland and had invested them with a prominent London mercantile firm. Now, just when John wanted to withdraw his money, the firm went bankrupt and John was left with a $7,000 obligation to Tufts that he was unable to pay.

Abigail was devastated. Such financial reverses happened to other people—people who speculated unwisely, trusted their money to fools, or lived beyond their means. When men like Nabby's husband, for example, went bankrupt because they had invested money with other men who then mishandled it, she accused them of gullibility no matter how much they seemed to be the victims of circumstance. Now she and John themselves were victims, despite their years of frugality and careful management. She feared any sort of debt, and the obligation to Tufts loomed like a calamity.

In her distress, Abigail painted the whole affair as worse

than it really was. She talked about the dire "sacrifices" she and. John would have to make. But the London firm had agreed to make good at least some of the money, and in any case their existing land holdings were still extensive. They wanted the Quincy farm badly, however, and decided to sell other holdings, if necessary, to close the deal with Tufts for his share.

John Quincy felt guilty about his part in the setback. He blamed himself for having entrusted the money to that particular firm, even though it was a reputable one and there had been no reason to believe it would go bankrupt. He felt it was his personal responsibility to make good his parents' loss, so he sold his house in Boston—for $7,000, exactly the sum owed Tufts. He turned the money over to his parents, who in turn sold him the house and farm where he had lived as a child and where John Briesler now lived as a tenant.

The arrangement actually worked out quite well for John Quincy. He had been elected United States Senator in April 1803, just about the time of his parents' financial reverses, and beginning in November he would be spending about half the year in Washington. He would no longer be able to maintain his law practice, and the farm in Quincy would be a more pleasant place to spend his summers than Boston. He also felt it incumbent upon himself to spend more time with his parents as they got older, and living near them was much to his liking. Louisa, one may suppose, was less delighted about spending future summers in a tiny farmhouse practically in her in-laws' backyard.

Louisa was expecting her second baby in early July. She had a history of miscarriages, and her first delivery had been a difficult one, so she and John Quincy were both nervous about her condition. Abigail commented to Thomas, a bit testily, that John Quincy hadn't been out to visit in two weeks, spending every moment fretting over Louisa. "He looks as anxious as though he had the trouble himself to pass through," she wrote, and added that a man choosing a wife ought to look for one with a strong constitution. It was ironic that John Quincy was visiting his parents when Louisa delivered their second son, appropriately enough on July 4. They named the baby John.

Having decided to move closer to his parents, John Quincy now joined the battle to get his brother to forsake Philadelphia. He told Thomas that his prospects would be brighter in New England and informed him of his own decision to move into "the old paternal mansion." Clearly, he was suggesting that Thomas's duty lay closer to home. When John Quincy and Louisa journeyed to Washington in November, they stopped in Philadelphia, and he renewed his admonitions in person.

Finally all the family solicitations had their effect. Before he left Philadelphia, John Quincy was happy to inform his mother that Thomas was wrapping up his affairs and planned to be in Quincy by December. Sensitive to both his brother's feelings and his mother's foibles, he suggested that she leave Thomas alone and offer no advice on "his mode of life and his pursuits." Only then would he be able to feel that he preserved his independence.

Thomas was distressed at the thought of being dependent on his parents again, but he was clearly not making much headway in his career by staying in Philadelphia. He went to Quincy confused and uncertain about his future. He decided to continue to study law, if not to practice it, and to do some work on the farm in the spring. At that moment he felt totally unequipped to undertake the management of a farm of his own.

Despite her professed wishes that her sons would stay out of politics, Abigail was proud of her son the Senator. His long, detailed letters about politics and Louisa's gossipy accounts of Washington social life satisfied her craving to be part of the world beyond Quincy.

Meanwhile, she looked after John Quincy's farm, seeing that repairs were made and preparations completed for their return in the early spring—just as Mary Cranch and Cotton Tufts had done for her in years past.

When Congress adjourned at the end of March, however, John Quincy went home alone. Like his parents, he and Louisa found living in two places 500 miles apart impossibly wearing and expensive. With two small children, the difficulties were even greater. Every year during his term as Senator they tried a different arrangement, but none of them was fully satisfactory.

John Quincy's solution to the problem was to do as his parents had done: leave Louisa in Quincy with the children, while he traveled back and forth to Washington. But Louisa did not have family and friends in Quincy, she did not look upon it as home, and she was much less inclined to "sacrifice" her husband for half the year than Abigail had been. John Quincy, who thought all women should be like his mother, never quite understood Louisa's point of view. When he told her that he couldn't afford to bring her and the children back to Washington the next winter, she replied that, if she had to be separated from him half the year, she "prefer'd passing the summer months with my family to living alone at Quincy through five dreary winters." She also observed that when they were both at Quincy, they spent less time together than anywhere else. Abigail, John, and the multitude of relatives left them little time for their own privacy.

John Quincy interpreted her decision to mean that she preferred being separated from him to being separated from her family. Louisa had to remind him that, one way or the other, she was going to be separated from him anyway. But she felt insecure about John Quincy's affection, and the injured tone of his letters completely destroyed her determination to have some say in her domestic arrangements. "To insure your affection, and esteem there is no sacrifice . . . I would not make with pleasure," she wrote him. To prove it, she was prepared to go to Quincy immediately and stay there through the winter.

John Quincy, in the meantime, had decided to rent his house again and move in with his parents, inasmuch as his family had not come with him. When he received Louisa's offer to join him, in mid-May, he thanked her but replied that the summer was already "far advanced" and that she would no sooner reach Quincy than they would have to think about going back to Washington again. As it turned out, he didn't leave Quincy until late October, so this objection was rather hollow. In any case, her joining him would would increase, rather than decrease, their expenses. Louisa, left to suffer her loneliness, resolved not to allow such a separation again. The children missed their father, too. "George is very angry with you he says you are very naughty to go away and leave him," she reported.

Abigail didn't help matters by telling Louisa how much she missed her grandchildren and how important she believed children's early attachment to their grandparents to be. Nor did it do much for Louisa's peace of mind to receive Abigail's pointed letters about John Quincy's poor health, all but accusing Louisa of failing to care for him properly during the previous months. He worked too hard, she wrote; he didn't get enough exercise; he went too long between meals. Louisa should see to it that he took crackers with him to Congress to nibble between meals;

she should also get him to pay more attention to his personal appearance, which was inclined to be slovenly.

Louisa, who felt that she had little enough influence over her husband, resented the implications of Abigail's remarks. When John Quincy returned to Washington in the fall, she retaliated by writing to Abigail about the noticeable lack of improvement in his health.

Abigail was equally free with advice about her grandchildren. She thought John Quincy tried to force his children to grow up too quickly. Although George was only three, his father worried about his short attention span. "You must not look for an old head upon young shoulders," Abigail admonished him. "A grave sedate Boy, will make a very mopish dull old man." Remembering her own grandmother's sympathy for her childish moods, she announced, "I . . . am really rejoiced to hear that he is a wild Boy."

William and John Smith were another story. They continued to board with Abigail's sister Elizabeth and attend school nearby. John displayed academic promise and gave close attention to his studies, but William had trouble sticking with any task for more than a short time. What was normal in a three-year-old child was not acceptable in an adolescent preparing for college. Abigail felt confident that William's faults would be corrected, and John's promise encouraged, under her sister Elizabeth's care, so she was outraged when William Smith decided to take his sons home. "It is a pitty two such fine Boys should be in a way to be ruined," she complained. "Their Father has no Head for to plan out their Education." But William was tired of having his children so far away and decided that they could enter Columbia College, close to home. Their grandmother, of course, thought they should be prepared for Harvard.

The summer of 1805 was one of the most pleasant Abigail could remember. John Quincy returned from Washington, this time bringing Louisa and the children. Thomas married Nancy Harrod, a young woman he had met years earlier when he lived in Haverhill. They moved in with Abigail and John. At last Thomas seemed to be happy, and Abigail was pleased to have at least one of her children living under her roof. She and Nancy liked each other immensely. New England born and bred, long acquainted with the Adams family, Nancy fitted into the Quincy household easily. There was none of the tension between them that existed between Abigail and Louisa.

Nabby and her children visited in August, completing the family circle. Surrounded by her children and grandchildren, Abigail felt happier than she had for many years. She relished being the mistress of a large household. The frequent comings and goings of children and grandchildren might have exhausted most people, but Abigail loved every minute of it. She was as busy as she ever had been, supervising the servants, tending her garden, running the dairy, fussing over John and the children. The old political debates and disappointments had receded into the background; although Abigail continued to follow political news and continued to rail against the folly of the Federalists, the partisan battles and crises over foreign policy seemed much less critical now.

In the fall Abigail had yet another addition to her household. George and John stayed in Quincy when John Quincy and Louisa returned to Washington. George boarded at the Cranches and attended a school nearby; John stayed with his grandparents.

This decision intensified the friction between Abigail and Louisa. John Quincy and Abigail together decided that it was too expensive and too complicated to take the boys back and forth to Washington every year, and that they would be better off going to school in Massachusetts. In the Adams family, of course, there was plenty of precedent for such a decision. Sending the children to board with relatives while they went to school was a family custom. Louisa, however, had grown up in a much different atmosphere, one where children were indulged and kept close to home as long as possible. She hated to leave her children behind, a decision she felt John Quincy had foisted on her with Abigail's connivance.

When Louisa wrote Abigail about how much she missed her children, she received a rather stern response on the proper atmosphere for raising children. In a boarding house in Washington, Abigail asserted, children would be too "confined" and might mix with the wrong sort of people. Making the long trip between Quincy and Washington twice a year did them no good either. "I should suppose that your own judgment experience and good sense would have convinced you of the propriety of the measure without compulsion," she told Louisa. She herself had often been separated from her children and had felt just as anguished as Louisa did, but she always thought it most important to consider the best interests of the children first. On the definition of the children's best interests, Abigail was certain there could be no dispute.

From that point on, Louisa was determined not to be separated from her children again. She finally gave in and accepted John Quincy's original plan for them. Beginning the following fall, she stayed in Quincy with the children while he journeyed back and forth to Washington alone. The separations from her husband were painful, but she refused to give up control over her own children.

For the time being, however, Abigail enjoyed having a small child around the house again. Three-year-old John and his grandmother were inseparable companions. He hated it when she wrote letters, because then he had to be quiet and make do with less than her full attention. George spent every weekend with them; both boys seemed to adjust quickly to their parents' absence. When Louisa and John Quincy returned in the spring, it was all they could do to get the boys to stay home with them. To Louisa's chagrin, they always wanted to run off to visit their grandparents.

In the spring a new family crisis erupted. The ever unreliable William Smith had become involved in the visionary schemes of one Francisco Miranda, who wanted to free the people of South America from Spanish rule. Miranda had tried to enlist the support of the American government, playing on American dreams of expansion, and had received some private encouragement but no official sanction. The daring and adventure of his plans appealed to Smith, who became involved in the planning of the proposed attacks in South America. His current work as Surveyor of the Port of New York kept him from joining the expedition himself, but he sent his son William, who was eighteen, when Miranda and his band sailed to Colombia early in 1806.

Nabby and William did not tell Abigail directly about her grandson's adventure. William Senior wrote rather vaguely that his son had long wanted to go to sea and that a good opportunity had presented itself. Abigail, who had been following the reports of Miranda's activities with a suspicious eye, instantly guessed that young William had shipped out with him, on a "don Quixot expedition," as she called it.

Bad news turned into worse. Miranda's expedition was a disaster; he and several of his men were arrested for insurrection and thrown into jail at Bogotá. William Senior was arrested for his role in encouraging the expedition and stripped of his federal appointment. Once again, Nabby and her family were without any means of support, and the entire family worried about the fate of young William. To their relief, it turned out that he had somehow escaped capture and was safe on the island of Aruba in the West Indies. His father's troubles, however, could not be so easily solved. He was in prison awaiting trial. Nabby was living in a small house on the prison grounds to be near him. John Quincy stopped in New York on his way home and urged her to go home with him, but she was determined to stay with her husband.

William was tried and acquitted at the end of the summer, but his reputation was tarnished and he could not hope for any more federal appointments. With his investments fairly well depleted, he had no way of supporting his family. Abigail worried constantly about Nabby through the fall and winter. Letters from her were infrequent and evasive; Abigail could not understand how the Smiths were supporting themselves. Confiding her concern to John Quincy, she asked him to stop in New York on his way home in the spring and try again to persuade Nabby to come to Quincy for the summer. This time he succeeded. Nabby and Caroline spent the summer and early fall in Quincy. William was off in upstate New York, where he owned some land, building a house and preparing to settle there permanently. With no other prospects of earning a living, he had decided to resort to farming on the frontier.

The summer of 1807 was even more hectic than usual for Abigail and John. Thomas and Nancy still lived with them; now they had an infant daughter, Elizabeth. Nabby and Caroline were there, and John Quincy came every Sunday with his family. William and John Smith came for briefer visits, as did Sally and Abbe. Susan was home from school for the summer. In August, Louisa had a third son, Charles Francis.

The Sunday before John Quincy left for his annual trip to Washington, the entire family gathered for dinner. It was a memorable occasion for Abigail, for she had around her dining room table more of her family than ever before. All her children were there and all her grandchildren except John Smith—sixteen of them in all.

Abigail was determined that Nabby and Caroline should stay with her through the winter. The house William was building for them would be ready by late fall, but, Abigail noted, "I cannot think of her going into the wilderness at this season of the year." When William wrote in December to ask Nabby and Caroline to meet him in Albany, Abigail would not hear of it. Undaunted, William went to Quincy to fetch his family. At that point Abigail could no longer interfere; and she admitted that Nabby had done exactly what she herself would have done: followed her husband, "however less eligible his situation was than that I had before experienced."

Still, it was a bitter blow to have her only daughter so far away. She was convinced that Nabby would suffer in her wilderness existence. Abigail missed Caroline too, almost as much as she missed Nabby. At twelve, Caroline was already turning into a young lady, and Abigail contrasted her grace and manners with Susan's temperamental nature. Susan had always been something of a difficult child, and her grandmother couldn't help showing a preference for Caroline. There was something contradictory about Abigail's judgments of her granddaughers, however. Caroline had all those docile, feminine qualities that she admired in young women, whereas the difficult, temperamental Susan was much more like herself. Abigail recognized this fact but criticized Susan for her headstrong behavior nevertheless.

Absorbed as she was in her children and grandchildren, Abigail did not lose interest in the world outside Quincy. She still read several newspapers and eagerly awaited John Quincy's letters describing the debates in Washington. In February 1808 she was shocked to read in a newspaper that her son had attended a Republican caucus to choose candidates for the coming Presidential election.

Federalist-dominated New England newspapers blasted John Quincy as a turncoat. Abigail could not believe that the reports were true. Her son, a party intriguer? And for the Republicans? She wrote him a letter expressing her disbelief and asking for an explanation. No lover of the Federalists, she still could not bear to think that John Quincy would ally himself with the Republicans. More serious, however, was her objection to caucuses in general, which she considered unconstitutional. They seemed to be a way of institutionalizing the political parties that she abhorred.

John Quincy responded that he had indeed attended the caucus. He was distressed at his mother's disapproval but proceeded to outline, point by point, the reasons he thought she was wrong about the unconstitutionality of caucuses. His most telling reason, and the one most likely to appeal to his mother, was the need to achieve some unity in nominating candidates. Without caucuses to narrow the field, he told her, elections would be even more "tumultous" than they already were. John Adams agreed with his son. He wrote him privately that he thought Abigail was wrong on this issue. Eventually Abigail came around too; a few months later she defended John Quincy's attendance at the caucus.

The caucus was the beginning of John Quincy's conversion to Republicanism. His parents, too, leaned in that direction as the Federalists became more and more obviously pro-British and as the doom they expected under a Republican administration failed to materialize. Abigail approved of the caucus's choice of James Madison, although she still expressed some lingering distrust of Republicans and of Virginians—the two were virtually synonymous in her mind. Revealing how much of a politician she could be, she observed that the Federalists had so alienated themselves from the majority of the voters that they could not possibly hope to win the Presidency. Under the circumstances, "to obtain the Best and least exceptionable on the other side is a desirable object." She was not yet ready to admit, however, that a Republican might be a positive choice rather than the lesser of two evils.

John Quincy was rewarded for his support of the Republicans by losing his Senate seat when he came up for reelection in the spring of 1808. Senators were chosen by state legislatures, and the Federalists dominated the legislature in Massachusetts. Abigail had seen the Federalist party turn against her husband, and now she watched it turn against her son. This new example of "base ingratitude" unleashed her fury at party rivalry in full force.

Ever since John's defeat for reelection Abigail had deplored the behavior of the Federalist party. No longer did she view the Republicans as "partisans" and the Federalists as disinterested supporters of the government. She finally recognized that there were two contending parties in the nation, and that they looked very much alike in their tactics. She could even admit that the Federalists had been every bit as partisan as the Republicans from the beginning—although she still refused to admit that either John or John Quincy had ever been a party man. She became increasingly disillusioned with the Federalists not only because of their tactics but also because of their continued extreme pro-English policies, which, she believed, threatened American neutrality and independence. In the fall she supported James Madison's election as President. To support a Republican, a Virginian, and Jefferson's hand-picked successor represented a drastic change of heart. Like John Quincy, she was slowly becoming a Republican.

Spring came early to New England in 1808, and the sight of her garden helped cheer up Abigail when she had dwelled too long on the state of the country. She couldn't remember an earlier spring. They cut the first asparagus on April 24; "our daffies Bloomd" on the twenty-fifth; and peach, pear, and "plomb" trees were in full bloom by the first week in May.

She had more grandchildren to fuss over; Nancy's and Thomas's second daughter was born in February, and Susan's sister Abbe came to stay for several months. Abigail continued to write regularly to her absent grandchildren, showering them with advice, but she also admitted for the first time that grandparents might not, after all, be so well-suited for bringing up children. She feared that she was becoming "too indulgent" toward her brood.

John Quincy spent little more than a year as a private citizen. In July 1809 Madison appointed him Ambassador to Russia. John Quincy accepted with little hesitation and began making hasty preparations for his departure. It was imperative that he leave by August in order to arrive at Saint Petersburg before its harbor froze and closed the city to contact with the outside world. Louisa and Charles Francis would accompany him;

Nabby's son William would go along as a secretary. George and John would go back to boarding with the Cranches.

Abigail and John were dismayed at their son's appointment. They had come to depend on his weekend visits and had counted on having his companionship for the rest of their days. Diplomatic assignments generally meant a minimum of three years away from home—his last assignment had lasted seven years. Saint Petersburg was the most distant post to which he could be sent, and the ice that closed its harbor for half the year would make communication infrequent.

Still, Abigail could not bring herself to persuade her son to turn down the job. She was inured to the idea that patriotic men served their country no matter how great the hardships, although her faith was sorely tried by this appointment. She disguised her unwillingness to part with him by arguing that he would be more useful to the country at home and that the "intolerant spirit of party" had forced him to accept this assignment. Booted out of the Senate for standing up to the Federalists, he was, in effect, being exiled to Russia—or so it seemed to Abigail. "Of the few children I have had, how they have been divided, brought together again & then scattered," she lamented.

On August 5, John Quincy, Louisa, and their companions sailed from Boston. Abigail could not bring herself to go into town to see them off, so heavy was her grief. Of all the many times she had said goodbye to her children, this time was the most difficult. Her age, her poor health, the distance, and the usual length of diplomatic assignments all made her fear that she and John would die before their son returned. This parting "was like takeing our last leave of him," she wrote. Having Nabby at such a distance made John Quincy's departure all the more difficult. She was left with only Thomas for comfort in her old age.

Chapter 18

The Curtain Falls

John Quincy's departure made Abigail feel very old and lonely. At sixty-four she was already an old woman by the standards of the time, and she had good reason to wonder whether she would ever see her son again. Every week seemed to bring word of the death of another friend. Her own health was generally poor, although she was rarely too sick to be up and about, supervising her household and writing her letters. She increasingly felt the infirmities of age but on the whole she faced her last years calmly and cheerfully. She counted herself fortunate that she still had John, in remarkably good health despite his seventy-three years.

The grandchildren were a never ending source of diversion. She had ten of them now, ranging from Thomas's infants to Nabby's nearly adult sons. At the moment five of them lived with her and John: Thomas's family, with two daughters; Charles's older daughter, Susan; and George and John, left in their grandparents' care while John Quincy, Louisa, and baby Charles went to Russia. Abigail loved children and was never too tired to play with them or too impatient to tolerate their exuberance. Her grandchildren kept her young.

As she got older, Abigail became more tolerant in her opinions and behavior. She reduced somewhat her efforts to dominate her children and grandchildren; she became more moderate in her political views and less hostile to political opinions different from her own; and she patched up quarrels with old friends. Being out of the political limelight ultimately had a beneficial effect on her. Removed from the arena of battle and no longer compelled to defend her husband's actions, she could take a more rational, balanced view of national events.

The winter of 1809–10 was the coldest in memory in New England. Even the largest fires could not keep the rooms of the Quincy house warm. The water in the bedroom wash basins froze every night, and it was all Abigail could do to keep her ink flowing freely enough to write letters. Uncomfortable as she was, she thought how much colder John Quincy and Louisa must be in Russia. She stayed close to her fireside "to keep myself from quite congealing to a statue" as she read a popular traveler's account of Russia and Sweden. The book helped her visualize her children's surroundings and made her feel a bit closer to them.

In January, five months after John Quincy and Louisa left Boston, she finally learned of their safe arrival in Saint Petersburg. From then on, letters came with surprising frequency, although they took three or four months in transit. Louisa wrote at length about how much she hated Saint Petersburg. They spent months in bad lodgings, because housing was altogether too expensive for John Quincy's salary. The manners and morals of the people were terrible, and the weather, of course, was wretched. She wanted to go home in the spring, but John Quincy said he couldn't affort to support her there, even in the little house in Quincy.

Abigail fully understood their plight, for she had felt exactly the same way when she lived in France and England, and indeed, in Philadelphia and Washington. But she was less willing to see her son endure such trials than she had been to endure them herself. When John Quincy, who usually confined his letters to political news and observations about Russia, also complained about his inadequate salary, she jumped to the conclusion that he wanted to return home. Confident that he himself would never ask permission to leave his post, she decided to do it for him. She wrote to President Madison (without telling John) asking him to give John Quincy permission to return home. It was not fair for him to live in disgrace on an inadequate salary, she argued, or to have to dip into his small stock of assets to support himself. She had been taught to sacrifice everything for her country, but she had lived in more difficult times; those days of necessary sacrifice were past.

Madison responded graciously. He had never intended his Ministers to make undue sacrifices in pursuing their duties, he wrote, and he would give John Quincy permission to return home if and when he requested it. John Quincy, of course, did not want such permission. Complain as he might, his sense of public duty was just as strong as his mother's, and he was determined to finish his mission. She ought to have recognized his complaints about salary and the difficulty of his job for what they were—rhetorical statements of his own self-sacrifice—because they were exactly like the complaints she had made all through her life in politics. About a year later, when John Quincy indirectly found out about his mother's meddling, she sent him copies of her correspondence with Madison and apologized. If she had done wrong, she wrote, it was only because of her "zeal" for his welfare.

She took comfort in John Quincy's sons. George reminded her more and more of his father as a boy, especially in his stubborn disposition. She tried, gently, to correct his "positiveness," just as she had with the young John Quincy, but felt confident that he would grow out of it or at least learn to keep it under control. At the tender age of ten, he already showed an interest in politics. John continued to be small for his age, but what he lacked in size he made up for in energy and affection. Abigail delighted in describing to Louisa how he "claps me round the neck and says o! how I do Love you Grandmamma."

In June, after five years of living under Abigail's and John's roof, Thomas and his family moved out. With three children and a fourth expected, it was time for them to have their own home. They moved into the cottage next to John Quincy's so they were close by and Abigail still saw her grandchildren almost daily.

As the years went by, Abigail mourned the deaths of more and more of her "ancient Friends." She grieved for them but took comfort in their long and useful lives and their release to what she believed was the better life ahead. Their deaths were a sharp reminder of her own mortality, but this too she faced with equanimity.

Abigail's fortitude in the face of sickness and death was sorely tried, however, in the summer and fall of 1811. Mary Cranch took sick in July, and everyone believed she was dying—except Mary, who remained optimistic about her recovery. Abigail spent every possible moment nursing her sister. When she couldn't go herself, she sent other family members or servants.

Even more serious, Nabby was suffering from breast cancer, an extremely rare disease at the time. As early as March Abigail had expressed alarm at her daughter's symptoms; she wrote Benjamin Rush for advice and urged Nabby to come to Boston to consult doctors there. Nabby tried to make light of her illness and refused to leave her family. Finally, at the end of June, she was persuaded to make the trip, accompanied by John and Caroline. Abigail had not seen her daughter in three and a half years and had often despaired of ever seeing her again, so great was the distance between Quincy and central New York State.

At first Boston doctors questioned whether Nabby was suffering from cancer at all and advised doing nothing for the time being. Nabby and her children made plans to return home in October. But her symptoms worsened, and finally her doctors reluctantly advised surgery. Without anesthetic and without any general understanding of antiseptic methods, surgery was a dreaded last resort in the early nineteenth century. But when her doctors told her that it was the only hope to save her life, Nabby submitted to the operation.

Surgery appeared to cure her. She convalesced rapidly but decided to spend the winter in Quincy. Travel through the remote parts of New York would be difficult in November, and it seemed advisable for her to stay close to her doctors and to her mother's constant care. So William, who had arrived in Quincy shortly after the surgery, and John went home alone; Caroline stayed with her mother.

In the midst of the crisis over Nabby's illness, Mary Cranch continued to worsen. Then Richard took sick too, in mid-October, and within four days he was dead. Mary, who had persisted in her conviction that she would recover, died two days later. She had struggled to live for the sake of her husband and children, Abigail believed; when Richard died, she gave up the struggle. They were buried together on the same day.

Their deaths were the most serious blow Abigail had suffered since Charles's death ten years earlier. Mary and Richard had been her constant companions. They had cared for each other's children and grandchildren and had relied on each other in every crisis. Their loss was irreparable. Yet Abigail berated herself for her "selfish grief" at their deaths. They had lived long and full lives; they had died before becoming "burdensome and helpless"; and they had died together. Each had been spared the grief of living without the other, and that was the greatest blessing of all.

By December Abigail herself was sick. The combination of caring for sick relatives and trying to make most of the food for Christmas herself finally proved her undoing. "I am really so self sufficient as to believe that I can do it better than any of my Family—so I am punished for my self conceit & vanity," she wrote her sister Elizabeth. Looking back on the year 1811, she considered it one of the most trying she had ever experienced—a constant round of sickness and death.

As death claimed many of her old friends, the ones remaining became more precious. She continued to write occasionally to Hannah Green, who had been her earliest friend. Reminiscing about the days of Calliope and Diana, she observed, "As our Lamp of Life is nearly burnt out, I feel a sympathy drawing me nearer & nearer to those dear surviving Friends who began the race with me." Typically, she did not dwell too long on the past but devoted much of her correspondence with Hannah to tales of her grandchildren.

Advancing age also inspired Abigail to bury the hatchet and renew friendships that had fallen victim to differences of political opinion. At the end of 1811 she wrote Mercy Warren a letter expressing her respect and affection despite their disagreements in the past, and the following summer she extended her friendly overtures by visiting Mercy for the first time in years.

The Adams–Warren friendship had faded in the years after the Revolution, although the two households remained on cordial terms, because of disagreements about governing the new nation in the 1780s and 1790s. What was left of their friendship collapsed in 1805 when Mercy published her *History of the*

American Revolution, which included a severe attack on John's administration. Abigail broke off all contact with Mercy. She remained so angry that she even refused to write a letter of condolence when James Warren died in 1808. By 1811, however, old passions had cooled; when a friend came to visit, bringing greetings and expressions of affection from Mercy, Abigail softened and wrote a friendly reply. She could not forbear to remind Mercy of the reasons for her long silence, but Mercy—now eighty years old—ignored the remnants of Abigail's resentment, and the two women once again entertained each other with their letters.

About the same time, she and John patched up their old quarrels with Thomas Jefferson. Years earlier, in 1804, Abigail had broken their long silence with Jefferson by writing him a letter of sympathy after the death of his daughter Polly, the child Abigail had cared for in London. Jefferson responded politely, reaffirming his feelings of friendship for both Abigail and John, but he also mentioned some of the old political disagreements between them. Abigail had not intended to reopen a correspondence, but she could not let Jefferson's remarks pass. As a result they continued to write each other for several months, airing their old political disagreements. Still unable to resolve their differences, they finally ended their correspondence. John knew nothing of it until it was over.

Now, eight years later, Jefferson had retired from politics too, and the old issues that had divided them seemed much less serious. For several months Benjamin Rush, who was close to both Adams and Jefferson, urged them to end their long silence. Finally John wrote to his old friend, beginning a correspondence that lasted until their deaths. Abigail joined their exchange occasionally too. In the end, the deep friendship they felt for each other conquered the political animosities of years past.

Time dimmed the memory of her differences with Jefferson, but also Abigail's political ideas in general had changed. In 1800 she had predicted that the country would not survive a Jefferson administration; now she supported the policies of James Madison, Jefferson's hand-picked successor. She rejected the Federalists, who had become increasingly extreme in their views, as narrow-minded politicians pursuing their own selfish interests. She became particularly upset with the Federalists for their continued uncritical support of Britain despite that country's renewed assaults on American shipping in 1811 and 1812. This new American–British conflict finally pushed Abigail and John forever away from the Federalists and into the Republican camp. Long a proponent of close ties between the United States and Britain, Abigail now blasted the British in terms strikingly similar to those she had once reserved for the French.

Abigail's turnabout on foreign policy issues was not quite so contradictory as it appears. She had always been suspicious of political parties, and she had always opposed any foreign interference in American affairs. It mattered not whether it was the Federalists or the Republicans who engaged in dirty politics, or the British or French who threatened American rights. In April 1812 Congress voted a sixty-day embargo on all trade with England in an effort to force them to stop the impressment of American sailors. Federalists, and most New Englanders in general, opposed the embargo vigorously and advocated a policy of appeasement toward Britain; but Abigail thought Congress had not gone far enough and should be preparing for war as well. Always bellicose when it came to foreign relations, she preferred war to continued submission to British atrocities on the high seas. When the United States finally did go to war in July, she thought the government prosecuted the war too slowly. Throughout the War of 1812 her views stood in sharp opposition to those of most New Englanders, who bitterly opposed the war.

Abigail worried that the war would make communication with John Quincy difficult and would delay his return home. She turned out to be right in surmising that the war would delay his return, although not because of the difficulty of crossing the ocean in wartime. In the spring of 1813, just when John Quincy was thinking of going home, he was appointed one of three Commissioners to negotiate an end to the war with Britain. James Monroe, then Secretary of State, wrote to Abigail and John expressing his hope that they would encourage John Quincy to accept this new appointment. Abigail, who desperately wanted her son at home, responded by referring to her history of sacrifice in the name of public duty. She had raised young children alone while John served in the Continental Congress; she had traveled to Europe alone; she had twice parted with her son on diplomatic missions. Unlike the appointment to Russia, which she had never really approved, the peace commission was exactly the sort of difficult, tiresome, thankless, but important service that she considered a public duty.

The beginning of peace negotiations did not end the war. The British attack on Washington in September and Andrew Jackson's triumphant victory at New Orleans in January were yet to come. During the summer of 1814, however, personal tragedy pushed all thought of war and politics out of Abigail's mind.

Nabby was sick with rheumatism through the spring and summer, and Abigail could not suppress the nagging fear that her ailment was not rheumatism but a recurrence of cancer. In June her worst suspicions were confirmed when Nabby's children reported that she had a tumor in the other breast and that she was so ill she could scarcely walk across the room. Abigail could hardly bear to think that her daughter would die so far away. But she was too old to make the 300-mile journey to central New York State, and Nabby was too sick to come to Quincy. Abigail despaired of ever seeing her daughter again.

Nabby, however, was determined that it would not be so. Knowing that she was dying, she decided to travel to Quincy even though she could barely move. With John and Caroline, she made the trip in a bumpy carriage and arrived in Quincy the last week in July. Two weeks later, her husband arrived from Washington, where he had been attending congressional sessions. Nabby lasted only a few more days and then died on August 15, at the age of forty-nine.

It was the severest blow yet for Abigail. She had been closer to Nabby, her only daughter, than to any of her other children. She marshaled all her resources of religion and philosophy and told herself that it was God's will, that Nabby was happier released from her suffering, that it was selfish to wish her on earth longer. But no amount of fortitude or faith could overcome the harsh reality that her beautiful, selfless, devoted daughter, still in the prime of life, had been taken from her. Only Caroline seemed to be able to assuage her grandmother's grief. At nineteen, she was maturing into a lovely woman, and she reminded Abigail of Nabby as a young woman. Always one of her favorite grandchildren, Caroline now became doubly precious.

Caroline continued to live with Abigail until her marriage two years later. William stayed in Quincy too, until it was time for him to return to Washington, and he came back to Quincy when Congress adjourned the next spring. The big house in Quincy was like a magnet, drawing in and sheltering children, grandchildren, nephews, nieces, and cousins. No matter how many already lived with Abigail and John, there always seemed to be room for more.

Deaths of close friends and relatives came with increasing frequency now. Benjamin Rush had died unexpectedly in April 1813; Mercy Warren and Elbridge Gerry died within days of each other in October 1814. In December she and John fell seriously ill themselves—John was sicker than he had been for twenty years—and both remained housebound until late February. As usual when she was sick, Abigail turned to books to amuse herself, but problems with her eyes limited the amount of reading she could do. Worse, age made her memory "like a sieve." She tried harder than ever to concentrate on what she read, "yet the impression is like a press copy, faint, difficult to retrace, and often escapes me."

In April 1815 Abigail's sister Elizabeth died suddenly. Now, with her brother and sisters all gone, Abigail felt terribly alone. A few months later another of her most cherished relatives, Cotton Tufts, died. He had survived to the venerable age of eighty-four and died just as suddenly as Elizabeth had.

Abigail hardly needed any more reminders of her own mortality, but the deaths of Elizabeth and Cotton Tufts made her more aware than ever before that death could come without warning. She brooded over the fact that she might never see John Quincy again. She wrote Louisa that she had hoped to see them once more, but "I now despair of it." She brooded the more because John Quincy had again lengthened his stay in Europe. The Peace Commissioners' work ended when the Treaty of Ghent was signed on Christmas eve, 1814. But shortly thereafter President Madison appointed John Quincy Ambassador to Britain. Abigail was distressed that he would remain in Europe still longer, but she could not help feeling a certain satisfaction at the appropriateness of his appointment. John had negotiated peace with the British after the Revolution and had been the first Minister to Britian; now John Quincy had done the same thing. "Britain must feel that she has been foild a second time; and that as it were by Heredatary descent," she commented.

Knowing that he would be in Europe for another year or two

at least, John Quincy decided that it was time for George and John to join him. Abigail hated to give them up, but she made no protest. It was best for the boys to be with their parents, she admitted; they would benefit from their father's guidance and would have an opportunity to see a bit of the world.

Abigail was by now an expert on packing for trans-Atlantic voyages. By early April she had the boys ready to go. As she prepared her grandsons for their journey to England, she couldn't help reminiscing about her years there. Louisa's complaints about the high cost of living in London and the unsociability of its residents came as no surprise. Abigail remembered English society in just the same way: "distant haughty and impolite." Despite her disdain for the royal court, she could not suppress her curiosity and asked Louisa for her impressions of the now aging Queen and for an account of current court fashions. Did the ladies still wear hoop skirts? And did they still wear feathers in their hair—feathers so ridiculously tall that they barely cleared the roof of a carriage?

George and John wrote about their sightseeing, and Abigail responded by comparing her impressions of the same places thirty years earlier. She was delighted that John liked Clapham, a pretty village near London, because she had fond memories of visiting friends there. When John wrote that he didn't like England as much as his native land—like a little echo of his father and grandfather before him—she was even more pleased.

As she got older, Abigail had to face the fact that even her grandchildren were no longer children. George, in school near London, was preparing for college, while Abigail still urged John Quincy not to force him to grow up too fast. Nabby's daughter, Caroline, married in September 1814. Abigail liked her new grandson-in-law, John Peter DeWint; he was handsome, modest, of good character, and the sole heir to his family's substantial estate. His only failing was that he lived in New York and would take Caroline away from Quincy. "She was the prop of my Age, my solace, my comfort," Abigail wrote sadly after Caroline's wedding.

A few weeks later, she picked up a New York newspaper and read, to her astonishment, that her granddaughter Abbe had been married a few days before. Abbe and her mother, Sally, had left Quincy some years before to live in New York, while Susan had remained with her grandparents. Although Sally and Abbe had not been in frequent contact with Abigail and John, it seemed rude and unkind not to notify the Quincy relatives of Abbe's impending marriage.

More surprises awaited her. About two weeks after she read about the marriage, Abigail returned from visiting a friend to find Abbe and her husband waiting for her. They planned to visit for a few days, but they had engaged lodgings at a nearby boarding house and refused to stay with Abigail and John! "I was thunder struck," was Abigail's reaction. Abbe's husband protested that he didn't want to be a burden to the family. John was all for throwing them out immediately, but Abigail tried to persuade them to change their minds. Still Abbe's husband was adamant, and there was nothing to do but submit to the bizarre arrangements. Offended as she was, Abigail had to admit that she liked Abbe's husband.

Neither age nor the threat of illness slowed down Abigail's daily pace. She was seriously ill in the winter of 1816 but had barely recovered when, according to John, she was back to her old habits of working too hard around the house and trying to keep track singlehandedly of all the members of her far-flung family. "Your Mother," he observed to John Quincy, "is . . . restored to her characteristic vivacity, activity, witt sense and benevolence. Of consequence she must take upon herself the Duties of Granddaughter, Neice, Maids, Husband and all. She must be allways writing to you and all her Grand children." He worried that she would damage her health with all her activity but added on reflection that such fears were silly, "for there can be but a few minutes before both of us must depart, and but a few seconds between her departure and mine, or between my departure and hers."

Visitors were always welcome. On a moment's notice, Abigail would drop everything to entertain a houseful of company. "Your Father, and I have Lived to an Age, to be sought for as Curiositys—accordingly we have more strangers to visit us, and more company, than for years past," she told John Quincy. Relatives came and stayed for several weeks, a month, or more.

Normally, she and John did not go out much, but the summer of 1816 seemed to be a constant round of parties. John wrote to John Quincy an account of a party they attended "with . . . the bon ton, of our beloved Town of Quincy." A bit amused at his sociability, he added, "Bless my heart! how many feet have your

Mother and your Father in the Grave? and yet how frolicksome We are?"

Later that summer they set Boston tongues wagging when they attended a dinner party at the Harrison Gray Otises. Otis was one of the extreme Federalists who had bitterly opposed John and later John Quincy. The two families had not spoken in years. But when one of the women of the family asked Abigail whether a visit from the Otises would be welcome, she urged them to come. An invitation to dinner followed. John and Abigail went and enjoyed themselves immensely, but the spectacle of the former political enemies around the same dinner table was the talk of the town. "It was a subject of speculation . . . whether the stocks have risen or fallen in concequence," Abigail observed. It was said the Otises had ulterior motives—that they wanted some political favor—but Abigail believed they were motivated by "the benevolent desire of extinguishing all party spirit." John, himself surprised at the reconciliation, asked his son, "Do you ascribe it to the Eclipse of 1806, to the Comet or to the spots in the sun?"

Party spirit indeed seemed to be on the wane not only in Boston and Quincy but throughout the country. It was widely expected that James Monroe would succeed Madison as President in the fall, with little opposition. By following Washington's and Jefferson's example of retiring after two terms, Madison helped establish a principle of regular, orderly turnover in the nation's highest office. With the Federalists in decline, the Republicans took on the character of a broad national party. With the country at peace and in a period of prosperity, there was little to excite party animosity.

Abigail continued to take an optimistic view of her country's future. She supported Monroe's election, although she thought he was not so able a leader as Madison, and she no longer railed against political parties and frequent elections. "I am determined to be very well pleased with the world," she remarked, "and wish well to all its inhabitants. Altho in my journey through it, I meet with some who are too selfish, others too ambitious, some uncharitable, others malicious and envious, yet these vices are counterbalanced by opposite virtues—. . . and I always thought the laughing phylosopher a much wiser man, than the sniveling one."

Coming from one who had predicted the country's imminent destruction only a few years earlier, such a statement represented a major change of heart. Part of the change was wrought simply by getting away from politics; no crisis looked quite so threatening from the peaceful countryside of Quincy. But part of it was the result of Abigail's realistic observation of the changes in her country. She had lived through the critical years of fighting a revolution, establishing a new government, and testing its stability against foreign and domestic opposition. Now, fifteen years after she had bowed out of public life, the crisis of the young republic appeared to be past.

Monroe was elected in November, to no one's surprise. Immediately rumors started that he would appoint John Quincy Adams Secretary of State. The newspapers confidently announced as much at the end of November, but Abigail would not allow herself to believe that the reports were true.

Both she and John had been urging John Quincy to come home for several months. Abigail emphasized over and over the fact that neither of them could live much longer and that they wanted to see him again before they died; John stressed the importance of educating their children in America rather than Europe. But John Quincy was not to be coerced. Like his father, he did not want to appear too eager for office; and going home right after a Presidential election might make him look like one of the hungry multitude of office seekers.

But Monroe did in fact appoint John Quincy Secretary of State shortly after the election. As soon as they received the news, John Quincy and Louisa began making plans to go home. They reached New York on August 6, 1817, nearly eight years after they had left home. John Quincy wrote to Abigail immediately and set out for Quincy as soon as they could collect their luggage and hire a carriage. Abigail calculated the travel time and counted the days until she might expect to see them, but no one could say for sure when they would arrive.

It was Louisa Smith who first spotted a carriage drawn by four horses coming down the hill on a sunny morning two weeks later. "I ran to the door," Abigail recalled. "It arrived in a few moments. The first who sprang out was John, who with his former ardour was round my neck in a moment. George followed half crazy calling out o Grandmother—o Grandmother." Charles, who was too young to remember his grandparents, hung back shyly.

Abigail had warned John Quincy that eight years had wrought great changes in her appearance, and he had made similar observations about himself. But all such concerns were forgotten in the excitement of the reunion. The children were in fine health; Louisa looked younger than ever, Abigail thought, and all of them had survived their long journey remarkably well. Although the new administration was now in its sixth month, John Quincy did not rush off to Washington but stayed at home for a month, entertaining his parents with tales of life abroad.

George was admitted to Harvard soon after they arrived in Quincy, and the younger boys were sent to school in Boston. John Quincy and Louisa set off for Washington in September, leaving Abigail once again in charge of their children.

The first day John and Charles were sent to school, they were back again in Quincy by evening. Their pretext, Abigail reported to Louisa, was retrieving a forgotten book. Neither one wanted to go back to Boston. If allowed to stay with her just a day or two more, they promised to return and study very hard; but the first weekend found them back in Quincy again. Although Abigail thought they shouldn't be running home all the time, she hadn't the heart to tell them not to come. "I must wean them by degrees," she told Louisa. She would limit their visits to every other week, and then every third week—but the system never worked. The boys insisted on coming home to their grandmother, and she loved their company too much to stop them.

Winter seemed to bring out company in Quincy. Heavy snows made excellent sleighing, and Boston friends who wanted a pleasant day's outing were likely to ride out to Quincy to call on the Adamses. Abigail always felt compelled to feed them, and somehow extra food could always be found. One day she produced dinner for nine guests on the spur of the moment. By March she was telling John and Charles that they couldn't come every weekend; she and John needed some peace and quiet.

The informal, impromptu entertaining at Quincy contrasted strikingly with Louisa's accounts of Washington society. She wrote long letters to Abigail describing the parties, the visits, and the squabbles over who should visit whom and when. Elizabeth Monroe was making herself unpopular by refusing to hold "drawing rooms," and Louisa herself got involved in a flap over visits between the wives of Cabinet members and the wives of Senators. Abigail well remembered similar problems in her own day and was full of advice for Louisa. Mrs. Monroe would never get away with eliminating the drawing rooms, she predicted. If she had followed Jefferson, who was a widower and did relatively little entertaining, she might have managed it. Coming after the popular Dolly Madison, however, she would have to follow her example and continue to entertain lavishly.

Abigail was right. She was amused to learn later that Mrs. Monroe not only reinstituted the drawing room but did it in a much more formal style than her predecessors. "In my day, if so much stile, pomp and Etiquette had been assumed the cry of Monarchy, Monarchy would have resounded from Georgia to Maine," she told Louisa. As for Louisa's own problems, Abigail urged her not to lose any sleep over whether Cabinet members' wives made the first visit or waited for Senators' wives to call first. Watch what other people did, she suggested, and follow the lead of the men.

John Quincy was so busy during his first few months as Secretary of State that he thought he and Louisa would have to forgo their summer vacation in Quincy. Abigail repeatedly urged them to come, and at the end of August they finally managed to get away for about a month. A few days after they left, Abigail fell ill with typhoid fever. Louisa Smith, Susan, Nancy, and other friends and relatives took turns sitting by her bed, trying to make her comfortable. John was so distracted with worry that he paced the house, unable even to read. After several days Abigail appeared to improve, but then she took a sudden turn for the worse. On October 28, a few days short of her seventy-fourth birthday, she died.

Abigail died as she would have wished. Her illness was brief and without pain. Her mind and her wit remained sharp to the end, even if she did complain about forgetfulness. Occasional problems with her eyes and stiffness in her fingers never stopped her from her favorite occupations of reading and letter-writing. She supervised every detail of her vast household until her last illness, and she never became dependent on anyone. Most important to her, she died with most of her family around her, and she had lived to see John Quincy one more time.

Epilogue

Abigail's death shocked everyone who knew her. Despite her frequent illnesses, people close to her saw only her boundless energy and determination. She had survived so many sicknesses, nursed so many members of her family through illnesses, and buried so many others that no one was prepared for her death.

John could hardly contemplate life without Abigail, and yet he took the blow with remarkable tranquility. Through fifty-four years of marriage they had loved each other with an intensity that never diminished. One of the obituraries noted aptly that "The worthy President always appeared as the friend, who had lived himself into one with the wife of his bosom." It was as if part of himself went to the grave with her.

The children, grandchildren, neighbors, and friends all tried to support him through his grief, and yet they found him providing an example of strength to them. "How shall I offer you consolation for your loss, when I feel that my own is irreparable?" John Quincy asked. His father replied, "My consolations are more than I can number. The seperation cannot be so long as twenty seperations heretofore. The Pangs and the Anguish have not been so great as when you and I embarked for France in 1778." Fully convinced that he would follow her soon, he would not let his grief overwhelm him.

But even though John was nine years older than Abigail, he survived her by nearly eight years. He lived quietly at Peacefield, with the company of Louisa Smith and an ever changing complement of children and grandchildren. He remained in remarkably good health and continued his regimen of study and writing. For the last two years of his life he had the immense satisfaction of following John Quincy's career as President.

Through the spring and summer of 1826 John's health weakened steadily. On July 4, the fiftieth anniversary of the Declaration of Independence, he died. He was ninety-one. Thomas Jefferson, his lifelong friend and sometime political enemy, died the same day. They were the last survivors of the men who made the American Revolution.

Abigail did not live quite long enough to see her son elected to the nation's highest office, making her the first and only woman ever to be both wife and mother of American Presidents. John Quincy succeeded James Monroe to the Presidency in 1824. He was elected on the Republican ticket, an irony that his mother would have appreciated. She would not have been surprised that he, like his father, was a one-term President, or that he lost in 1828 to Andrew Jackson, widely hailed as the successor to Jefferson in the battle to make the United States more democratic.

Sixty-one when he left the Presidency, John Quincy was no more ready to give up politics than his father had been; but instead of retiring to Quincy, he won election to Congress and began a second career as a legislator. Abigail would have looked askance at such a decline in status, but she would have changed her mind had she been able to watch him become one of the leaders of the fight against slavery. And she would have understood his determination to keep up the fight, remaining in Congress until his death in 1848 at the age of eighty-one.

Thomas continued his solid if undistinguished career as a judge and leading resident of Quincy. He fathered seven children and died young, by family standards, at age sixty. He survived his father by only six years.

Caroline Smith DeWint kept her mother's memory alive by publishing selections from Nabby's journal and letters in 1841. Abigail would have been pleased at the memorial to her daughter. If her sex prevented her from shining as a politician or judge, at least she could leave, through her writings, some record of a woman's impressions of the years of revolution and nation-building. As an advocate of education and self-expression for women, Abigail would have thought such a memorial the most appropriate way to remember her daughter.

But Abigail was extremely self-conscious about her own writing. She often told correspondents to burn her letters. No doubt she would have scolded her granddaughter for including some of her letters in the collection of Nabby's writings—to say nothing of all the later generations who lovingly preserved her letters among those of all the other family members. What she would have thought of her biographers—reading her correspondence, prying into her mind, publishing the story of her life for anyone to read—one can only conjecture. Despite her strong views on the need for improvements in women's status, she always considered her own life and works far less important than those of her husband and son, or even those of women whose lives were less traditional than hers—like Mercy Otis Warren and Catharine Macaulay.

Probably Abigail would have been astonished to find herself transformed into something of a celebrity one hundred fifty years after her death. She knew that members of her family would go down in history, but she hardly believed that she herself would be one of them. Yet surely she would have approved of the reasons for her fame: the interest of a later age in the history of family and domestic life, as well as the history of politics; and, above all, its interest in the emancipation of women and in the discovery of women in the past who spoke out on behalf of their sex.

Sources for
Quotations

For fuller citations of published sources and collections, see the "Note on Sources" following this section.

Page	Quotation and Source
ix	"heroine": July 7, 1775, *AFC* I:247.
xi	"tyranny," "Egyptian bondage": AA to JA, January 4, 1795, AP #379.
xiii	"busy world": AA to JA, November 30, 1794, AP #378.
	"sausy Lad," "As to points and comma's": January 27, 1803, AP #402.
4	"Nabby, you will either make": AA to Elizabeth Shaw Peabody, June 10, 1801 (actually 1808), LC.
6	"to say all the handsome things": *JA Diary*, II:72.
10	"Wild colts make": AA to JQA, December 30, 1804, AP #403.
11	"In youth the mind": February 2, 1762, Smith–Carter Papers, MHS.
12	"Creator": Ibid.
13	"Good nature": *JA Diary*, I:108–09
14	"Tender feelings": Ibid., I:234.
15	"I never did": n.d. (1762 or 1763), *AFC* I:2.
	"I saw a Lady": August 1763, *AFC* I:8.
	"Apparitions": September 12, 1763, *AFC* I:8.
16	"Cruel, Yet perhaps": February 14, 1763, *AFC* I:3.
	"Patience, my Dear": April 20, 1763, *AFC* I:5.
17	"cast in the same mould": September 12, 1763, *AFC* I:9.
18	"I know of nothing": November 23, 1763, AP #343.
	"must permit the little Villains": JA to Cotton Tufts, April 9, 1764, *AFC* I:20.
19	"I am not affraid": April 2, 1764, *AFC* I:13.
	"Did you ever see": April 7, 1764, *AFC* I:17.
	"Dont conclude from any Thing": April 26, 1764, *AFC* I:40.
	"sending . . . a Nest": April 12, 1764, *AFC* I:24.

Page	Quotation and Source

19   "The Nest of Letters": April 13, 1764, *AFC* I:26.

         "I would not you should": April 13, 1764, *AFC* I:29.

         "Did you never": April 19, 1764, *AFC* I:37.

20   "Miser like I hoard": April 15, 1764, *AFC* I:31.

         "too severe," "You sometimes view": April 12, 1764, *AFC* I:26.

         "Gentleman and his Lady": April 30, 1764, *AFC* I:41.

         "'Were I imprison'd": May 4, 1764, *AFC* I:43.

21   "I have this Evening": September 30, 1764, *AFC* I:47–48.

         "a Number of bauling Lawyers," "Oh my dear Girl": September 30, 1764, *AFC* I:48.

26   "Your Diana become a Mamma": c. July 14, 1765, *AFC* I:51.

28   "Tis a hard thing": October 13, 1766, *AFC* I:56.

         "I would give a great deal": January 15, 1767, *AFC* I:59.

         "a Sight here rare": January 15, 1767, *AFC* I:59.

30   "What strang Ideas they have": January 15, 1767, *AFC* I:60.

31   "awful admonitions," "plants," "raised and cultivated": James Fordyce, *Sermons to Young Women* (Boston, 1767), I:25.

38   "I considered the Step": *JA Diary*, III:294.

         "burst into a flood of Tears," "She was very sensible": *JA Diary*, III:294–95.

40   "our (cruel) Mother Country": April 20, 1771, *AFC* I:76.

         "From my Infancy," "Domestick Beings": Ibid.

         "The Natural tenderness," "prevent their Roving": Ibid.

         "If your Gay acquaintance," "instructive": January 4, 1770, *AFC* I:68–69.

Page	Quotation and Source
67	"America . . . is like a large Fleet": June 11, 1775, *AFC* I:216.
	"I want you to be": June 22, 1775, *AFC* I:225.
	"the most abject slaves," "A Lady who lived": July 25, 1775, *AFC* I:261.
68	"You had prepared me": July 16, 1775, *AFC* I:246.
69	"I . . . fear least a degree": AA to Mercy Warren, July 24, 1775, *AFC* I:255.
	"I have received": July 5, 1775, *AFC* I:239.
	"I want some sentimental": July 16, 1775, *AFC* I:247.
70	"I find I am obliged": August 27, 1775, *AFC* I:276.
71	"patience and submission," "At times": October 1, 1775, *AFC* I:288.
	"I have been like a nun": November 12, 1775, *AFC* I:323.
	"I . . . ruminate upon": Ibid.
72	"parent State," "Let us renounce them": AA to JA, November 12, 1775, *AFC* I:324.
	"I am more and more convinced": AA to JA, November 27, 1775, *AFC* I:328–30.
73	"I soon get lost": Ibid.
	"but whether her Eyes": November 4, 1775, *AFC* I:320.
	"if I could write": October 23, 1775, *AFC* I:312.
	"commend me to the Ladies": July 5, 1776, *AFC* II:34.
74	"the most accomplished Lady": September 16, 1775, *AFC* I:285–86.
	"Whom God has joined": December 3, 1775, *AFC* I:332.
	"I found his honour": January 1776, *AFC* I:422–23.
76	"one who wishes": AA to JA, March 2, 1776, *AFC* I:352.
77	"The sound": March 2, 1776, *AFC* I:353.

Page	Quotation and Source

88   "The Town of": June 15, 1777, *AFC* II:265.

"a most ungratefull": Ibid.

89   "an eminent, wealthy, stingy": July 30, 1777, *AFC* II:295.

"was like to outshine": JA to AA, May 15, 1777, *AFC* II:238.

"the Lindsey Woolsey": March 1, 1777, *AFC* II:166.

90   "tis a constant remembrancer": March 8, 1777, *AFC* II:173.

"I must summon": April 17, 1777, *AFC* II:212.

"I look forward": June 1, 1777, *AFC* II:250.

"I . . . some times . . . immagine": June 8, 1777, *AFC* II:258.

91   "shaking fit": July 9, 1777, *AFC* II:277.

"It appeard to be": July 16, 1777, *AFC* II:282.

"My Heart was much set": Ibid.

"Is it not unaccountable": July 28, 1777, *AFC* II:292.

"endeared to me": August 12, 1777, *AFC* II:308.

92   "A smart Wife": August 11, 1777, *AFC* II:306.

"the Movements of How": September 17, 1777, *AFC* II:343.

"If Men will not fight": October 20, 1777, *AFC* II:354.

93   "I have patiently": October 25, 1777, *AFC* II:358–59.

95   "Can I Sir consent": Ibid.

"we may profit": January 2, 1778, *AFC* II:376.

97   "Cannot you immagine me": AA to John Thaxter, February 15, 1778, *AFC* II:390.

98   "I resign my own": February 15, 1778, *AFC* II:390.

"sacrifice to the glorious": March 6, 1778, *AFC* II:400.

"to exclude him": AA to John Thaxter, February 15, 1778, *AFC* II:391.

Page	Quotation and Source
117	"My habitation": AA to JA, November 14, 1779, *AFC* III:233–34.
119	"There are so many persons": November 29, 1779, *AFC* III:240.
120	"I grow more and more": March 1, 1780, *AFC* III:292.
	"The People are Lazy": *JQA Diary*, January 3, 1780, AP #5.
	"My affections I fear": January 16, 1780, *AFC* III:258.
	"They behave": June 17, 1780, *AFC* III:366.
121	"very acceptable": April 15, 1780, *AFC* III:321.
	"A little of what you call": May 1, 1780, *AFC* III:335.
122	"15 yards of thin black": July 5, 1780, *AFC* III:372.
	"26 yards of Dutch": November 13, 1780, *AFC* IV:17.
	"They say two Cows": November 13, 1780, *AFC* IV:15–16.
123	"You will greatly oblige": January 3, 1781, *AFC* IV:58.
125	"disagreeable," "alarming": July 5, 1780, *AFC* III:371.
	"are not dismayed": July 21, 1780, *AFC* III:380.
126	"How ineffectual is the tye": October 8, 1780, *AFC* IV:2.
	"Unprincipled wretches": Ibid.
	"I trust we shall": October 15, 1780, *AFC* IV:6.
127	"however this Belief": Ibid.
	"The fate of the Southern States": March 19, 1781, *AFC* IV:94.
129	"You must not be": January 21, 1781, *AFC* IV:68.
	"blackening": Alice Lee Shippen to Elizabeth Welles Adams, June 17, 1781, *AFC* IV:154.
	"You will send me": June 30, 1781, *AFC* IV:164–65.
130	"when he is wounded": AA to James Lovell, June 30, 1781, *AFC* IV:166.
	"I am pained": August 4, 1781, *AFC* IV:193.

Page	Quotation and Source

143   "tender passion": January 22, 1783, AP #360.

144   "and I would have this observed": January 20, 1783, AP #360.

        "your Amelia is the same": December 1782, Cranch Papers, MHS.

145   "I feel too powerfull": December 23, 1782, AP #359.

        "reformed Rake": January 22, 1783, AP #360.

        "Professor of belle Letters": Ibid.

        "My 'Princess'": January 29, 1783, AP #360.

146   "I dont like this method": January 22, 1783, AP #360.

        "voilent opposition never yet": April 7, 1783, AP #360.

148   "almost at the world's end": July 23, 1783, AP #361.

        "great flow of Spirits": December–January, 1783–84, AP #362.

        "I am too much": November 19, 1783, AP #361.

149   "the object my Heart": December 7, 1783, AP #362.

        "I know not whether": Ibid.

150   "I have no reason": July 1, 1783, BPL.

        "Love and the desire": Ibid.

        "My Heart swelled": December 15, 1783, AP #362.

152   "You invite me to you": February 11, 1784, AP #362.

        "but . . . my fears": Ibid.

153   "but let no person": May 25, 1784, AP #362.

        "that once great Nation": AA to JQA, April 25, 1784, AP #362.

155   "What should I have thought": July 6, 1784, AAS.

        "a sweet situation": AA to Elizabeth Shaw, n.d. (1784), LC.

156   "the most odorifferous": Ibid.

        "To those who have never": AA Diary, in *JA Diary* III:155.

Page	Quotation and Source
156	"Going to a Good Husband": Ibid., p. 157.
	"As I found I might reign": AA to Elizabeth Shaw, n.d. (1784), LC.
	"dress his victuals": AA Diary, in *JA Diary*, III:158.
	"which had been enough": Ibid.
157	"If I did not write": Ibid., p. 164.
	"a great cradle": Ibid., p. 159.
	"I begin to think": AA to Mary Cranch, July 6, 1784, AAS.
	"partial prison": AA Diary, in *JA Diary*, III:164.
	"high monarchacal man": Ibid., pp. 155, 158.
158	"mortifying," "mechanics & mere husbandmen": AA to Mary Cranch, July 6, 1784, AAS.
	"Your letter of the 23d": July 26, 1784, AP #363.
	"But do you know": August 21, 1784, BPL.
159	"He is the same": AA to Elizabeth Cranch, August 1, 1784, Essex Institute.
	"I saw upon the table": AA2 Journal, I:viii.
160	"poets and painters": January 1785, AAS.
161	"There is a rage": AA to Mary Cranch, July 6, 1784, AAS.
	"The fellow staird": AA to Elizabeth Shaw, December 14, 1784, LC.
162	"One thing I know": AA to Lucy Cranch, September 5, 1784, AAS.
	"Boston cannot boast": Ibid.
163	"Etiquet," "a pack of Lazy": AA to Cotton Tufts, September 8, 1784, AP #363.
164	"where she shew more," "you see that manners": AA to Lucy Cranch, September 5, 1784, AAS.
165	"every appearance indicates": AA to Mercy Warren, September 1784, AP #363.
166	"seperate appartments": Ibid.

Page	Quotation and Source

166   "Appetites & passions": Ibid.

"grown old in Debauchery": AA to Elizabeth Shaw, January 11, 1785, LC.

"the lowest and most obscure": Quoted in Dumas Malone, *Jefferson and the Rights of Man*, 2:9.

168   "He is one of the choice": AA to Mary Cranch, May 8, 1785, AAS.

"seem rather calculated": AA to Cotton Tufts, 1784, AP #363.

"a good representation": AA2 Journal, I:19–20.

"had rather be amused": AA to Mary Cranch, February 20, 1785, AAS.

169   "O! the Musick": Ibid.

"I felt my delicacy": Ibid.

"This people are more": AA2 Journal, I:18.

170   "I turn my thoughts": AA to Royall Tyler, September 1784, AP #363.

"I had rather dine": April 15, 1785, AAS.

171   "What a sad misfortune": February 20, 1785, AAS.

"You can never feel": May 8, 1785, AAS.

172   "It is a bold stroke": March 5, 1785, AP #364.

"I love to feel free": JA to Cotton Tufts, March 5, 1785, AP #364.

"He chuses I should": AA to Cotton Tufts, March 8, 1785, AP #364.

173   "I think I have somewhere": June 6, 1785, *A–J Correspondence*, I:28.

175   "publick & noisy": AA to Mary Cranch, June 24, 1785, AAS.

"I consider your boasts": June 21, 1785, *A–J Correspondence* I:33–34.

176   "We have not taken": AA to ?, 1785 or 1786, AP #366.

Page	*Quotation and Source*

187   "Indeed he searches": March 18, 1786, AP #367.

"The favourite of the *Muses*": Ibid.

188   "a more martial": Ibid.

190   "For what have we been": AA to JQA, November 28, 1786, AP #369.

"Ignorant, wrestless desperadoes": January 29, 1787, *A–J Correspondence*, I:168.

191   "The spirit of resistance": February 22, 1787, Ibid., 173.

"A *levelling* principal": AA to Mary Cranch, February 25, 1787, AAS.

192   "The lower class": AA to Cotton Tufts, 1786, AP #369.

194   "I spent a fortnight": January 20, 1787, AAS.

"Virgin": December 25, 1786, AP #369.

"An old Man": Ibid.

"bedfellow," "You recollect in France": December 30, 1786, AP #369.

"To derive a proper": AA to Mary Cranch, January 20, 1787, AAS.

195   "What is the chief end": Ibid.

"prodigious expence": Ibid.

"You may put up with that": April 29, 1787, AP #369.

196   "The study of the Household": AA to Lucy Cranch, April 25, 1787, AP #369.

197   "My Pappa has talked": AA2 to Lucy Cranch, October 15, 1786, AAS.

198   "much more entertained": AA to Mary Cranch, September 15, 1787, AAS.

"You will smile": Ibid.

"twit us of being": AA Diary, in *JA Diary*, III:204.

"experiment," "rage," "national evil": September 15, 1787, AAS.

Page	Quotation and Source

199   "Thus is the landed property": Ibid.

"Poverty hunger & nakedness": October 10, 1787, AP #370.

"The ease with which property": Ibid.

"Deprecate that restless": Ibid.

200   "private man": November 6, 1787, AP #370.

201   "I have lived long enough": February 26, 1788, *A–J Correspondence*, I:228.

"'Tis domestick happiness": AA Diary, in *JA Diary*, III:215.

203   "Believe me I am not": May 25, 1786, AAS.

"I feel that I can": AA to Mary Cranch, February 25, 1787, AAS.

204   "Garden was a wilderness": August 1788, AP #371.

"In height and breadth": July 7, 1788, *AA2 Journal* II:85.

206   "I suppose you will tell me": November 16, 1788, AP #371.

209   "I would not change": July 12, 1789, *New Letters*, 17.

"I can no more do": August 9, 1789, ibid., 20.

210   "a grace dignity & ease": AA to Mary Cranch, August 9, 1789, *New Letters*, 19.

"I have a favour": July 12, 1789, ibid., 14.

211   "gravely misled," "I feel it": ibid., 17.

212   "This is no more state": August 9, 1789, ibid., 20.

"If any person": January 24, 1790, ibid., 8

214   "make and receive": October 3, 1790, *New Letters*, 59.

"It is my destiny": October 10, 1790, ibid., 60.

215   "I have the vanity": ibid., 61.

"acute rheumatism," "in the midst of all this": December 12, 1790, ibid., 66.

Page	Quotation and Source

Page   *Quotation and Source*

216   "*decent woman* who understands": January 9, 1791, ibid., 68.

"one continued scene": AA to Mary Cranch, February 5, 1792, ibid., 77.

217   "I feel that day a happy one," "a cleaver, sober": December 18, 1791, ibid., 75.

"insignificant office": December 15, 1793, AP #376.

218   "I firmly believe": AA to Mary Cranch, April 20, 1791, *New Letters*, 83.

"the V President": Ibid.

221   "This Day decides": December 5, 1792, AP #375.

"tomorrow will determine": December 4, 1792, AP #375.

222   "Four years more": December 28, 1792, AP #375.

223   "I hope Brisler minds": November 26, 1792, AP #375.

"I have the advantage": December 29, 1792, AP #375.

225   "the Tellegraph of the mind": February 13, 1795, AP #379.

"However great the Blessings": AA to Mrs. Paradice, n.d., 1791, AP #375.

228   "unless mankind were": AA to JA, February 26, 1794, AP #377.

"all Ages and Nations," "enlightened": Ibid.

"eternal Indecision": February 9, 1794, AP #377.

229   "There are some": AA to JA, May 3, 1794, AP #377.

"so valourous and noble": April 1, 1794, AP #377.

"I want to hear": January 24, 1794, AP #377.

230   "I check every rising wish": May 10, 1794, AP #377.

"at a very early period": June or July 1794, AP #377.

"ardent for another": November 2, 1794, AP #378.

231   "Antifederalism, Jacobinism": Ibid.

"There is scarcely animation": December 7, 1794, AP #378.

Page	Quotation and Source

231   "I wish I had a farm": December 5, 1794, AP #378.

"innocent," "I know not what": Ibid.

"buisy world": November 30, 1794, AP #378.

"amusements," "great relief," "but dont you know": December 6, 1794, AP #378.

232   "Paternal Acres": December 23, 1794, AP #378.

233   "He is ingenious enough": January 4, 1795, AP #379.

"much yet remains": Ibid.

"disciple of Wollstonecraft": January 22, 1794, AP #377.

234   "However brilliant": AA to JQA, May 20, 1796, AP #381.

"after all the Hair Breadths scapes": October 26, 1795, AP #380.

235   "to allarm & terrify": AA to JQA, November 19, 1795, AP #380.

"humble all Jacobinical wretches": AA to JA, December 15, 1795, AP #380.

"Tho I am not certain": December 27, 1795, AP #380.

"You know the Consequence": January 5, 1796, AP #381.

236   "duty," "It is no light thing": January 7, 1796, AP #381.

"I am Heir Apparent": January 20, 1796, AP #381.

"If the succession": JA to AA, February 15, 1796, AP #381.

"My Ambition leads me": January 21, 1796, AP #381.

"I think what is duty": February 20, 1796, AP #381.

237   "patience prudence discretion": Ibid.

"I am weary": February 2, 1796, AP #381.

"No man even if he is": March 2, 1796, AP #381.

"Oh that I had": March 11, 1796, AP #381.

238   "quiet and retired," "has ever been": AA to TBA, August 16, 1796, AP #382.

Page	Quotation and Source

239   "Prudence is a sorry": JQA to AA, August 16, 1796, AP #382.

"The die is cast!" AA to TBA, September 25, 1796, AP #382.

240   "on the decision": December 7, 1796, AP #382.

"I laugh at myself": Ibid.

241   "You may recollect": December 31, 1796, AP #382.

"a narrow squeak": December 20, 1796, AP #382.

"Luckily for you": December 27, 1796, AP #382.

"Retirement at Peace Field": December 23, 1796, AP #382.

244   "Tho wrong in politicks": AA to JA, January 15, 1797, AP #383.

"We shall be put": March 3, 1797, AP #383.

245   "I have however": January 11, 1797, AP #383.

"our *dernier* resort": January 28, 1797, AP #383.

"bird of passage": AA to JA, February 13, 1797, AP #383.

"more than I dare tell": AA to JA, March 29, 1797, AP #383.

246   "attacking the principle," "Tell them": AA to JA, February 13, 1797, AP #383.

"I am a Being": March 9, 1797, AP #383.

247   "the most affecting": March 17, 1797, AP #383.

"It will not fail": March 18, 1797, AP #383.

"but there are many": April 6, 1797, AP #384.

248   "It seems as if": AA to JA, April 12, 1797, AP #384.

"My reflections upon prospects": AA to Mary Cranch, May 16, 1797, *New Letters*, 89.

"I wish they were," "prettily but frugally": Ibid.

"a discreet woman": Ibid.

"was like a ploughd feild": Ibid., 90.

Page   *Quotation and Source*
249   "Mrs Tufts once stiled": Ibid.

            "I keep up my old Habit": May 24, 1797, ibid., 91

            "I shall have got": AA to Mary Cranch, June 23, 1797, ibid., 98.

            "You will not wonder": Ibid., 98–99.

251   "One might as well": October 22, 1797, *New Letters*, 108.

252   "I was fully sensible": AA to Mary Cranch, December 26, 1797, ibid., 120.

253   "The President had": July 3, 1798, ibid., 199.

            "the President would not": Charleston, S.C., *City Gazette*, March 5, 1800, quoted in Donald Stewart, *The Opposition Press in the Federalist Period*, p. 514.

254   "I am at a loss": AA to Mary Cranch, January 20, 1798, *New Letters*, 124.

            "I hope we may be": February 13, 1798, LC.

256   "The people are daily": March 27, 1798, AP #387.

            "war with union": April 14, 1798, AP #388.

            "I hope we shall": AA to AA2, April 11, 1798, *AA2 Journal*, II:151.

257   "shaved and pared": December 2, 1798, AP #392.

258   "I know you have": December 10, 1798, AP #392.

259   "The poor child": November 15, 1798, AP #392.

            "I have done all": December 17, 1798, AP #392.

            "With respect to what": December 28, 1798, AP #392.

260   "If he has none": January 12, 1799, AP #393.

            "one, of whose reformation": AA to JA, February 14, 1799, AP #393.

            "I dont like": January 18, 1799, AP #393.

261   "wisht the old woman": AA to JA, February 27, 1799, AP #393.

            "The old woman can tell": Ibid.

Page   *Quotation and Source*

261   "to ensure any kind": Ibid.

262   "delicate," "maternal care": April 1, 1799, AP #394.

263   "Did he, indeed": August 26, 1799, AP #396.

          "would stand all day": October 31, 1799, *New Letters*, 211.

          "I want to have them": AA to Elizabeth Shaw, February 4, 1800, LC.

264   "I wish any thing": November 26, 1799, *New Letters*, 218.

265   "every eye in the Room": March 18, 1800, ibid., 241–42.

          "One or two more": AA to Mary Cranch, March 5, 1800, ibid., 237.

266   "What ungratefull Beings": AA to William Smith, December 25, 1799, Smith–Townsend Papers, MHS.

          "There is something": February 27, 1800, *New Letters*, 234.

269   "I acted . . . as your proxy": May 22, 1800, AP #397.

270   "but not so fast": AA to JA, June 2, 1800, AP #398.

271   "little General," "Electioneering": AA to TBA, July 12, 1800, AP #398.

          "Anglo–American faction": AA to TBA, August 15, 1800, AP #398.

          "Brittania & Gallia": AA to Catherine Johnson, August 20, 1800, AP #398.

          "we may get on": AA to TBA, August 15, 1800, AP #398.

272   "Services rendered": September 1, 1800, AP #398.

273   "Weep with me": December 8, 1800, *New Letters*, 261–62.

274   "I halted but could not": AA to Mary Cranch, November 21, 1800, ibid., 256–57.

          "where I was received": Ibid.

          "I arrived . . . at this place": Ibid.

Page   *Quotation and Source*
275   "the very dirtyest Hole": Ibid.

"a castle of a House," "for ages to come": Ibid., 259

276   "the universal character": AA to Cotton Tufts, November 28, 1800, AP #399.

277   "Two of our hardy": Ibid.

"The lower class": Ibid.

278   "At my age": November 13, 1800, AP #399.

"We will live": AA to TBA, January 15, 1801, AP #400.

279   "unstable fluctuating": AA to Cotton Tufts, December 15, 1800, AP #399.

"infidel," "If ever we saw": AA to Mary Cranch, February 7, 1801, *New Letters*, 266.

281   "I would strive": January 15, 1801, *New Letters*, 263.

282   "a hotbed": AA to JQA, January 29, 1801, AP #400.

"monarch of stoney field": JA to TBA, September 15, 1801, AP #115.

283   "appears to enjoy": AA to TBA, June 12, 1801, AP #401

"with a total indifference": AA to TBA, April 22, 1801, AP #400.

284   "the post of honour": AA to TBA, July 5, 1801, AP #401.

285   "fine Lady": LCA, "Adventures of a Nobody," AP #269.

"The old gentleman": Ibid.

"Had I steped into": Ibid.

286   "An accomplished Quincy lady": Ibid.

288   "He looks as anxious": AA to TBA, June 20, 1803, AP #402.

289   "the old paternal": August 19, 1803, AP #402.

"his mode of life": November 7, 1803, AP #402.

290   "prefer'd passing the summer": LCA to JQA, April 17, 1804, AP #403.

Page	Quotation and Source

303   "As our Lamp": February 20, 1810, Samuel Abbot Green Papers, MHS.

307   "like as sieve," "yet the impression": AA to JQA, February 27, 1814, AP #416.

"I now despair": April 14, 1815, AP #423.

"Britain must feel": AA to LCA, May 9, 1815, AP #423.

308   "distant haughty and impolite": AA to LCA, September 2, 1815, AP #426.

"She was the prop": AA to Elizabeth Shaw Peabody, September 13, 1814, AP #419.

309   "I was thunder struck": AA to Harriet Welsh, October 30, 1814, AP #420.

"Your Mother": June 25, 1816, AP #432.

"Your Father, and I": August 27, 1816, AP #432.

"with . . .the bon ton": July 26, 1816, AP #432.

310   "It was a subject": August 27, 1816, AP #433.

"Do you ascribe it": August 26, 1816, AP #433.

"I am determined": AA to JQA, November 5, 1816, AP #434.

311   "I ran to the door": AA to Harriet Welsh, August 18, 1817, AP #438.

312   "I must wean them": September 15, 1817, AP #439.

313   "In my day": January 24, 1818, AP #442.

315   "The worthy President": November 1818, AP #445.

"How shall I offer you": November 2, 1818, AP #445.

"My consolations": November 10, 1818, AP #445.

A Note on Sources

A Note on Sources

Basic Primary Sources

Abigail Adams and her family were prolific letter writers, and they also had a sense of their importance in history. As a consequence, they saved most of their letters, and later generations carefully preserved them. The majority of their letters, diaries, and other papers are contained in the Adams Papers in the Massachusetts Historical Society. A microfilm edition of this collection has made it widely available throughout the country.

Most of Abigail's letters in this collection through 1782 have been published in the *Adams Family Correspondence*, ed. Lyman H. Butterfield et al., 4 vols. (Cambridge, 1963, 1973). Some additional letters from 1783 and 1784 appear in *The Book of Abigail and John*, ed. Lyman H. Butterfield et al. (Cambridge, 1975). Also published in this series is the *Diary and Autobiography of John Adams*, ed. Lyman H. Butterfield et al., 4 vols. (Cambridge, 1961). Abigail's two brief diaries, kept on her voyage to Europe and during part of her stay there, are included in Volume 3.

Other important manuscript collections are located at the American Antiquarian Society, the Library of Congress, and the Boston Public Library. The Massachusetts Historical Society has a substantial number of Abigail's letters that are not included in the Adams Papers but are scattered through several other collections. The Essex Institute has a small but important group of her letters; others are scattered in several archives. Part of the American Antiquarian Society collection has been published as *New Letters of Abigail Adams, 1788–1801*, ed. Stewart Mitchell (Boston, 1947).

Other published collections include the *Adams-Jefferson Correspondence*, ed. Lester J. Cappon, 2 vols. (Chapel Hill, 1959), and the Warren–Adams Letters, Vols. 72 and 73 of Massachusetts Historical Society *Collections* (1917, 1925). Nabby's diary and some of her letters appear in *The Journal and Correspondence of Miss Adams, daughter of John Adams*, ed. Caroline Smith DeWint, 2 vols. (New York and London, 1841–1842). These volumes also include some of Abigail's letters not available elsewhere, since the original manuscripts have been lost.

General Secondary Sources

There have been surprisingly few biographies of Abigail Adams. Charles Akers has made a start at rectifying this deficiency with his brief *Abigail Adams: An American Woman* (Boston, 1980). The older biographies, none of them very satisfactory, are Janet Whitney, *Abigail Adams* (Boston, 1947); Dorothie Bobbé, *Abigail Adams, the Second First Lady* (New York, 1929); and Laura Richards, *Abigail Adams and Her Times* (New York, 1917). Two recent Ph.D. dissertations focus on the early period of her life: Rosemary Keller, "Abigail Adams and the American Revolution," University of Illinois, Chicago Circle, 1977, and Edith B. Gelles, "Abigail Adams: Domesticity and the American Revolution," University of California, Irvine, 1978.

Page Smith's two-volume biography of John Adams (Garden City, N.Y., 1962) discusses Abigail at length. Peter Shaw's *The Character of John Adams* (Chapel Hill, 1976) is extremely helpful for understanding John Adams's pysche and his relationship with Abigail. Catherine D. Bowen, *John Adams and the American Revolution* (Boston, 1950), is an exhaustive study of the early period of his life. John Howe, *The Changing Political Thought of John Adams* (Princeton, 1966), is useful for understanding Abigail's political thought as well, since her ideas were so closely linked with John's. The Adams–Jefferson relationship is illuminated in Merrill D. Peterson, *Adams and Jefferson: A Revolutionary Dialogue* (New York, 1976).

Marie B. Hecht, *John Quincy Adams* (New York, 1972), is

the most useful general treatment of his life. Samuel Flagg Bemis concentrates primarily on his public career in *John Quincy Adams and the Foundations of American Foreign Policy* (New York, 1949) and *John Quincy Adams and the Union* (New York, 1956). His relationship with his mother is treated in Joseph E. Illick, "John Quincy Adams, The Maternal Influence," *Journal of Psychohistory* 4 (1976): 185–195, and David F. Musto, "The Youth of John Quincy Adams," *Proceedings* of the American Philosophical Society 113 (1969): 269–82. The only biography of any of the other children is Katherine Roof, *Col. William Smith and Lady* (Boston, 1929), which provides a rather insubstantial treatment of Nabby's adult years.

Specific Primary and Secondary Sources

The literature on the Revolutionary and early national periods is vast. The books and articles noted here have been helpful in describing the context in which Abigail Adams lived, but they are not by any means an exhaustive bibliography of the subject.

Childhood and Courtship (Chapters 1 and 2)

The Massachusetts Historical Society has a microfilm edition of the manuscript records of North Parish, Weymouth, as well as a variety of memoirs and pamphlets on the town. The *History of Weymouth, Massachusetts*, 4 vols. (Weymouth, 1923), provides substantial detail on the early history of the town. Some useful works on other rural New England towns in the colonial period include Kenneth Lockridge, *A New England Town: The First Hundred Years* (New York, 1970), and "Land, Population and the Evolution of New England Society, 1630–1790," *Past and Present* 32 (1968), 62–80; Philip Greven, *Four Generations* (Ithaca, N.Y., 1970); and Linda Auwers Bissell, "Family, Friends and Neighbors: Social Interaction in Windsor, Connecticut," Ph.D. dissertation; Brandeis University, 1973. Daniel Scott Smith analyzes in detail one of Weymouth's neighboring towns in "Population, Family, and Society in Hingham, Massachusetts, 1635–1880," Ph.D. dissertation; University of California, Berkeley, 1973. John J. Waters, *The Otis Family in Provincial and Revolutionary Massachusetts* (Chapel Hill, 1968), also sheds light on the region in which Abigail grew up.

A biographical sketch of Abigail's father appears in John

Langdon Sibley, *Biographical Sketches of Graduates of Harvard University* (Cambridge, 1873–1956), 7:588–91. Other relatives, including John Quincy, Cotton Tufts, Isaac Smith, Jr., and Richard Cranch, are also included in this reference work. William Smith's diaries are in the Massachusetts Historical Society, as are those of Cotton Tufts; selections from them were published in the Massachusetts Historical Society *Proceedings*, 42 (1908–09): 440–70 (Smith) and 479–87 (Tufts). Unfortunately these diaries consist of a string of brief, rather uninformative notations; but they do give some flavor of daily life in the Smith husehold. On ministers in general in the eighteenth century, J. William T. Youngs, Jr. *God's Messengers: Religious Leadership in Colonial New England, 1700–1750* (Baltimore, 1976), is useful. Information about Abigail's mother is sparse; she is discussed briefly in Sibley's sketch of William Smith. Evidence on the Smiths' disapproval of Abigail's marriage to John comes from the "Memoirs of Dr. John Pierce," Massachusetts Historical Society *Proceedings*, 2d ser., 19 (1905): 386.

Information on women's education in the eighteenth century can be gleaned from the following: James Axtell, *The School upon a Hill: Education and Society in Colonial New England* (New Haven, 1974); Lawrence Cremin, *American Education: The Colonial Experience, 1607–1783* (New York, 1970); and Robert Middlekauff, *Ancients and Axioms: Secondary Education in Eighteenth Century New England* (New Haven, 1963).

Motherhood and Politics (Chapters 3 and 4)

On childbirth and childrearing, see Catherine M. Scholten, "'On the Importance of the Obstetrick Art': Changing Customs of Childbirth in America, 1760 to 1825," *William and Mary Quarterly*, 34 (1977): 425–45; Dorothy C. and Richard W. Wertz, *Lying In: A History of Childbirth in America* (New York, 1977); and Philip Greven, *The Protestant Temperament: Patterns of Child-rearing, Religious Experience and the Self in Early America* (New York, 1977). In contrasting Abigail's childrearing practices with those common in the seventeenth century, John Demos, *A Little Commonwealth: Family Life in Plymouth Colony* (New York, 1970), is helpful.

Books that Abigail read which gave advice to young mothers include the Reverend James Fordyce, *Sermons to Young Women*

(Boston, 1767 and many other editions); [John Hill], *On the Management and Education of Children, . . . By the Honourable Juliana-Susannah Seymour* (London, 1754); and John Locke, *Some Thoughts Concerning Education* (London, 1693 and many subsequent editions).

Remember the Ladies: Women in America, 1750–1815, ed. Linda Grant DePauw and Conover Hunt (New York, 1976), provides a variety of information on housekeeping practices and women's dress. Further detail on the colonial housewife may be found in Alice Morse Earle, *Home Life in Colonial Days* (New York, 1898), and in other books by the same author.

For general descriptive material on colonial Boston, see Carl Bridenbaugh, *Cities in Revolt: Urban Life in America, 1743–1776* (New York, 1955), and G. B. Warden, *Boston: 1689–1775* (Boston, 1970). On the physical appearance of Boston and its changes over time, Walter Muir Whitehill, *Boston: A Topographical History* (Cambridge, 1959), is essential. Esther Forbes provides a wealth of detail on life in Boston during the Revolutionary era in *Paul Revere and the World He Lived In* (Boston, 1942).

The political disturbances in Boston in the 1760s are discussed in Edmund S. Morgan and Helen M. Morgan, *The Stamp Act Crisis* (Chapel Hill, 1953); Pauline Maier, *From Resistance to Revolution* (New York, 1972); and Hiller Zobel, *The Boston Massacre* (New York, 1970). On John Adam's work on the Boston Massacre case, see *The Legal Papers of John Adams*, ed. L. Kinvin Wroth and Hiller Zobel, Vol. 2 (Cambridge, 1965). Richard D. Brown, *Revolutionary Politics in Massachusetts* (Cambridge, 1970), discusses the radical political organizations of the 1770s.

Background for Abigail's political ideas in the Revolutionary period may be found in Bernard Bailyn, *Ideological Origins of the American Revolution* (Cambridge, 1967), and Caroline Robbins, *The Eighteenth Century Commonwealthman* (Cambridge, 1959). Katharine Anthony's biography of Mercy Otis Warren, *First Lady of the Revolution* (Garden City, N.Y., 1958), sheds light on Abigail's frinedship with Mercy. Catharine Macaulay's political ideas are discussed in Lynne Withey, "Catharine Macaulay and the Uses of History: Ancient Rights, Perfectionism, and Propaganda," *Journal of British Studies*, Fall 1976, pp. 59–83. More general information about Macaulay may be found in Lucy Martin Donnelly, "The Celebrated Mrs. Macaulay," *William and Mary Quarterly* 6 (1949): 173–207.

The Revolution (Chapter 5–8)

For a general overview of the Revolutionary years, see Lawrence H. Gipson, *The Coming of the Revolution, 1763–1775* (New York, 1954), and Edmund S. Morgan, *The Birth of the Republic, 1763–1789* (Chicago, 1956). John R. Alden, *The American Revolution, 1775–1783* (New York, 1954), is especially useful on military aspects of the conflict. Robert Gross describes the events at Lexington and Concord in *The Minutemen and Their World* (New York, 1976). Charles Francis Adams, *Three Episodes of Massachusetts History* (New York, 1892), provides detailed information on the effects of the war in Braintree.

Diplomatic issues, and John Adams's role in them, are discussed at length in Samuel Flagg Bemis, *The Diplomacy of the American Revolution* (Bloomington, Ind., 1957). E. James Ferguson, *The Power of the Purse* (Chapel Hill, 1961), is an excellent treatment of the financial problems of the war.

For background on Abigail and her family's inoculation for smallpox during the war, see John B. Blake, *Public Health in the Town of Boston, 1630–1822* (Cambridge, 1959), and, for a more general treatment, Richard H. Shryock, *Medicine and Society in America: 1660–1860* (New York, 1960). The latter is useful also for a general view of medical problems in Abigail's time, as is John Duffy, *Epidemics in Colonial America* (Baton Rouge, 1953).

Europe (Chapters 10 and 11)

George Rudé, *Paris and London in the Eighteenth Century* (London, 1952), is a good introduction to those cities during the time Abigail lived there. Rudé gives a much more detailed picture of London in his *Hanoverian London* (Berkeley, 1971). Orest Ranum, *Paris in the Age of Absolutism* (New York, 1968), discusses the physical appearance and social problems of Paris in the seventeeth century; Howard Rice, *Thomas Jefferson's Paris* (Princeton, 1976), gives a detailed description of the Adams's home in Auteuil and their surroundings. More information on Jefferson during these years, and his relationship with the

Adamses, may be found in Dumas Malone, *Jefferson and the Rights of Man*, Vol. 2 of *Jefferson and His Time* (Boston, 1948–62).

Charles R. Ritcheson, *Aftermath of Revolution: British Policy Toward the United States, 1783–1795* (Dallas, 1969), discusses the economic problems Americans experienced after the Revolution as a result of restrictive British trade policies. The debates over the constitution of Massachusetts, essential for understanding the unrest there in the in the 1780s, are detailed in Oscar and Mary Handlin, *The Popular Sources of Political Authority* (Cambridge, 1966), and Robert J. Taylor, *Massachusetts, Colony to Commonwealth* (Chapel Hill, 1961). Both books include documents demonstrating the objections of several towns to the constitutions, as well as useful interpretative introductions. The literature on Shays Rebellion is substantial; Marion Starkey, *A Little Rebellion* (New York, 1955), is a useful overview.

National Politics (Chapters 13–16)

John C. Miller, *The Federalist Era* (New York, 1960), is a good general summary of the years of John Adams's service in national office. More specific works on the framing of the Constitution and the establishment of the new nation include Gordon S. Wood, *The Creation of the American Republic, 1776–1787* (Chapel Hill, 1969); Merrill Jensen, *The New Nation* (New York, 1950); and Forrest McDonald, *We the People: The Economic Origins of the Constitution* (Chicago, 1958). On opposition to the federal constitution, see Jackson Turner Main, *The Antifederalists* (Chapel Hill, 1961).

Forrest McDonald, *The Presidency of George Washington* (Lawrence, Kan., 1974), is a helpful summary of the political issues of the first Presidential administration. Douglas Southall Freeman, *George Washington: Patriot and President* (New York, 1954), provides more detail on Washington's administration.

The formation of the first political parties is discussed in Joseph Charles, *Origins of the American Party System* (Chapel Hill, 1956), and William Nisbet Chambers, *Political Parties in a New Nation, 1776–1809* (New York, 1963). Donald Stewart, *The Opposition Press of the Federalist Period* (Albany, 1969), is an exhaustive study of the "Jacobin" newspapers that Abigail hated so much.

John's Presidential career is analyzed in detail by Stephen Kurtz, *The Presidency of John Adams: The Collapse of Federalism, 1795–1800* (Philadelphia, 1957), and more generally in Ralph Adams Brown, *The Presidency of John Adams* (Lawrence, Kan., 1975). Manning Dauer, *The Adams Federalists* (Baltimore, 1953), discusses political party conflicts during his administration.

John Reps discusses the planning of the new capital city in *Monumental Washington* (Princeton, 1967). James Sterling Young, *The Washington Community, 1800–1828* (New York, 1966), is extremely useful not only on the physical appearance of early Washington but also on political and social interaction there.

Mary Benson, *Women in Eighteenth Century America* (New York, 1935), is helpful in understanding Abigail's reading on women's issues in the years after the Revolution. Nancy Cott, *The Bonds of Womanhood* (New Haven, 1977), which focuses specifically on New England women, provides a good general treatment of changes in women's social roles in the postwar years. Kathryn Kish Sklar, *Catharine Beecher* (New Haven, 1973), is an excellent study of a nineteenth-century woman who carried some of Abigail's ideas about women and their domestic role to their logical conclusion. Linda Kerber discusses Abigail's pet topic, improvements in women's education, in "Daughters of Columbia: Educating Women for the Republic, 1787—1805" in Stanley Elkins and Eric McKitrick, *The Hofstadter Aegis* (New York, 1974). Her article "The Republican Mother: Women and the Enlightenment—An American Perspective," *American Quarterly* 28 (1976): 187–205, is also useful on changes in perceptions of women in this period.

Retirement (Chapters 17 and 18)

Useful discussions of the politics of the early nineteenth century include Marshall Smelser, *The Democratic Republic, 1801–1815* (New York, 1968), and George Dangerfield, *The Era of Good Feelings* (New York, 1952) and *The Awakening of American Nationalism, 1815–1828* (New York, 1965). The decline of the Federalists is discussed in David Hackett Fischer, *The Revolution of American Conservatism* (New York, 1965), and Linda Kerber, *Federalists in Dissent: Imagery and Ideology in Jeffersonian America* (Ithaca, N.Y., 1970). John Quincy Adams's diplomatic missions are discussed in Samuel Flagg Bemis's biographies noted above.

Material Evidence

In addition to books and manuscripts, what little remains of Abigail's physicial environment is helpful in understanding her life. Only the small, original part of her childhood home survives today, and it has been moved from its original site. It is maintained by the Abigail Adams Society and is open to the public. The house she and John lived in after they were married, as well as the neighboring house where John lived as a child, have recently been acquired by the National Park Service and are being restored. All three of these houses, which date from the seventeenth century, are instructive to the twentieth-century observer, who often does not realize that large families in an earlier time managed to live comfortably in very small spaces.

Peacefield, the home Abigail and John bought while they were in Europe, is much larger and grander. More than any number of words, it demonstrates the Adamses' upward mobility in the years after the Revolution. It is maintained by the National Park Service as the Adams National Historic Site; knowledgeable guides point out to visitors the limits of the original house, the various additions, and the specific furnishings acquired by Abigail and John at different times.

Abigail and John's house in Auteuil is now an apartment building, hemmed in by stores on a busy street. But the grandeur of the original house is still obvious, and the nearby Bois de Boulogne still exists in much the same form as in the eighteenth century.

Abigail's lovely vistas from Richmond Hill have been thoroughly swallowed up in the growth of New York City, and the muddy streets and shacks of early Washington have long since been covered with concrete. But in all the cities in which she lived, a few buildings and often the street plan give some flavor of the eighteenth century. The basic layout of the central part of

Washington has not changed since Abigail's time. London's parks and squares remain much the same also. And in Boston it is still possible to walk the narrow, crooked streets that Abigail walked, from the old Town House to Fanueil Hall and the waterfront, through the back alleys of the North End, past the house where Paul Revere once lived and the North Church, where lights once warned of the redcoats' march toward Lexington.

Index

Index